PC Upgrading & Maintenance

No experience required.

PC Upgrading & Maintenance

No experience required.™

PC Novice/Smart Computing

SYBEX®

San Francisco • Paris • Düsseldorf • Soest

Associate Publisher: Gary Masters
Acquisitions Manager: Kristine Plachy
Acquisitions & Developmental Editor: Peter Kuhns
Editor: Vivian Perry
Project Editor: Davina Baum
Book Designers: Patrick Dintino, Catalin Dulfu
Desktop Publisher: Maureen Forys
Production Coordinator: Robin Kibby
Proofreaders: Katherine Cooley, Eryn Osterhaus
Indexer: Matthew Spence
Cover Designer: Ingalls + Associates

Screen reproductions produced with Collage Complete.

Collage Complete is a trademark of Inner Media Inc.

SYBEX is a registered trademark of SYBEX Inc.

No experience required. is a trademark of SYBEX Inc.

PC Novice, the PC Novice logo, Smart Computing, and the Smart Computing logo are trademarks of Sandhills Publishing.

TRADEMARKS: SYBEX has attempted throughout this book to distinguish proprietary trademarks from descriptive terms by following the capitalization style used by the manufacturer.

Netscape Communications, the Netscape Communications logo, Netscape, and Netscape Navigator are trademarks of Netscape Communications Corporation.

Library of Congress Card Number: 97-69405
ISBN: 0-7821-2137-3

Manufactured in the United States of America

10 9 8 7 6 5 4 3 2 1

Contents at a Glance

Table of Contents

Introduction

Personal computers are a peculiar type of appliance. They have few moving parts, so they last a long time. But product development in computers is so rapid, the minute you buy your PC it starts to fall behind the technology curve.

The weird juxtaposition of longevity and light-speed obsolescence creates a problem for some computer owners: The system you buy today may not do everything you want it to do next year. Although the computer works just as well as it always did, technologically speaking, the rest of the world has passed it by.

At least it can seem that way. Actually, unless you have some compelling need to process information a bit faster, or do something via software that you couldn't do before, there's no reason to play a continual game of catch-up with your computer. You can keep on chugging away with your current PC until something new comes along that you really can't live without.

At that point, you'll have two choices:

- You can buy a new system with all the latest bells and whistles.

- You can upgrade—or add new capabilities to—your current PC.

Most people don't want to spend $2,000 every year buying a new computer, and that explains the popularity of upgrading. Adding a component or two to your computer is a relatively inexpensive way to greatly extend its useful life. Luckily, upgrading most components on a PC is not that difficult. It does help, though, if you have a knowledgeable friend available who can lend a hand. That's where we come in. *PC Upgrading & Maintenance: No experience required.* will take you step-by-step through the process of upgrading virtually every component on your computer. We explain the benefits of particular upgrades, how difficult they are, how long they take, what they cost, and which tools you'll need. We even walk you step-by-step through the upgrading process.

This book covers software upgrades as well, so if you're looking for some tips about upgrading applications, or want to know how to install a new operating system, you'll find it here. For those people who would like to get more out of their computers without having to worry about adding new hardware, we introduce some software alternatives to adding hardware.

All the material in this book is presented in an easy-to-read, plain-English style. Even if you're a fairly inexperienced computer user who has never "popped the top" off a PC, you'll be able to understand and follow along as we walk you through the upgrade process.

What Will You Learn from This Book?

This book aims to get you comfortable getting down and dirty with your computer. We will teach you how to understand the needs of your computer and judge what is best for you; that is, what will fit your budget *and* maximize the use of your computer. *PC Upgrading & Maintenance: No experience required.* will guide you through a safe and effective installation of new hardware and software, including expanding performance with more RAM, or new hard drives, CPUs, and diskette drives, bringing your computer into the latest technology via multimedia, video, modems, and operating systems, as well as going through the more prosaic everyday maintenance, that every computer, like every car, needs in order to last longer.

Skill 1 will get you situated, and start you thinking about what's right for you, and how to go about getting what you need. Skill 2 will go more in depth on this issue, and will get you familiar with Microsoft Diagnostics, which will be a helpful tool in figuring out the capabilities of your system. A computer is an electrical appliance, however advanced. Safety is a big issue in any installation, and Skill 3 addresses it in a clear and easy-to-understand manner. Skill 3 will also show you how to back up your system, a handy thing if anything goes wrong! Skill 4 gets into the meat of the matter; the upgrading begins, with Random Access Memory. Skills 5, 6, and 7 continue in this manner, addressing the installation of CPUs, hard drives, and diskette drives, all aimed at getting you the most efficient and fastest computer for your buck. Skills 8 and 9 get into the fun stuff: multimedia. These skills will prepare your computer for the sights and sounds of the latest software. Skill 10 will delve into the other big topic of the day, the Internet. Installing a modem is the first step!

The next few skills will focus on the external stuff that will complement the technology booting up inside. Skill 11 will deal with keyboards and joysticks. Printers are covered in Skill 12, and Skill 13 deals with scanners. Skill 14 will make sure that you have all the right places to plug in your new hardware. Next, we'll get into the nitty-gritty. That aging PC can get a real boost with a new motherboard/processor upgrade; Skill 15 will equip you with the knowledge and proficiency you need. Skill 16 will guide you through installation of a new power supply. Skill 17 will focus on upgrading your PC card for that laptop of yours. Skill 18 will move to the bigger picture, with instructions on how to set up an Ethernet network. Skill 19 will look into the viability and ease of actually building your own PC.

Skill 20 will go into how you can maximize the hard drive space that you do have, and Skill 21 will address a sister issue: memory. With all the speed that you'll have, you will be ready for Skill 22, in which you will learn what it takes to upgrade or change operating systems. Skill 23 will look at how you can get the most from the Internet, by taking advantage of all the capabilities of your Web browser. Finally, Skill 24 will look at all the problems that typically come up along the way, and the best way to deal with them. But that's not the end! You'll see, along the way, many references to companies that can provide you with the hardware and software that we're talking about; in the Appendix, you'll find a quick reference and an easy way to contact many of the biggest and best-known companies around.

Conventions Used in This Book

Here are some items that you will see throughout this book:

- When we ask you to type a word or a phrase, we'll put the word or phrase in **boldface** font.

- New terminology can sometimes be confusing—particularly when you don't know that it's new. For this reason, we'll use *italics* to signal the first appearance of an important word or phrase.

These are some other elements that you will become familiar with:

 NOTE   This is a note. It provides a piece of additional information about a topic.

THIS IS A SIDEBAR

Occasionally, we'll discuss a topic that requires more space than a note. If putting the discussion into the main body of the text would disrupt the flow, we'll present it to you in a sidebar that looks like this.

TIP This is a Tip, which is intended to be a shortcut or a trick that helps you be more productive.

WARNING This is a Warning. It indicates a condition or an action that could be potentially harmful to your work or your computer.

Ready, Set. . .

No experience is required, but motivation and curiosity is. Upgrading your PC can increase your productivity at home and at the office (as well as letting you play the latest 3-D game). We hope this book helps you extend the useful life of your computer. Let's go!

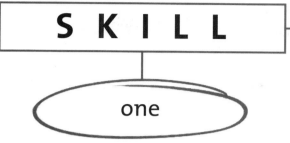

S K I L L

one

Avoiding
Upgrading Pitfalls

- ❑ Educating yourself before you buy

- ❑ Backing up your data

- ❑ Upgrading your drive quickly and efficiently

- ❑ Getting the most from Plug and Play

- ❑ Upgrading your Flash BIOS for Plug and Play

- ❑ Troubleshooting device drivers in Windows 3.1 and Windows 95

Upgrading your hardware or software can be cost-effective, educational, and easy—or costly, confusing, and nightmarish. The outcome depends partly upon luck and partly upon smarts, but you'll want to educate yourself before you undertake an upgrade. Here are some tips from experienced upgraders that can save you time, money, and grief.

Before You Buy

There are some things to consider before you head to the computer store. Ask yourself what you want to upgrade, why you want to upgrade, and what you hope to achieve by upgrading. If you're happy with your system, don't be swept up with marketing slogans. If you have a very old system, compare the cost of upgrading to what a new system or subsystem costs. For example, it often makes more sense to buy a new motherboard than to upgrade the old board's central processing unit (CPU), or to replace the computer rather than upgrade the motherboard. New purchases often can provide more benefits than upgrading individual parts.

Don't worry about long-term improvements. In three years, anything you install will seem ancient. Rather than installing the fastest CPU and the most memory you can afford to protect against obsolescence, consider buying products you can use now, such as a better printer, a modem, or a tape backup.

Think about what you can install yourself and what you should leave to an expert. For example, 90 percent of modem installations go smoothly, but 10 percent of them will bring experienced technicians to tears. It might be worth a $25 store installation fee to avoid being among the 10 percent.

Check into the technical support a company offers, before buying its product. A faster and cheaper product isn't better if the company won't help you keep it working.

Go online, and see what others say about the upgrade you're considering. Forums on commercial online services and Usenet newsgroups on the Internet are excellent places to read about problems and fixes others report. Ask what they wish they had known before purchasing and installing the product. The only dumb questions are the ones you didn't ask.

Try to buy your components from one vendor. If you buy a sound card from one vendor and a CD-ROM drive from another, and they don't work together properly, you can count on each vendor claiming the problem lies with the other vendor's parts.

When a dealer performs an upgrade for you, insist that he or she test everything. Make sure all parts are working before leaving the store.

Building Your Safety Net

Although most upgrades go smoothly, sometimes a routine installation causes chaos to break loose. If you build a safety net, you'll have a minor nuisance instead of a catastrophe. Make sure all mission-critical data and programs on your PC are backed up. A common mistake, for example, is to back up accounting data, but not your programs and system software. If this is lost, it can take days to reconfigure.

Here's how to build your safety net:

- Fully back up important files.

- Obtain a screen shot or other record of your CMOS (complementary metal-oxide semiconductor) setup. (A screen shot is a "snapshot" of a screen image that can be printed or saved as a file.)

- Keep a copy of your backup software outside your computer. If your computer chokes with your only copy of the backup software installed on its hard drive, your backups are useless.

- In case you get into a jam, perform the upgrade when your technical support or favorite PC expert is available.

- Make an emergency boot diskette. A bootable (or system or DOS) diskette contains your computer's minimal operating system. If it's inserted in the diskette drive during startup, you may get your computer at least partly operating if the hard drive won't start normally. A clean boot system diskette contains the minimum data needed to start your computer, but will not necessarily run everything normally. Another type of boot diskette, and the one an upgrader needs most, contains as many of your computer's normal pre-upgrade startup configuration files as possible. It's designed to temporarily let you run your PC normally if your upgrade procedure fails or prevents your computer from starting normally. Another type of boot diskette contains a working copy of your backup program.

- Test your emergency boot diskette—before you need it—by restarting your computer with the diskette in your A: drive. If your computer restarts, and your DOS C> prompt appears, your boot diskette is working. If you can then perform your PC's normal operations, your emergency boot diskette is operating fully.

- After each step of your upgrade, and when a component is successfully running, perform another backup. For example, if you're installing a multimedia kit, and your CD-ROM drive is working but your sound card isn't, run a backup. Without this backup, your attempt to get the sound card working could cause more problems.

To perform a partial backup after each step, look in your backup software for a mode called "differential," which backs up your system without performing a full backup after each step.

Differential backups exist in the Windows 3.1 and MS-DOS 6.20 and newer versions of MSBACKUP. Differential backups also are available in most backup software, but are not always called "differential." A differential backup is useless until you have backed up your whole system because the differential backup refers to your full backup, and ensures that items added or changed since your last full backup are updated. After you create a full backup, a differential backup is a quick way to keep your backups current. Don't confuse differential with "incremental," which doesn't work as well. (For more information about backups, see Skill 3.)

Your safety net is now in place, and you are ready to begin upgrading.

If You Don't Back Up

If you choose not to back up your data, you should at least follow these recommendations.

Put a formatted diskette in your A: drive, and type these commands:

```
c:
cd \
copy autoexec.bat a:
copy config.sys a:
copy \windows\win.ini a:
copy \windows\system.ini a:
```

You need to do this after every successful step of your installation, on a separate diskette. This preserves older copies of your crucial system files (such as AUTOEXEC.BAT, CONFIG.SYS, WIN.INI, and SYSTEM.INI); if anything goes wrong, you'll be able to use this diskette.

Starting Up

There are a number of things you need to do as you begin the upgrading process. This section covers tasks you'll want to perform before moving on. The first thing you'll want to do is to clean up your system before installing new upgrades. You remove an old DOS program from your hard drive by using the DELTREE command in DOS or File Manager in Windows 3.1, both of which let you delete entire directories.

Properly removing old Windows programs and drivers is tricky business: You are fooling yourself if you remove an icon without removing its program. If you don't remove a Windows program cleanly, you could end up with unwanted files or you might accidentally remove something you shouldn't. Windows uninstall utilities are available to remove unwanted programs. These include Microhelp Inc.'s UnInstaller, Quarterdeck Select's Uninstall-It, International Microcomputer Software Inc.'s WinDelete, Quarterdeck Corporation's CleanSweep, and Vertisoft Systems' Remove-It.

Run SCANDISK or another disk checker, such as Norton DiskDoctor, before installing new software. These utilities check for errors in your hard drive's File Allocation Table (FAT), which is your disk's filing system. If you add new software to a drive that already has problems, you're asking for trouble.

Run DEFRAG (or another disk defragmenting utility, such as Norton Speedisk) before installing new software. This neatly packs the existing files on your hard drive, providing an "open," contiguous space into which your new software can load. This lets it load faster with less wear on your drive.

In short, be sure everything is working before you upgrade.

Don't use pre-Windows 95 versions (DOS 6.22 or earlier) of DEFRAG and SCANDISK on drives larger than 528MB. They weren't designed for this purpose and can cause problems.

Check to make sure you have enough hard drive space before you try to install something new. An upgrade that is aborted for a lack of space will likely leave you dead in the water unless you know how to cleanly uninstall the upgrade. You may not even be able to restore from backups. But don't always believe those *Insufficient Disk Space* messages during a software upgrade. Some programs usually don't recognize they are being installed on top of an older version. For example, a message while installing Ami Pro 3.10 might say it needs 12MB free when it really only needs 4MB if installed over an older version of Ami Pro.

Read the README.TXT files that come on the diskettes with your hardware or software. While books and even quickstart sheets are printed months before your product was shipped, these informational files are usually updated with information that will make your installation easier or safer. Check to make sure you have the latest version of your software. There might be updates and fixes since your version was manufactured. Carefully mark the location from which you disconnected your cables. With flat ribbon cables, note which way edges are facing.

Be careful with static electricity. Even a mild charge from your body can seriously damage cards and chips. Exposed electronics on new hard drives are particularly sensitive to static. Touch the bare metal frame of the computer case before touching electronic parts, and keep chips and cards in their anti-static bags until you begin the installation.

Consider running a software installation monitor program such as INCTRL, WinDelete, or LogIt, which is part of Remove-It. These programs will record what the installation program is doing to your computer, which is invaluable if you need to troubleshoot or remove software.

Don't install everything at once. Leave that newly installed modem running for a few days before tackling that multimedia kit upgrade. Install products with components that come in stages. For example, if your modem comes with fax software, communications software, and a free copy of an online service's software, don't install them all at once. Get the modem running, back up your programs, and then tackle the next step. Adding a CD-ROM and a video card at the same time, for example, could leave you wondering which one is causing your network card to stop working.

This divide-and-conquer strategy protects you when adjusting hardware settings (such as DIP switches) or software settings (such as CONFIG.SYS file settings). Change one thing, and see if it works. If not, reset it, and try something else. This will prevent you from getting lost in a maze of changes with no way out.

If you run out of interrupt request lines (IRQs), you can re-use the IRQ5 and IRQ7 lines that belong to the printer ports LPT1 and LPT2. You usually can assign them to use other gadgets although they're already "occupied." Printer ports rarely use these IRQs. (IRQs are hardware lines over which devices can send requests for service to the microprocessor.) Consider using IRQ/port analyzers (install helper software) such as Touchstone's Setup Advisor (714/969-7746). If not, learn how to use MS-DOS' MSD command, which most PCs have.

Try moving deviant add-in cards to different slots. All slots are supposed to be equal, but occasionally they're not.

 NOTE   Remember to reboot your computer when you want to test the effects of an installation. Many program installations don't go into effect until after you restart the PC.

Here are a couple of things you should steer clear of: Don't install similar programs with overlapping functions, especially programs that work through modems or fax cards. Don't upgrade from diskettes copied from your friends' directories. You could unwittingly copy incompatible configuration information between machines and make your PC crash. If things don't work, it will be impossible to tell if the problem is you, your computer, or the irregular software.

Mopping Up

After the upgrading process is complete, you still have some work to do.

Make sure everything is running correctly before replacing the case's cover, but don't put fingers and screwdrivers in an open case if your PC is running. By leaving the case open, you don't have to reopen it to change just one setting. Consider taping the new documentation to the inside of your computer's case. After all, the only time you will ever need a chart of the jumpers on your sound card is when you're adjusting it inside the case. Tape notes to the inside of the case documenting what you did. Label ports and wires on the back of your case. Three months later, they'll all look the same.

If you encounter trouble, simplify your system. Stop loading CD-ROM drivers and network drivers, and set your video to VGA. After the problem is resolved, reload drivers one by one until you find which one is giving you trouble. When installing hardware to replace an older item, Windows 95 has preconceptions about your old hardware, and insists on holding a place (IRQ, port, etc.) for the old item, even if you've removed it. For example, it might think you're adding a new modem and still own the old one. You might get a message such as *There's no room for two modems in this computer.*

The solution: When you remove a piece of hardware, but before you rerun the "new hardware detection" step, enter Device Manager, and manually remove your old device there.

Some Tips for Upgrading Your Drive

Some typical hard drive problems can be avoided by following a few general guidelines.

Don't use hard drive partition manager drivers such as Micro-House's EZ Drive or DiskManager, even though they come packed with upgrade hard drives, unless using these drivers is the only way you can run your new hard drive.

These managers allow pre-1995 computers to run drives larger than 528MB, but they sometimes impair performance, thus locking you out of your drive when they conflict with other software. First check with the dealer or drive manufacturer to see if there's any other way your computer can run that drive. If not, at least make sure you have the latest version of the software.

Partition your upgraded, larger hard drive before you start loading programs onto it—or have the dealer partition it for you. (A partition is a section of a drive that your computer reads as a separate drive.) Effective partitioning can create a tremendous amount of usable space, as large drives are forced to allocate space for files in increasingly larger, minimum-sized chunks called "clusters" or "allocation units" (see Table 1.1). For more information on partitioning, see Skill 6.

T A B L E 1 . 1 : Partitioning a Hard Drive

Size of Disk (Partition Size)	Minimum Size Allocation Unit DOS Permits	Typical Slack (Unusable Wasted Space)
17 to 127MB	2KB	4%
128 to 255MB	4KB	8%
256 to 511MB	8KB	16%
512 to 1023MB	16KB	28%
1024 to 2047MB	32KB	49%

The effects of partitioning are so dramatic that, unless you partition, you probably will have no more usable space on a 1.2GB drive than on a smaller, cheaper 850MB drive. Even partitioning a 1.08GB drive into a single partition of 1023MB and ignoring the leftover 23MB would create 186MB of usable space.

Upgrading with Care

Deciding whether to upgrade to a new version of your favorite software usually requires some serious thought. Should you stick with the stalwart version you know inside and out or spend money on a new version with gaudy "New And Improved" stickers splashed all over the box?

It's like deciding whether to trade in your trusty blanket that has provided warmth for years for a new electric blanket. Giving up that old blanket and its comfort seems like an impossible proposition—until you spot the list of benefits the electric blanket provides. Then you can't get that electric blanket home quickly enough.

Software upgrades are similar—the list of new features is usually enough to make your final decision on whether to upgrade easy. Taking advantage of those new features isn't always as simple as it might seem, though. Upgrading to a software package's new version can cause some headaches; you must install the new program, convert older data files, and learn to use new features. Some tips will ease the transition from your old software to "New And Improved."

System Preparation

It's important to remember that upgrading to a new version of a program is like installing an entirely new program, and you need to follow the same precautions and rules you would with a new program. Many people think a software upgrade is simple, but it's just as complicated as installing from scratch.

"There are a lot of customers that we find in support who upgrade, and they haven't prepared their system for the installation," says Paul Coffin, manager of worldwide technical support for Corel Corporation, which manufactures CorelDRAW and other programs. "They have a lot of applications running in the background; they haven't done any housecleaning on their hard drive. That kind of stuff is very important."

Most programs, especially popular programs from well-known manufacturers, have extremely smooth upgrade installation procedures. Most programs will give you a choice of either storing the program files for the new version in a new directory on your hard drive or storing the new program files in the same directory as the old version and overwriting the program files from the old version. You'll need to choose the installation procedure that works best for you.

"One of the things we suggest to customers when upgrading is that because you're upgrading to a whole new package with a whole bunch of new features, you're going to be relearning some of the stuff because different things have changed," Coffin says. He suggests keeping the old software version until you've mastered the learning curve on the new application. You should delete the old version once you're comfortable with your new software.

Delete with Care

Manually deleting files and directories requires plenty of care; haphazard deletion of directories can be hazardous to your computing health.

The worst scenario is when users delete files they realize they shouldn't have after they reinstall a program. They can't undelete them because the installation has just overwritten all of the sectors on the hard drive in which those files were contained.

You can avoid such potential deletion problems by storing the new and old versions of the programs in different directories. That isn't always possible, though, especially if storage space on your hard drive is cramped. And if you store the two versions in different directories, chances are you'll have to manually move your personal data files from one directory to the other. When you overwrite the old version with the new version, usually the new version will automatically find and use your data files.

Whether your old data files can be read by the new version of the software usually depends upon whether you've kept up with previous version upgrades. If you are faithful about upgrading your software, your data should be read easily. "If you're going from version one to version seven, though, then it's a roll of the dice," Coffin says. "If you go from two to three, three to four, four to five, five to six, all the way up, then usually it's a pretty clean transition. Certainly a lot of software vendors try to ensure that it's as clean as it can be."

Many of these tips may sound obvious, but many people forget about them. If you take them for granted, but you're lucky, you'll still have a successful installation. If you're unlucky, you may end up calling someone like Coffin.

"I think that maintenance and housecleaning—always making sure you know what's on your hard drive—are key," he says. "It sounds like a simple, little thing, but screens are popping by them, they're hitting OK or Continue, and they're not paying any attention to what's going on," Coffin says. "There's a reason that information is there. You definitely should be watching it and reading it." Preparing the system for installation and reading instructions are key to a hassle-free installation.

Backing Up Key Files

Before upgrading any software, we recommend you copy any data files for that particular program onto diskettes. (Data files contain information you've created, such as a word processing document you typed.) Although most programs provide extremely smooth upgrade installations, you'll encounter the occasional program that goes haywire because of a certain setting on your computer or because you have extraneous programs running.

Unless you are a very tidy hard drive keeper, though, finding all of the data files for the backup could be problematic.

"The biggest difficulty is [when customers say], 'Well, I saved my CorelDRAW files in some directory, but I can't remember where.' The questions then become, 'How can we find them?' and 'How can I make sure I don't accidentally delete a directory that they are contained in?'" says Coffin. Don't count on the software's upgrade installation program to help you find those data files.

With most programs, the software creates a working directory inside the actual program directory, and it automatically stores all data files in this working directory. For example, Sidekick from Borland stores all of your files in its DATA directory (see Figure 1.1).

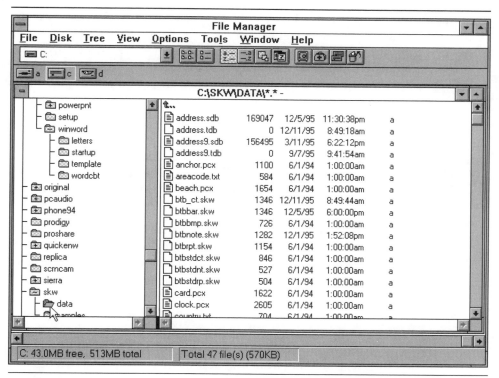

FIGURE 1.1: Sidekick stores all of you data files in the DATA folder inside the program folder.

To make a backup copy of all files in the working directory when using Windows 3.1, enter File Manager, click the icon of the directory you want to copy, hold down the mouse button, and drag the icon to the A: diskette drive icon along the top of the screen. In Windows 95, you can follow the same directions using the My Computer feature. If the diskette can't hold all of the files inside the directory, you'll have to copy them individually to several diskettes by dragging each file icon onto the A: drive icon.

If you're not lucky enough to have that type of working directory, there are a couple of techniques you can use to find your data files.

You can search the entire hard drive for data files unique to each program. Most programs use a default extension (the portion of the filename to the right of the period in the traditional eight-plus-three filename format used with MS-DOS and Windows 3.1) to identify their data files. For instance, CorelDRAW uses a .CDR extension and Excel uses .XLS.

In Windows 3.1, go to File Manager, click the File menu, and select the Search command. In the Search For box, type *. followed by the extension you want. File Manager will list all occurrences of files with these extensions in a search window, and you can copy them to a diskette from that window. In Windows 95, enter the Windows Explorer, and use the Find command under the Tools menu.

NOTE   The filename extensions aren't automatically visible in Windows 95. To see them, select the Options command from the View menu in Windows Explorer.

If you usually change the default extension when saving data files, there's still hope. Sort all files in the program's directory by date. If you can remember the approximate date you installed the older version of the program, you can copy all files to diskette that have changed since the installation.

When installing a major application, the dates usually are the same for all files. But if the dates have changed, drag those files into a backup directory, and then you'll know you can go back to those files that have changed.

To sort files by date in Windows 3.1, enter the File Manager, and select the Sort By Date command from the View menu (see Figure 1.2). Files that have changed most recently will be listed at the top of the screen. From the Windows Explorer in Windows 95, click the View menu, then select the Arrange Icons command followed by the By Date command.

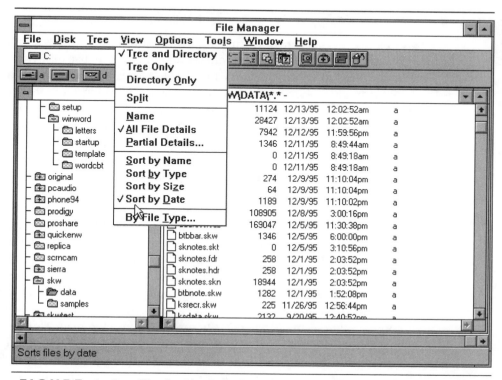

FIGURE 1.2: The Sort by Date Command in the Windows 3.1 File Manager can help you locate the files that have been changed most recently.

Plug and Play Makes Installing Devices Easy

Would you buy a TV that needed to have its components adjusted before you could watch it? How about one that let you watch one program, but needed to be adjusted to work with other programs and different VCRs? Of course not! You expect these devices to work perfectly as soon as you plug them in and press the power button. But these hassles have come to be expected from personal computers. Getting a PC's hardware to work together can involve the risky business of adjusting conflicting DIP switches, IRQs, and device drivers. Installing new peripherals can be difficult and time-consuming, and there is always the fear that adding a new sound card might knock out a previously working modem or printer.

Industry officials have long discussed this problem and have sought a way users could add peripherals quickly and easily. Their solution is Plug-and-Play technology, which is designed to improve integration of hardware and software to let computers automatically recognize and immediately use hardware components after they are installed. Even while Apple's Macintosh touted its own version of Plug and Play, no one in the PC industry did anything about it until 1993 when a Plug-and-Play industry standard was promoted by four companies—each dependent upon the other to deliver on the Plug-and-Play promise. Microsoft promised a new operating system that would incorporate Plug-and-Play expansion architecture; Intel promised Plug-and-Play chips; Compaq Computer promised Plug-and-Play PCs; and Phoenix Technologies promised Plug-and-Play Basic Input/Output System (BIOS) chips.

Plug-and-Play versions of these components are designed to work together to make configuring any hardware device—keyboard, monitor, printer, sound card, CD-ROM, anything—automatic and easy to understand. Plug in the new device, fire up your PC, and the system senses the new peripheral, automatically adjusts hardware settings, and loads the required device drivers to make everything work. No more device conflicts, fiddling with jumpers, or tweaking CONFIG.SYS files.

When Plug and Play was first developed, four advantages were immediately obvious, says Russ Madlener, Microsoft's product manager for desktop operating systems. Automatic installation and configuration of add-in devices would reduce the costs of owning a PC. It would require fewer calls to technical support and let users spend more time using their PC instead of getting it ready to use. Even more appealing was the possibility that users would buy more devices if they were easier to install.

Eagerly anticipated, the new technology was sometimes derided as "Plug and Pray" because of its hit-and-miss performance. But since the release of Windows 95, the first PC operating system to support Plug and Play, plus hundreds of new Plug-and-Play-compatible devices, the Plug-and-Play dream has become a working reality. Although it's not perfect, it makes owning a PC and installing hardware add-ons and peripherals as simple, in most cases, as using a television.

Making Plug and Play Work

For optimum, long-term Plug-and-Play performance, you need:

- A Plug-and-Play operating system
- Plug-and-Play-certified hardware add-ons

- 32-bit virtual device drivers as opposed to 16-bit, Real-mode drivers used under DOS and Windows 3.*x*

- A Plug-and-Play-compliant-BIOS (a routine stored in read-only memory that controls communication between a microprocessor and a computer's software)

Working with device drivers, a specially tuned Plug-and-Play BIOS is smart enough to detect hardware, communicate with it, and manage configuration changes.

Obtaining three of the four components of Plug-and-Play technology is simple. Upgrading to Windows 95 gives you the operating system you need. Certified Plug-and-Play hardware is easy to recognize because it must meet certification standards and will sport "Designed for Windows 95" and "Built For Plug and Play" logos on its box. For a complete list of all Windows 95–compatible software and hardware products, check out Microsoft's Windows Hardware Quality Labs (WHQL), formerly known as the Microsoft Compatibility Labs (MCL), on the World Wide Web at `http://www.microsoft.com/hwtest/`. The site gives you the option of searching for certified hardware (see Figure 1.3).

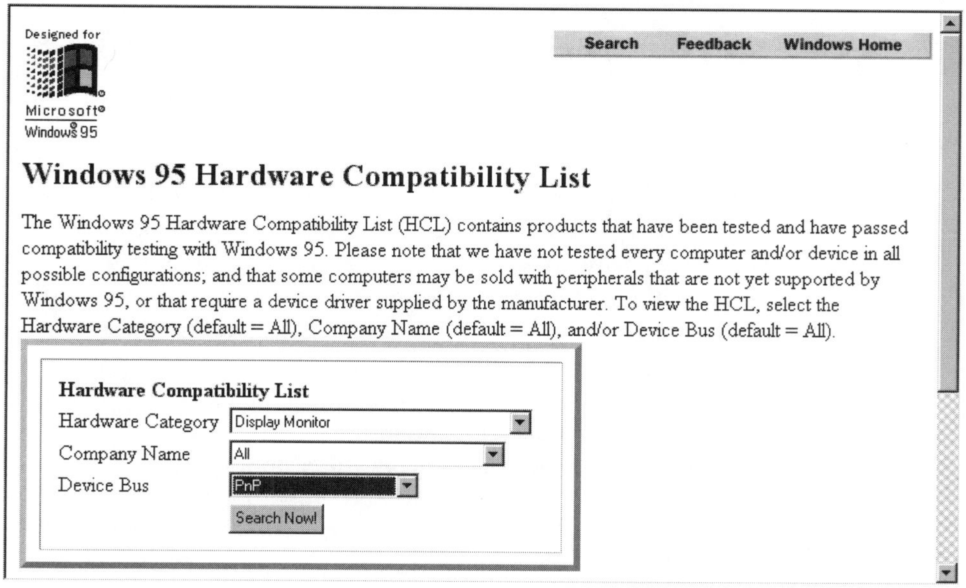

Designed for
Microsoft®
Windows® 95

Search   Feedback   Windows Home

Windows 95 Hardware Compatibility List

The Windows 95 Hardware Compatibility List (HCL) contains products that have been tested and have passed compatibility testing with Windows 95. Please note that we have not tested every computer and/or device in all possible configurations; and that some computers may be sold with peripherals that are not yet supported by Windows 95, or that require a device driver supplied by the manufacturer. To view the HCL, select the Hardware Category (default = All), Company Name (default = All), and/or Device Bus (default = All).

Hardware Compatibility List

Hardware Category   Display Monitor
Company Name   All
Device Bus   PnP

Search Now!

FIGURE 1.3:   The Windows 95 Hardware Compatibility List at Microsoft's World Wide Web site lets you search for Plug-and-Play-certified hardware.

Plug-and-Play device drivers usually come on the installation diskette(s) shipped with Plug-and-Play hardware. To get the latest device driver, check the manufacturer's Web site or call the company. In most cases, the manufacturer will mail you an updated driver for free.

However, determining if you have a Plug-and-Play BIOS or Plug-and-Play PC is a bit trickier. Generally, most major manufacturers' systems built in 1995 or later have Plug-and-Play capabilities. Check your manual or the BIOS identification message that appears on your screen at bootup to see if it says "Plug and Play." If it doesn't, call the system vendor.

For Windows 3.*x* and older systems, another solution is to check your system's setup utility by interrupting the boot process—usually by pressing the F1 key.

NOTE   Check your user's manual for particulars about interrupting the boot process. When in doubt, consult expert help.

Checking your BIOS is much simpler if you're using Windows 95:

1. Click the Start button, select Settings, then Control Panel, and double-click System.

2. When the System Properties window appears, click the Device Manager tab.

3. Click the System Devices icon to expand the list. If you see a Plug-and-Play BIOS listed, you're in business.

Although you can upgrade to Windows 95 and use Plug-and-Play devices without a Plug-and-Play BIOS, experts suggest that you make sure all future computer hardware you buy is Plug-and-Play-compliant.

Replacing a BIOS chip is cheap—generally about $100 including installation at a local computer store or chain. Many manufacturers will send you a free upgrade depending on when you bought your PC. Newer PCs with a Flash BIOS can actually be upgraded by running special software you can download from the company's Web site or have mailed to you.

Finally, instead of replacing your BIOS chip, which does nothing to increase PC speed, consider upgrading your motherboard, advises Los Angeles-based system consultant William Goldstein. "You can pick up a 486 Plug-and-Play motherboard for a hundred bucks, while Pentium-powered boards hover between $100 to $300," he says.

If you don't have Windows 95, you still can quickly find out more about your BIOS by using a built-in utility called Microsoft Diagnostics (MSD)—provided you're using Windows 3.*x* or DOS 6.*x*. To run this program, type **msd** at the DOS prompt, and press ↵. Press **P** for Computer, and you'll see the BIOS manufacturer and version number. For more information about BIOS upgrades, call your BIOS manufacturer or a software retailer.

How Plug and Play Works

Under Plug and Play, your entire system is checked every time you boot up to see if any new devices have been installed. It identifies both the devices on the motherboard and external devices, such as diskette drives, keyboards, video displays, and adapter cards. It determines the resource requirements for each device and provides the proper interrupt request lines (IRQs), direct memory access (DMA) locations, and input/output (I/O) and memory addresses.

First, the system looks for older non-Plug-and-Play hardware devices, called legacy devices, because these devices have fixed resource requirements. This means Windows 95's Plug and Play cannot automatically configure them to work in the system. However, Windows 95 can detect more than 800 pieces of legacy hardware, according to Madlener. So even though Windows 95 can't change IRQ or I/O address settings on legacy devices, it can detect them and load the proper device drivers. As a rule of thumb, if your hardware worked under Windows 3.*x*, it will work under Windows 95.

Plug and Play then seeks out Plug-and-Play peripherals, which are more flexible than legacy devices. It finds the proper device drivers and loads them. Therefore, you should always have your original Windows 95 installation diskettes available before you allow your system to detect a new device. This is because after Windows 95 detects the new hardware, it will need to install it from the Windows 95 installation diskettes. When it's finished, all the devices you have installed and their resource allocations are stored in Windows 95's Registry (the registration database), Hardware Tree, and Device Manager.

In addition to detecting, loading, and configuring a dizzying array of hardware, Windows 95's Plug and Play is smart enough to remember different hardware profiles. For example, if you hook your Plug-and-Play laptop into a docking station, Windows 95 can sense that your laptop is docked or undocked and will load the proper devices. More importantly, the Plug-and-Play system allows for hot docking, which means you don't have to reboot your portable PC each time you pop it in or out of its docking station.

Right now, adding or removing devices on the fly, while your system is turned on, is limited to laptop docking stations and PC Cards. Desktop systems require you to turn the system's power off before installing new equipment. However, using new Universal Serial Bus (USB) technology, you'll be able to connect devices in a daisy chain to a single port (while the system is running) without risking damage to your PC or the devices themselves. Industry experts predict a wave of new USB-compliant modems, keyboards, scanners, and other input devices to be released—though it's expected to take years before they become mainstream products.

Plug-and-Play SOS

But whether you have a complete Plug-and-Play PC and Plug-and-Play add-ons or a hybrid PC with a mixture of Plug-and-Play and legacy devices, Plug and Play doesn't always work. One reason is because neither a Plug-and-Play BIOS nor Windows 95 has any leeway in configuring fixed legacy hardware. Obviously, the more legacy devices in use, the fewer resources left for Plug-and-Play devices and the more likely a problem could occur, Madlener says. "What generally happens is the system tries to automatically configure itself by moving a peripheral to a location that's already occupied by another device," he says.

Another source of potential Plug-and-Play problems is simply the thousands of systems, configurations, old BIOSs, off-brand equipment, and obsolete and bad device drivers tossed into computers.

Experts point out that Plug-and-Play specifications are still evolving. As they settle down, there will be fewer conflicts. Most initial Plug-and-Play conflicts have been eliminated as manufacturers created new device drivers that bridged the gap and worked with their older legacy hardware and Windows 95.

A final reason is technology itself. With the number of computer-equipped U.S. households expanding rapidly, hardware and software companies are working overtime to make whatever they sell more consumer-friendly. Older, slower non-Plug-and-Play printers, modems, and other add-on devices are reaching the end of their technological lifespan and are being replaced by newer, faster, slicker Plug-and-Play equipment that comes standard on today's multimedia PCs. As these non-Plug-and-Play components fade from existence, so will problematic installations.

But even if Windows 95 doesn't recognize your hardware because it's too old or too new and doesn't have the proper device drivers, you still can install new hardware using Plug and Play and Windows 95's New Hardware Installation Wizard and Device Manager.

Saving Time with Wizards

So you've upgraded to Windows 95. After plugging in your keyboard, mouse, external modem, and laser printer, you fired up your system. You held your breath and waited patiently as the new operating system clunked around and, to your amazement, recognized one component after another, automatically installing the proper device drivers. But while Windows 95 recognized most of your components, it failed to detect one or two. Here's what you can do to solve this problem using Windows 95's Add New Hardware Wizard:

1. Close all programs, then click the Start button, select Settings, and then click Control Panel.

2. In the Control Panel window, double-click the Add New Hardware icon. When the Add New Hardware Wizard window appears, click Next.

3. The screen will ask if you want Windows to do the work and search for new hardware. Select Yes (recommended), then click Next.

4. Before Windows searches for the new hardware, it tells you that the detection process may take several minutes. Click Next.

5. If Windows 95 finds your hardware (or failing that, takes a guess), it displays the name of the hardware in a box. If it's correct, click Finish, and Windows 95 will automatically install the proper device driver.

6. If Windows 95 did not detect your new hardware, a dialog box will ask you to manually install the device. Click Next, and you'll see a list of hardware types, such as CD-ROM controllers, display adapters, floppy disk controllers, hard disk controllers, keyboards, and modems.

7. Select the hardware type you're trying to install. If, for example, you choose printers, clicking Next displays a list of printer manufacturers. (If you still don't see your hardware type, select Other Devices.)

8. Click the manufacturer and model number of your printer, for example, IBM/Lexmark 4039 Plus. To see if Windows 95 has a driver, click Next. If it does, it will automatically install it. When the setup is complete, click Finish.

9. If Windows 95 does not have the driver, or if you have the driver on diskette (which is the preferred way to do this), click Have Disk. Then enter the name of the drive and the folder that contains the device's driver (usually your diskette drive or CD-ROM drive), click OK, then Next.

10. When the setup is complete, click Finish.

Troubleshooting

Not everybody in the computer business is a Plug-and-Play convert. Consultant Goldstein maintains Plug and Play is a flat-out failure. "It's about 90 percent (successful)," he says, "but because of the 10 percent that's not there, it causes more people more problems than if Plug and Play did not exist."

He recommends that you make sure any device you buy has a manual override. Before installing any Plug-and-Play device, back up your system, and be sure to have a clean bootable diskette handy. Using Windows 95's Device Manager, see which IRQ and I/O addresses are in use, and write down those addresses.

Here's how to see information about the devices installed on your system:

1. Right-click the My Computer icon on the Windows 95 Desktop, then select Properties.

2. Click the Device Manager tab (see Figure 1.4).

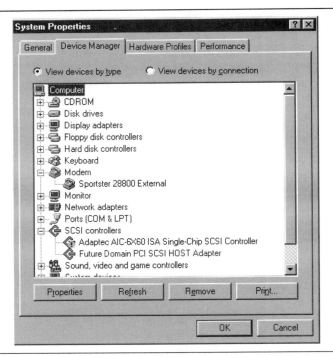

FIGURE 1.4:   The Windows 95 Device Manager tab on the System Properties dialog box lists all the hardware devices on your PC.

3. Select Computer, and click Properties to display a complete list of your devices and their settings. To find the settings for IRQs, I/O and DMA locations, and memory, for example, click the category desired (see Figure 1.5). When you're finished, click Close.

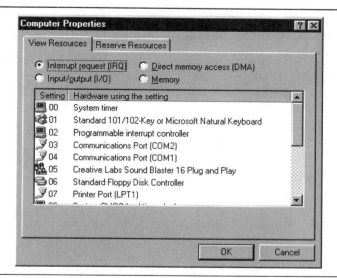

FIGURE 1.5: In the Computer Properties window, you can determine how your computer's interrupt request lines, direct memory access, input/output, and memory are allocated.

4. Back in the Device Manager page, Windows 95 also lists the installed device for categories including CD-ROM drives, disk drives, modems, and SCSI controllers. To expand the list, click the plus (+) sign next to any item. Clicking Monitor, for example, might reveal drivers for a NEC MultisyncXE-17.

5. Select an item, and click Properties to display additional information about the selected device, including device type, manufacturer, hardware version, and device status (which should say *The device is working properly*).

6. A yellow exclamation point over any Device Manager listing means there's something wrong. The message will say the device is not working properly. To manually change a device setting, click the Resources tab, then select Change Setting. Double-click the setting you want to change, such as

Input/Output Range or Interrupt Request. You then can enter a specific value manually. The conflict information box will tell you if your new setting conflicts with other devices.

NOTE When manually changing a setting, you may first have to click the Use Automatic Settings box. Also, not all devices have a manual override.

7. When you're finished, click OK to exit the Properties page, and click OK again to close the System Properties window.

NOTE Remember that you must restart your computer before any new hardware changes take effect.

In theory, as you add and change hardware devices, Plug and Play is supposed to automatically uninstall and remove older device drivers no longer in use. In practice, Goldstein asserts, Plug and Play misses the boat. The result is that Windows 95 loads several drivers and slows down your system.

To see which device drivers are being loaded, follow steps 1, 2, and 4 in the preceding list. If you see device drivers that are no longer on the system, such as an older modem or printer that you no longer use, you can delete the old driver by highlighting it, and then clicking Remove.

WARNING Be careful not to remove drivers for your mouse, CD-ROM drive, or CD-ROM controller because you might have trouble reinstalling Windows 95 if something goes wrong.

For the best long-term results, buy only Plug-and-Play-compatible hardware from major manufacturers. Download and install new up-to-date device drivers.

Driver's Ed

Whether you have a legacy device or a new Plug-and-Play peripheral, your best bet is to get a Windows 95 driver directly from the manufacturer. Even if the device came with a new driver, chances are that a better one is already available. You can usually download it from the manufacturer's Web site, bulletin board system, or a product support forum on America Online, the Microsoft Network, or CompuServe. Look in the user's manual for information. Otherwise, call the manufacturer and have the new driver mailed to you.

According to Madlener, the diskette version of Windows 95 supports more than 2,000 devices—roughly 80 percent of all devices on the market, while the CD-ROM version supports even more. Additional CD-ROM extras and updated drivers are available from Microsoft's Knowledge Base on America Online (Keyword: knowledge base), CompuServe (Go: windows), The Microsoft Network (http://www.msn.com/), or directly from Microsoft (http://www.microsoft.com). These sources offer a broad range of information on product support for Windows 95 (see Figure 1.6).

FIGURE 1.6: CompuServe's WinSupport Forum is a comprehensive index of Windows 95 product support, updates, and technical information.

Finally, on the slim chance that neither the hardware manufacturer nor Microsoft has a driver for your device, Windows 95 literally takes a guess and installs a compatible driver. Generally, the device will work, but because the software wasn't specially written for the device, expect a few glitches. Another temporary solution is to use the device's Windows 3.x driver.

Plug-and-Play Diagnosis

With Windows 95 running on a new Pentium-powered multimedia PC with Plug-and-Play-compliant hardware, you can add, remove, and even swap new devices by simply plugging them in and turning on your PC. Installing and configuring various combinations of legacy devices will continue to cause conflicts. Plug and Play isn't perfect—until you remember the old way devices were installed under Windows 3.*x* and DOS—then it seems like magic.

Upgrading Your Flash BIOS for Plug and Play

Your computer's BIOS (basic input/output system) is a routine stored in read-only memory that controls communication between the PC and its hardware. When you turn on the central processing unit (CPU), programming code in the BIOS takes inventory of system hardware and prepares various installed components for work. Without the BIOS, the CPU doesn't know how to control basic hardware operations, such as information being read from or written to a disk or interactions with the keyboard and hard drive. Similarly, without BIOS code, the CPU can't communicate with the system clock or video board.

Earlier, we mentioned some of the advantages of a BIOS upgrade. You should consider upgrading your computer's BIOS when you want to add to your PC new components that can't be recognized by your current BIOS system. Upgrading your BIOS also can let your computer take advantage of Plug and Play.

BIOS programs typically are stored in read-only memory (ROM) chips located on the motherboard because information stored in conventional random-access memory (RAM) disappears when you turn off a computer. (ROM can be read, but not modified. RAM is a temporary memory storage area used to load program instructions and store files currently in use.) When you turn on your computer, the BIOS version number is often one of the first messages that appears on-screen. For example:

```
AMIBIOS (C)1992, American Megatrends, Inc.
```

In the Beginning

The collection of BIOS programs stored in ROM determines how a computer starts. The BIOS performs the same set of routine operations every time. When you turn on a computer, a programming code in the main system BIOS determines what hardware is installed. The built-in program checks if this hardware is

BIOS: NAME, RANK, AND SERIAL NUMBER

When designing programs, software developers frequently use and build upon data stored in the BIOS. If the BIOS in your computer has a bug or lacks the ability to run a new peripheral, you may have to replace it. That's why the BIOS date and version number are so important.

A particular BIOS version can significantly affect PC performance. Two machines with identical hardware but with different BIOS firmware (the software permanently stored in hardware chips), might exhibit different personalities. For example, Gateway 2000, a leading manufacturer and direct marketer of PC-compatible systems, confirmed in 1993 that some of its local bus systems with a particular BIOS had problems running certain memory-resident applications. The BIOS in these faulty systems used an area of memory reserved for communication among applications. If users ran applications that occupied this part of memory, they were forced to reformat their hard drives. A corrected BIOS eventually was built into Gateway's newer models, and the problem was resolved.

working and then searches for other BIOS-like programs installed on add-on boards in your system. If it recognizes any, it yields control of the system to those BIOS programs so they can perform their initial inventory and tests. When expansion board BIOSs have completed their startup routines, the main system BIOS continues with its tests, checking the computer's low memory area and initializing those components it's designed to control.

Most of these operations occur very quickly, without users being aware of them. Sometimes, however, you may notice a particular stage in the BIOS power-on self-test (POST). For example, since a video graphics array (VGA) controller adapter typically has its own BIOS chip, the software contained in video board ROM runs before the main system BIOS. As a result, you may notice a video board sign-on message before the main system BIOS copyright notice, date, and version number appear on-screen. When the main system BIOS tests low memory, a memory test message appears. When it inventories the hard drive, diskette drives, and keyboard, lights flash on those devices.

Once preliminary tests are complete and everything checks out, the BIOS pulls up additional information by loading the operating system into memory. It does this by reading a series of small boot files (MSDOS.SYS, IO.SYS, CONFIG.SYS, and AUTOEXEC.BAT) from the active drive (usually drive C:, which is the hard drive). Operating system software and applications take over from there.

The First Steps

When you purchase a computer, its BIOS firmware knows how to work closely with the system's installed components. To add new components, such as a large 1.2GB hard drive, to an older PC, you may have to upgrade your system BIOS so it can recognize drives with more than 1,024 cylinders. Computers manufactured in the early 1980s require a BIOS upgrade to use an enhanced graphics adapter (EGA) board, hard drive, local area network (LAN) card, or any ROM-equipped expansion board. Similarly, if you installed Windows 95 and want your computer to use its new Plug-and-Play features to manage installed peripherals or to recognize peripherals you add later, you must upgrade to a BIOS with built-in Plug-and-Play features. A common reason to upgrade a BIOS is to allow computers built before 1995 to properly run the new larger and faster Enhanced IDE hard drives.

Many BIOS upgrades require replacement of the old BIOS chip on your motherboard, which is the computer's main circuit board that contains the computer's CPU, RAM chips, and expansion slots. Old 80286, 80386, and 80486 machines typically have two BIOS chips rather than one. A Pentium system, on the other hand, doesn't require chip replacement. It stores its BIOS on a special kind of memory chip called a Flash ROM, or Flash EPROM, chip. If Flash ROM chips are used in the BIOS, the BIOS is often called a Flash BIOS. To upgrade Flash BIOS, Flash ROM chips simply run an update program and let the software perform the modifications. While making these changes doesn't require much skill, an incorrectly installed Flash BIOS will prevent the computer from starting, so pay close attention to update instructions that are shipped with the software.

Last year, Gateway 2000 issued Flash BIOS updates to integrate Plug-and-Play capabilities into its P5-75 through P5-100 systems and its P5-60 and P5-66 Rev 3 and 4 motherboards. To add improved Plug-and-Play capabilities to a P5-90 system, for example, a system must have BIOS version 1.00.12.AX1T. The newest Gateway Pentium systems have Plug-and-Play BIOS revisions already installed.

You must take two precautionary steps before you can safely update a system's Flash BIOS. First, ask your computer manufacturer's technical support department which BIOS version your computer should be running. You don't want to download or install the wrong BIOS. The technician will want to know which Pentium motherboard is in your computer. You'll find this information on the packing slip that was shipped with your system.

Second, turn on the computer and watch the screen for the message that tells you how to enter your computer's Setup program. On a machine with an American Megatrends Inc. (AMI) BIOS, you might have to press Delete or F1 at startup. On a computer with a Phoenix BIOS, you may have to press Ctrl+Alt+Esc. Other computers use different methods to access their Setup programs.

A built-in Setup program is the portion of your computer's BIOS that lets you determine several of your system's basic characteristics. It also tells the computer which type of diskette and hard drives are installed, the system bootup sequence (which determines the drives the system checks when it looks for the operating system), serial and parallel port addresses, and more. This vital configuration information is stored in a complementary metal-oxide semiconductor (CMOS) chip. CMOS is generally used for RAM and switching applications, and operates at high speeds while using little power. Since CMOS memory is volatile, the chip must be connected to a working battery to retain information. If the battery fails, CMOS data dissolves, causing you to see either an *Invalid Configuration* or *CMOS Failure* message at startup.

Since updating the BIOS might accidentally modify or erase current CMOS settings, you should run the Setup program and write down all CMOS information, noting the settings for equipment installed in your system. As an alternative, you can document your computer's CMOS by moving through each CMOS screen display and pressing the Print Screen key on your keyboard.

Using the Print Screen key prints a hard copy of the computer's current screen display. This approach is more reliable than jotting down notes by hand because it eliminates the possibility of making an error. Be sure to print settings for both Standard (Main) and Advanced CMOS configurations. If a problem occurs later, you can re-enter the Setup program and use the printout to reconfigure those settings.

Getting BIOS Update Files

Every BIOS upgrade is different. In this section we describe a BIOS upgrade for a Gateway PC running Windows 95. The specific commands and filenames used in this installation may differ from your BIOS upgrade, but the general chain of events will be the same. Use the following instructions as a general guideline, but contact your computer's manufacturer for specific details on upgrading your BIOS.

If your computer doesn't have a modem, request that the manufacturer mail you the BIOS update on diskette. If you have a modem-equipped computer, you can get updated BIOS files by contacting the manufacturer's BBS. Files may be downloaded free of charge, but you'll need to download the data onto a bootable, high-density system diskette. Depending upon the version number of the BIOS currently installed in your computer, you even may need to perform two BIOS updates.

To imitate how we performed our upgrade, prepare two bootable system diskettes in the following way:

1. Place the diskette to be formatted in drive A:.

2. Double-click Windows 95's My Computer icon.

3. When the window opens, click the A: drive icon.

4. Choose Format from the File menu.

5. Select Full from Format Type, then check Copy System Files from the Other Options menu.

6. Click Start.

Repeat the procedure to format a second diskette, then contact the manufacturer's BBS.

To obtain a BIOS update from the Gateway BBS via modem:

1. Use the modem to dial the Gateway BBS.

2. At the screen prompt, choose a language/protocol (press **1** for English/ANSI, the standard English language version), then press ↵.

3. Log in with the user ID guest.

4. Press **L** to access Gateway's driver library.

5. When the Driver File Download Library appears, choose **2** for Motherboard Utilities.

6. From the Motherboard Utilities menu, choose **5**, for Flash BIOS Updates For All Systems.

7. After the Flash BIOS Update Menu appears, choose the update for your particular system. Since we were running a P5-90 with a P54C Plato motherboard, we selected **C** (the P5 (1.00.12.AX1T) BIOS option) to add Plug-and-Play capabilities to our main system BIOS.

A BIOS update will occasionally require two steps. The procedures for each step are essentially the same. For our two-stage BIOS update, follow these steps:

1. When the Flash BIOS Update Menu displays, choose **B** (P5-90 Flash BIOS (1.00.09.AX1T)). A message appears stating that you'll be downloading a self-extracting file containing the BIOS update AX1T for P5-90 systems. This update will work only on systems with the BIOS revision 1.00.09.AX1 and prior .AX1 revisions. Once your system has been flashed with this version, it isn't possible to return to an earlier version.

2. You're now ready to download the first BIOS update. Verify download settings for your telecommunications program. Since you are going to download a file that could harm your system if executed incorrectly, you want to ensure that your download directory is set correctly.

3. Choose a download option (such as Z for the Zmodem transfer protocol).

4. Press ↵ to begin the download process.

When you've finished downloading the 1.00.09.AX1T update, you're ready to download the second file.

1. Choose **C** for P5 (1.00.12.AX1T) BIOS (updates for .AX1T BIOS only).

2. A notice tells you this file is an updated BIOS for the P5-75, P5-90, and P5-100 BIOS and that users must first upgrade to 1.00.09.AX1T before using this update. While you haven't yet upgraded to 1.00.09.AX1T, you've already downloaded the archived file, so you're all set.

3. Choose a download protocol (such as Z for Zmodem), then press ↵ to initiate the download process.

4. After the 12AX1T.EXE transfer is complete, the computer returns to the Flash BIOS Updates menu. Press Alt+F4 to quit and disconnect. You also can type **x**, then press ↵ to exit. Repeat the command three more times, then type **y** to automatically disconnect your modem from the Gateway BBS system.

Updating the BIOS

Each BIOS update is transferred to your download directory as a self-extracting archive. To install these updates, proceed as follows:

1. Place the first bootable diskette in drive A:.

2. Copy the P5AX1T.EXE file to that diskette, then double-click the drive A: icon to verify that a copy of the file now resides on the diskette. If you see an icon labeled P5AX1T.EXE, you're ready for the next step.

3. Drag the original P5AX1T.EXE archive file from the download directory on your hard drive to the Recycle Bin.

4. Right-click the Recycle Bin, then choose Empty Recycle Bin to delete its contents.

5. Return to drive A:, and activate it by clicking the drive A: icon.

6. Double-click on the P5AX1T.EXE file icon in drive A:. The archive automatically self-extracts, copying its contents to the diskette. Scroll through the files to see what's there, making sure to print out and read files with the .TXT filename extension for installation instructions.

7. Leave the diskette with the P5AX1T files in drive A:, then restart the computer.

8. Follow the on-screen directions. After completing all steps, reboot once more, and a new BIOS copyright message will be displayed on-screen.

You're now ready to perform the second BIOS update. Follow these steps:

1. Place the second bootable diskette in drive A:.

2. Copy the 12AX1T.EXE file from the download directory on your hard drive to the startup diskette. Double-click drive A: to verify that there is a copy of the archived file. If you see an icon labeled 12AX1T.EXE, you're ready for the next step.

3. Drag the original 12AX1T.EXE archive file from the download directory to the Recycle Bin, then empty the Recycle Bin to delete its contents.

4. Return to drive A:, and make it active by clicking the drive A: icon.

5. Expand the 12AX1T.EXE archive as you previously expanded the P5AX1T.EXE upgrade archive. Remember to print out and read the .TXT files for installation instructions.

When the computer restarts with the second bootable Flash BIOS diskette in drive A:, the Flash Memory Update Utility screen appears. Press ↵ to continue and then follow these steps:

1. After the Main menu appears, use the Down Arrow key to highlight the option labeled Update Flash Memory Area from a File. Press ↵ to continue.

2. When the Update Flash Area window appears, Update System BIOS should be highlighted. If it isn't, use the Down Arrow key to scroll to and highlight this option. After it's highlighted, press ↵.

3. When the Enter Path/Filename window appears, use the down arrow to highlight 1012AX1T_.BIO in the Files box. Press ↵.

4. When the Verify Image window appears, make sure that Continue with Programming is highlighted, then press ↵.

5. Finally, after the Continue message appears, remove the bootable Flash BIOS diskette from the diskette drive, then press ↵. The system will reboot, displaying the message *BIOS Version 1.00.12.AX1T*.

To ensure that the CMOS settings are still correct, enter the CMOS configuration setup at system startup, and check the settings against your printed copy. If there are any discrepancies, modify the settings to match the printout. Be sure to save changes when you exit.

Troubleshooting

If you inadvertently expand the archived BIOS upgrade files in the download directory, do not run any of your BIOS-updating utilities from your hard drive. If you do, you could trash your computer's CMOS settings, which then would have to be reconfigured manually from the emergency printout you created. In addition, you might trash a crucial operating system file, prompting a startup error message that reads *Bad or missing Sys file* or *Non-system disk*. If this message appears, insert your Windows 95 Emergency Start Disk in your boot drive (drive A:), restart the computer, then type **sys a: c:** at the C> prompt. The SYS command transfers IO.SYS and MSDOS.SYS (crucial DOS operating system files), as well as the COMMAND.COM file, to your hard drive without requiring reformatting. Once this transfer is complete, you can safely reboot. Everything should be back to normal.

The most serious problem with trashed CMOS settings is if your Disk Type setting has been trashed. In this instance, you won't even get a C> prompt, and the above repair method won't help. To remedy this, you need to have previously made a record of your disk parameters so that you can manually re-enter them into the CMOS setup screen. Without this information, you'll have to call the computer or drive manufacturer to find out these parameters. On many newer Plug-and-Play computers, the BIOS can automatically analyze your hard drive and put the correct disk parameters in your CMOS setup on the fly.

Troubleshooting Device Drivers

Imagine yourself at the helm of an old-fashioned telephone switchboard. Your job is to keep track of every incoming and outgoing call, and if two or more calls need to be on a conference line, you must make sure everyone talks to the right person. Now, add another switchboard and maintain the same level of performance as you had with the first.

This example is simplistic in computer terms, but it's similar to what happens with your computer's hardware devices. Conversations between a hardware device and its computer must be exact—or problems occur.

Drivers are the link between your computer and the devices connected to it. When working with peripherals such as printers, modems, and monitors, any feature specific to a manufacturer's product will generally require a separate driver to make that feature work. CD-ROM drives, sound cards, graphics adapters, and input devices are good examples of hardware that needs manufacturer-specific drivers.

Besides controlling hardware, drivers can be used for software emulation and control. ANSI.SYS, a DOS driver that bridges the gap between text and graphics, is a good example. With ANSI.SYS loaded in a system, you can access features normally unavailable to the DOS user, such as control over cursor position and screen foreground and background colors. Few programs use this driver anymore, and you should not load it when you work with Windows.

MS-DOS Device Drivers

There are two levels of device drivers in DOS. The first, or low-level, system device drivers connect your computer with the keyboard, printer, monitor, serial port, system clock, and disk drives. The second level represents device drivers installed by command lines listed in the CONFIG.SYS file. Any file in CONFIG.SYS with a .SYS extension is a device driver. These driver files control devices that DOS does not cover with its low-level drivers and add control over the devices DOS is aware of. To view a list of the system device drivers in your computer's memory, type:

mem /d /p

at the C> prompt, and press ↵. The MEM/D command (the /P switch tells DOS to list information one screenful at a time) displays all of the internal drivers and other information stored in memory.

Device drivers use extensions other than .SYS. EMM386.EXE and SETVER.EXE, for example, are device drivers loaded from CONFIG.SYS but which control built-in utilities. As mentioned before, device drivers can control components of your computer other than hardware. Third-party memory managers such as QEMM (Quarterdeck) and 386 Max (Qualitas) are device drivers that control memory that is not an add-on, but is integral to the system.

Installing DOS Devices

During startup, drivers load from the CONFIG.SYS file. The syntax for loading a device is:

```
device= [path] [filename] parameters
```

The path is the location of the driver file (directory and, if applicable, subdirectory). Filename is the full name of the driver file (name plus extension), and parameters indicate additional information or switches needed by the specific setup.

Because there are so many manufacturers and types of devices, DOS offers basic support, but the manufacturers must supply drivers for their devices.

The following command line loads the driver CSP.SYS for a sound card:

```
device=e:\sb16\drv\csp.sys
```

In our example, the driver resides in the subdirectory \DRV located in the directory \SB16 on the E: drive of this system. Without this driver, the sound card will not work. The driver tells DOS how to instruct the computer to integrate the device into the system for access. The device driver loaded in our example CONFIG.SYS file is that bridge.

Memory Issues

Each driver you install requires a certain amount of memory. If you install the driver without a memory manager, it loads into conventional memory (the first 640KB of memory). Since this area of memory is always in demand by DOS, we can use another type of driver to access high memory (above 640KB).

HIMEM.SYS is the memory manager included with DOS. After installation, this driver provides access to high memory, letting you install programs without using conventional memory. The syntax for loading HIMEM.SYS is:

```
device=c:\windows\himem.sys
```

 NOTE You must load HIMEM.SYS before loading any other driver; drivers loaded before HIMEM.SYS will not have access to high memory.

Once HIMEM.SYS is loaded, you can load your drivers into high memory with the DEVICEHIGH command. For example, we would load our sound card driver into high memory by adding this line to CONFIG.SYS:

```
devicehigh= device=e:\sb16\drv\csp.sys
```

This driver now resides in high memory, freeing conventional memory for other needs.

Windows 3.1 Device Drivers

Unlike DOS, Windows 3.1 is designed around device drivers. Because of the myriad drivers and their integration within the operating system, two computers may have different devices but everything will work the same in either one. This flexibility and integration also makes system expansion easier. After being properly installed, new hardware automatically integrates into every Windows-based application. Most Windows drivers are stored in the WINDOWS\SYSTEM directory and can have one of three extensions:

- .DRV denotes a typical Windows driver.

- .386 denotes a driver used for Enhanced mode operation.

- .DLL denotes a dynamic-link library driver file.

Drivers loaded from the SYSTEM.INI file reside in four sections: [boot], [drivers], [mci], and [386enh]. You may find drivers in other sections, but those sections are specific to the driver and not standard SYSTEM.INI sections. Some driver information is in the WIN.INI file, but that data is generally the specific driver's settings and options. (A *dynamic data link,* or DDL, is a feature in Windows that links information in one file to information in another file. For example, a DDL can be used to link information in a spreadsheet to information in a project management program. Changing information in one program would automatically update the information in the other.)

Real Mode and Virtual Mode

Device drivers residing at the DOS level are called *Real-mode drivers* and include mouse drivers and sound card drivers. These drivers are typically device-specific and often are manufacturer-specific, and must be loaded into memory before these devices will operate. The way Real-mode drivers access the system eliminates the possibility of multitasking operation.

Windows supports two operating modes: Standard mode and 386-Enhanced mode. The default operating mode depends upon your computer. Computers with CPUs lower than an 80386 will only run Windows in Standard mode, while computers with an 80386 or higher CPU can run in either Standard or Enhanced mode.

Windows does not use virtual memory when in Standard mode, which means it cannot use multitasking with DOS-based applications (that means you cannot open a DOS window inside a Windows-based application).

Virtual drivers let Windows separate tasks into their own virtual machines. For example, each DOS window you open essentially acts as though it is being accessed by a separate machine. In the virtual world, it is. Most virtual device drivers manage your equipment's hardware so more than one application can use a single device at the same time.

The term *VXD* is used to identify a general virtual device driver. The V stands for Virtual, the X represents the type of device the driver is for, and the D stands for device. For example, in the [386enh] section of SYSTEM.INI, the virtual mouse driver is called out as "VMD" with the X replaced by the M (for mouse). A "VDD" represents a display driver, and so on.

Installing Drivers

When you add a peripheral to your system or receive an updated driver for an existing device, you need to install the new device driver in Windows.

 NOTE   When you add hardware to your system, you should always install the device before installing the driver.

Diskette-based driver installation can add or update an existing driver in one of the following ways:

- Run an installation program that automatically sets up the driver in the SYSTEM.INI file.

- Install the driver from the Control Panel.

- Install the driver using the Windows Setup program.

- Manually edit the SYSTEM.INI file.

Most new software uses the automatic installation method. If the software does not make all the necessary changes, you will have to set up the hardware with either the Control Panel or Windows Setup.

When adding or updating drivers in Windows Setup, one of the options is *Other <device type> requires diskette from OEM (Original Equipment Manufacturer)*, where <device type> is any one of the four selections (display, keyboard, mouse, or network). This option indicates that Windows will look for the file OEMSETUP.INF on the installation diskette. This information file contains the information Windows needs to properly install the driver.

Getting Rid of Drivers You Don't Need

There is no reason to run Windows in Standard mode. If your computer has an 80386 or higher processor, stay in Enhanced mode for optimum performance. Therefore, you don't need files for Standard mode or a 286 processor cluttering your drive; you can safely delete the following files located in the WINDOWS\SYSTEM directory:

- DOSX.EXE
- DSWAP.EXE
- Files with .2GR extension
- KRNL286.EXE
- WSWAP.EXE
- WINOLDAP.MOD

Problems and Conflicts

It's possible to load the wrong driver. Windows is not intelligent enough to know if a driver will work with a particular device. For example, in Windows Setup you can change the Display device to a mode your video card doesn't support and Windows will accept the change. When you restart Windows, you'll receive a blank screen instead of the Windows logo. If you load the wrong printer driver, you may get only a page of garbled text.

Another situation may come up, if your device is not supported by Windows, as is sometimes the case with older printers or specialized peripherals. Windows usually gives you an alternative to this problem. Even though your device's specific model or brand may not have a specific driver, you can probably use a generic counterpart. In the case of a printer, almost all older printers have a default setting for emulating an Epson FX, and Windows supports several of these models. If your printer has any special features, you probably won't have access to them when you use a non-specific driver, but at least your printer will work.

If you are having problems making a peripheral work and are sure it is not the device itself, try using a generic Windows driver. For example, most modems are termed "Hayes-compatible." (Hayes was the cornerstone in the modem world and set a standard that is still adhered to today.) Again, if you cannot find a driver specific to your modem, it should work with a Windows generic Hayes driver.

Windows also can load a driver that accesses an address being used by another device. The driver that loads first takes priority. Sometimes Windows displays a warning message alerting you to the conflict, dumps you into DOS before Windows loads, or loads everything but the conflicting device. Most problems of this nature occur right after you've added new hardware or updated a driver. If this is the case, it is easy to locate and fix the offender.

If Windows starts up but, after installing new hardware or a driver, a device that worked before the installation stops working, this indicates something is awry in the SYSTEM.INI file. To find the culprit, open Program Manager's File menu, and select Run. When the Run dialog box appears, type **sysedit** in the Command Line box. This launches the Windows System Configuration Editor, which is a text editor that lets you work with your system files (CONFIG.SYS, AUTOEXEC.BAT, SYSTEM.INI, and WIN.INI). You can edit or view these files easily from this program. Be careful not to make a change that could keep Windows from restarting.

From the Window menu in System Configuration Editor, select the System.ini window. When you have SYSTEM.INI on-screen, look in two or more sections for a file or group of files that is causing the problem. Because you know the type and name of the hardware, you may be able to find it, since the driver file will probably have some portion of that name in its file specification. The first place to search is in the [boot] section. (The driver file will probably have a .DRV extension.) If the conflict is, for example, a mouse that stopped working, look for the MOUSE.DRV line. If the information there doesn't match the mouse you are using, that's the problem.

Other sections to search are [386enh] and any sections created specifically for a device (as in the case of a sound board or CD-ROM drive). These device-specific sections will often have section headings indicating which device they support.

 **WARNING** Be very careful editing the file that you think is causing a problem; if you are unsure what a command line is for, don't delete it.

To make it invisible to Windows, add a semicolon in front of the first character on the line. For example:

```
; device=c:\cbw\cmswtape.386
```

Windows will ignore the line with the semicolon during the startup process. If, after restarting your system, you cannot re-enter Windows or other problems occur, you can load SYSTEM.INI into the text editor and remove the semicolon.

LOCATING UPDATED DRIVERS

For various reasons, manufacturers often update drivers. If you mailed in your warranty card, you should be notified of the latest driver updates. Many manufacturers have their own bulletin board system (BBS) from which you can download the latest device drivers (you can find the number in the product's user manual). Other places for finding updates are online services such as CompuServe and America Online. Most major manufacturers maintain their own forum where users can get the latest information and files for their products.

To locate a supporting forum on CompuServe, use the Find command and enter either the product type or the manufacturer name. For example, to locate the forum for an ATI graphic card, enter **ati** or **graphics**. On America Online, enter the computing section and select the topic to enter the forums.

Not all updates, however, will necessarily be important to you. Sometimes an update repairs problems that plague specific equipment and does not apply to anything installed on your computer.

As you've seen from our look at device drivers, they give access to a wide range of applications that may otherwise have limitations. And even if they start to cause problems, you should now find them relatively easy to fix.

Are You Experienced?

Now you can. . .

- ☑ make smart choices when buying hardware for an upgrade
- ☑ back up your data so nothing is lost
- ☑ upgrade your drive with a minimum of hassles
- ☑ install hardware and peripherals that meet Plug-and-Play standards
- ☑ upgrade your Flash BIOS for Plug and Play
- ☑ identify and solve problems with your Windows 3.1 and Windows 95 device drivers

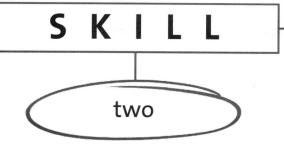

S K I L L

2

two

Using Microsoft Diagnostics to Learn About Your Computer

- ❑ Getting started with Microsoft Diagnostics (MSD)
- ❑ Using MSD to find upgrade and configuration information
- ❑ Trying out alternatives to MSD
- ❑ Decoding error messages
- ❑ Looking for help

Before you plunge headfirst into adding hardware to your computer, determine the capabilities of your system. This can help you know which components to buy and which ones to avoid. But where can you turn to learn this vital information? When you installed MS-DOS or Windows, a terrific program called Microsoft Diagnostics (MSD) was included to provide the information you need.

MSD gives you information to help you decide about upgrades and help you configure your computer more effectively. In fact, MSD will reveal more computer information than you probably need to know. MSD, for example, can tell you which type of processor runs your computer, how many diskette drives your computer has, and—most important—which type of Basic Input/Output System (BIOS) chip is found in your PC.

Starting MSD

To use Microsoft Diagnostics, you first have to locate the program. If you have both MS-DOS and Windows, you probably have two different versions of the program. If you have MS-DOS 6.0 or newer, the latest version of Microsoft Diagnostics (2.11) resides in your C:\DOS directory. Earlier versions of MS-DOS have version 2.11 in your C:\WINDOWS directory.

To start Microsoft Diagnostics, go to the proper directory by typing either **cd c:\dos** or **cd c:\windows**, then type **msd** and press ↵. MSD then will inform you it is "examining your system." Depending upon the speed of your computer, this will take from a few seconds to nearly a minute.

 WARNING   Do not launch Microsoft Diagnostics from the Windows File Manager, because you will get some inaccurate information. To get the correct information, exit Windows, and then start Microsoft Diagnostics.

Exploring a Wealth of Information

After Microsoft Diagnostics has finished its investigation, the Summary Screen will appear with 14 information blocks and three menu items (see Figure 2.1). There usually is information at the right of each block, but there's even more lurking behind the scenes.

Microsoft Diagnostics includes information about nearly every aspect of your computer. You can use Microsoft Diagnostics to help you upgrade your computer yourself, or you can print the document to show the salesperson as you shop for hardware. Either way, you will be better prepared for the upgrading process. This section gives you a play-by-play description of the information available.

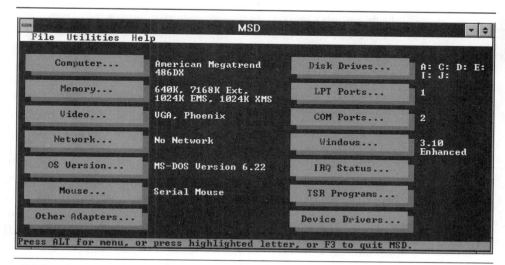

FIGURE 2.1: You can learn about your computer's components and capabilities from the main menu of Microsoft Diagnostics.

What Makes Your Computer Tick

To the right of the block marked Computer you'll see two lines. The top line indicates the manufacturer of your read-only memory Basic Input/Output System (ROM BIOS). These built-in instructions control the computer's configuration and tell your computer how to operate. The bottom line indicates your processor type, but this information is not always accurate. For example, if you have a 486DX2 or DX4 processor, Microsoft Diagnostics will list it as a 486DX. Some other manufacturers' processors (such as the AMD 486DLC processor) may be reported as a completely different system.

The P in the Computer box is red. Press P on your keyboard, and a large white box will pop up that gives you information about your computer's configuration. The first five lines of information are about your system's BIOS. Microsoft Diagnostics will tell you who made the computer, who made the BIOS, the BIOS version, the type of computer for which the BIOS was designed, the BIOS ID Bytes, and when the BIOS was released. If the BIOS version is blank, this means that Microsoft Diagnostics wasn't sure which version you have. There's another place to get this information, which we'll discuss later.

BIOS information is important because computer capabilities have changed dramatically in recent years. If you have an older BIOS, the size of the hard drive your computer can accept might be limited, and some expansion boards might not work in your computer. Generally, if your BIOS release date is more than three years old, you'll have to be careful when you upgrade. (See Skill 1 for more on working with your BIOS.)

After the BIOS information, Microsoft Diagnostics will tell you your processor type, whether a math coprocessor is installed (486DX and Pentium processors will say *Internal*), which kind of keyboard you have, and which kind of expansion bus (the connections between the motherboard and peripheral devices) your computer has. Microsoft Diagnostics recognizes these buses: Industry Standard Architecture (ISA), Extended Industry Standard Architecture (EISA), and IBM's Microchannel. If you have Peripheral Component Interconnect (PCI) or VESA Local Bus (VL-Bus or VESA Local Bus), it won't detect them. The last three lines in this box consist of technical information that would only be used by a technical support representative trying to help you. To exit out of the processor information, press the Esc key or ↵.

MSD won't tell you whether your processor is upgradeable. You need to look at the central processing unit (CPU) inside your computer to determine which type of socket it's plugged into. (See Skill 5 for details.)

The Lowdown on Memory

The first line beside the block marked Memory shows how much MS-DOS Mode memory your computer has, which is almost always 640KB, or 640 thousand bytes. The next line shows how much physical memory you have beyond the first 640KB. Adding these numbers together will give you your computer's actual physical total random access memory (RAM). For example, 640KB + 7,168KB = 7,808KB. The actual physical memory in this example is 8MB. The total is smaller than the actual amount of memory because your computer's hardware reserves memory that Microsoft Diagnostics can't detect. Buying more RAM for your computer often is the least expensive and most effective way to boost your computer's speed. This section of MSD will tell you how much RAM your computer has. (For more information about installing RAM, see Skill 4.)

If your computer has loaded an Expanded Memory Specification (EMS) or an Extended Memory Specification (XMS) program (called a driver), Microsoft Diagnostics will tell you how much RAM has been reserved for the driver. (A driver is a hardware device or program that controls another device.) If you're running Microsoft Diagnostics under Windows 95, it will tell you that all RAM has been reserved for XMS. That's perfectly normal.

Pressing the M key will give you detailed memory information about your computer that's cryptic, fascinating, and not very useful. This data is crucially important to a troubleshooter, but you won't need it for an upgrade.

Taking Stock

The Computer and Memory areas are just the beginning of what the MSD main menu has to offer. The following is a run-down of what you can find out from the rest of the blocks on the menu, starting with Video, the one that follows the Memory block.

Video This block provides the basic display type and the name of the manufacturer of your Video BIOS, which usually is not the manufacturer of the video card. To get that information, press the **V** key. The two important pieces of information here are the Display Type and the VESA OEM name (the original equipment manufacturer of the VESA Local Bus), which will list the true manufacturer of your video display. If you don't have a late-model video adapter, a new adapter in a VL-Bus or PCI expansion bus could speed your computer's video performance.

Network This box tells whether your computer is linked to a network. Usually, you'll see the words *No Network.* If you are on a network, you can read details about the network by pressing the N key.

OS Version This block gives you the version of MS-DOS you are using (if you are running under Windows 95, this box tells you you're running MS-DOS 7.0, which doesn't exist). Pressing O gives you the details. The most important detail here is where in the computer's memory MS-DOS is located: Low, the High Memory Area (HMA), or Upper Memory Blocks (UMBs). Storing MS-DOS in the wrong location will hurt your computer's performance. If MS-DOS is loaded in low memory, it takes up room other programs could use.

Mouse At this box, you'll see one of these messages: *Not Detected, Serial, Bus,* or *PS/2.* If you have a mouse, and see *Not Detected,* press **U** to see more information, and Microsoft Diagnostics should give you the information you need. Note the interrupt request lines (IRQ) and the port the mouse is plugged into. The rest of the information is irrelevant to the upgrading process. (IRQs are lines that enable hardware to request service from the microprocessor.)

Other Adapters You'll need one piece of information from this block. If your computer has a game adapter (usually used for a joystick), Microsoft Diagnostics will note it and at which hardware interrupt it resides. If you want to buy a joystick or flightstick, check here to see if you have a port to plug it into.

PRINTING MSD INFORMATION

MSD can print the information you retrieve from it for you. At the menu bar at the top of the screen, go to the File menu, and select the Print Report option. You can select any section of the program. To enter information about yourself that will print on the report, make sure the Customer Information box is checked.

Disk Drives This box is probably the most valuable. Here you'll see the drive letters of your diskette and hard drives. You might see drive letters you didn't think existed. These are the "host" drives created when you installed DoubleSpace, DriveSpace, or Stacker. To see the details, press **D** (see Figure 2.2). You'll see the size and type of each installed diskette drive, hard drive, and any CD-ROM or optical drives. Every piece of information on this screen is valuable, especially the Fixed Disk information that gives specific hard drive configuration information. This information and the BIOS information will tell you your options for increasing your computer's storage space.

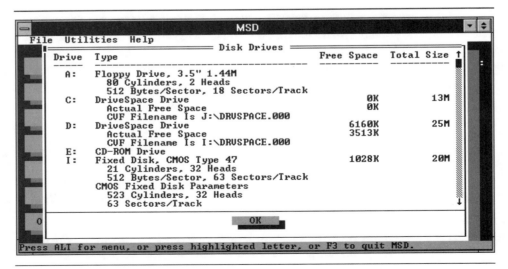

FIGURE 2.2: This screen in Microsoft Diagnostics tells you what resides on each of your disk drives.

LPT Ports and COM Ports   These boxes provide the number of each type of port installed on your computer. LPT ports are parallel ports (an external connector that accepts parallel cables from devices that need high-speed data transmission, such as printers) and COM ports are serial ports (ports for cables that transmit data one bit at a time, used for peripherals such as modems and mice). Pressing L or C provides more information, and the only item you'll need to know for both types is the Port Address, which is a hexadecimal number such as 0378H. This tells you whether you have the appropriate connectors for new external additions to your computing setup.

Windows   This box provides interesting information, but not about Windows. The lower portion of the box lists filenames with extensions such as .386 and .VXD. These are extra "driver" programs that other manufacturers have added into the Windows environment, usually incorporated when you install a custom video driver. If you have trouble with your computer when it's running Windows, these are likely suspects.

IRQ Status   Here you can learn which devices are using which hardware interrupts, and which IRQs are still available. Be careful, because Microsoft Diagnostics won't always catch all interrupts in use. It commonly overlooks CD-ROM controllers, for example.

TSR Programs and Device Drivers   Skip these boxes. This information is valuable only to an experienced troubleshooter or customer support representative.

WHAT MSD DOESN'T TELL YOU

There are some items Microsoft Diagnostics doesn't tell you about, and they're important. Microsoft Diagnostics won't tell you who made the chips in your computer's motherboard. If you have a generic clone computer, this can be important in determining compatibility with some upgrade cards and kits. To find out this information, open the computer case, and read the company name off the second biggest chip on the computer's motherboard. (For information about locating your computer's motherboard, see Skill 15.)

Microsoft Diagnostics also won't tell you about your cache RAM. This will require a knowledgeable friend or a more sophisticated diagnostic program.

Skill 2

Powerful Alternatives to MSD

Microsoft Diagnostics is a diagnostic tool with two shortcomings: The information you get is scattered, and some important information is missing. To see better information about your computer in a more usable format, you might want to consider using other programs.

Norton Utilities from Symantec is a large collection of programs that reveals what's in your computer, organizes it, rates it against other computers, and fixes it. It also can save your hide when you accidentally reformat your hard drive or delete a important file.

Another excellent tool for investigating the inner workings of your computer is WINCheckIt 4.0 from Touchstone Software. This program gives you all the details you could ever want in a unique format. This program displays a representation of your computer. You get information about an individual component by clicking it with your mouse.

If your computer uses the American Megatrends BIOS (you can confirm this with Microsoft Diagnostics next to the Computer box), you might want to look at AMIDiag. This program looks at any computer system with the AMI BIOS in intricate detail. AMIDiag can identify the type and speed of any cache memory you have as well as the newer expansion bus types such as PCI and VL-Bus. Because this program is expensive, it isn't one you would pick to use just once.

Quarterdeck Corporation offers WinProbe 4.0. This program is primarily intended to make your Windows and Windows 95 installation smooth, but it also performs comprehensive diagnostic tests on your hardware. If you're thinking about purchasing a product that can help you identify what you have now and enhance what you'll end up with later, this one may be for you.

The cream of the crop is QAPlus from DiagSoft. This DOS-based application is an incredibly complete program for delving into the depths of your computer. Every conceivable piece of information you could ever want is here, organized in a simple and understandable manner. It also lets you rate your computer's performance against others and includes a number of utilities to fix common problems with hardware and software. There's also a QAPlus for Windows.

Decoding Your Computer's Error Messages

In this world of vastly different software and computers, there can be many ways for modern technology to trip up, presenting you with challenges that may seem a bit daunting. For example, you might be working along fine when Windows 95 turns its screen to deep blue, announcing that you have experienced a *Fatal Exception Error.* Windows 95 will suggest that you press ↵ to recover, and that you may be able to continue as usual.

Fat chance.

Windows 95 has its own suite of problems that demand solutions. Arcane error messages are often displayed by even the latest and most competent versions of DOS. Windows 3.1 displays messages that seem coherent to the few who delve into memory management.

We'll tell you how to deal with many of the common failings of modern PCs. Some problems can be created solely by your computer, others by your operating system or applications. Knowing which of these products is the culprit can be the first step in resolving any issue. How do you know which part of your PC is struggling? Most problems can be solved by understanding the cryptic error messages that your PC displays on-screen.

Signs of Hardware Trouble

Your computer can detect if it's in trouble, then tell you what's wrong. Your PC considers its condition every time you turn on the power switch—even before the computer runs its operating system software.

The diagnostic process is called the Power On Self Test (POST). Your computer may display screwy error messages only an engineer could understand (see Table 2.1). Knowing what those error messages mean can help you decide which user manual to consult or which technical support line to call.

When you see the error messages in Table 2.1 displayed as simply numbers and letters alone, your PC's POST is telling you that you're in trouble. These error codes tell you something is amiss, but they don't tell you what to do. Your PC may be able to tell you in understandable sentences, but the messages can vary among PCs. If your PC doesn't give you a clearer message than those listed below, take your computer to a technician for best results.

TABLE 2.1: Common Hardware Error Messages

Error Message	Hardware Component
02x	Power supply
1xx	Motherboard
2xx	Memory (specific location also listed)
3xx	Keyboard (specific key may also be listed)

TABLE 2.1 CONTINUED: Common Hardware Error Messages

Error Message	Hardware Component
4xx	Monochrome video
5xx	Color Graphics Adapter (CGA) video
6xx	Diskette drive
7xx	Math coprocessor
9xx	Printer adapter card
10xx	Secondary printer adapter card
11xx	Serial (RS-232) adapter card
12xx	Secondary serial adapter card
13xx	Game, A/D, controller card
14xx	IBM graphics printer
17xx	Hard drive
18xx	Expansion unit
24xx	Enhanced Graphics Adapter (EGA) video
25xx	Secondary EGA video
28xx	PC/XT 3278/79 emulation adapter
29xx	IBM color graphics printer
30xx	Network adapter
31xx	Secondary network adapter
33xx	IBM compact printer
36xx	IEEE 488 adapter
38xx	Data acquisition adapter
39xx	Professional Graphics Adapter (PGA) video
48xx	Internal modem
49xx	Alternate internal modem
71xx	Voice communications
73xx	3.5-inch external drive
74xx	Video Graphics Array (VGA) video
85xx	IBM expanded memory adapter
86xx	PS/2 mouse or pointing device

MS-DOS Error Messages

MS-DOS, like your computer's hardware, can identify many problems that arise. Most problems DOS will tell you about are ones you've caused, such as typing errors, a DOS-compatible program that won't run because it was installed improperly, or not having all the hardware the program requires. The following are some error messages DOS displays:

- **Bad command or file name:** Filename errors mean you either typed incorrectly or are trying to access a path, directory, or file that doesn't exist. In the case of a command error, you either made a typing error or your DOS version doesn't recognize the command.

- **Cannot find system files:** Displayed when you try to make a (bootable) system diskette and DOS can't find the system files. Switch drives or directories so that the current DOS prompt indicates you're in the boot directory, then try the SYS command again.

- **Cannot load Command.com, system halted:** You started your computer with a system diskette in a diskette drive. You've also been running a program from a diskette, and that program needs to find COMMAND.COM. Put that system diskette back in the drive, and try again.

- **Existing format differs from that specified:** Appears when you are reformatting a disk or diskette to a different capacity. This is a "good" message. You'll have to tell DOS it's OK to continue.

- **File creation error:** Either the filename you specified is already in use or the disk is write-protected. If you're sure the diskette is not copy protected (you can find out by checking the tab on the diskette), try using a different filename. If these solutions don't work, try creating your new filename on another diskette or drive. You may simply have too many files located in the root directory of the disk.

- **Incorrect DOS version:** The version of the COMMAND.COM file doesn't match the version expected to be found by a program you're trying to run. You may have more than one version of some DOS files on your PC, and the program you're trying to run is finding an older (or newer) version by mistake. You may have to reinstall DOS to fix this problem.

- **Insufficient disk space:** The disk is full. You have to delete some files to create more free disk space.

- **Insufficient memory:** Close programs running in the background to give your PC more memory to work with.

- **Invalid drive in search path:** You must have made a hardware change. This message is telling you that you need to update your PATH statement to reflect drives that exist in your computer.

- **Invalid parameter:** You've used a command DOS does not understand. Type the name of the utility program you want to use, followed by the /? parameter, and then press ↵ to review a list of acceptable command parameters.

- **Non-system disk or disk error:** You're trying to start your computer, but it can't find a system diskette. Place a bootable diskette in your A: drive, and press ↵.

- **Out of memory:** A program can't complete its task because there is not enough free memory. Close some other running programs to free up memory. If no other programs are running, you may have to add memory capacity to your computer or consider buying a memory-management program.

- **Stack overflow—system halted:** Reboot your computer, then edit your CONFIG.SYS file so that the value of STACKS= is increased by 10.

When you see any of these messages, or the myriad others we don't have space to cover here, refer to your DOS documentation, or to one of the many third-party DOS manuals, such as *Mastering Dos 6 Special Edition*, also published by Sybex, to learn how to remedy the problem. Either source will tell you what's causing the problem.

Messages about Your Applications

If there is any sort of "Wild West" in personal computing, it exists in the diversity of programming methodology. Programmers, for example, can word an error message so it means something to them when they design the software, then forget to change the message so it makes sense to the user. The result is a garbled message. If an error message is displayed, you might identify that the message is created by your application if the program's name appears in the error message or on the title bar of the error message box. To solve the problem, refer to the users manual or call the application's technical support line.

Windows 3.1 Error Messages

Windows 3.1 has several error messages indicating that something needs to be done. The four most common ones are: *General Protection Fault* (GPF),

System Error—Divide by Zero or *Overflow Error*, *Application Execution Error*, and *Out of Memory*.

In the case of GPFs, System Errors, and Application Execution Errors, Windows has determined that an application has fumbled, resulting in some sort of trouble. Windows 3.1 names the culprit for you, and it's usually one of the applications currently running. These messages are displayed by Windows 3.1, but it's usually your application that needs fixing, so call *only* the technical support line for the program named in the error message.

If Windows 3.1 says you are out of memory, read the user manual to learn if it's a swap file issue, a system resource problem, or the effect of memory-hungry applications.

Windows 95 Error Messages

In virtually all error messages displayed by Windows 95, an application is named as the culprit. Click on the button that gives you more details to learn which of your programs is failing. Look for a filename with an .EXE (executable) or .DLL (dynamic link library) filename extension, then search your hard drive for that file. The application that "owns" the problematic program should be identifiable. If that program file is located in one of Windows 95's directories, call Microsoft for help. If the program named is not located in one of Windows 95's directories, call that application's technical support line.

Windows 95 also offers genuine Help at the click of a button. If a button is not displayed when trouble arises, press your keyboard's F1 key.

Are You Experienced?

Now you can. . .

- ☑ find and start MSD
- ☑ use MSD to find information for upgrading and configuring your computer
- ☑ work with alternatives to MSD
- ☑ make sense of the error messages your computer produces
- ☑ find help for problems with hardware, MS-DOS, and Windows

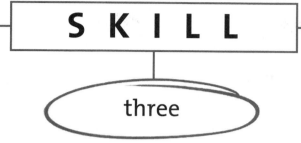

SKILL

3

three

Taking Precautions before You Begin

- ❑ Creating a system diskette
- ❑ Backing up your system files in MS-DOS or Windows
- ❑ Restoring backed-up data
- ❑ Understanding backup options and setup file strategies
- ❑ Developing a backup schedule
- ❑ Creating a bootable diskette
- ❑ Removing your computer's cover

Before you do anything to your computer, there are some precautionary steps you'll need to take. For some installations, these steps may seem like overkill. We cannot, however, stress strongly enough how important these measures are. This skill covers the precautions you'll need to take to make sure you don't get left out in the cold if something goes wrong during an installation. You'll learn how to create backup disks to store crucial system information and the data you can't afford to lose, and how to restore your system after a crash or conflict disables it. By the time you're finished, you'll be able to design a backup system to fit your needs, and you'll have a bootable diskette on hand. You'll even be able to open up your computer—that preliminary step that is so important to performing many of the upgrades outlined in this book.

Making System Diskettes

Installing new devices means installing new drivers (the software that tells a PC how to communicate with its peripherals), which in turn means configuration files get updated. Murphy's Law dictates that when these files get updated, things can go awry. If you load a new device, but can't get it or your PC to run properly (or at all) when you reboot your PC, it's very likely the new device has created a conflict. Having backups of system files can spare you hours of frustration.

If you have problems accessing your hard drive, you'll need a system diskette with which you can boot up your system. To create this diskette in MS-DOS, type **sys a:** at the C> prompt, and press ↵. The SYS command copies four mission-critical files: COMMAND.COM, IO.SYS, MSDOS.SYS, and one file needed for accessing DOS-compressed hard drives. DOS hides the latter three files from view so they can't be accidentally edited or deleted. As a general rule, you should never mess with these files except to copy them to a system diskette.

In Windows 3.1, open File Manager's Disk menu, and select Make A System Disk to copy the same files. In Windows 95, open Control Panel, and select Add/Remove Programs. In the Properties window that appears, click the Startup Disk tab, then Create Disk. This copies such files as COMMAND.COM, FDISK.EXE, FORMAT.COM, REGEDIT.EXE (Windows 95's Registry), and UNINSTAL.EXE (Windows 95's uninstaller utility).

DOS and Windows 3.x users also must copy their AUTOEXEC.BAT and CONFIG.SYS files, which contain critical information about what the computer needs upon startup to ensure normal operation. Copying the FORMAT.COM and FDISK.EXE files is also recommended. To copy these files, type the following commands at a DOS prompt:

```
copy c:\autoexec.bat a:
copy c:\config.sys a:
copy c:\dos\fdisk.exe a:
copy c:\dos\format.com a:
```

and press ↵ after each one. Windows 3.*x* users also should copy their WIN.INI and SYSTEM.INI files. To copy these files in DOS, use the above COPY command at the C:\WINDOWS> prompt. Or, in File Manager, highlight the files, and press F8. In the Copy dialog box's To field, type the destination to which the files should be copied.

Windows 95 users should copy their SYSTEM.DAT and USER.DAT files to diskettes. You can find these files in the Windows folder; these files, however, are hidden. To change the attributes of the files, go into Windows Explorer, and click the Windows folder icon. Then, open the View menu and select Options; in the resulting dialog box, click the View tab. Find the Hidden Files section and click the radio button next to Show All Files. When you scroll through the file listing, you will see SYSTEM.DAT and USER.DAT listed.

Backing Up

Backing up (making copies of) files can be tedious, but by doing it, you can avoid a host of more serious problems farther down the road. Backing up and then restoring the files on your system presents remarkably fewer hassles than you would encounter if you installed everything from scratch or tackled misconfiguration problems file by file. We can give you a score of reasons why you should back up, but in short: Trust us. Some day you'll need a backup.

Restoring Your Backup Files

In the event of a system crash, you'll need to restore your backup files to your hard drive. Every restoration process is different. On one occasion, you'll need to restore a single file. Another circumstance may require you to restore your entire system, just your WINDOWS directory, or all the files in your WordPerfect directory except your documents. The point is, if you have the backups, you can get inside your backup software and figure out how to restore files when you need to. But if you didn't make backups, you're out of luck. By the way: if you call

WHY DO YOU NEED TO BACK UP DATA?

Think about the data you store on your hard drive each day: your son's homework, your family's financial records, that sales presentation you've been working on for weeks. Is this data you want to lose? If you did lose it, how quickly could you re-create it?

Not convinced? Remember that all your hardware settings are stored on your hard drive in such files as AUTOEXEC.BAT, CONFIG.SYS, SYSTEM .INI, and WIN.INI. If your hard drive crashes and you don't have a backup of these settings, you can count on spending hours reinstalling device drivers and reconfiguring their Settings menus so they can run together without causing memory problems.

Still not convinced? Think of the new computer you just bought that was preloaded with an office suite, some games, online software, and diagnostic utilities. Most new computers with preinstalled software don't ship with diskettes you can use if the applications need to be reinstalled. Without backup copies of these programs, you're dead in the water. By backing up your applications, whether they were installed by you or the PC's manufacturer, you not only save yourself in a hard drive crisis, you've also saved the settings you've made so your word processor can print and your graphics software can access the graphics you scan. You can back up your applications with the same utility software you use to back up your data files.

technical support and have a complete, reasonably current set of backups, say so. Technical support will probably assume you don't have a backup, and may walk you through a far more tedious and dangerous repair than might be necessary with backups available.

Performing Backups in Windows and DOS

Be careful with your words and your time. Once they're gone, you can never get them back. Which is why we've stressed backing up your computer files on a regular basis. When files are lost, you not only lose the words and data they contain, but you also lose the time it took to accumulate that information. Fortunately, you don't need to look far for backup software. These programs are bundled with Win-dows 3.*x*, Windows 95, and all newer versions of MS-DOS. They provide everything you need to make backups of your files.

We'll describe how to make backups using the programs bundled with Windows 3.*x*, Windows 95, and MS-DOS 6.2. You'll learn how to select which files to back up, how to create and work with setup files, and how to use all the options in these programs. You should have at least three newly formatted diskettes available before proceeding with this tutorial.

From Windows 3.*x*

Depending upon your computer, Microsoft Backup for Windows 3.*x* can be found in the program group (a group of computer programs) labeled either Microsoft Tools or Microsoft Applications. Find the icon labeled Backup, and double-click it.

The first time you launch Microsoft Backup, the program needs to configure itself and run some tests to ensure the program's compatibility with the computer's diskette drive. It also will run a test to make certain that information from the hard drive is accurately copied to the diskette. The computer will tell you when to insert and change diskettes.

 **NOTE**   If the computer tells you to change diskettes, remove the full diskette and insert the next diskette. Don't hit the ↵ key to restart the process. The computer automatically recognizes when a new diskette is inserted and restarts the test itself. Hitting the ↵ key pauses the program.

Whenever Microsoft Backup is launched, it takes some time to read the contents of the hard drive. Then it will display a control panel with five large square buttons labeled Backup, Compare, Restore, Configure, and Quit (see Figure 3.1). Click the Backup button.

The next step is to pick a setup file to use. For now, use the DEFAULT.SET setup file. (More on setup files later.)

Next, choose which drive you will back up. Usually, there will be just one option, the C: drive. However, you may have additional choices if you have compressed your hard drive using Stacker, DriveSpace, or another disk compression utility, which is a program that compresses data so a hard drive can store more information. These choices, called virtual drives, don't really exist. They are simply a portion of a hard drive that has been set aside for storing

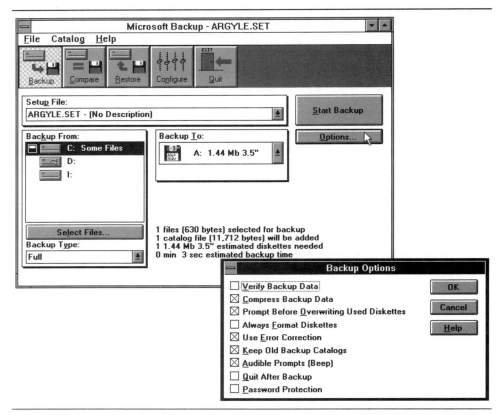

FIGURE 3.1: Backup for Windows makes it easy to select the drives and files that you want to back up.

uncompressed data. The program also may detect a CD-ROM drive or any additional hard drives.

A complete backup can take several hundred diskettes (and several hours) to copy all the data on today's large hard drives. You won't want to back up your entire hard drive very often. Rather, you'll back up a few important files, directories (a group of files and programs), or subdirectories (a directory contained in another directory) on a regular basis. Here's how to select them:

1. From the Microsoft Backup program, click the Select Files button. This opens a diagram showing all the directories, subdirectories, and files on your computer. The left side of the diagram shows directories and subdirectories. Clicking a different directory or subdirectory changes the list of files shown.

QUICK START: BACKING UP IN WINDOWS 3.*x*

To start a backup in Windows 3.*x*:

1. From File Manager, select Tools, Backup.

2. As with the MS-DOS utility, it may run a compatibility test to ensure the reliability of the backup. Follow the prompts.

3. Click Backup. A window pops up with options to customize your backup.

4. Select a drive to back up from and a drive to back up to.

5. Click Select Files.

6. The Select Files screen displays all directories, subdirectories, and files.

7. To select a file or directory, highlight it and double-click.

8. You can back up the entire hard drive by choosing Select All from the File menu or, on some systems, by pressing Ctrl+7.

9. To do a partial backup, highlight a file or directory, and click Include or Exclude. You'll be asked to select the files to be included in or excluded from your backup. Again, consider using the Differential backup mode.

10. When ready, click the Start Backup icon.

2. Scroll through the list of directories on the left to find the yellow icon for the WINDOWS directory, then click it. On the right side of the diagram, click the file named ARGYLE.BMP. (This is a bitmap file of the image used in the Argyle background pattern.)

3. Now click Include near the lower-left corner to open the Include/Exclude window. Click Add to add ARGYLE.BMP to the list of files that will be backed up. Click OK to close the Include/Exclude window.

4. A small black box next to the ARGYLE.BMP filename shows it has been selected for backup. A note in the lower-right corner, Selected Files, shows how many files (one) have been selected and how much data (630 bytes) they contain. Click OK.

5.   Choose a backup type. For this tutorial, choose a full backup.

6.   The box marked Backup To: contains the list of available diskette drives. Clicking the arrow opens a list of the types of drives and the type of diskettes (such as 1.44MB diskette or 720KB diskette) that can be used. Choose the appropriate drive and diskette option (probably 1.44MB, 3.5-inch).

At this point, you'll want to change the setup file. If you attempted to make a backup now, the computer would try to save the current settings in the DEFAULT .SET file. Instead, you should create a new setup file:

1.   Open the File menu, and choose the Save Setup As command. In the File Name: box, type **argyle** and click OK. The Setup File box should now read Argyle.set.

2.   Put a formatted, blank diskette in your computer's diskette drive, and click Start Backup. (Be prepared for a warning that says you can't use the diskette drive while making backups. It's nothing to worry about.) Microsoft Backup will make a backup copy of the ARGYLE.BMP file on the diskette.

Backup Options

These instructions can be used to back up anything from a single file to the entire hard drive. However, there are some options that can make Microsoft Backup even more useful.

The Backup Type list can be used to select one of three backup methods: full, incremental, or differential. A full backup is just what it sounds like: a complete backup of all the listed files. A differential backup makes copies of files that have changed since the last time a full backup was performed. An incremental backup makes copies of files that have changed since the last time a full or differential backup was performed.

The Options button offers nine more choices that can be turned on or off:

- **Verify Backup Data:** As each file is backed up, the computer pauses to compare the copy against the original file. This provides added security but slows down the backup process.

- **Compress Backup Data:** Backup copies can be compressed as they are copied to reduce the time it takes to transfer files to a diskette and to reduce the number of diskettes needed to back up data. The extent to which files can be compressed depends on the type of file.

- **Prompt Before Overwriting Used Diskettes:** This safety feature protects files from accidental erasure.

- **Always Format Diskette:** This is useful if you back up with unformatted diskettes.

- **Use Error Correction:** This is another useful feature that makes it possible to restore data even if a diskette is damaged. Although error correction can take up to 10 percent of a diskette, Microsoft recommends that it always be activated.

- **Keep Old Backup Catalogs:** Every backup creates a list, or catalog, of the files that were copied. The catalog is recorded on both the diskette and the hard drive. Old catalogs can eventually consume lots of space on the diskette and hard drive, but it's still a good idea to leave this feature activated.

- **Audible Prompts:** The computer beeps to remind you to change diskettes during a lengthy backup.

- **Quit After Backup:** Automatically closes Microsoft Backup after the backup is completed.

- **Password Protection:** You can use passwords to prevent files from being stolen and restored on someone else's computer.

Microsoft Backup can be programmed to automatically seek out and back up files created during a given time period regardless of what type of backup is selected. For example, it could be used to back up all files created during the current week.

To back up files created during a selected time period, click Select Files to open the list of directories and files. Click Special to open the Special Selections window.

In the section marked Backup Files In Date Range, click Apply Range. Type in the starting and ending dates for files you want to back up. Microsoft Backup will save all files created or modified during that period, including the starting and ending day. Be cautious with this option, however. Files will not be backed up if they are not contained in directories or subdirectories that are already marked for backup.

The Special Selections window also can be used to exclude certain types of files from the backup process. Click the window's Help button for an explanation of these options.

Setup File Strategies

Together, all the details used to perform a backup are memorized in a setup file. That includes the files chosen for backup, the files excluded from the backup, the type of backup, and all the other possible options. These details are memorized any time the File menu is used to create a new setup file (Save Setup As) or save an existing setup file (Save Setup).

Creating and saving setup files are essential to a sound backup strategy. For example, different setup files can be used for annual, bi-annual, monthly, weekly, and daily backups. Different setup files also could be created to back up database files, spreadsheet files, or document files.

A good practice is to fully back up critical files at least once a week and make differential or incremental backups on a daily basis. For a home-based business, that might mean executing a full backup once a week and differential backups daily. A graduate student might use the same strategy for backing up thesis or dissertation data. A home PC user, though, might get by with full backups of essential files once a month and differential backups once a week.

The determining factor in devising a backup strategy is not the amount of data involved, but the time involved in rebuilding the data if something should happen to it. (For more information on backup strategies, see "Creating a Backup Schedule" later in the chapter.)

From Windows 95

The backup program bundled with Windows 95 is similar in many ways to the Windows 3.*x* program. It offers almost the same options and also uses setup files. The most notable change is the step-by-step approach it takes to leading users through the backup process.

To find and start the backup program:

1. From the Start menu, choose Programs.

2. From the Programs list, choose Accessories ➤ System Tools.

3. Finally, click the Backup command to launch Microsoft Backup for Windows 95.

Launching this utility for the first time opens a box explaining the three-part backup process. Click OK to close this box. Then another box appears on-screen to explain the importance of the Full System Backup setup file. Read it, and then click OK.

A diagram of all the drives, folders, and files on the PC will appear on-screen. A plus or a minus sign appears on each folder icon. A minus means the folder is open and its contents are visible. A plus means it is closed and the contents are hidden. Click a plus sign to open a closed folder or a minus sign to close an open folder.

NOTE   Folders are the Windows 95 equivalent of directories and subdirectories.

Quick Start: Backing Up in Windows 95

1. From the Start menu, select Programs ➤ Accessories ➤ System Tools ➤ Backup.

2. The first screen you'll see provides a rundown of the steps in the backup process: selecting the files to be copied, choosing the destination drive, and beginning the backup process.

3. The next screen lets you choose to perform a full system backup.

4. Next, you arrive at the window where you're prompted to select the files to back up. Click the white box to the left of the file or directory to be backed up.

5. Once you've selected the files, click Next Step. At the resulting screen, select the destination drive.

6. After the drive has been selected, click Start Backup, and follow the prompts.

The next step is identifying the folder and files you want to back up. For this tutorial, follow these steps:

1. Click the My Computer icon, then the Windows 95 [C:] icon. Scroll down the diagram to find a folder marked Windows. Use the mouse and cursor to highlight it.

2. In the right side of the diagram, locate a file named GENERAL.TXT. Mark it for backup by clicking the box in front of the filename. (Clicking it again will deselect it.) After the file is selected, a note near the lower-right corner of the screen shows how many files have been selected and the size of the file.

   When a file is selected, a checkmark appears in a box next to the file name. A checkmark also appears next to the Windows folder icon, but that doesn't mean the entire folder will be backed up. It simply means that at least one file in the folder has been tagged for backup.

3. Click Next Step to open a new window where you will choose the destination for the backed-up file. Put a blank, formatted diskette in the computer's A: drive, select the A: drive, and click Start Backup.

4. A window labeled Backup Set Label appears. This creates a setup file that can be used for repeating the backup. For this tutorial, type **my test backup** in the space provided and click OK to start the actual backup. A window shows the progress of the backup and another appears when the backup is completed.

5. Click OK, and the backup is done.

Streamlined Options

The Windows 95 backup program offers fewer options than its Windows 3.*x* counterpart, and this makes for a program that's easier to operate. For example, instead of three types of backup (full, differential, and incremental), there are only two types (full and incremental). Some of the options that were eliminated have been replaced by two options for using tape backup drives.

Unlike the Windows 3.*x* backup program, the Windows 95 program lacks an Options button. To open a list of available backup options, open the Settings menu and select the Options command. Use the cursor to select the Backup tab. The available options are:

- **Quick backup after operation is finished**

- **Full backup**

- **Incremental backup**

- **Verify backup data by automatically comparing files after backup is finished:** This can slow down the backup process, but offers added protection.

- **Use data compression**

- **Format tape backup drives when needed:** This option automatically detects and formats unformatted cassettes.

- **Always erase on tape backups:** If the tape is unformatted or if the drive doesn't recognize the tape format, this option automatically erases the tape before recording backup files to it. If this option is not chosen, the computer attempts to back up files to the unused portion of the tape.

- **Always erase on diskette backups:** This option automatically erases all data on a diskette before making a backup. If this option is not chosen, the computer attempts to back up files to the unused portion of the diskette.

As with Windows 3.*x*, the Windows 95 backup program can back up files added or modified within a given date range. To back up files within a range of dates, open the Settings menu at the top of the screen, then click the File Filtering command.

Use the Last Modified Date option to program the computer to back up files created or modified within a given range of dates. This window also can be used to exclude entire types of files, such as batch files or executable files, from a backup.

From MS-DOS 6.2

The Microsoft backup program bundled with MS-DOS 6.2 is remarkably similar to the backup program bundled with Windows 3.*x*. (See Figure 3.2.) It uses the same commands, the same menus, and the same options. It even uses setup files created by its Windows cousin. So why create a duplicate backup program that runs in DOS, but not Windows?

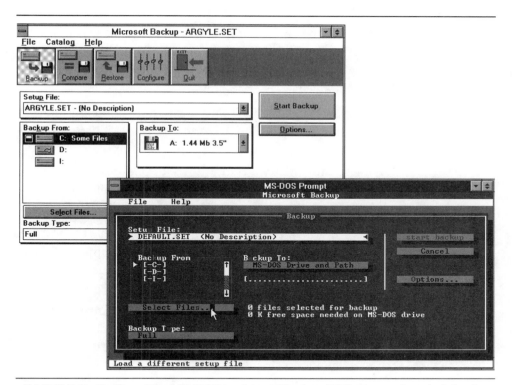

FIGURE 3.2:   The MS-DOS backup utility lets DOS users select their backup options with the same ease enjoyed by Window 3.*x* users.

One good question deserves another: What happens if the files that need to be restored are the files used to launch Windows? The DOS version of Microsoft Backup can be used to restore Windows if it cannot be launched.

To start Microsoft Backup, type

msbackup

at the C> prompt and press ↵. If the computer cannot find and launch the program, it may be necessary to find the directory and subdirectory that contains the

QUICK START: BACKING UP IN DOS

To run a backup from MS-DOS:

1. At the C> prompt, type **msbackup**. At this point, you might be asked to Autoconfigure; just follow the prompts.

2. Select a drive to which MSBACKUP can copy the files, such as your diskette drive.

3. A Compatibility Test prompt may appear if the system has not yet run one. Run it every time you install new hardware. To run the test, follow the on-screen prompts.

4. After the test, a menu will appear with five options: Backup, Restore, Compare, Configure, and Quit. Choose Backup.

5. In the Setup File box, select the default.

6. Using the Tab key, go to the Select Files box, and press ↵. On the Select Files screen, choose the drive from which to copy the files. In this case, select your hard drive (usually C:), then the directories you want to back up.

7. The Select Files box lets users customize the backup to the specific files or groups of files that change most frequently. The Differential backup type will copy just the files added or changed since your last full backup.

8. Once the variables have been adjusted, select Backup, and follow the prompts.

If you have MS-DOS 6.21, you can get a free (or at least very inexpensive) "step-up" diskette to MS-DOS 6.22. The backup utility in version 6.21 has no compression ability, which seriously impairs its practicality.

MSBACKUP.EXE file and include it in the DOS command line. If the MSBACKUP .EXE file is in the DOS directory, for example, you would type

c:\dos\msbackup

at the prompt and press ↵.

Like the Windows backup utility, the MS-DOS backup program must configure itself the first time it is run. Use the mouse and cursor to select Start Configuration to run the configuration. After the program configures itself, it will execute a self-test. Then, use the mouse and cursor to select Start Test. Have a couple of formatted diskettes ready for the test.

If the mouse doesn't function, use the Tab key until the Start Configuration button is highlighted, then press ↵. You can use the Tab and ↵ keys throughout the DOS program to open menus or execute commands. In some instances, you can also use the arrow keys and the spacebar to navigate the menus and select options.

BACKING UP APPLICATIONS

Copying applications and their customized settings is more difficult than backing up data files. Backing up programs is rarely as simple as copying the program's directory to another device; you often have to search through other locations, such as subdirectories under your /WINDOWS directory, to find other important files essential to the program's operation. A program's custom settings are stored in initialization files, and those files aren't always stored where you think they are. Your word processor might store settings in a .DOT or .INI file that could be stored in its own directory or in your WINDOWS directory. Windows itself also may save its .INI files in a directory other than its own. Consider sorting your directory listings to group all your .INI files together so you can copy them; the extra effort will be well worth the frustration you'll save yourself in the event of a hard drive crash.

Making Backups: Time Well Spent

Making backup files on a regular basis may seem like a nuisance, but it's no different than inspecting a car's brakes regularly. If you ever have an emergency, you'll be glad you took the precaution. There are ways to lessen the inconvenience. Some popular utilities can schedule backups to run by themselves. Many users schedule automatic backups late at night when no one is using the PC.

There are trade-offs with unattended backups. For one thing, there's no one around to switch diskettes. Consequently, unattended backups work only with incremental or differential backups that require a single diskette. If you need to run an unattended backup on a large hard drive, consider a tape drive. With this equipment, you can turn your drive on, click a few settings in your backup program, and then head home for dinner knowing your computer has everything under control.

Creating a Backup Schedule

There's a saying in our industry: "There are two kinds of people who use computers: Those who have experienced a drive crash, and those who will." If you take care of your hard drive, most of the time it will take care of you. Even so, things happen. There's no way to know when catastrophe is going to strike, so make sure you have copies of your important files in a safe place.

That's where backup schedules come in. Using the built-in utility programs in your operating system, or even using standalone packages, you have a variety of ways with which to protect your bytes before they hit the fan.

What Should I Do?

Excellent question. That depends on how you use your computer, and what you use it for. If you're using the computer for business, the information stored there is valuable and needs to be aggressively protected. For most home users, the information may not require as much protection.

There are three kinds of business backup schedules: light, moderate, and heavy. This applies to the amount of work you're going to perform and to the number of backup tapes or diskettes you're going to use. The heavier the schedule, the safer your data will be; for complete safety, you need some kind of backup every day.

Light Backups

This method uses just three sets of diskettes. Typically, you'd use a light backup on a weekly basis. Each Friday, for example, you do a full backup of the entire hard drive using one of three sets of backup media. This method requires the least effort and the smallest amount of media, but it is the riskiest.

For example, if your hard drive crashes on Friday morning, you'd have to use the previous Friday's backup to restore it. This means that you could lose up to a full week's worth of work.

Sometimes a failure can occur which you don't recognize for a while. A bad disk error might destroy the contents of a file but leave the file looking okay from the outside (directory listings and such). If something like that happened and it was three or more weeks before you noticed, you would already have overwritten good backups with bad ones; so make an extra backup at the end of each month and store it for three to six months. If your data is more valuable, a moderate or heavy backup approach might be best for you.

Moderate Backups

These provide more protection but take more time and backup media. Here, you would do a full backup every Friday and incremental backups of the new or changed data every other workday. The same diskette sets are used each week, and a fresh set is used for a full monthly backup.

How you use these diskettes to restore depends on what happens. Assume you accidentally erased a file from the hard drive on Wednesday, and the file was modified on Monday afternoon. Just grab the Monday disks, and restore that file. But what if the hard drive crashes on Thursday afternoon? After replacing the hard drive, you now have to restore all the data. You could use the Friday full backup and restore it to the new hard drive. Then grab the Monday incremental to restore the changes made that day, and so on through the following days. However, anything you did Thursday before the crash is gone for good. But you'd still only have to redo a morning's worth of work.

Heavy Backups

These provide the ultimate protection. You're going to use a lot of backup media, but it's worth it because you can recover from virtually any catastrophe. With a heavy backup schedule, you'll use a separate set of diskettes for each week of the month including incrementals for Monday through Thursday and full backups for each Friday, as well as a separate monthly backup.

With a heavy backup schedule, you can restore any file or directory on the hard drive from any day in the last five weeks by using the appropriate Friday backup and layering restored incrementals on top of each other. This is the ultimate in flexibility and security, but also in cost.

Do I Really Have to Do All This?

Your need for backups depends on how willing you are to be inconvenienced. Keep your backups small by only backing up data, not the programs used to create it. Your backups will be smaller and easier to manage, but if a crash occurs, you'll have to reinstall your programs from scratch.

You might want to think about making regular backups as cheap insurance. A few minutes here and there and a few dollars in the pot may save you a lot of time, effort, and frustration later.

Creating a Bootable Diskette

When disaster strikes, there's no need to panic. Even if you've changed a few system parameters and now you're unable to start your computer, you can remain calm. Just grab that bootable diskette you made as a backup when you first installed your system. You did make one, right?

It's always a good idea to make a backup of all your system files before problems arise. In fact, it's more than just a good idea; it's vital to your sanity and your computer. The best backup comes in the form of that aforementioned bootable diskette.

Every time you switch on your PC's power, your computer looks for something that will tell it what to do. The first thing it seeks is a bootable diskette, which has been specially prepared with important system files that are read during startup.

There are several reasons to keep bootable diskettes handy. First and foremost, the diskette would save your computer if your hard drive were unable to start itself because of system errors. A bootable diskette also is handy when you enter your directories and start deleting files. If you delete something important to your computer's operation, such as a startup mechanism, the bootable diskette will restore your original files. Bootable diskettes also are convenient if you think your computer may have contracted a virus. A final case for a bootable diskette occurs when you want to run a program that requires a lot of random-access memory (RAM), and your computer doesn't have enough space available. (RAM is the temporary memory storage area used to load program instructions.)

In addition to being useful, a bootable diskette is a breeze to use. Simply insert it in your diskette drive, and turn on your computer (or reboot, which means restart, if your computer is already on). That's it. Your computer will look for any diskettes before it goes into the hard drive to start itself.

In this section, we'll show you how to create one of these bootable diskettes. But before you can create a diskette, you must learn how to format one.

Formatting a Diskette

All diskettes must be formatted before your computer can read or write data to them or use them to start up. Formatting prepares the surface of the diskette to receive magnetic information transferred there by the heads in the diskette drive. If you try to read a diskette that isn't formatted, you'll see an error message on the computer's screen. If you try to save data to an unformatted diskette, the computer's operating system may tell you to format the diskette first.

 **WARNING** Formatting is a useful way to revitalize diskettes that have been used repeatedly. Formatting diskettes destroys all data saved to them, so use the FORMAT command carefully.

After you format a diskette, you can tell the computer to create a bootable diskette, adding hidden files to the diskette so you can start it from the diskette drive. For instance, in MS-DOS, the essential files IO.SYS, MSDOS.SYS, and COMMAND.COM. IO.SYS and MSDOS.SYS are called *hidden files,* although they can be accessible. These files are called hidden because they're not copied or listed with the general files, and they are ignored if a program is asked to display all files.

IO.SYS and MSDOS.SYS are the core program system files for DOS and are essential to making your computer work properly. COMMAND.COM tells your computer how to react to internal commands and executes the commands. Basically, these files set up the system so you can at least get a C> prompt. For this reason, you need a few other files on your diskette so that you can run your computer in the usual manner.

The extra files that belong on a bootable diskette are CONFIG.SYS and AUTOEXEC.BAT. CONFIG.SYS contains information about device drivers, buffers, and other miscellaneous commands. AUTOEXEC.BAT contains instructions that are carried out every time the computer is started.

The process used to format diskettes varies slightly with the type of operating system installed on the computer. Formatting diskettes in either MS-DOS or PC DOS requires entering a series of cryptic commands at the prompt. Windows 3.*x*, Windows for Workgroups (WFW), and Windows 95 use essentially the same menu structure. OS/2 Warp, the operating system designed by IBM, uses a slightly different procedure. Follow the step-by-step processes below to format and create bootable diskettes for your computer's operating system.

Creating Bootable DOS Diskettes

To create a DOS system (bootable) diskette, use the FORMAT command. The command line, as typed at the C> prompt, looks like this:

format <*x*:> /s

The FORMAT command tells DOS to prepare the diskette. Add a space and the drive letter where the diskette is located. In the example above, replace *x* with the letter of the drive holding your diskette. This usually will be either drive A: or drive B:. Always include a colon after the drive letter.

Make sure you specify the drive holding the diskette you want formatted. If you omit the drive letter DOS formats the diskette in the current drive, potentially erasing data. The /S switch tells DOS to add COMMAND.COM (a file that contains internal DOS commands and recognizes DOS as an executable program) and the two hidden files on the diskette after formatting is completed.

When the computer has finished formatting, the system will ask you for a volume label. Here, you can name your diskette in 11 characters or less.

To copy the AUTOEXEC.BAT and CONFIG.SYS files to a diskette in drive A:, type

copy c:\autoexec.bat a:

and press ⏎. When that file is copied, type the same command again, only replace the word *autoexec.bat* with *config.sys* and press ⏎. Your DOS bootable diskette is now complete.

Creating Bootable Windows Diskettes

Windows makes formatting diskettes as simple as pointing and clicking. You don't have to enter command line parameters like you do in DOS. Instead, follow these steps:

1. Double-click the File Manager icon in the Program Manager's Main program group.

2. If you installed Windows 95 over Windows 3.*x*, you should find File Manager listed in the Windows directory as WINFILE.EXE. Double-click this file to start File Manager, or check out Windows 95 Help to learn how to create a Start menu shortcut to File Manager.

3. Select the Disk option on the menu bar. The drop-down menu gives you four choices: Label Disk, Make System Disk, Format Disk, Select Drive.

4. Click the Format Disk option. It contains all of the other choices in one window.

5. Click the drive holding the diskette you want to format. The selection window lists the drive letters for only the drives capable of being formatted. These are usually only drives A: and B:.

6. Next, click diskette type. Windows automatically reads the type of drive you've selected, but you have to select the double-density or high-density size.

7. If you want to give the diskette a name, click in the options box marked Label, and type the name you want to give the diskette.

8. Click the mouse pointer in the other options boxes to perform a quick format or make a system diskette.

9. Finally, click OK to begin formatting.

To copy the AUTOEXE.BAT and CONFIG.SYS files in Windows:

1. Highlight the C:\ root directory in the left window of File Manager.

2. Locate the AUTOEXEC.BAT file in the right window, and click it. Then choose Copy from the File menu. A dialog box will appear. The Current Directory box should read C:\.

3. In the From: box, type **config.sys**. In the To: box, type **a:** or **b:** (depending on which diskette drive you use). After typing the destinations, press ↵.

Windows 95 offers two other methods for formatting diskettes. One uses Explorer, which is on the Desktop. Double-click the Explorer icon, and scroll the left column to see the diskette drive icons for A: and B:. Then right-click the icon representing the drive holding the diskette to be formatted. This opens a menu. Click the Format option, and select the options as described earlier for File Manager. Click the Start button to begin formatting.

The second method uses the My Computer folder on the Desktop. Double-click the folder, then right-click the drive icon. On the options menu that opens, select Format and the options described above for volume and storage capacity.

To make a bootable diskette, click the Copy System Files Only option.

To copy the AUTOEXEC.BAT and CONFIG.SYS files, click the My Computer icon and find the files here, making sure the diskette drive location is visible. Press the Ctrl key, click one of the files, and drag it to the desired destination. Repeat the procedure for the other file.

Creating Bootable OS/2 Warp Diskettes

To format an OS/2 Warp diskette, follow these steps:

1. Open the OS/2 System folder by double-clicking it.

2. Click the drives icon to open the drives folder. This folder shows an icon for each drive in your computer, including the hard drive and CD-ROM drive.

3. Double-click the icon for the drive holding the diskette to be formatted.

4. Open the formatting options menu by clicking the diskette symbol in the upper-left corner of the drive window. Then select Format Disk.

5. Finally, type a volume name in the label window. You may leave this line blank if you want. Select the type of format you want to perform. The choices are HPFS (High Performance File System) or FAT (File Allocation Table). Click the System Diskette option to create a bootable diskette. (Note that the format choices and the System Diskette option may not appear in the dialog box in some versions of OS/2.)

6. Start the formatting process by clicking the Format button at the bottom of the options box.

 **WARNING**   Be careful when selecting the drive to format in all three operating systems. It is easy to choose the C: drive and click the Format button by mistake. This erases all files on the hard drive, causing a fatal data loss.

OPENING THE HOOD: LOOKING INSIDE YOUR COMPUTER

You're now ready to pop open your computer's hood. Most of the installations in this book will require you to do this. The only tool you'll need is a Phillips screwdriver. This procedure isn't difficult but it requires some concentration and an adequate space for working.

First, unplug your computer and all its peripherals. You can leave the plugs connected to the back of your computer and devices, but remove all the plugs from their electrical sockets. This will eliminate the possibility of you getting zapped by an electrical surge. Look at the back of your computer. Most systems will have screws running along the very edge of their cases. These are the screws you need to remove. Do not remove any screws near your computer's fan, AC connection, or ports.

Your computer case's cover will probably slide off toward the back of the computer along its tracking. Some computers, however, may require you to slide the cover back slightly, then lift it off.

continued ▶

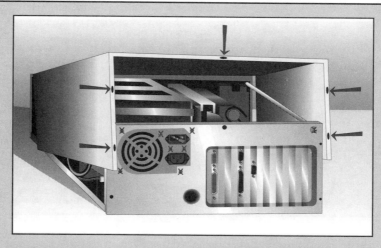

Before performing an installation, ground yourself by touching the metal frame of your PC to eliminate any static you might be carrying. Static discharges, no matter how mild, can damage cards and chips on the motherboard (the main circuit board of a PC). To protect your new components, leave them in the anti-static bags they were shipped in until the last possible moment.

You're now ready to proceed with the installations covered in this book.

Are You Experienced?

Now you can. . .

- ☑ create a system diskette
- ☑ back up system files in MS-DOS, Windows 3.1, and Windows 95
- ☑ restore data after disaster strikes
- ☑ choose among many backup options and use a setup file
- ☑ deveop a backup schedule that fits your needs
- ☑ create a bootable diskette
- ☑ remove your computer's cover

S K I L L

four

4

Installing Random Access Memory

- ❏ Evaluating the current amount of RAM in your machine

- ❏ Understanding upgrade options with RAM

- ❏ Identifying the different types of RAM and RAM boards

- ❏ Locating the SIMM sockets on the motherboard

- ❏ Removing and replacing RAM

In the old days of computing with DOS, PC users didn't need to know much about memory. If a problem with memory developed, they could adjust the settings in the AUTOEXEC.BAT and CONFIG.SYS files and reboot the computer. If they wanted more memory, they installed a memory card and ran a memory management program. That's not the case now. Almost nobody runs just DOS anymore.

Windows, which slaps a graphical menuing system on monitors, runs on top of DOS (or, in the case of Windows 95, replaces it altogether). But the Windows environment has a ravenous appetite for memory. It doesn't matter whether you run Windows 3.1 or Windows 95. If you don't have enough memory, your computer will run sluggishly, even if you have a fast Pentium processor.

The Fastest, Easiest Upgrade of All

So, if you want to improve your computer's operation, feed it a healthy diet of more memory. No other upgrade will better enhance your computer's performance, whether it is an older system or a new 266 megahertz (MHz) Pentium II. With Windows 3.1, you need 4MB of random access memory (RAM). Although that's a big jump in memory needs compared to the 640KB required by the early DOS-based computers, Windows limps along on 4MB. Pop in another 4MB and Windows 3.1 runs much better. With Windows 95, you need at least 8MB of RAM to handle all the advanced graphical tasks and to run one or two programs at a time.

Windows 95 Needs at Least 16MB

To get satisfactory performance from Windows 95, your computer needs at least 16MB of RAM. Although Windows 3.1 doesn't get much faster with more than 8MB of RAM, Windows 95's performance improves with each megabyte of memory. That's because Windows manages available memory by sharing what it needs to run multiple programs, print files, operate the diskette drives and monitor, and so on. When it runs low on memory, Windows converts the overflowing data into a temporary file, called a *Windows swap file*, in space it reserves on the hard drive. As you can imagine, offloading data to and then retrieving it from the hard drive takes a toll on the computer's efficiency because getting data from the hard drive is a considerably slower process than retrieving something from RAM. When there is a large supply of RAM, however, Windows can bypass the swap file on the hard drive and maintain its speed.

Many computing novices confuse the capacity of the hard drive and the amount of RAM a computer has. Aside from electricity, memory is what drives your computer. The size of the hard drive only limits how many programs and how much data you can save to it. Having an overly large hard drive for storage won't help much if your computer is starving for memory.

It is relatively easy to install more memory. Even if you've never ventured inside a computer, you can slip more RAM chips into the waiting slots on the motherboard. If you have an older computer, such as one with an 80286 or 80386 microprocessor, you will be limited to how much memory you can add.

TIP   The "Steps to Installing RAM" section walks you through the process of installing RAM.

For example, Windows 3.1 works best on a 486DX or higher central processing unit (CPU). Adding more memory to a slower system won't give you a huge performance boost. Similarly, Windows 95 is designed to run best with the added features built into a Pentium processor. Windows 95 isn't as proficient at handling more memory on slower CPUs because of the way the software was designed. Windows 3.1 still relies upon DOS to manage its memory; specifically, a DOS program called Microsoft Expanded Memory Manager 386 (EMM386.EXE) does this job. Windows 95 uses a new system to manage memory usage; although it still runs DOS in the background, the DOS version is redesigned to work exclusively with Windows 95.

Choosing Memory Modules

Memory is a vital component in all computers, but all memory isn't the same. Before you can upgrade memory, you must find out which type of memory chips your computer uses. You also must decide which kind of memory you want to upgrade.

Memory chips are measured by their RAM speed, which is the rate at which the modules work. RAM speed is expressed in nanoseconds (ns); rather than bog yourself down in technical definitions, remember simply that the smaller the number of nanoseconds, the faster the chip. You can install slower RAM than the other chips in your computer if you are adding to what's already there. But you cannot install a faster chip than your computer is rated to use. Check your computer's documentation to see which type and memory speed the system needs. You'll have to buy chips in multiples equal to the total memory you want. For instance, if you have 4MB now and want to upgrade to 16MB, see how many vacant memory slots there are. If the existing 4MB module is in one slot and there is only one slot remaining, you have to remove the existing module and buy two 8MB modules, one for each socket. If you only want to upgrade to a total of 8MB, just add an additional 4MB module into the available slot.

Here are the RAM types you'll encounter:

- **DRAM:** Dynamic random access memory. This is the most common and cheapest type of memory chip. This is also the slowest type of memory because it is made up of capacitors. The computer must constantly refresh its memory by recharging the capacitors. Usually DRAM chips are hard-wired to the motherboard and can't be removed without an expert's help. You can only add more chips in the available accessory slot.

- **SRAM:** Static random access memory. This memory chip is made of transistors, which do not need refreshing. Because it doesn't need constant refreshing, SRAM is about four times faster than DRAM. SRAM chips are larger than other types of memory so they are used to meet only some of the memory needs in a computer.

- **EDO RAM:** Extended data out random access memory. This is the fastest but most expensive memory chip. It handles memory access about 30 times faster than SRAM because it can move data in and out from different addresses at the same time.

- **VRAM:** Video random access memory. VRAM is used on video boards. It is much like DRAM but has a second port to speed up the access time. Adding more video memory speeds up the time it takes the motherboard to place colors, images, and text on-screen. If the video board is slow (meaning it only has 1MB of memory), the computer's motherboard has to spend too much time creating the image on-screen. The result is a slower response to programs and other functions.

When you upgrade RAM, you must add more of the same type of memory modules. For example, if your computer has DRAM, you cannot replace it with faster SRAM or EDO RAM chips because the electronic circuits can't handle this kind of design change. However, if your video card will accept more VRAM chips, adding them will measurably speed up the computer's performance even if you don't increase the overall RAM on the motherboard.

Installing Additional RAM

Computers use three types of RAM chips, depending upon their design. Older computers use dual inline chips (DIPs) that must be pushed directly in their sockets. DIP chips are the most difficult to install. These chips have two rows of eight "legs" called contacts. To install them, you must first remove the existing DIP chips with a special tool called a chip puller. Use the puller to grab the chip firmly and then rock gently from side to side to dislodge the contacts. Insert the new DIP chips very carefully to make sure all 16 contacts are centered in the socket. Then press firmly until the chip is seated against the top of the socket. If even one contact is bent during installation, your computer will not start.

Newer computers use single inline memory modules (SIMMs), which have single rows of chips soldered to a narrow circuit card with contacts on the bottom edge. SIMMs come in two varieties: 30 pins and 72 pins. To install them, hold the SIMM at an angle to match the plane of the holder in the socket. Then align the plastic pin in the socket with the hole at one end of the SIMM; SIMMs only fit in the socket one way. Push the metal contacts at the bottom of the SIMM into the socket. Finally, press the SIMM firmly into the socket, and press the SIMM back until the tabs on either side slide into position.

The newest type of memory is the dual inline memory module (DIMM), but unless you have a new PC built to the latest design standards, you won't have this type. DIMMs are installed the same way as SIMMs, but are thicker than SIMMs because the chips are stacked one atop another. The advantage is that DIMMs can provide more memory per module at only a slightly higher cost than SIMMs.

WARNING Before you touch the inside of the computer or handle the memory chips, make sure you discharge static electricity. If you don't, even a tiny static charge (unnoticeable to you) can permanently zap the electronic components. If you walk across a carpet while working on your computer, always re-ground yourself.

Planning Ahead

Upgrading computer memory is one of the best ways to give your system a longer, more useful life. Spending a few hundred dollars for memory is much better than buying a new computer. Memory slots are limited, though, so buy a module with enough memory to handle your future needs. Otherwise, you'll waste what you spend now if you decide to upgrade again later. Also, buy memory from a reliable dealer. Bargain basement deals can cost you big bucks if the memory chip goes bad or if it isn't the right type of memory for your computer.

To help consumers, Kingston Technology Corporation analyzed the memory demands of common applications to create a list of recommendations for a variety of tasks (see Table 4.1). Although each category is demarcated with minimum and maximum amounts, any of the tasks discussed here can be run on less RAM than is specified. However, running these applications at or near the recommended maximum amounts helps ensure optimum performance.

TABLE 4.1: How Much RAM Is Enough?

Amount of RAM	Applications in Use
8MB to 12MB	Light word processing, e-mail, and database use with one to two applications open simultaneously.
12MB to 16MB	Medium administrative uses including word processing, e-mail, fax and communications, spreadsheets, and business graphics with one to two applications open at once.
16MB to 24MB	Light number crunching involving spreadsheets, e-mail, and accounting software with one to two applications open at once for heavy administrative work.
24MB to 32MB	Heavy number crunching involving spreadsheet and statistical applications, large research databases, and more than three applications open at once.
32MB to 64MB	Light graphics involving word processing, page layout, and illustration or graphics software with one to two applications open at once.
64MB to 128MB	Medium graphics involving basic photo editing, presentation software, font packages, multimedia, word processing, page layout, illustration/ graphics software, and more than three applications open at once.

How to Install RAM

Here are two reasons to perform a memory upgrade. First, memory takes less than ten minutes to install. And second, it can help even a weak computer immensely. That's because random access memory (RAM) is like a large library where the CPU comes to gather the data it needs to make the applications run. As mentioned above, the more RAM your PC has, the less time the CPU has to spend searching for data in the swap file, which switches some of the data from RAM to the hard drive. The less swapping you do, the faster the CPU works.

A few years ago, the average PC was equipped with 4MB of RAM. That standard was upped to 8MB, and then to 16MB. Users who play computer games or work with desktop publishing programs might need as much as 128MB of RAM, though. Along with the progression of RAM size, chip technology has changed to the point where it's become fairly difficult to know what type of RAM is needed. *EDO, parity, non-parity, single inline memory modules,* and *dual inline memory modules* are some of the phrases you'll need to understand. The irony is that it's actually more difficult and time-consuming to become familiar with these terms than it is to install RAM on your PC.

Finding the Current Amount of RAM

There are three ways to discover how much memory is now in your computer.

- Type **mem** at the DOS prompt. Look under the Total column for the amount of memory you have. The amount will be listed in kilobytes (KB); eliminate the numbers after the comma to convert it to megabytes. For example, if the amount is 16,192KB, remove the 192 and add MB to the 16. You have 16MB of RAM.

- Watch the screen as the PC boots up. The BIOS, which is built into a computer's circuitry, controls the start-up routines for peripheral devices, such as the keyboard, display, and disk drives, and runs a diagnostic test on the PC's peripheral hardware. In the process, it tells you how much RAM you have.

- Right-click the My Computer icon on the Windows 95 Desktop. From the menu that appears, click Properties. The amount of memory your PC has will appear on-screen.

 NOTE   Adding memory will help a computer only so much. For example, we upgraded from 16MB to 56MB of RAM. After the upgrade, we saw improved performance, but only to a degree. Despite the infusion of RAM, performance was limited by the 66 megahertz (MHz) CPU installed in our PC. Therefore, you may be better off saving the money to invest in a newer computer.

Regardless of the limitations inherent in increasing your PC's RAM, there are obvious benefits to this type of upgrade RAM. For example, tests show that a 100MHz Intel Pentium processor with 32MB of RAM will outperform a 133MHz Pentium with 8MB of RAM.

First Step: Open Up

There's an easy way and a hard way to know what kind of RAM you need to buy for your upgrade. The easy way is to go to the computer manual and research what kind of memory is already inside the PC. The more complicated way is to open your computer's case and determine what type of memory you need by investigating the chips that are already there.

Since the easy way needs little explanation, let's focus on the difficult path. The first step in locating your RAM is to close all open applications and turn off the power to your PC. Also, as an extra precaution, you should unplug the computer. Then follow the instructions in Skill 2 to remove the case to prepare for installation.

Try to determine which screws (if any) you need to unscrew in order to remove the case. On the system we upgraded, we didn't have to remove any screws; the case slid off after pinching two tabs in front. Your computer might be configured similarly. Make sure you don't remove any screws near your computer's fan, electrical connection, or ports—all of which can be found at the rear of the system. After the screws are removed, slide the cover toward the front or back to remove it. Ground yourself by touching the computer's metal case or power supply box.

Finding the RAM

Now we can begin to explain what you might be looking for. The first items to locate are single inline memory modules (SIMMs), which are slender circuit boards dedicated to storing RAM. They're usually green with a row of rectangular, gray chips attached to them. SIMMs fit into sockets that have metal clips on either end. The sockets are usually located near the CPU on the motherboard (see Figure 4.1). We had to remove the power supply on our computer to access the SIMMs. Other computers may allow straight access to the SIMMs.

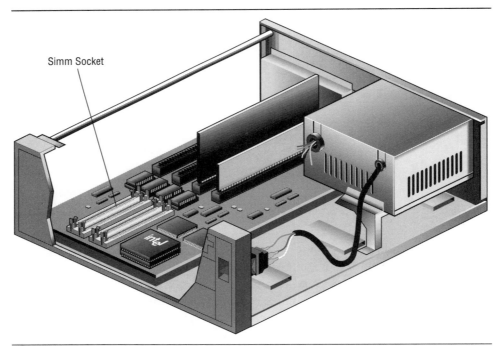

FIGURE 4.1:   The SIMM Sockets are usually long, white parallel channels.

If you have a newer computer (one powered by a Pentium or an IBM PowerPC microprocessor), it will have dual inline memory modules (DIMMs) instead of SIMMs.

You'll be able to tell the difference between the SIMMs and DIMMs by the number of pins on each type of module. The two types of SIMMs are 30- and 72-pin modules (see Figure 4.2). DIMMs for desktop PCs come in a 168-pin variety, and currently are much more expensive than regular 72-pin SIMMs.

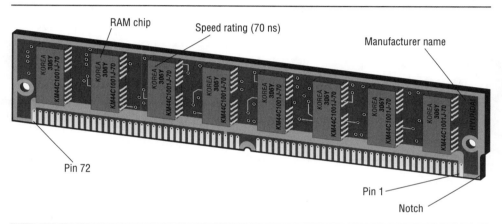

FIGURE 4.2:   A typical 4MB 72-pin SIMM.

A pin is a metal attachment on the module that allows data to pass from the PC to the rows of memory chips. Pins look like a number of little fingers running along the bottom of the module. The number of pins is crucial because 30-, 72-, and 168-pin modules will be different lengths, and consequently are incompatible with one another. In short, you must have the correct number of pins on your module or the RAM won't fit into your computer's sockets.

No Room for More SIMMs

When you find the RAM sockets in your system, you may discover that the PC has no memory modules. In this case, your computer is hard-wired with a small amount of RAM on the motherboard, and you'll have to look in the user's manual to determine the type of RAM your system requires. On the other hand, you may find that your system doesn't have any empty sockets. This doesn't necessarily mean that you can't add more RAM. You'll just have to take out some of the modules already in place.

Before you do this, we need to issue one caveat. Some computers require sockets to work in tandem, meaning that two sockets must have memory modules in place in order to function. This requirement is called a *bank*. A bank of RAM could be one socket, two sockets, or four sockets. If a computer requires a two-socket bank, but only has one socket filled with SIMMs, it will fail to boot up.

Solving a RAM Space Crunch

How can you tell which type of banks your computer requires? Here's a shortcut: If you have an older computer—one with a 386 or an early-model 486 CPU—it probably has a four-socket bank of 30-pin modules. Late-model 486s require one socket of 72-pin modules. Computers equipped with Pentium chips require two sockets of 72-pin modules.

 NOTE DIMMs can be installed individually, but to take full advantage of interleaving (a technology that reduces the amount of time the microprocessor must wait to access RAM), they must be installed in tandem.

Another shortcut is to deduce what kind of module you have by what is already in the PC. Assuming that you've never upgraded your RAM before, if your computer has two sockets of memory modules, it's likely that your computer has a two-socket bank. If all four of the sockets are filled, the PC probably has a four-socket bank. If only one is filled, the PC has a single-socket bank. To be absolutely safe, call the manufacturer, ask a salesperson, or consult the user's manual.

OKAY, NOW FOR A MATH QUIZ

Let's say you have a Pentium-equipped computer, and you want to add 16MB of RAM to it. You could buy one module of 16MB, but you would be making a mistake. Why? Because one module will fill only one socket, and from this discussion, you know that Pentium-equipped computers must have two sockets filled. Thus, you must buy two modules of 8MB, which equals the 16MB you desire.

Proper Identification

Here are four other things that you'll need to know when buying memory for your computer.

Access Speed   The speed rating of the memory chip is measured in nanoseconds. For the CPU and RAM to communicate, they have to have a speed that matches one another. Memory chips are rated at 60, 70, and 80 nanoseconds (ns).

To find the access speed of your system, find the tiny numbers and letters printed on the side of your memory chips. There's usually a series of characters followed by a dash and then a number. The number will be the chip's access speed. If there's only a one-digit number, such as a six, seven, or eight, that's okay; these numbers represent 60, 70, or 80, respectively.

 NOTE   It's okay to add faster chips but not slower ones. And in this case, the lower number is faster (that is, 60ns is faster than 70ns)

EDO or Non-EDO   This is something that mainly applies to owners of Pentium-equipped computers. EDO stands for extended data out, which is a shortcut designed in some RAM chips to decrease the amount of time the CPU and memory interact. Putting EDO chips in a non-EDO computer won't do any harm. Putting non-EDO chips in an EDO computer won't hurt anything either; however, the computer won't boot up, or it will operate more slowly than if you used the proper EDO chips.

Parity Bits   Your computer may also require RAM to support what's known as *parity*, which is a method used by some PCs to check the accuracy of a data transmission. With this system, an extra bit (known as a parity bit) is attached to the end of each byte (eight bits). This parity bit, like all other binary data, is a 0 or 1. Odd parity means the extra bit makes all of the bits add up to an odd number; even parity means the extra bits add up to an even number. Most computers in the home market use non-parity checking.

Tin or Gold   Pins are composed of either of these elements. You'll want to be consistent with the materials in your computer. Mainly, it's the high-end PCs that have modules with pins made of gold. A failure to match metals properly will deteriorate the connections in a computer.

Time to Change

After you've purchased the RAM, it's time to install it. Here are the steps you'll need to follow:

1. Ground yourself again by touching the computer's metal case or power supply box. Remove the module from its antistatic bag, being careful not to touch any metal parts on the chip. Try to hold the module from the sides.

2. One end of the module has a small notch so you know which way to align it in the socket. The socket has two posts, one on each side. One of these posts has a small plastic tab at its base that will just fit the notch of the module. Depending on the socket type, you'll need to bring the module in either horizontally or at an angle, then lift it to an upright position. On our computer, we pushed the module into the socket at a 45-degree angle, then moved it to a vertical position (see Figure 4.3). You shouldn't have to push very hard to get the module into the socket.

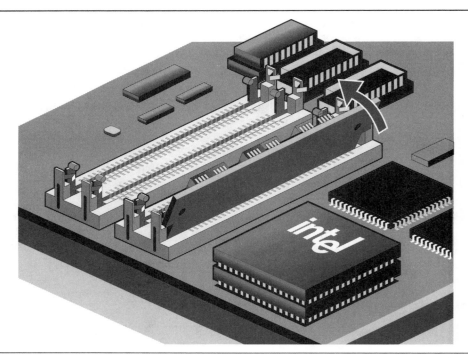

FIGURE 4.3:   SIMMs are installed at an angle, then snapped into the metal clip holders.

3. When the module is in place, two metal prongs attached to the plastic posts should fit evenly into the slot; one end should not be higher than the other. If everything looks okay, replace whatever components you had to move to install the RAM. You might want to test the machine before replacing the cover.

You'll probably receive some sort of error message as your computer boots up. All setup programs are a little different, so you should follow the directions on-screen or in the user's manual. The bottom line is that your computer needs you to update the amount of memory it now has. The setup program might detect the amount of new RAM automatically or you might have to enter the new value yourself.

If you try to boot your PC and nothing happens or your computer recognizes an amount of memory less than you installed, go back over the checklists above to ensure that you are using the right type of memory for your system. If that doesn't shed some light on the problem, try to reseat each of the modules following the steps above.

Once everything is working correctly, you should find that your applications run faster, and your computer generally performs better. And if nothing else, at least you won't have to worry about RAM prices for a while.

Are You Experienced?

Now you can. . .

- ☑ determine the amount of RAM in your computer
- ☑ upgrade your PC with more (or faster) RAM to achieve faster Windows performance and eliminate Windows bottlenecks
- ☑ figure out the difference between SIMMs and DIMMs
- ☑ determine if your computer uses 60 ns, 70 ns, or faster RAM chips
- ☑ pull out and re-install RAM SIMMs safely

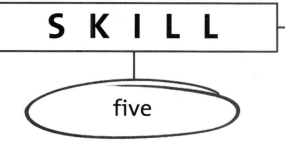

S K I L L

five

Installing CPUs

- ❑ Removing CPUs, fans, and heat sinks
- ❑ Understanding ZIF and LIF sockets
- ❑ Substituting a new heat sink
- ❑ Replacing an old CPU with a new one
- ❑ Adding an OverDrive CPU
- ❑ Updating software for a new CPU

The central processing unit (CPU), or microprocessor, is the most vital piece of hardware in your computer. Responsible for running every function of a computer, the microprocessor also interprets and carries out your instructions.

Every instruction to the computer travels through the microprocessor, which completes and routes the instructions to the proper component of your system. The CPU consists of a tiny, square silicon chip—often enclosed in a plastic casing. By upgrading it, you can make your computer operate much more efficiently. (The actual amount of improvement you'll notice may be slightly limited depending upon the type of computer you're upgrading. Some older computers, for example, can't be upgraded to Pentium performance. Also, only certain Pentium processors—and no 486s—can be upgraded at all to take advantage of MMX technology.)

NOTE MMX technology is Intel's latest enhancement to its processors. It delivers greater speed, as well as refined graphics and video.

Types of Upgrades

The type of CPU upgrade kit you'll want depends upon the type and speed of the computer you want to upgrade. CPU upgrades fall into three basic categories: chip-for-chip upgrades, piggyback upgrades, and daughtercard upgrades. Each of these upgrades is relatively easy to perform—you should be able to upgrade your computer's CPU yourself, without any unusual or expensive tools. (You should only need a small Phillips screwdriver to remove the computer's case, and possibly a chip removal tool to remove the existing microprocessor. If you need a chip removal tool, it will be included in the upgrade kit.)

NOTE It's always a good idea to have a phone and the technical support phone number for the upgrade manufacturer within reach. If you run into trouble, technical support personnel can walk you through the installation process.

Chip-for-Chip Upgrades In this type of upgrade, the old microprocessor is removed, and the new processor is inserted in the empty socket. Intel's OverDrive Pentium chip with MMX technology is one example where you completely replace the original chip. A variation on the chip-for-chip upgrade, however, occurs in some computers with special (pre-MMX) OverDrive sockets. The

OverDrive processor from Intel is a special upgrade for 486 and Pentium processors. Instead of removing the original microprocessor, the OverDrive processor pops into the "extra" OverDrive socket on the motherboard. This type of upgrade is designed to boost your system's performance, but may not raise it to the level of the next generation of CPUs.

These sockets let you place the new processor on the motherboard (the circuit board at the bottom of the computer case to which all the electrical components are attached) without removing the old one. They are usually found in computers where the original microprocessor can't be removed from the motherboard.

Piggyback Upgrades   This type of upgrade is performed by stacking the new processor on top of the old one. These upgrades are the easiest to do because you don't have to remove the old processor before performing the upgrade. Unless you run into trouble, it shouldn't take more than 15 minutes to perform a piggyback upgrade.

Daughtercard Upgrades   These upgrades are sometimes called card replacements or board replacements. Instead of installing a new chip, you install a daughtercard, which is a small board with a CPU chip attached. This type of upgrade is only slightly more difficult to perform than the other types of upgrades; it should take less than 30 minutes.

Types of Sockets

The type of socket in which your current CPU is installed will help determine the type of upgrade you'll perform. Nearly every Pentium computer will have its microprocessor in either a zero-insertion force (ZIF) or a low-insertion force (LIF) socket. (In the past, LIF sockets have commonly been called standard sockets. Some manuals still use this term.) You will find ZIF sockets in most Pentium computers. With a ZIF socket, a tension arm holds the microprocessor chip in place, and the chip pops out when you release the tension arm. No force is required to remove or install a chip in this type of socket. The tension arm applies the pressure needed to hold the chip in place.

If you have a LIF socket, the procedure will be a little more difficult, but it's still easy enough that you shouldn't need help from a professional. Upgrade kits often include a chip removal tool, similar to a miniature crowbar, for removing chips from this type of socket. Installing a new microprocessor in a LIF socket requires some pressure; it's important that you apply even pressure from above to avoid damaging the small pins on the bottom of the chip (see Figure 5.1).

Skill 5

Standard socket   ZIF socket

FIGURE 5.1: CPUs should be removed from their sockets with care.

 NOTE Some experts recommend having a technician perform this type of extraction and installation, but computer users with no previous experience replacing microprocessors were able to perform the upgrade in less than half an hour without any difficulty. With a LIF socket there is more risk that you may damage the computer than if you have a ZIF socket, but following the instructions that come with the upgrade kit should prevent errors. You should never use a tool other than the one provided with the kit to remove a chip from a LIF socket. If you are uneasy about performing an upgrade because your CPU is in a LIF socket, consider having it done by an expert.

Climate Control

Another factor that will affect the difficulty of your installation will be whether the old or new processor has a heat sink and, if so, what type it has. A heat sink is a device, usually made of metal, that absorbs and dissipates heat generated by an electrical component.

With millions of electrical currents blazing through a microprocessor every second, some heat is generated. This heat is dissipated through the heat sinks, which usually are anodized metal fins. Some chips come with heat sinks attached to their tops by epoxy, while others come as a separate part—and must be installed on the chip after it is attached to the motherboard, usually by way of an adhesive backing on the heat sink (see Figure 5.2).

FIGURE 5.2:   A heat sink for a CPU

"Essentially, metal conducts heat very well, so this takes the heat from the center of the chip where the die sits, and distributes it out," says Greg Meythaler, Intel's Pentium processor installation supervisor. "Because there are a lot of fins sticking up in the air, there's more surface area over which to dissipate the heat. The air flows down through the fins and the heat is dissipated."

The design of components in some computer brands is such that the regular air flow through the computer (generated by the computer's main fan) is enough to dissipate the heat from the fins and keep the chip cool. Such systems are called *passive heat sink*s. Other computer manufacturers mount a fan on the chip's heat sink to move air through the fins, and such systems are called *active heat sink*s. These computers have built-in fans along with the heat sinks to make certain they stay cool enough to work properly. While this will add a few steps to the upgrading process, in most cases it shouldn't make it any more difficult.

Installing the CPU

The first step in any CPU upgrade is to determine what type of upgrade kit you need. To do this, you need to determine what type of processor your computer is currently equipped with (for example, 386DX, 486SX, or Pentium) and its clock speed.

If you don't know your computer's processor type and clock speed, there are several ways to find this information. The easiest way to do this is to check your computer's documentation for system information. Another option is to run a program called Microsoft Diagnostics (MSD), which comes with DOS. To run this program, type **msd** at a DOS prompt, and press ↵. The program will display information about the various components of your computer, including the processor.

NOTE   You also can run MSD in Windows by opening Program Manager's File menu, selecting Run, and typing **msd** in the Run dialog box. While this provides the basic information you need for your microprocessor, if you're using MSD for other system information—such as memory or IRQ values—you may get a more accurate report if you exit Windows and run MSD from the DOS prompt. (Skill 2 discusses using MSD in detail.)

A third method is to turn off the computer, unplug all the cables from the back, open its case, locate the processor, and read the string of numbers on it. (This string will contain all the information you need; for example, it might say "Intel 80386SX-25." This means you have a 386SX processor chip from Intel, with a clock speed of 25MHz.) While this is the most difficult method, it's also the most reliable. Once you have the information you need, you can choose an upgrade from any of several companies.

However, if you have a Pentium chip and want to upgrade to MMX technology, you'll have to find out whether your computer can support the upgrade. Because of a voltage difference, the OverDrive chip is the only recommended way of upgrading an existing system to take advantage of MMX, and the chip will work in most—but not all—"classic" Pentium systems. Consult Intel's Pentium OverDrive Processor upgrade guide, available through a local computer dealer or Intel's Web site (http://www.intel.com). You'll also need to use a diagnostic utilities diskette that comes with the chip or can be obtained at the Web site. This process checks the BIOS compatibility, reviews processor information, and makes sure everything is working correctly before you upgrade.

NOTE   The upgrade kit you purchase will include specific directions for the upgrade you're performing; the following instructions don't replace those more detailed directions. As with any hardware installation, you should read the instructions thoroughly before beginning. We give an overview of how the upgrades are performed. There will be some variation among different brands of upgrades and different computer systems. The same rule applies to the figures included here. Your system's configuration may differ slightly from what we show.

It is important that you read Skill 3, *Taking Precautions Before You Begin* before proceeding with this upgrade. And don't forget to ground *everything* before removing the case.

Find the CPU   Locate the processor. It will be a square chip installed on the motherboard. The location of the chip on the motherboard will vary from computer to computer. Once you've located and exposed the processor, you're ready to proceed with the upgrade.

 NOTE

In some cases, you may need to remove some hardware (for example, adapter cards or drive bays) to get at the processor. If this is the case, be sure to make a note of where each piece goes and how it is installed, so you can put everything back where it belongs when you're done.

Is the CPU ZIF or Surface Mount?   Next, check to see if the current processor is socketed (in either a ZIF or a LIF socket) or if it's surface-mounted (soldered to the board). A socketed CPU's sides will be flush with the sides of the socket. A surface-mounted CPU will have fine wires radiating from it to the board. You shouldn't attempt to remove a surface-mounted CPU because you can cause permanent damage to the computer. If your computer's processor is surface-mounted, look for an OverDrive socket. (This is an empty socket next to your current processor, and it does not apply if you're upgrading to an OverDrive chip with MMX technology.)

 NOTE

If you are performing a piggyback installation, skip the next item and proceed to the "Piggyback Chip Installation" section.

Removing CPU Chips: Time for Special Tools   If you're performing either a chip-for-chip or a daughtercard upgrade, and the chip is socketed, you'll need to remove the existing CPU so you can insert the upgrade in its place. (If the chip is surface-mounted and you have an OverDrive socket, skip to the following section, "ZIF Socket Installation".) If your old microprocessor has a fan, you'll need to disconnect it from the computer's power source before removing the chip. Disconnecting the chip from the power source should be as simple as unplugging the cord. Some will be more difficult, though, and may require help from a service center.

The method you'll use to remove the old processor will depend upon whether the CPU is in a LIF or ZIF socket. If it's in a LIF socket, pry up the chip using the tool provided in the upgrade kit. Be sure you are only removing the chip itself, and not attempting to pry up the actual socket. Gently loosen the processor chip one side at a time until you can remove it with your fingers, taking care not to bend the pins on the bottom of the chip.

If the chip is in a ZIF socket, there will be a side lever, overhead bar, or retaining screw holding it in place. (Most have tension arms, so we'll focus on that type of ZIF socket.) You should be able to use your fingers to move the tension arm, but if your microprocessor is tucked into a corner of the computer's case you might need a screwdriver to get to it. Taking care to avoid contact with other portions of the computer, slowly lift the arm (it should move easily) until it's at a 90-degree angle to the chip. You now should feel the chip release from the motherboard socket. Don't touch or bend the delicate connector pins on the underside of the chip (see Figure 5.3).

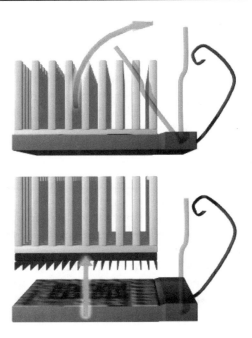

FIGURE 5.3:   The connector pins can easily be damaged during removal of the chip.

ZIF Socket Installation   Once you have removed the CPU, or located the OverDrive socket if the CPU is surface-mounted, you're ready to install the new processor. The installation should be fairly simple in most cases. (Some types of ZIF sockets will make it necessary for you to use a socket extender; this part and its directions are usually included in the upgrade kit.) On several types of computers, the chip acts like a key, only fitting in the socket one way. The microprocessor's pins make a square point on three sides and are beveled on the fourth side. Some processors have a corner marked *Pin 1,* which is lined up with Pin 1 on the socket. When you have the chip properly aligned, it will fit snugly into the socket. Before pressing the chip into the socket (if you have a LIF socket) or lowering the tension arm on a ZIF socket, verify that the pins on the chip are aligned with the holes in the socket (see Figure 5.4).

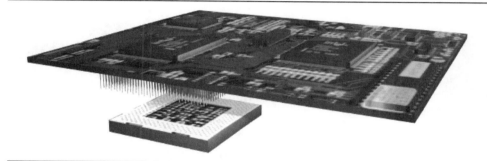

FIGURE 5.4:   Installing a CPU in a ZIF socket isn't complicated.

 NOTE   If you're performing a daughtercard upgrade, sometimes other items on the motherboard will interfere with the proper seating of the daughtercard. If this is the case, an extra piece of equipment is necessary to make the card fit correctly. This will be discussed in the upgrade manual, and the part will be available through the company that produced the upgrade you're using.

If the socket is a ZIF socket, make sure it's unlocked and in the open position. Don't force the chip into the socket because you could damage the connector pins. If the chip isn't fitting into the ZIF socket properly, check to be sure you have it lined up correctly, and that the tension arm is still at a 90-degree angle. If it has fallen, it will prevent you from installing the chip correctly. Once the chip is seated properly, close the socket to a locked position.

If the socket is a LIF socket, press the upgrade processor into the socket with firm, even pressure. You will be able to feel and hear when it has snapped into place.

Piggyback Chip Installation   If you are performing a piggyback installation, align the upgrade processor over the old processor, with the logos facing the same direction, or as directed in the upgrade kit's instructions (see Figure 5.5). Correctly aligning the processors is extremely important; installing the upgrade in the wrong position will permanently damage both processors. Press the upgrade processor down onto the old processor until you hear it snap into place.

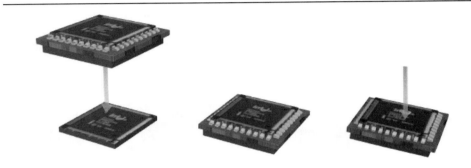

FIGURE 5.5: Proper alignment of chips is crucial to a successful piggyback installation.

Adding Heat Sinks and Fans If your new processor has a fan in addition to a heat sink, you now need to connect the fan to the computer's power supply. (If you're installing an OverDrive chip with MMX, the integrated fan is powered through the CPU, so you can skip this step.) With most computers, this should be as easy as plugging it into an existing power supply cord. If all the power cords inside your computer are occupied, the fan's cord can be plugged into the middle of an existing cord. Temporarily disconnect a power cord from its device. Plug the fan cord into the free end of the power cord and then connect the other end of the fan cord to the device originally connected directly to the power cord. Again, some computers will present difficulties and you may need a professional's help.

Reconnecting Everything At this point, you can plug the power cord back into the computer, reconnect it to the monitor, and turn them both on. If the computer powers up and runs normally, you've done the upgrade correctly. If there are no additional parts to install, turn the computer back off, push aside any cords that are in the way, and replace the case on the computer.

If you haven't installed the chip or daughtercard into the socket properly, your computer will probably experience one of the following problems: You won't be able to boot the computer at all; the computer may lock up after running for a few minutes because the chip expands slightly as it warms up and loses contact with the socket; or you'll receive general protection faults (GPFs) in Windows. In short, your computer may boot up, but it won't work properly if the chip or daughter-card is installed incorrectly.

If you have any of these problems, either start over with Step 2 or call technical support for assistance.

Completing the Installation   If there are other parts to be installed, turn the computer off, and unplug it again before continuing to work. One of the upgrade kits we used contained a plastic shroud to protect the processor; if the upgrade is working properly, you can install this shroud now. The kit also included a heat sink, which is installed after the shroud is in place. Once you've added any such additional parts, you're ready to reassemble the computer and perform any necessary software installations.

Once you've replaced any hardware that was removed to make the processor accessible, the physical installation is complete. Replace the computer's cover, reattach the power cords and peripherals, and start up the computer with your monitor turned on.

Software Update: Don't Forget This!   Many upgrades require a software installation after the hardware has been installed; the directions for the upgrade you're performing will tell you whether this is necessary. If it is, the software will be included in the upgrade kit, along with installation instructions.

The types of upgrades we've described cover CPU upgrades from 286 systems up to and including upgrading 486 systems to Pentium performance, in addition to upgrading a Pentium chip to one with MMX technology. The upgrades involving Pentium performance use an OverDrive processor, and feature either chip-for-chip upgrades, or the insertion of the OverDrive process upgrade into a special socket.

Once you've performed the upgrade, the fun part begins. Your computer should show improvement in speed and performance, giving you a new system to work with.

Are You Experienced?

Now you can...

- ☑ **find the CPU on the motherboard**
- ☑ **distinguish between a ZIF socket and a LIF socket**
- ☑ **remove and replace heat sinks and CPU fans**
- ☑ **remove CPUs from a motherboard and replace them**
- ☑ **upgrade a PC's software settings for a newly added CPU**

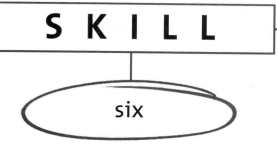

SKILL

six

Installing a Hard Drive

❑ Choosing a new hard drive

❑ Installing the drive: step by step

❑ Partitioning and formatting the drive

❑ Installing a second hard drive

❑ Understanding the options for data storage

Once you've made the decision to upgrade your hard drive, the process of choosing a hard drive begins. When shopping for a hard drive, you should learn about a drive's formatted capacity, speed, and, most importantly, its ease of installation before making your upgrade purchase. It's equally important that you make sure your new drive is compatible with, and suitable for, your computer.

Although most hard drives today range in capacity from 1GB (gigabyte) to 4GB, you may not need that much—and your computer might not work with drives that large. With many PCs built before 1995, you can avoid considerable hassles and costs by staying with a small drive of less than 528MB. (A gigabyte is a unit of computer storage equaling about one billion bytes; a megabyte equals about one million bytes). To determine your future needs, ask yourself these questions: How long do I plan to keep my PC? What programs or accessories do I want to use? Is my current hard drive almost out of storage space? Do I have a pre-1995 PC that won't let me install a larger-than-528MB EIDE drive without technical hassles? (For more information, see "Stockpiling Your Data" later in this skill.)

Another important criterion is speed. It's difficult to compare drive speeds because drives often are not tested under the same conditions, causing reported speeds to vary. As a crude rule of thumb, the faster the spin speed of a hard drive, the faster the drive will be. Insist on a Fast ATA-2 drive. The phrase "Enhanced IDE" used to describe a drive means essentially the same thing as Fast ATA-2. These are the latest, fastest drive standards on the market.

Finally, consider such things as whether there is a concise installation manual and whether the drive comes with new screws, brackets, and cables; though in many instances you can use the ones included with your old drive. In some cases, however, the two hard drives won't be the same size, especially if you are replacing an older model hard drive.

In terms of drive interface, your computer most likely will use either Integrated Drive Electronics (IDE), the pre-1995 standard drive interface (or Enhanced IDE, or EIDE), or Small Computer Systems Interface (SCSI). IDE drives are the most common type of hard drive used in PCs. IDE drives are the most compatible, and all modern IDE drives have automatic translation (meaning your system will detect the new hard drive's bit size and make the needed changes).

While there are many reasons for not using larger-than-528MB drives on pre-1995 computers, we'll just give you the moral to this story. If your PC doesn't have support for Enhanced Integrated Device Electronics (EIDE), Fast ATA, or larger than 528MB drives in its BIOS, think twice about installing one of the larger drives.

TIP   If you're unsure about what you currently have, or what you need, talk to a knowledgeable salesperson or a qualified technician. You can save yourself some frustration later by dealing with this issue before you plunk down any money for a new drive.

Installing the Drive

We installed a Medalist 1080 EIDE (Fast ATA) drive from Seagate Technology Inc. on a Hewlett-Packard Vectra 33 megahertz (MHz) 486. The illustrations of our computer may look different from your computer; the components illustrated are in all computers, you just may need to look carefully to find some of them (see Figure 6.1).

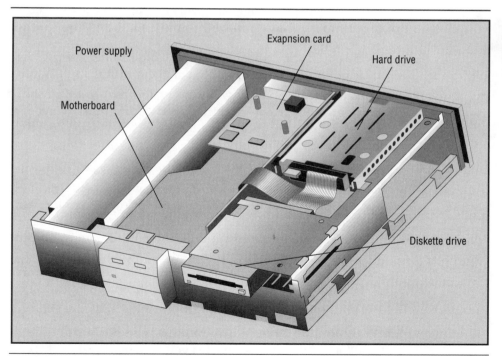

FIGURE 6.1:   All computers have the same basic components.

NOTE   The instructions in this section do not apply to SCSI installations.

New Drive Setup

The process of installing a drive is outlined in the following sections. Before you do anything else, read Skill 3, *Taking Precautions Before You Begin*.

 **WARNING**   If you don't follow the instructions for creating backups and system diskettes outlined in Skill 3, you will lose *everything* on your current drive.

Your Hard Drive   Locate your hard drive, which probably will be mounted to the side, bottom, or back of your diskette drives. The hard drive should look a lot like the one you just bought and will be inside a metal bracket. If you have your computer manual handy, consult it to see if it has a diagram showing where the hard drive is.

Look at your new drive. You should see a flat (usually gray) ribbon cable and a multicolored power cable connected to the drive. Look at your new hard drive, and make sure these cables will work on the drive. If they don't, it's a good indication that your current hard drive adapter card (the circuit board that controls your drive) is incompatible with the new drive. You may need to upgrade your adapter card as well as your drive.

Where's the Hard Drive?   Look at how the hard drive is placed in the computer. Which direction is it facing? Where and how are the cables connected? How is it connected to the bracket? Writing down this information and sketching how your system looks will make this installation much easier. Look at the edges of the ribbon cable(s). One edge is lightly marked in red (or at least has red dashes on it). Note which direction the red edge is facing.

If your old drive is smaller or larger than the new one, you may need to find a new bracket. The new drive may come with its own bracket; if not, you can purchase one from your computer retailer.

Removing the Screws   Remove the screws holding the drive's bracket in place. You should then be able to gently remove the drive bracket from the computer. Do not pull on the drive. If it doesn't come out easily, you've either left a screw in place, or one of the drive's cables may be caught. Find the problem, and try again.

Cables and the Drive   Carefully disconnect both cables from the drive. The drive still should be in its bracket to prevent damage to the drive. The cables may be difficult to disconnect, but don't pull too hard because you may permanently damage the cables or the drive. If the cables do not pull off easily, try disconnecting one side of the cable, then wiggle the cable until it pops off. Don't disconnect the cables from the computer unless you plan to replace them.

Removing the Drive   Remove the drive from its bracket by loosening the screws. The old hard drive should now be free. (See Figure 6.2.) Set the screws and hard drive aside.

Grounding Yourself   Ground yourself by touching the inside of the computer case. Remove the new hard drive from its packaging, touching only the sides of the drive. Slide it into the bracket or bay from which you removed the old drive. If there is a difference in size between your new and old drives (the new one most likely will be smaller, if there is a difference), you may need to purchase side brackets to make the drive fit.

Replacing the Screws   Replace the screws that hold the drive in the bracket. Be sure the drive is facing the right direction, or the cables may not reach the drive.

The Interface Cable   Reconnect the 40-pin interface and power cables. There is only one way these power cables will connect, but the flat cable on some systems can indeed be plugged in backwards (either on the drive or on the adapter card), which will cause the drive not to work. That's why it's crucial to pay attention to the red edge on the cable. Flipping these cables the wrong way rarely does permanent damage, but it will disable the drive.

Attaching the Bracket   Put the bracket and hard drive in the computer and replace any screws you removed. If you don't replace the screws, the drive may move around and be damaged.

Putting Things Back Together   Replace the computer's cover by tightening the screws or latches. Reconnect the monitor to the computer, and plug both in. You now can turn on your computer, with your system diskette in your diskette drive, and begin the system setup.

Skill 6

Software Setup

Virtually all pre-1995 computers only allow for 528MB of hard drive space, unless some special change is made, preferably in the PC's BIOS. If you are installing a drive larger than 528MB, you may run into problems when configuring the drive. If you do encounter problems, call a qualified technician or the technical support line for your computer's manufacturer.

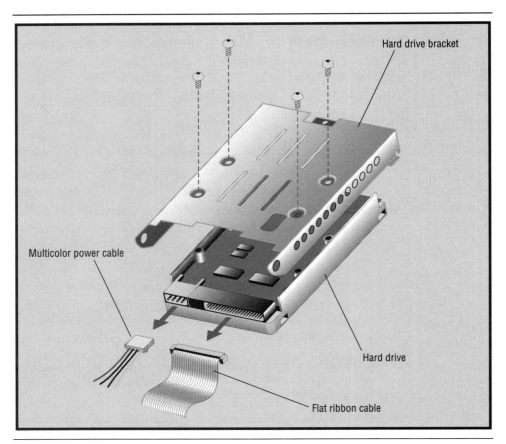

FIGURE 6.2: Removing the screws on the bracket frees the hard drive.

Although you've installed the drive, it's not ready to store data. You must change your system's BIOS settings, and partition and format the disk before the computer will recognize the drive. (As we mentioned earlier, the basic input/output system is a set of instructions that tells your computer how to perform basic functions, such as booting up or communicating with the disk drives. These settings are stored permanently inside your computer.)

Partitioning and formatting the drive prepares the disk inside your drive so you can save data. While partitioning divides the disk into separate storage areas, formatting clears the disk and prepares it to store data.

There are two ways you can approach editing your BIOS and partitioning and formatting your hard disk. The first is to use an automatic setup utility, which should accompany your drive, such as DiskManager or EZ-Drive. If your drive doesn't have a diskette that contains this utility, call the company or access its bulletin board system or World Wide Web site to download the software. The utility will make necessary changes to your BIOS settings, then it will partition and format your hard disk; these utilities will require less input from you and will take less time than if you manually configured everything. However, don't let an automatic setup utility install DiskManager or EZ-Drive software onto a drive that doesn't need it. This applies to drives with less than 528MB (including ones marked as 540MB), PCs with EIDE adapters, or newer computers with EIDE support in their BIOS.

The second way to configure your new drive is to do it manually. This method will require you to enter the BIOS, change all the settings, and then run the DOS FDISK and FORMAT commands to prepare the hard disk to receive directions. The following are the necessary steps for manually configuring a new hard disk:

1. Insert the system diskette you created according to the instructions in Skill 3 into the A: drive, and turn on the computer. While the computer is booting, you'll want to watch for the hotkey combination to invoke the BIOS setup. In our case, we had to press the F2 key.

2. Press the hotkey(s) to enter the BIOS setup, and locate the hard drive setup screen. In some computers, the settings automatically adjust for the new hard drive, so you may not need to enter information about the drive's model, cylinders, heads, and sectors per track. However, check these settings to make sure they are correct.

   If you need to enter drive information, it can be found in the drive's documentation or on the drive itself. Our setup screen also included lines for the drive's park location and landing zone, though the drive will work fine as long as you enter information about the heads, cylinders, and sectors correctly.

3. When you've finished entering the information, save it, and exit the BIOS setup (consult the BIOS menu for the keys you need to press to do this; it probably will be a key such as Esc or a function key). Shut off your computer, and restart it.

From this point on, instructions will vary depending upon whether you have a built-in utility. When in doubt, follow the drive's documentation.

TROUBLESHOOTING TIPS

If you've finished the installation and your hard drive doesn't work or isn't being recognized by the computer, check the following:

- Are cables connected properly?
- Did you turn the ribbon cables 180 degrees so that the wrong sides meet?
- Did you enter the wrong information regarding drive parameters and drive type in the Setup screen?
- Is the power connector firmly attached to the hard drive?

You should also make sure that you correctly transferred the startup files to your hard drive. If you partitioned the drive with FDISK, ensure that all the partitions are formatted.

Are you getting "Incorrect version of DOS" messages? Did you install a new version of DOS from factory diskettes onto your new drive and then restore from a backup that has an older version? If so, reinstall the new version again, run the DELOLDOS command (see your DOS manual), and remove the remnants of the old version.

Once you've checked these things, look for any other troubleshooting techniques in your drive's manual. When everything else has failed, call the technical support number in your installation manual.

Preparing the Disk for Data

Once you have restarted your computer with the system diskette in your A: drive, you're ready to run MS-DOS's FDISK command. FDISK lets you do three things to your hard drives: determine the amount of space that will be occupied by DOS, designate what will be contained in the remaining hard drive space, and further divide that space into other "drives."

The first partition is called the primary DOS partition. This will always be your C: drive and cannot be subdivided. This partition is also called the active partition because this is where DOS boots from when you start your computer. You can have only one active partition.

The second partition, if you opt for one, is called an extended partition. This is the space left over after you've designated your primary partition. Extended partitions must have one or more designated logical drives (named D: through Z:).

Start FDISK by typing **fdisk** at the A> prompt, and pressing ↵. This is the moment of truth. If your drive isn't really running and connected to the PC, FDISK won't start, and you'll see an error message.

Setting Up a Primary Partition   The first thing to do is set up your primary DOS partition. When FDISK starts, you'll see a Fixed Disk Setup Program menu. If you have not run FDISK before, choose Option 1 (Create a DOS Partition or Logical DOS Drive). In the next menu, choose Option 1 to create your primary partition. You now can make your entire C: drive the primary partition or only a part of it. If you're only going to use part of the drive, you can specify how much in either megabytes or percentages, but if you use percentages, make sure you follow your specified number with a percent sign (%). If you don't, DOS will assume that you mean megabytes and you'll wind up with a partition of a different size.

Your next step is to make your primary partition active. To do this, return to the main FDISK menu, and select Option 2 (Set Active Partition). The DOS prompts will guide you through the process. You must specify which partition is active; DOS does not have a default setting that would automatically make the primary partition active.

Setting Up an Extended Partition   To set up an extended partition, return to the main FDISK menu, and choose Option 1 again. In the Create DOS Partition menu, choose Option 2 (Create Extended DOS Partition). You'll be asked to specify in megabytes or percentages how much hard drive space will be given to an extended partition.

Skill 6

NOTE   Remember, you can only have one active drive, so don't try to make your extended partition active.

Setting Up Logical Drives   After you set up your extended partition, you'll automatically be given the Create Logical Drive(s) option in the Extended Partition menu.

You can specify up to 23 logical drives and how much space will be given to each one. Remember that A: and B: are reserved for your diskette drives, and C: is your primary partition, leaving D: through Z: for your logical drives, though D: is often used to designate CD-ROM drives. DOS's on-screen instructions will guide you through each step, making it unlikely that you will get lost in the process.

Viewing partition information   When you put an active status on your primary partition, you saw a screen similar to the Display Partition Information screen. To view this screen, choose Option 4 (Display Partition Information) from the main FDISK menu.

The display is fairly easy to understand. When you view it, it will list all the partitions that have been created. An "A" in the Status column means a partition is active. The next column is Type. PRI DOS means primary DOS partition, and EXT DOS means extended partition. Make sure the "A" status is in the same line as the PRI DOS type. If not, you'll have to go back to the FDISK menu and start over. Volume Label will be blank unless you've given it a name during the creation process. Mbytes tells how many megabytes the partition was allotted. System refers to the kind of filing system used for the partitions. The Usage column tells you how much space (in percentage form) has been allocated to that partition, not how much space has been used.

Formatting Your New Drive

Now that you've set up your new partitions and logical drives, you're almost done. Next, you have to format each new drive.

You first have to format your C: drive. To do this, put your system diskette into your diskette drive, type **format c: /s,** and press ↵. The /S parameter tells DOS to load your system files onto your C: drive. When done, remove the diskette and restart your PC. If DOS starts, your C: drive is bootable.

During this format process, you may run into a snag. If, for example, you are formatting a drive that is larger than 528 million bytes and you've created a single partition, and you receive an on-screen message that says only 504MB is being formatted, this is an indication that your PC's BIOS doesn't recognize the features that would let it use the full capacity of the drive. If you have a larger drive with multiple partitions and FDISK only sees 504MB, then you also have a BIOS problem. When this happens, do you:

1. Cry and throw out the drive?

2. Go back into the BIOS and re-enter information about your hard drive?

3. Call the drive manufacturer's technical support department?

You do want to enter the BIOS and look for the terms LBA (for logical block addressing), ECHS (extended cylinder head sector addressing), or Large; you should not enter any information. If you don't see one of these terms, run the software that came with your drive to set it up. If the problem reoccurs, call your PC's manufacturer and ask for a BIOS that will recognize your new drive. You shouldn't call the technical support line for your drive's manufacturer, because the problem lies with your BIOS and not with your drive.

If you haven't hit the above snag, you can format your other partitions, starting with your D: partition. At the DOS prompt, type **format d:** and press ↵. Notice that you're not using the /S parameter here because you don't want system files loaded anywhere but your C: drive. Repeat this command for each logical drive, making sure to change the drive letter in the command line.

Now that you have "installed" your logical drives, you can access them by typing the drive's identifier at the DOS prompt.

Lastly, you need to install your backup software and use it to restore your programs and data to the new drive (see Skill 3 for details).

Installation of our drive and system setup took about 45 minutes, not counting the time required to restore our backups. Read the drive's documentation before installing, and re-read it if you have problems. Before long, you'll have the drive installed and will be enjoying the increased storage space.

Installing a Second Hard Drive

So, you've bought a new hard drive, and figure you'll leave the old hard drive in your computer and use it for backups. You'll save money by not having to buy a tape drive or diskettes. It sounds logical, right?

Don't forget computing's No. 1 rule: Few things are as easy as they sound. None of the hard drive experts we spoke with recommended this procedure for beginners, and, after performing the installation ourselves, we have a hard time recommending it either. Our experts recommended—unless you're extremely comfortable with hardware installations and system software manipulation—having a professional add the second hard drive and reconfigure your software to run in the "new environment."

 NOTE Unless you are confident of your abilities, adding a second hard drive is not a good idea without complete backups that you have tested to ensure that all data is present and accessible.

Why Install Another?

Aside from the obvious bonus of more storage space, adding a second hard drive provides other benefits:

- If you run both Windows 3.1 and Windows 95, having two drives lets you isolate each operating system so you have a better chance of pulling off that tricky stunt.

- The two-drive setup provides an easy way to move data and programs from your old drive to the new one.

- Improved backup capabilities—your old drive can store copies of your crucial data. But a second drive isn't a total substitute for backup tapes; if your computer is stolen or burned, your backup is gone with it.

To run two hard drives in one computer, you'll need to specify one drive as master (the main hard drive from which your computer boots) and one as slave (the secondary drive). Unfortunately, some computers don't let you use the newer hard drive as the master, which can prevent you from taking full advantage of its improved speed. If the old drive isn't fully compatible with the new drive, the old drive may have to be the master.

Unfortunately, you won't discover the incompatibility until you've completed the installation. If you can't make your new drive the master, we recommend looking at the section on installing a hard drive at the beginning of this skill and following the steps there to replace your old hard drive with the new hard drive, rather than using the new drive as a slave.

 NOTE In our step-by-step instructions for installing a second hard drive, we'll often refer to the section on hard drive installation because many of the steps are the same.

The Installation

Set aside a minimum of one hour for installation; by the time you finish the data transfer, you could be pushing two or three hours if the installation is problematic. Be sure to read and follow the instructions for protecting your data in Skill 3. Even though you'll be transferring data from one hard drive to another, you would still be better off backing up all data on your drive.

 NOTE   Read all steps and warnings thoroughly before deciding whether you want to attempt this installation yourself.

Choosing a Location   Decide where you want to put your new hard drive. You have several options, depending upon your computer's configuration (see Figure 6.1 at the beginning of this skill). You'll want to keep it as close to the current hard drive as possible because of the cabling connections you'll need to make. Be sure you have a 40-pin ribbon cable that can connect to both hard drives and to the expansion card and a power cable that can be spliced. You may have to purchase cables with extra connectors.

Setting the Jumpers   Prepare to set the jumpers on the new drive and old drive. Depending upon the location of the old drive's jumpers, you might need to temporarily remove the old drive (following the steps in the earlier section on installing a hard drive). Setting the jumpers is the first step toward determining which drive is the master and which is the slave.

Many newer drives will contain documentation about the correct settings, but many older drives don't. If you can't find such documentation, you'll need to call technical support for the drive's manufacturer. Some drive manufacturers also place this information in technical libraries on their bulletin board systems.

 NOTE   For more information on hard drives, visit the following World Wide Web sites for Quantum (http://www.quantum.com) and for Seagate (http://www.seagate.com).

Connecting the Cable   Attach the 40-pin drive interface ribbon cable to the two drives and to your expansion card, and connect the power cable to the two drives. Then mount the new drive, following the steps in the section "Installing the Drive." Replace the computer's cover.

Checking the BIOS Setup   Refer to the steps outlined in the "Software Setup" section earlier in this skill for information on entering the basic input/output system (BIOS) Setup. After entering the BIOS Setup (Step 2), you'll see two listings for Hard Disks, sometimes referred to as 0 and 1. Hard Disk 0 is the master disk, and Hard Disk 1 is the slave.

Your old hard drive will be listed as the master. Enter the master drive setup screen (following the keystrokes required for your BIOS Setup), and write down the old hard drive's numbers for mode or type, cylinders, heads, and sectors per track. Without the correct numbers in the BIOS Setup, your hard drive(s) won't work properly.

Type the parameters for the new hard drive in the master drive setup screen; the parameters for the old hard drive should be entered into the slave drive setup screen, if you've chosen that configuration. Some older BIOS Setups will request write precomp and landing zone parameters, but you can usually set these to zero because newer hard drives don't use them. After making the changes, exit the BIOS Setup.

 NOTE   The BIOS Setup controls many aspects of your computer, and inadvertent changes—particularly to "disk type"—can cause the PC to function improperly.

Formatting the Disk   You now must prepare the drive to store data by partitioning and formatting it. Some new hard drives contain software utilities that will automatically perform this task. Read your hard drive's documentation for more information. Don't format or use FDISK on the new drive until you've safely copied these utilities to diskette.

Follow the earlier instructions in the "Preparing the Disk for Data" section to run FDISK on your drives. After booting your computer using the system diskette, you must make sure you're using FDISK on the new hard drive. If you use FDISK on the old drive, you'll erase its data. While running FDISK, choose the Display Partition Information option to make sure you're using the new drive. This will either show the presence of some partitions, or will say there aren't any partitions. You want to make sure you're on the drive without partitions.

Rebooting the Computer   After creating partitions on the new drive, you'll need to reboot your computer again using the system diskette before beginning the formatting process. See the "Formatting Your New Drive" section earlier for more information.

Again, formatting requires care. Your two hard drives will be C: and D:. Make sure you format the new hard drive. If you format the old drive, you'll destroy your data because the FORMAT command erases all data. You can use the DIR command to figure out which drive needs formatting. If you have more than one partition (drive letters beyond D:) on either drive, the location to which DOS assigns letters is usually not what you'd expect. If you have, for example, C:, D:, E:, and F: partitions scattered between the two drives, you must check to see which letter is on which drive before doing any copying or formatting. If you run the DIR command on a drive, and it shows that files are present, you know you're on the wrong drive.

After completing the formatting, reboot your computer. It should boot from the master drive.

Copying Data   You now need to copy information from your old drive to the new one using the XCOPY command. If you're copying information from the D: drive to the C: drive (we'll assume each drive has only one partition), type

xcopy d:*.* c:\   /s /e /v

at the DOS prompt. The /S switch in the above command line tells XCOPY to copy all subdirectories contained in the source directory that aren't empty. The /E switch directs the XCOPY command to also copy all the subdirectories in the source directory that don't hold any files. The /V switch can slow down XCOPY's operation a bit; it verifies that the information you just copied was stored correctly on the new medium. When the information you're copying is crucial, the peace of mind offered by using the /V switch is worth the slight delay it causes. Depending upon the type of programs you're using, though, using the XCOPY command to move files between drives can be troublesome, too. In short, problems arise when programs are moved to the new drive because they can get confused about their location and refuse to run. If you run into this problem, you may have to call the tech support number for your applications.

Skill 6

CD-ROM PROBLEMS

If an older computer has a newer ATAPI- or IDE-type CD-ROM drive, yet has only one IDE port, it can't accommodate two hard drives because the ATAPI CD-ROM drive runs off the same IDE plug the second hard drive would use. Also, after the new hard drive is assigned its drive letter, any CD-ROM's drive letter will change (from, for example, D: to E:), and some programs will then be unable to locate the CD-ROM drive.

Stockpiling Your Data

With each new software release and upgrade, data storage requirements get larger. The computer you bought as recently as a year ago might be hard-pressed to keep up with the flow of new goodies you're pressing into service or with the data those new goodies produce. We'll look at the various data storage options available and show you how to use them appropriately and cost-effectively. Table 6.1 will help you to sort out your options when deciding what type of storage device to buy.

TABLE 6.1: Pros and Cons of Storage Devices

Storage Medium	Pros	Cons
CD-R Drive	Because of its large (650MB) capacity, the CD-R drive is ideal for storing, archiving, or backing up large files	Not rewriteable
	Excellent medium for distributing data, as it can be read by both CD-ROM systems and CD-R drives	Drive cost is still expensive
	Cheap price per megabyte of disks	Transferring files is not as easy as drag-and-drop on some
		Slow transfer rate
Hard Drive	Fast access to data	Once out of storage, you must buy an entirely new unit rather than inexpensive cartridges
	The practical choice for storing any type of file or program because of fast access time	Price per megabyte is high
Jaz Drive	Ideal for large file storage, data archiving, and backup because of the 1GB removable cartridge capacity	Price of disks the same as SyJet disks for a little less storage
		Proprietary cartridges can only be used in Jaz drives
Magneto-Optical Drive	Huge amounts of storage for large files, data archiving, and backup; can store up to 4.6GB on some removable MO cartridges	High start-up price for drives

TABLE 6.1 CONTINUED: Pros and Cons of Storage Devices

Storage Medium	Pros	Cons
CD-ROM Drive	Good cost per megabyte for 650MB of storage	Cannot write your own data to disk
	Because of large 650MB capacity, has become an ideal storage medium for large applications, such as reference and office suite software; also cheaper for manufacturers to distribute than multiple diskettes	
SyQuest EZFlyer	As easy to store files on as a diskette, but with lots more room (230MB)	Proprietary cartridges can only be used in EZ drives
	Can store and run your less frequently used programs (transfer rate causes some lag when program is operating)	
	Good cost per megabyte for 1.3GB cartridges	
Tape Drive	Cheap cost per megabyte of storage	Only ideal for backup purposes
Zip Drive	As easy to store files on as a diskette, but with lots more room (100MB)	Proprietary disks can only be used in Zip drives
	Can store and run your less frequently used programs (transfer rate causes some lag when program is operating)	Price of disks the same as LS-1200 diskettes for a little less storage

Fixed Hard Drives

Hard drives used to be large, expensive devices that weren't very reliable and stored only a fraction of the information that they do now. An average hard drive in 1978 was 8 inches wide, cost $3,000, and only stored 5 million characters (5MB) of information. Today, you can run down to your local computer superstore and pick a hard drive off the shelf that stores more than 2 billion bytes of information and costs less than $500.

Let's take a quick refresher course on hard drives.

Most hard drives today use a method of connecting to your computer's main board called Integrated Drive Electronics (IDE). That means the controlling circuitry for the drive is built into the drive itself. In the old days, you had to match the microprocessor, an expansion card called a hard drive controller, and the drive itself very closely. If you didn't have the right drive, the right controller, or the right computer, you were out of luck. Modern IDE drives remove that problem by putting all the electronics into the drive itself. All you need to install the drive is a cable and an IDE interface in the computer, either on the motherboard or on an adapter card that's nowhere near as complex as the older style.

The Two Personalities of IDE

There are two flavors of IDE drive. Standard IDE drives are compatible with virtually every computer under the sun and offer satisfactory but not spectacular performance. They come in sizes ranging from around 500MB to more than 2GB and cost from $200 to $500. Enhanced IDE (EIDE) drives are also available for a small premium. These drives offer much better performance than their predecessors, but require an EIDE adapter in the computer to take advantage of it. If you have an IDE adapter, your EIDE drive will behave like a normal IDE drive.

The major advantage of EIDE is called Mode Four. If your drive and adapter are Mode Four-capable, you'll be able to transfer information into and out of the drive at up to 2MB per second rather than the normal IDE speed of around 700,000 bytes (7KB) per second. That means multimedia applications with video and sound will run much more smoothly.

You can have two hard drives per IDE adapter, configured as a master and a slave with a simple jumper on the back of the drive. In most configurations, the first drive will be your C: drive and the second one will be D:. If you're adding a new drive to your existing setup, don't forget to move the jumper on the old drive from the standalone (SA) position to the Master (MA) position or Slave (SL) position. Check the drive's manual for the exact wording and the location of the jumpers; if you don't have a manual, call the company directly or access the company's bulletin board system or World Wide Web site.

If you need more than two drives, you have two choices. Some computers have not one but two IDE adapters, and you can put two drives on each of them. You might already have a CD-ROM drive attached to the secondary IDE adapter, though, so three drives may very well be your limit.

The Benefits of SCSI Drives

Do you need lots of hard drives? One really, really big hard drive? If so, you'll need to look at the Small Computer Systems Interface (SCSI, pronounced "scuzzy"). SCSI drives rely on a special controller card that is installed in an expansion slot in your computer.

There are three flavors of SCSI controller and drive. The simplest is called SCSI-2. It's a standard, reasonably fast controller that uses cables in a daisy chain to attach up to seven devices. Each device gets a SCSI ID, numbered from 0 to 7, and the controller itself usually gets ID number 7. SCSI hard drives range in capacity from around 1GB up to 9GB, and these hard drives usually cost a little more than IDE drives. SCSI controllers and drives are capable of moving information into and out of the computer at up to 10MB per second. Sometimes this data transfer rate is limited to 5MB per second by the computer's expansion slot, but that's still a lot faster than an IDE drive.

If you need speed—and you will if you want to run lots of high-end multi-media applications—consider Fast SCSI. Fast SCSI is similar to SCSI-2, but devices on the daisy chain can move information at up to 20MB per second, twice the fastest rate SCSI-2 can handle.

Do you really need a lot of storage? Does the storage method need to be blind-ingly fast? You'll need to look at Fast Wide SCSI (also called Ultra SCSI). Fast Wide SCSI doubles the width of the information bus that carries data in and out of the computer and also allows SCSI IDs from 0 to 15. Fast Wide SCSI hard drives are significantly more expensive than regular SCSI drives, though. Figure on spending an extra $100 for each drive.

There's one additional benefit to having a SCSI controller in your computer. SCSI is used for more than just hard drives, and you can mix and match on the same controller chain. You might, for example, have one or two hard drives, a SCSI CD-ROM drive, and a tape backup unit on a single controller. SCSI reduces the number of controller cards in your PC and makes configuring and using your system quite a bit easier.

Skill 6

A WORD ABOUT HARD DRIVES IN GENERAL

When selecting a hard drive, pay attention to the drive's rotational speed, which measures how fast the metal platters inside your hard drive's case rotate. The faster the rotational speed, the better the drive's performance. Most drives rotate at around 4,000rpm, but there are faster 5,400rpm drives and drives designed for multimedia that spin at 7,300rpm.

Removable Hard Drives

More storage is good, but how would you like to have unlimited storage? If you opt for one of the new high-capacity drives with removable cartridges, you'll have just that. There are quite a few choices for removable drives: You get to pick whether the drive goes inside or outside the computer's case, how it hooks up to the computer, and what capacity it will hold.

External drives have some very definite benefits but they also can come with a liability or two. The biggest benefit is that your spiffy new drive isn't tied to a single computer. If you have a machine at the office and one at home, you can migrate the drive to wherever it's needed at the time. Add a portable computer to the mix and you're really in fine shape.

The largest liability comes from how you're likely to connect that external drive to your computer. You have two choices: through the computer's parallel port, which it will share with your printer if you have one, or through an external SCSI connector. If you will be using the drive with multiple computers, a parallel port drive will be your best choice, since every computer has at least one parallel port. However, if this is your choice, you're going to be artificially limiting the speed of data transfers. The hard drive can move information in and out a lot faster than the parallel port can send or receive it. The alternative is a SCSI controller card and an external drive with a SCSI connector. This is a lot faster, but each computer to which you intend to attach the drive has to have its own SCSI controller and be configured properly. This can add up to a lot of work.

The most popular removable drive right now is Iomega Corporation's Zip drive. Each cartridge stores 100MB of data, and the cartridges cost $20 each or less. Several other manufacturers have licensed the Zip technology from Iomega, so you might see an Epson Zip drive or a Hewlett-Packard desktop computer with a built-in Zip drive. They're all compatible with each other, so you can exchange Zip disks with other computers. At about $150 each, the Zip drives themselves are relatively inexpensive.

Need more capacity? Take a look at SyQuest's EZ external drives, which can hold up to 230MB of data. Cartridges for these drives are a little pricier, selling for about $35 each, but the drives offer fast access times. If you need a lot more storage, you'll need to go back to Iomega and evaluate a Jaz drive. The drive costs around $400 and cartridges for it cost $100 each, but each cartridge stores 1GB of information. You can get even more storage from a removable drive, but you'll have to move to a different technology to get there (see Figure 6.3).

FIGURE 6.3:   Kingston Technology Corporation's Data Express DE100 is a removable frame and carrier system that supports SCSI hard drives, letting users add storage capacity.

NOTE   If you believe that more is better, and a lot more is a lot better, read the section a little further on about CD-Rewriteable drives.

There are some really good reasons to use removable hard drives and some of them might not be evident at first glance. If you have two or more computers and want to move data between them, removable drives are a good choice. But what if it's a program that you want to move between computers? Many programs can only legally be installed on a single computer at a time for use, but the license doesn't say the single computer has to be the same computer. If you install the software on a removable hard drive, you can simply carry the drive to wherever you'll be working that day, plug it in, and get right to work.

Be careful with this strategy, though, as some Windows-based software will install a portion of the program into a dedicated area and another portion in the Windows SYSTEM directory. If Windows is installed on a permanent hard drive, you might be leaving a chunk of your program behind when you travel. The best way to avoid problems with this configuration is to test it before you need it.

Storage Devices

When was the last time you backed up your computer? In other words, when did you last copy all the information on your hard drive onto another storage medium, such as floppy diskettes or magnetic tape? If you're like a majority of PC users out there, the answer is most likely, "not too recently." Why not? Because unless you have the right equipment, making a backup is hard to do and takes a long time.

Tape Storage

Tape drives take the drudgery out of backups and make the process a lot quicker. If you have a late-model computer, it could have up to a billion bytes of information and programs stored on it. For the sake of argument, we'll say you only have half that much, 500MB. If you were to back up the entire hard drive to diskettes, it would take 125 diskettes to store the entire contents of the hard disk—and that's with data compression that squeezes 4MB onto each floppy diskette. As if organizing and continually keeping track of 125 diskettes isn't reason enough to consider a different medium for backup storage, consider that the backup process for this 500MB hard drive would take around six hours.

With a tape drive in this scenario, you could put the entire hard disk onto a single cartridge—in less than an hour. Seagate and other manufacturers make drives that are compatible with 3M's Travan cartridge system. Each Travan cartridge stores at least 800MB of information, and their biggest cartridge, the TR-3, stores 1.6GB of uncompressed data and 3.2GB of compressed data. With that much storage you can put several complete backups on a single tape (see Figure 6.4).

One nice thing about Travan drives is that they're attached to the computer like a diskette drive. Most computers have an extra spot in their cases for a second diskette drive and the cable even has an empty connector just waiting to be attached to something. Having this setup in your system means that installing a tape drive is even easier than installing a second hard drive because there are no jumpers to reset.

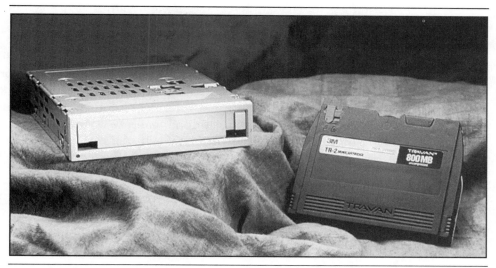

FIGURE 6.4:   The TEAC Supertape 1600 (at left) provides up to 1.6GB of storage capacity (compressed) or 800MB (uncompressed). An 800MB tape cartridge is on the right.

CD-ROM

If you don't already have a compact disc, read-only memory (CD-ROM) drive, you're lagging behind the rest of the pack. CD-ROM drives are fast becoming the distribution method of choice for software publishers. Programs keep getting bigger, and when faced with the choice of putting 12 or 13 diskettes or a single CD in the product box, publishers often choose the latter. Since CD-ROMs hold up to 650 million bytes of information each, a publisher can pack programs, data, and even multimedia tutorials onto a single plastic disc that costs less than $1 to produce.

When shopping for a CD-ROM drive, there are a couple points to consider. First, how fast is the drive? Original CD-ROM drives for microcomputers transferred information into the computer at 150KB/second. Manufacturers quickly learned that if they made the drives spin twice as fast they could make the information transfer twice as fast as well. These double-speed (2X) drives, which transferred data at 300KB/second, were very popular, but short-lived. They were followed in quick succession by quad-speed (4X, 600KB/second), six-speed (6X, 900KB/second), eight-speed (8X, 1200KB/second), ten-speed (10X, 1500KB/second), and twelve-speed (12X, 1800KB/second) drives. The faster the drive, the less time you have to wait for your programs and data to load into the computer, and the video and audio are displayed more smoothly as well.

The second major consideration is the interface, which is how the drive attaches to the computer. Older CD-ROM drives had proprietary interfaces and required that a special adapter card be installed in the PC. Newer drives use one of two interfaces: *Attachment Packet Interface (ATAPI)* or SCSI. ATAPI is actually the same interface used by your hard drive, and instead of a second hard drive, you can plug a CD-ROM drive into that vacant second connector on the data cable. This can slow down transfers from the hard drive, though, so if your computer has two IDE interfaces (most newer computers do) it's better to plug the hard drive into the first interface and the CD-ROM into the second one.

CD-R(ecordable)

CD-R drives have become less expensive in recent months. They work just like regular CD-ROM drives for reading information, but with the appropriate software you can format and create your own data and audio CDs. This is useful for people who have large quantities of information they need to store permanently; once the information has been stored on the CD it can never be changed. If you write computer programs or construct large databases that will be used by other people and you want a fairly inexpensive way to distribute them to these people, CD-R might be the way to go.

If you are considering installing a CD-R drive, your computer must be fast—a minimum 66MHz 486—and have at least one high-speed disk drive. Information has to flow from the hard drive to the CD-R drive in a quick and uninterrupted manner or the disk will be invalid. Blank discs for CD-R drives cost $12 to $15 each.

CD-Enhanced

This is a hot topic. There's a new generation of CD-ROM, with much higher access speeds and greater storage capacities. These drives are called DVD drives. While Sony, one of the principal manufacturers of DVD drives, says DVD isn't an abbreviation for anything, the media has been defining DVD as Digital Video Disc. A few models of DVD drives began to be available in 1997 with several manufacturers promising wider choices in the near future. The early DVD models store up to 8GB each. At the time of this writing, analysts were predicting that within a year we'd start to see DVD-R drives, which will let you record your own information. These drives will probably be rewriteable, meaning you can make changes after the information has been recorded.

Magneto-Optical and Optical Rewriteable Storage

If you need really large and changeable storage capacity, you need to look at magneto-optical (MO) drives or rewriteable optical drives. Although the end result is the same, these are different technologies. MO drives use a special disk in a cartridge that magnetically stores your information on one side and optically stores formatting information on the other side. This lets the actual data be written very closely together, making more room on the disk for data.

MO drives store the same amount of information as CD-ROM discs (650MB), and the information can be added to, edited, or erased. Most MO drives have one other benefit: They will accept and read standard CD-ROM discs when you put the discs in a carrier cartridge and feed them into the drive.

These days, the top-of-the-line optical storage unit is Pinnacle Micro's Vertex optical drive. For around $1,500, you can purchase a drive that uses optical media to store up to 2.6GB on each removable optical platter. The drive stores and retrieves information at almost the same speed as hard drives and the information is fully rewriteable. Additional disks cost around $130 each and provide the lowest price per megabyte of storage available. Pinnacle Micro makes another drive, the Apex, that stores more than 4GB, but it's normally used in ultra-high capacity and networked installations.

PC Cards

If you have a laptop PC, all the information you've just read was probably interesting but mostly irrelevant. Most laptop computers don't have expansion slots for SCSI adapters. They also don't have bays for CD-ROM drives or additional hard drives. Consequently, you're limited to using external devices that attach via the parallel port. Or are you?

Your laptop almost certainly has two small slots somewhere along its side into which you can slide PCMCIA adapter cards, also called PC Cards. There are PC cards for modems, network adapters, sound and video, SCSI controllers, and even hard drives.

The trick is to see what kind of slot you have. If the slot is only about a quarter-inch tall and looks like it will accept a single card, you have a Type II PC Card slot. You'll be able to expand your hardware options by installing PC Cards for SCSI controllers, external SCSI hard drives, and CD-ROM drives. If the slot looks like it's a half-inch tall and will accept two PC Cards, you actually have one Type II and one Type III slot. You can use all the options above and also install a PC Card hard drive. PC Card hard drives are only 1.8 inches wide and less than a half-inch tall and come in capacities up to 300MB. What's nice about these drives is that you can swap them in and out of the PC Card slot as you need them, and you generally won't have to restart your portable for it to recognize the new device. (For more information on PC Cards see Skill 17.)

Asking the Right Questions

As you can see, there are a lot of options for expanding your storage space. If you're like most computer users, you have limited room in your computer and are limited by your wallet in what you can buy. So, it will really pay to sit down and think about the kinds of information you'll be dealing with before you head for the computer store. Are you more likely to be working with large programs than data? Is the drive's access speed going to make a big difference in your ability to get the job done? Will you need to move information between computers regularly? All these questions will have a direct bearing on just how big that data stockpile is likely to get.

Are You Experienced?

Now you can. . .

- ☑ **make an informed choice of a new hard drive**
- ☑ **open up your computer and install a new drive**
- ☑ **configure and format the drive so it's ready to go**
- ☑ **install a second hard drive (if you're feeling confident)**
- ☑ **choose among the many options for data storage**

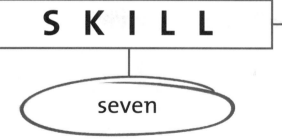

S K I L L

seven

Installing a Diskette Drive and Tape Drive

- ❑ Replacing a diskette drive: removal and installation
- ❑ Understanding how diskette drives work
- ❑ Installing a tape drive
- ❑ Troubleshooting diskette drive and hard drive problems

Installing a Diskette Drive

The overlooked and underappreciated diskette drive, the mechanism that reads data from and records data to a diskette (also known as a floppy disk), is seldom discussed as a vital element of the computer system. Hard drives with capacities of 1GB or more and CD-ROM drives with extensive multimedia capabilities garner most of the attention, and have overshadowed the modest and dependable diskette drive. Despite their lack of flash and muscle, though, diskette drives are used by millions of people each day, and users all around the world depend on the 3.5-inch diskettes for recording and exchanging business statistics, school reports, and personal information.

Their lack of complex parts is one reason diskette drives have been successful and popular among computer users. A diskette drive consists of a *spindle motor,* which spins the diskette; a *stepper-motor,* which moves the actuator arm; and the *actuator arm,* which positions the read/write head to retrieve or record data.

Diskette Drive Technology

The technological breakthroughs that endlessly redefine the capabilities of other computer components have not affected the fundamental mechanics of the diskette drive for years (see Figure 7.1). So while computer users struggle to determine when to upgrade their hard drives and CD-ROM drives, their diskette drives continue to faithfully and flawlessly perform the necessary function of small-capacity, portable data storage.

Because of the utility and dependability of diskette drives, few computer users ever find a reason to replace or permanently remove them. Nevertheless, there are four primary instances when you might decide to remove or install one:

- The diskette drive breaks and needs to be replaced. This rarely occurs, but if it does, a new drive is relatively inexpensive, usually costing less than $30.

- A second diskette drive is added as a way to easily back up diskettes.

- An older diskette drive is upgraded to take advantage of diskettes with greater storage capacities. There are 5.25-inch and 3.5-inch diskettes and diskette drives. The 5.25-inch diskette, which is encased in flexible plastic, has a maximum storage capacity of 1.2MB. These are nearly obsolete. The popular 3.5-inch diskette, which is encased in hard plastic, has a maximum storage capacity of 2.88MB, but most diskettes have a capacity of 1.44MB. The smaller size and rigid casing of the 3.5-inch diskette make it more

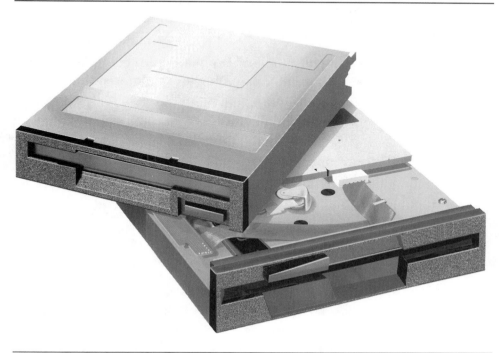

FIGURE 7.1:   Unlike some other computer components, the basic design of diskette drives has not changed in years.

convenient to carry and less prone to damage while being moved from one computer to another than the larger, flexible 5.25-inch diskette. (Some computer users incorrectly refer to the 3.5-inch diskette as a hard disk. A hard disk, which is found inside a hard drive, is a high-capacity storage medium inside your computer's case.)

- A diskette drive is replaced by another type of storage drive or a CD-ROM drive. Some computers are sold with multiple diskette drives, although this doesn't happen as often today as it did a few years ago. Many users, finding no need for the second drive, will replace it with a CD-ROM drive or a tape drive, which is used for large-capacity storage.

Regardless of why you need to install or remove a diskette drive, there's only one way to actually do it, and we'll show you how. If you don't need to remove an existing diskette drive, you can skip to the "Installing a Diskette Drive" section.

Finding the Best Diskette Drive

Buying a diskette drive after purchasing a computer is like buying a can of beans after purchasing a watermelon. The questions, tests, and maneuvers that are ceremoniously required before making a major purchase, such as a computer or a watermelon, have no place in the simple selection of smaller items, such as a diskette drive or a can of beans.

The most important factor to consider before you buy a diskette drive (or a can of beans) is whether you actually need it. For all intents and purposes, there are few reasons why a person would need a 5.25-inch diskette drive. Such drives have smaller storage capacities than 3.5-inch drives, and it has become nearly impossible to find new software applications that come on the larger diskette.

On the other hand, 3.5-inch diskette drives are ubiquitous—nearly every computer sold today comes equipped with a 3.5-inch drive. Although the storage capacity of a 3.5-inch diskette is limited (to 1.44MB), it is adequate for transporting small files and documents. Users who currently don't have a 3.5-inch diskette drive on their computers should seriously consider upgrading to one.

The best option for those who want to upgrade from a 5.25-inch diskette drive to a 3.5-inch drive is to replace the 5.25-inch drive with a 3.5-inch diskette drive. Such drives are fairly inexpensive—a used 3.5-inch drive found at a pawn shop usually proves to work just as well as a new drive purchased from a computer store—and can be installed easily at home. And for users who need to retain the data stored on their old 5.25-inch diskettes, many computer shops, libraries, and universities have equipment that will transfer data from the larger to the smaller diskettes.

The second upgrading option is to keep the 5.25-inch drive and add a 3.5-inch diskette drive. For users working with a limited number of drive bays, there are even dual drives that combine the two drives into one unit. These combination drives are twice as expensive as a single diskette drive, but require less space so you still have room to add a CD-ROM drive or a tape drive.

Removing a Diskette Drive

To remove a diskette drive, follow these steps:

1. Make sure your PC is turned off and all diskettes are removed from the drive. Read Skill 3 before you start this procedure. Follow the steps outlined in that skill to power down your computer and remove the computer case.

2. After you have completed the steps outlined in Skill 3, locate the diskette drive inside your computer. It is a metal box, approximately 4 inches wide, 6 inches long, and 1 inch thick, and its mouth (where the diskettes are inserted) will be visible on the front panel of the computer, as shown in Figure 7.2. The drive may be anchored to a metal casing with other drives. Do not remove any screws, cables, or wires until you have determined the exact position of the drive.

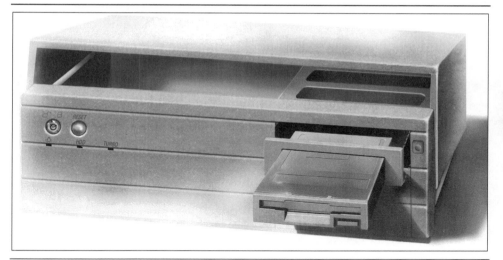

FIGURE 7.2:   The diskette drive resides in a metal box in the computer.

3. After you have located the diskette drive, you are ready to remove it. Try not to disturb the other drives as you extract the diskette drive; a pair of needle-nosed pliers will help you reach some of the tight areas. Disconnect the drive from the support brackets or casing, and then unplug the power source (a four-slot plug with multicolored wires extending from it) and the ribbon cable. Keep track of all loose screws and unplugged wires and

Skill 7

cables. Some computer manufacturers number the cables; write down these numbers to help you remember which cables connect to which plugs. Set the old diskette drive aside.

4. If you are removing a 3.5-inch drive that was located in a 5.25-inch drive bay (a drive bay is the system unit space, usually located on the front panel of the computer, reserved for the installation of any type of drive), you will have to remove the metal brackets that positioned the drive in the bay. Don't discard these brackets; you may find them useful during later installations. If you removed a 3.5-inch drive from a 3.5-inch drive bay or a 5.25-inch drive from a 5.25-inch drive bay, you won't have to deal with these brackets.

5. You are now ready to install your new diskette drive. However, if you aren't going to install a new drive, you will need to cover the open drive bay in the face of your computer with a fitted plastic panel. You can get these panels from a retail computer store or by calling the computer manufacturer. If you removed a 3.5-inch drive from a 5.25-inch bay, you may first have to remove a partial drive-bay panel that was situated to fit around the smaller drive in the larger open bay before you install the full-size drive-bay cover.

6. Physically removing a drive for good also requires you to remove it from your system's BIOS configuration. For more information, see step 7 in the following section.

Installing a Diskette Drive

Once you've removed the old diskette drive, you're ready to install the new one. Follow these steps:

1. Prepare your work area and remove the computer case. See Skill 3 before proceeding.

2. Locate the drive bay in which you will install the new drive, and remove from the face of the computer the plastic panel covering the mouth of the drive bay. Behind this plastic panel, which also is known as a drive bay cover, you may have to remove a metal, clip-out panel from the computer chassis. Store these panels in case you later decide to remove the new drive.

For a 5.25-inch drive, you must use a 5.25-inch drive bay (actual measurement is closer to 6 inches). For a 3.5-inch drive, use a 3.5-inch bay (actual measurement is closer to 4 inches), if you can. Since many computers only have one 3.5-inch bay, you may have to install the smaller drive in the larger 5.25-inch bay. Most diskette drives, however, come with brackets and a pre-formed front panel to adapt with little trouble to this odd fit.

3. Try fitting the diskette drive into the drive bay before connecting wires or installing adaptive brackets. Some 3.5-inch drive bays are positioned vertically rather than horizontally. Although technically it doesn't matter which way you position the drive into a vertical slot, determine which way will provide the most comfortable fit. Find and remove the screws you'll need to use to attach the drive to the chassis.

4. At this time, you'll also want to find the ribbon cable and power source designated for the diskette drive. If you just removed a drive, you can use these cables. Some computer manufacturers label the power cords to designate which cables are reserved for the diskette drive. Plug in the cords to make sure they fit. Each cord has only one correct way to connect to the drive. The striped or red edge of the ribbon cable must be aligned with Pin 1 on the diskette drive. Pin 1, which is always the leftmost pin on the bottom row, is usually denoted in the instruction manual and on the drive itself. Next, if you're using brackets, hold them in place and determine how they will secure the drive.

5. If you're using brackets, screw them on, and insert the diskette drive. If you have connected the cables, you'll probably have to disconnect them before installing the drive. Position the drive in the drive bay, then reconnect the cables, and screw the drive into place. Double-check your cable connections, and make sure you didn't accidentally disconnect any cables from the other drives in the process of installing this one.

6. Position the computer case and screw it on, or lock it down tight. Reconnect the power cord, the mouse, the keyboard, the monitor, and any other components connected to the back of your computer. Reposition the computer on your desk, and put the monitor back into place.

7. Finally, you must update your system's BIOS to recognize the presence of the new diskette drive. When you boot (start) your computer, enter the hotkey sequence needed to access your Setup screen before your computer's startup routine has a chance to open Windows or DOS. The hotkey sequence—which may be a single key, such as the F1 key or the Del key, or a combination of keys, such as Alt+Del—will be revealed to you in one of the first messages to appear on the monitor. The message may be as descriptive as *Hit the F1 key to enter the setup sequence,* or it may simply read *Setup = F1.*

Pressing the hotkey sequence will bring you to the Setup screen. Find the section that contains the statistics about the diskette drives. The first diskette drive on your computer is usually the A: drive. If you have only one diskette drive on your computer, it will be referred to as the A: drive. The second diskette drive usually is referred to as the B: drive. The size of the diskette drive (3.5-inch or 5.25-inch) does not affect the designation of an A: or B: drive.

Use the arrow keys, the Tab key, and the ↵ key to activate your newly installed drive. The drive configuration specifics will be found in the instruction manual. If you're not sure about the configuration specifics, call the manufacturer with the drive product number, which can be found on the drive itself. Generally, most 3.5-inch drives are 1.44MB, and except for older models, most 5.25-inch drives are 1.2MB. You also may need to change the Boot Options, which simply tell where the computer looks for startup information when the computer is booted. Usually, you'll want to set the Boot Options to *Check the A: drive first, then the C: drive.*

To deactivate a drive that has been permanently removed, follow the preceding steps for entering the Setup screen, but change the status of the removed drive (drive A: or B:) to *None* or *Not Installed.* If you've removed the primary diskette drive, you'll have to change the Boot Options to *C: Only.* If you removed a secondary diskette drive, you probably won't have to change the Boot Options at all.

When you've finished adjusting the Setup screen, follow the on-screen commands to Save and Exit. Your computer will then boot up, and your drive will be activated. To double-check activation, insert a diskette into the drive, pull up File Manager (or My Computer in Windows 95), and check for the presence of an A: (or a B:) drive. If you've set it up properly, the contents of the diskette should be registered on the monitor.

Installing an Internal Tape Drive

Hard drives are convenient places to store your important information, but relying on them exclusively can sometimes lead to the dark day when everything comes crashing down.

Fires, floods, and giant meteors from outer space would think nothing of crushing your poor computer, although more often a hard drive failure or human error is to blame for the catastrophe of data loss. Regardless of the cause, the result is the same. You probably have the original diskettes for most of your applications, but the data you've created with them—the spreadsheets, financial information, databases, and documents—would vanish.

Just ask yourself how much it would cost to replace everything on your hard drive in the event of a major crash. When you look at it that way, you may find a tape drive is well worth the purchase price and installation time. Most tape drives come bundled with software that lets you perform backups quickly, easily, and conveniently. And unlike many computer components, tape drives are relatively easy to set up.

Most tape drives come in both external and internal versions. Installing an external drive usually consists of nothing more than plugging a cord into the back of your computer and loading up some software. Unfortunately, external drives can be quite a bit more expensive than their internal counterparts, and they consume precious desk space. External drives are good for networks and similar situations when you want to back up multiple computers with one drive. With a typical home or small-business PC, the money saved by buying an internal drive makes the effort of opening up your computer worth it.

Setting Up

The installation of a tape drive is a fairly straightforward procedure. You won't have to deal with strange creatures such as COM settings or IRQs that appear when you attempt to install modems or sound cards. Basically, the process consists of attaching the drive to a slot inside an empty drive bay, connecting a couple of cables, and installing some software.

Drive bays are the spaces on the front of your computer where devices such as diskette and CD-ROM drives reside. (See Figure 7.3.) Most computers have at least three drive bays, although a few brands may only have two. Depending on the make of your computer and the components already installed, you may be running out of empty bays. Some tape drives are made to fit in either full-size bays designed to hold 5.25-inch drives, or half-size bays made for 3.5-inch drives. A model that can fit in either bay will give you a little flexibility if your bay situation is crowded. Look inside your computer and decide what space you have before choosing a tape drive.

In this exercise, we'll install an HP Colorado T1000 tape drive, a model that can fit in either size bay. While the various brands of tape drives are slightly different from each other, the basic installation process is similar. Still, it's a good idea to thoroughly read any materials included with your tape drive to see if the manufacturer has thrown in some curve balls. Pictures in this book or your manual might differ slightly from what you see inside your computer, but all computers have the same basic components somewhere inside the case.

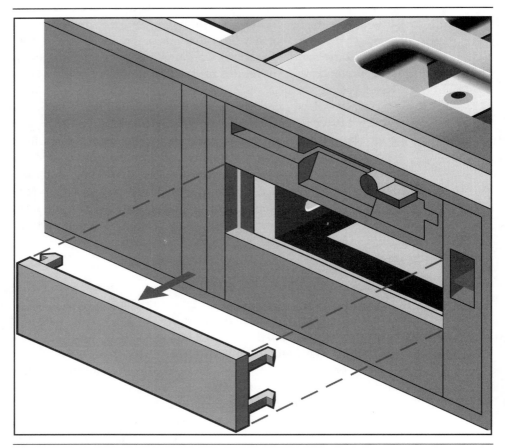

FIGURE 7.3:   Diskette drives are located in drive bays in the front of your computer.

In the tape drive package, you should find the tape drive in an antistatic bag. There also may be a data cable, a power cable converter, some screws, various manuals, and backup software. Make sure you have all the components mentioned in the installation manual before beginning.

 NOTE   The antistatic bag protects the sensitive electronic components of the tape drive from random electrical charges. Leave the tape drive inside the antistatic bag until you are ready for it. Static from your hands can damage fragile electronic components.

The only tool you're likely to need is a Phillips screwdriver. Depending on your computer, you also might want to have a flat-head screwdriver handy. Try not to use screwdrivers with magnetic tips; magnets and computers generally are a bad mix.

Installing the Tape Drive

Before beginning, make sure your PC is turned off. Be certain that you've carefully read Skill 3 before you start this installation. Follow the steps outlined in that skill to power down your computer and remove the computer's cover. Move the monitor away from the computer, and clear some desk space so that you have some room to work.

Making Room

Locate the drive in which you will insert the new tape drive. Unless you are swapping out something else to free a drive bay for the tape drive, you will need to remove one of the drive bay cover plates. Most drive bay covers are flexible pieces of plastic held in place by latches on either side. Usually, it is easiest to snap them out by pushing from the inside of the computer. Just press gently in the middle of the cover with your finger; or, if you can't reach it, try using a pencil.

In a few crowded computers, you may find it impossible to reach the cover because of other drives. A last resort would be to remove one of these drives temporarily in order to gain access to the free drive bay cover. Just be careful not to tear any wires connecting any of the drives to the other components of your computer.

Getting Plugged In

Locate the power cord that will plug into the back of the tape drive. Power cords start at the power supply and usually consist of a few wires topped by a small white connector. There may be a power cord hanging around in the drive bay area, or you may have to hunt for it near the power supply (see Figure 7.4). Snake the power cord through the open bay, and see whether it will connect with the power jack of the tape drive.

The power cord will fit into the smaller of the tape drive's two connectors. Depending on your computer and tape drive, there might be an adapter to fit between the tape drive and the power cord. The power cord should fit snugly into the connector on the drive. If it obviously won't fit, use the adapter.

 NOTE   As you handle the tape drive, remember to try not to touch any of the electronic components.

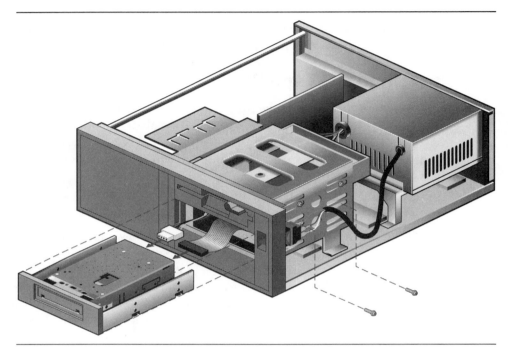

FIGURE 7.4: The power cord emerges from the open drive bay.

Hooking Up the Cable

Now attach the data cable, which is the wide, thin cable with a wide connector at either end. Many times, these cables are clearly marked as to which end fits into what device. Connect one end to the tape drive. It will probably only fit the correct way.

Carefully snake the free end of the data cable through the drive bay and into the computer. Lay it aside while you attach the tape drive to the computer.

Breaking Out the Screwdriver

On some computers, you'll need to use screws, probably supplied with the tape drive, to secure the tape drive to the inside of the computer. On the Hewlett-Packard computer we used, we needed to screw two brackets to either side of the drive, then slide the drive in and attach tabs on the front of the brackets to the front of the drive bay with two more screws. If you're unsure how to attach the drive to the computer, look at how other diskette drives or CD-ROM drives are attached.

Connecting to the Motherboard

Once the drive is solidly inside the bay, it's time to attach the main data cable. The tape drive will run off the same board that controls your computer's diskette drive, so look for a similar cable that connects the diskette drive to either a diskette drive control board or the *motherboard*. The motherboard is the main electronic board in the computer. It will be large, green, and encrusted with all sorts of electronic components. The control board either will be built into the motherboard or attached to it somehow. Avoid touching any of the electronic components to keep them clean.

On the T1000 drive we installed, the data cable from the tape drive connected directly to the motherboard's diskette drive controller, replacing the diskette drive data cable. The diskette data cable then connected to the tape drive cable through a black connector near the end of the tape drive cable.

The most important step when switching all these data cables is to note exactly how the diskette drive data cable is connected before you start. There should be a red stripe along one side of the cable. Write down whether this stripe is on the left or right side and on the top or bottom of the cable. Then disconnect the cable from the diskette drive and replace it with the cable from the tape drive (see Figure 7.5). The position of the red stripe should be the same for the new data cable connection as it was for the old data cable connection. For example, if the red stripe was on the top left side of the diskette drive data cable, then it should be on the top left side of the tape drive data cable.

On the Hewlett-Packard computer we used for this example, the data cable from the hard disk drive blocked our access to the diskette drive cable. In order to switch all of the cables around, we first had to pull out both the hard drive and diskette drive cables, plug in the tape drive cable, replace the hard drive cable, and then connect the diskette drive cable to the tape drive cable. There's nothing wrong with moving things around under a crowded hood in order to reach your objective, but always be sure you remember exactly where everything goes.

Putting It All Together

Once all the cables are connected, carefully fold down all the extra cable length into whatever free space you can find. Make sure that when you replace the computer's case, the data cables aren't pressing onto an expansion board hard enough to bend or break it. Then put the outer case back on the machine.

Reconnect the power cords to all of your equipment, and turn on the computer. It should boot as normal.

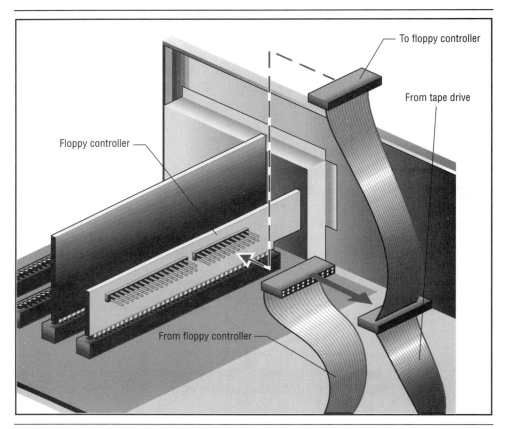

FIGURE 7.5:   The cable from the tape drive replaces the cable from the diskette, or floppy, drive.

Before you can test your work, you'll have to install the required software according to the manufacturer's directions. This will probably consist of putting a diskette in the diskette drive and typing **a:setup** or **a:install** at the Run command in the Windows Program Manager File menu. Then sit back and follow the on-screen instructions.

We found installing an internal tape drive to be an easy way to equip a home computer for major backups. The entire process only took about 20 minutes, and the software that came with our T1000 drive was easy to configure and use. Our tape was buzzing along happily in no time, and our small test backup worked as advertised.

Avoiding the Nightmare

The ultimate computer nightmare... seeing the computer screen go blank and knowing that you have just lost valuable information forever.

What might make you feel even worse is that you could have avoided such a nightmare simply by backing up your system, discussed here and in detail in Skill 3.

When you back up your computer system, you copy data from your computer's hard drive to a secondary storage unit, which gives you a copy to fall back on in case the original is corrupted or lost. The information you store on this secondary storage unit is called your system backup.

If you live in areas prone to natural disasters, system backups are crucial. However, Mother Nature is not the only reason to make a backup. Accidentally reformatting the hard drive or falling victim to a computer virus can have a more devastating effect. Even if your computer runs again, you still have the headache of re-creating the data. If you've backed up your data, that re-creation may take only a few minutes.

Besides tape drives, there are other options, including diskettes, compact discs, or secondary hard drives. Most tape drives come with software that lets you set the PC to automatically perform the kind of backup you want. A full backup saves all the files on a drive, while selective backups save only files that you've selected. Incremental backups save any files modified since the last backup. Many programs also let you choose when the backup should take place. The best times are usually nights or weekends when you don't need to use your computer.

Regardless of the backup method you choose, it is likely to be worth it. The cheap price of today's alternatives just make it that much more worth it. Whenever there is information on your computer that you would regret losing, it should be backed up.

Skill 7

Troubleshooting Disk Drives

The longer you work with computers, the closer you come to experiencing what all users fear—disk drive failure. Usually, disk drive trouble occurs without warning. You turn on your system only to see an error message saying the computer can't read the hard drive. Thus, your computer can't boot, and you can't access your data. Or you place a diskette in a drive only to get a message telling you there is no diskette in the drive.

Does this sound familiar? These mishaps can happen, and when they do, the error messages will produce panic. But if you act recklessly, you might make a bad situation worse. Chances are fairly good that if you keep a level head, you can get your drives working again.

The longer you use your computer, the more likely you will experience hard drive or diskette drive failure. However, you can avoid trouble by practicing effective drive maintenance regularly. And if disaster does strike, learn to troubleshoot the problem and get speedy relief.

Eliminating Causes

First, when you can't access one or more drives, check inside the computer. A common cause of drive problems is a loose connection. Connectors are loosened by vibrations, by bumping the computer, or by moving it. Also, conditions in the workplace often contribute to poor connections. Moisture, as well as excessive heat or cold, can weaken contacts. To fix this, you need to open the computer's case.

Roll up your sleeves, unplug your PC from the wall socket, and touch a nearby metal object to discharge static electricity. Look at the back of your computer; there should be two or more screws on the outermost edge of the cover that hold it in place. Use a Phillips screwdriver to remove the screws, and set them aside until you're done. (Make sure that nothing metal touches any other metal object inside the case.) Now, you can lift or slide the cover off the chassis (see Figure 7.6). While computers contain the same basic components, their location in the computer's case can vary. Consult Figure 7.7 for some ideas on where important components may be found.

Older PCs Use Controller Cards

Once inside, you'll need to locate the controller card, which is a special circuit board that connects the disk drives and the motherboard (the main circuit board of your computer). To find the card, follow the ribbon cable running from the disk drives to where the cable plugs into a vertical card; the drive cable is a wide, thin, gray wire bundle that connects the drives to the controller card.

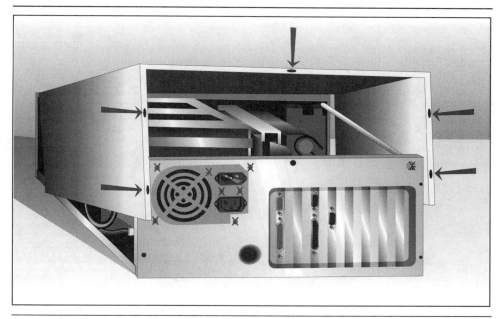

FIGURE 7.6:   When preparing to open the computer, remove only the screws that are near the edges of the cover.

After you find the card, note how it sits in its slot on the motherboard and how it fits through the groove on the back wall of the computer. Then compare the controller card to how the neighboring cards are seated to verify that it's positioned correctly.

To ensure the card is properly set, press down firmly, but gently, on both ends of the card; this will help you make sure all metal points make good contact. Also check the connections at the controller and the drives. Carefully pull the connecting plugs one at a time from their pins, then gently push them back on. Be careful not to bend the pins, or the connectors won't fit correctly. If pins become bent, take a nonconductive material with a straight edge, and insert it along the row of pins. Then gently press this edge against the bent pins until they straighten. Now, use a can of compressed air to blow out dust from inside the diskette drive. These cans are available from most stores that sell computer supplies. The cans come with a tiny tube that fits into the spray nozzle. Carefully hold this tube inside the drive, and spray the compressed air liberally. This dislodges dust that accumulates inside the drive and prevents the drive heads from reading the spinning diskette's surface.

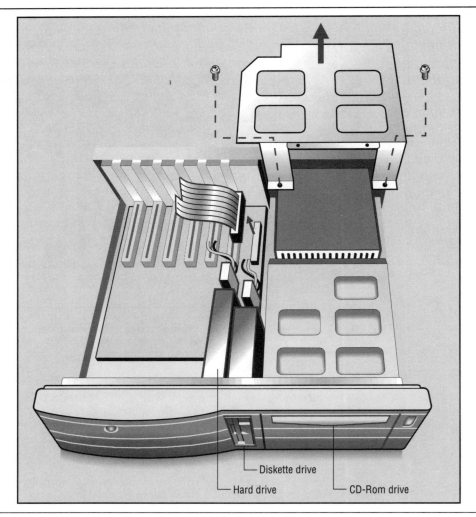

Diskette drive

Hard drive

CD-Rom drive

FIGURE 7.7: The location of components within different computers may vary.

 TIP

Periodically, you should use compressed air to blow dust out of the diskette drive and the computer case itself. A buildup of dust blocks airflow over crucial parts, causing them to overheat and damage the computer. Dust accumulating in the diskette drive will cause read/write errors.

If checking cable connections and cleaning debris from the drives fails to solve the problem, there are three other troubleshooting procedures to follow, one at a time: changing the drive cables, replacing the controller card, or replacing the failed hard drive or diskette drive.

Changing the Drive Cable

The cables to the diskette and hard drives work independently. Only replace the cable of the malfunctioning drive. You can get a replacement set from a computer parts store instead of calling the computer's manufacturer to get original replacement parts. The job itself is easy. Remove one end of the wire, and replace it with the same end of the new wire. Then disconnect the other end and reconnect the replacement, putting the wire in the same position in which you found the original. As long as you don't bend or twist it so that the cable creases, the placement isn't crucial. Take note of the red strip that runs along one edge of the ribbon wire, and install the replacement wire in the same direction.

Replacing the Controller Card

If changing the wires doesn't work, the controller card could be bad. Don't worry about testing the card to confirm that it's malfunctioning. Repair technicians troubleshoot by replacing suspected parts. To remove the controller card, carefully pull the cable connectors from the card. Then grasp the card at opposite ends, and pull firmly upward with both hands; gently rocking the card lengthwise will help dislodge the card from the motherboard.

 **WARNING**   Never rock a controller card sideways. That could make the connecting tabs break off—freeing the card but leaving the contact points behind.

The manufacturer's markings on the removed card will assure that you find a compatible replacement. Installing the new controller card is a two-step operation. First, carefully but firmly push the card into the vacant slot. Then, push the cable connectors onto their pin points. If the replacement card isn't an exact substitute, you may have to install new drivers from software that comes with the controller card. To install the drivers, type **a:setup** at the DOS prompt, and press ↵. In Windows 3.1, open Program Manager's File menu, select Run, and type **a:setup** in the dialog box. If you run Windows 95, double-click the Start button on the Windows 95 Desktop. Select the Run command from the menu that appears, and type **a:setup** in the dialog box.

NOTE You may find that you'll need to replace the diskette drive or the hard drive of your computer. Replacing a diskette drive is covered in detail earlier in this skill in the section called "Installing a Diskette Drive." For the nitty-gritty on replacing your hard drive, see Skill 6.

Looking for Other Antidotes

When the computer fails to boot from the hard drive, you may have a trashed boot sector. (The boot sector is a portion of the hard drive or diskette that has been reserved for a short program that loads an operating system.) You may still be able to save the rest of the hard drive. But this calls for stronger medicine, such as a disk repair utility. There are some excellent programs that can be found at any computer store and that find and repair such maladies. If you ever need one, you will be glad it's on your shelf.

TROUBLESHOOTING TIPS

When working inside the PC to troubleshoot drive problems, follow these basic precautions:

- Discharge static electricity before you touch the computer.
- Don't drop anything inside.
- Don't leave any spare parts when you're finished.
- Draw a diagram of plug connections before you remove them. Most wires are color coded, so taking notes is simple.

If you have a fatal crash instead of a bad boot sector, you can still breathe life into your computer if you have an emergency boot diskette (see Skill 3 for details on creating a bootable diskette). This will give you access to the hard drive if nothing else is damaged. You can copy your data files to diskettes and back up your program files. You even may be able to run your essential programs.

Don't rule out computer viruses when your drives malfunction. Unless you keep your system isolated from the outside world, it'll get a virus sooner or later.

Every time you swap diskettes with a friend or colleague or install a shareware program, you expose your computer to viruses. When your computer slows down for disk access or can't read a file anymore, the culprit might be a virus.

Viruses are rogue programs written by hackers. Many are annoying but otherwise harmless to your computer. Some are destructive, wiping out boot sectors on the hard drive or diskette, rendering data unreachable. Safeguard your drives by taking two quick and easy precautions. One, always scan diskettes you get from other people or your own diskettes that have been in somebody else's computer. Two, always start your computer with a virus scan. This checks the computer's memory, where a virus can hide until you access a program and the virus "leaps" from memory to the disk.

Keeping Disks Damage Free

To prevent delays in reading data on your hard drives and diskettes, you need to periodically run drive maintenance utilities. If you have DOS, Windows 3.1, or Windows for Workgroups (WFW), you have two handy programs called SCANDISK.EXE and DEFRAG.EXE. ScanDisk checks the directory indices DOS maintains so it can find programs and data and examine the condition of the disk surface. If ScanDisk finds any weaknesses on the disk's physical surface, it marks it and moves any data stored there to a safe location. To use this tool, type

scandisk x:

at the DOS prompt, where *x* is the drive you want to check. You can't run this program in a DOS window within Windows or WFW; you must exit Windows.

DEFRAG.EXE unclutters the disk storage system so drive heads don't slow down while making repeated passes for scattered bits and pieces of stored data. All hard drives and diskettes suffer from file fragmentation. Files are fragmented when DOS squeezes information wherever it finds open space on a disk. Saving and deleting files, especially during different work sessions, scatters data across the disk; eventually, fragmented drives can bring your system's performance to a crawl. The Defrag utility places all the parts of a file in contiguous areas on the disk. To use this tool, type

defrag x:

at the DOS prompt, where *x* is the drive you want defragmented. Again, do not run this program from a DOS window within Windows.

Windows 95 comes with new versions of ScanDisk and Defrag. Unlike the pure DOS versions, you can run these disk maintenance tools within the Windows

Skill 7

environment. You can put these utilities on a predetermined schedule to run ScanDisk. (You should run Defrag once or twice a week.)

Windows 95 makes regular drive maintenance an automatic operation. If you don't run it, you must establish a regular maintenance schedule to run manually. If you do, your hard drive will stay healthy. In addition to running ScanDisk and Defrag, get a quality virus-checking program, and use it often. That way, you minimize the chance of disaster striking your hard drive and diskettes.

Dead Batteries

Another possible cause of hard drive failure is a worn-out CMOS battery. This battery sends currents to the CMOS chip, which is responsible for keeping the settings the motherboard needs upon startup, such as which type of hard drive and other system components exist. When the battery runs down, the microprocessor can't find vital information about the structure of the hard drive. The complementary metal-oxide semiconductor (CMOS) consists of two field transistors contained on a silicon chip. (CMOSs are high-speed devices generally used for RAM and switching applications.) Normally, batteries are drained only when your computer is off or if it hasn't been used for a long time (this includes new computers that you've just bought). The more you use your computer, the longer your battery lasts.

An early warning of a dying battery is your clock losing time. Type **time** or **date** at the DOS prompt occasionally to check and reset your time and date. If your clock loses more than, for example, one minute a day or you get occasional *Clock failure* or *Clock error* messages upon startup, a dying battery might be the cause. Also, try resetting your CMOS without replacing the battery. Then, when your PC is running, turn it off and restart it. If you can restart it fine after turning it off for three minutes, but leaving it off overnight causes lost or changed CMOS settings, your battery needs replacing.

NOTE   For information about changing CMOS settings, consult your PC's manual or call the manufacturer. For more information and instructions about changing or installing your system's battery, contact your computer's manufacturer.

Keeping your computer in top shape is similar to keeping yourself fit and trim. You have to use a bit of preventive medicine, a dash of diagnostic care, and a dose of first aid. Only when these procedures fail is it time to call the technical experts.

Are You Experienced?

Now you can...

- ☑ replace an old diskette drive or simply install a new one
- ☑ understand how diskette drives work
- ☑ install a tape drive to back up data
- ☑ troubleshoot diskette drives and hard drives

Installing Multimedia

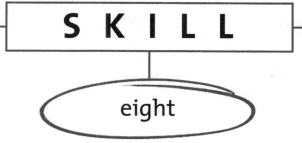

- ❑ Getting ready for a multimedia upgrade
- ❑ Understanding multimedia standards
- ❑ Installing a sound card
- ❑ Installing a CD-ROM drive

The evolution of multimedia is arguably the pinnacle of computer development so far. The ability to combine audio and video into a single interactive medium, coupled with the higher data-storage capacity and increased retrieval speed of CD-ROMs, has provided computers with capabilities unheard of 10 years ago and unimaginable 50 years ago. Gone are the days when computers were simply glorified typewriters. Today's computers are stereos, recording studios, theaters, arcades, telephones, and more. That is, if your PC is equipped to handle your multimedia demands.

Although most new computers come equipped with multimedia capabilities, not all computers are multimedia ready. Computer users who decide to upgrade can buy individual components, such as a CD-ROM drive or speakers, or they can buy a complete upgrade kit, which offers all the components necessary to turn any computer into a multimedia extravaganza of sounds and images. We've outlined some of the considerations you should make before purchasing a multimedia kit as well as some things to consider after you've decided to upgrade.

Is Your PC Prepared?

Multimedia clearly is the future of computing. But before you rush out to buy your first multimedia kit, consider whether you actually need an upgrade. Despite all the hype about multimedia, if you only use your computer for simple tasks, such as writing letters and balancing your checkbook, you probably don't need to upgrade. Considering the high price of upgrading and the speed at which technology moves, it's not worth spending a lot of money on a product that will soon become outdated.

Another important element to consider before deciding to upgrade is whether your computer can handle an upgrade. Because of the voluminous amounts of information that can be stored on a CD-ROM—a single compact disc can hold more than 300,000 pages of text—the central processing unit (CPU) of a computer needs to be able to process data at an extremely high rate of speed. Although some CD-ROM drive manufacturers claim their products will run on a PC with a 386 CPU, a 25MHz 486SX CPU with 4MB RAM is generally considered the absolute minimum. A VGA color monitor or better is required for video playback.

NOTE These are minimum system requirements. A faster CPU, additional RAM, and an SVGA monitor all will enhance multimedia performance.

After deciding to upgrade to a multimedia system, determine which type of upgrade best suits your needs and which one will be most compatible with your existing system. If you foresee the need to replace your PC soon, the first and best option is to purchase a complete multimedia computer system. Although this is the most expensive option, buying a complete multimedia system eliminates all installation and compatibility problems. It also costs less than purchasing a computer and components separately.

If you don't plan to replace your computer system and you already own some multimedia components, you can purchase individual components for your computer. This method lets you build your computer according to your particular needs.

For advanced computer users with extraordinary demands, it's practically a necessity. For novices or recreational computer users, however, purchasing individual components can cause major compatibility dilemmas. Because each piece is purchased individually, the price is usually higher than buying a kit.

Another option is buying an upgrade kit. For the average computer user, purchasing a complete kit, which usually includes a CD-ROM drive, a sound card, speakers, and several software titles, is the most convenient option and will adequately handle almost all recreational multimedia needs. Furthermore, purchasing an upgrade kit solves many compatibility dilemmas; in compiling the packaged unit, the manufacturer has already determined which components work best together. Also, the price of a packaged kit is considerably cheaper than purchasing the components separately.

Building the Perfect Beast

Upgrade kits fit into many price ranges and offer a variety of components. If you take the time to shop carefully, you should find a kit that will satisfy all your computing needs. Doing a little homework before you head to the store also will help you select the right upgrade kit.

First, you should consult either your computer's manufacturer or your local computer vendor to determine which multimedia kits are recommended for your PC. The manufacturer or vendor should be able to tell you which CD-ROM drive will best complement your computer so you can expect peak performances from both. Also, conferring with the manufacturer helps ensure that you avoid hardware incompatibility problems.

As an additional precautionary measure before you buy, you should check your computer to make sure you have an expansion slot available for the sound card and a 5.25-inch drive bay for the CD-ROM drive. The expansion slot needs

Skill 8

to have a corresponding port that opens on the back panel of your computer. And you'll recognize the presence of an available drive bay by the removable plastic panel (approximately 6 inches wide and 2 inches tall) on the front of your computer. If you don't have an available drive bay, you'll have to buy an external CD-ROM drive.

Finally, another good reason to check your computer is to make sure you don't already own something you plan to buy. Don't forget about those speakers you received as a Christmas present or that sound card you installed two years ago.

Making the Buy

As you stroll the aisles of your local computer store, searching for the upgrade kit that will satisfy your multimedia desires, you'll be accosted by large boxes adorned with portraits of neatly arranged CD-ROM drives, speakers, sound cards, and small armies of software.

Flashing software titles around is an easy way for computer companies to catch the consumer's attention. After all, getting 22 titles with your kit sounds more appealing than receiving a mere six or 12 titles. Although the bundled software that comes with an upgrade kit is one factor to consider when making your final purchasing decision, don't forget to look at the whole package.

One kit may include a microphone, while another includes speaker mounts. This package may offer headphones and 24 software titles, but that one offers a better sound card and a voice recognition program. The possible combinations are endless, and each upgrade kit has something unique to offer prospective buyers.

 NOTE   Remember this: No kit includes free parts. In other words, when you buy a kit you're paying for everything in the box, so you should determine what you need before you buy.

Which kit you decide to buy will ultimately depend upon your multimedia intentions. Generally, it's better to choose a multimedia kit that offers superb hardware and mediocre software than one with mediocre hardware and excellent software. Extra features, such as a microphone or speaker mounts, also are beneficial.

With multimedia becoming increasingly prevalent, it's important to equip your PC with multimedia capabilities. When choosing your upgrade option, however, don't become overwhelmed by facts and figures; the best upgrade for you may not be the best product on the market. The bottom line? It's best to buy a kit based upon how you want to use your computer and not how manufacturers want you to use it.

Multimedia Standards

For several years, the Multimedia PC Working Group has established multimedia PC guidelines that address the quality of the end-user experience. This Software Publishers Association (SPA) group, composed of members from PC industry companies and organizations, first released its multimedia PC (MPC) specifications in 1991. The original guidelines, known as MPC1, were considered the basic multimedia extension of the PC standard, and they helped hardware manufacturers create an installed base of multimedia-ready computers. In 1993, growth in multimedia functionality and an industry-wide review of which standards should be changed prompted the development of MPC2 specifications. Unless a product met all MPC2 requirements, it still was considered MPC1.

MPC3, released in 1996, is the latest set of specifications and takes the multimedia experience one step further. If your hardware bears the "MPC3 Certified" logo, you can be sure the system is capable of providing full-screen, full-motion video and enhanced CD-quality sound while running even the most complex multimedia programs. Software packages that display the MPC3 logo can be run on machines that comply with the MPC3 standard. Previously released MPC2 multimedia software can run on the new MPC3-compliant hardware. MPC3 simply is the next stage in the evolution of the industry's qualification standards.

Table 8.1 outlines the specifications of the three MPC standards.

TABLE 8.1: The Evolution of MPC Standards

Component	MPC1 (1991)	MPC2 (1993)	MPC3 (1996)
Processor	16MHz 386SX	25MHz 486SX or compatible	75MHz Pentium or compatible
RAM	2MB	4MB	8MB
Hard Drive	30MB	160MB	540MB
Display	VGA	VGA, 64K colors	VGA, full-motion video
CD-ROM	1X (150KBps)	2X (300KBps)	4X (600KBps)
Average Seek Time	1 second	400 milliseconds	250 milliseconds
Sound Board	8-bit	16-bit	16-bit
MIDI	Yes	Yes	Yes
Speakers	Yes	Yes	Yes (3 watts/channel)
Operating System	Windows 3.0	Windows 3.0	Windows 3.11/DOS 6.0

Skill 8

What Do I Really Need?

Multimedia kits, like computers in general, seem to be saturated with excesses. And yet, as time passes, upgrades become necessary because what once was considered exorbitant is now substandard. So although it might seem like retailers and computer manufacturers are encouraging you to purchase something you don't need, in many cases they're providing honest advice about what you should buy. To make shopping easier, we'll briefly explain why you might need that extra component.

4X, 6X, 8X, or Faster?

The amount of data stored on a compact disc is, perhaps, the main reason for the success of the CD-ROM drive. Considering that the standard diskette contains 1.44MB of information, it's no surprise that the compact disc, which can store up to 650MB of data, has overshadowed its predecessor.

Furthermore, CD-ROM drives have extremely fast data access rates, which expedite the presentation of information and improve video performance. Video presentations demonstrate a remarkable improvement in clarity and a decrease in frame stuttering—the skipping of a frame during video playback—when played on faster CD-ROM drives.

Software developers have used CD-ROM technology to expand the depth of their programs, packing them full of video footage, sound bites, photographs, and extensive text in order to create a comprehensive presentation of information. Programs such as Microsoft's Encarta96 Encyclopedia and Creative Wonder's 3D Atlas, with 649MB and 643MB of data respectively, demonstrate that developers fully intend to give you the most bang for your buck.

With software developers improving the performance capabilities of their products, a faster drive is recommended for those who plan to use educational and entertainment software. Buying an 8X or faster drive may cost more now, but it will save you money in the long run by postponing future upgrades.

Speakers

Some manufacturers and retailers recommend purchasing speakers to replace the pair that comes with your multimedia kit. The truth is, however, that unless you really want to shake the walls when you play Quake, the small speakers included with a multimedia kit will be sufficient. Perhaps one day, when computers have replaced the stereo, it might be worth buying bigger speakers. But for today's average user, bigger speakers are simply superfluous.

Microphones

As an additional feature, some multimedia kits include a microphone for use with any sound recorder program. Although microphones now are used for entertainment, they promise eventually to serve in a more important capacity.

Voice communication programs, which allow person-to-person telecommunications via modem, have already been developed by some companies. These programs use a microphone and speakers to act as a receiver and transmitter. Because calls are made through a local telephone number, the only cost for making an Internet telephone call is the per hour cost charged by your Internet service provider. Although this technology has not been perfected yet, great strides have been made recently and will undoubtedly continue to be made as this form of communication gains popularity.

For a peek at this technology, visit VocalTec's World Wide Web site at `http://www.vocaltec.com` to download a free copy of Internet Phone.

Software

Finally, the tantalizing software that comes with a multimedia package can be a good reason for choosing one upgrade kit instead of another. In addition to providing cheap entertainment, the software bundled with a multimedia kit often is carefully selected by the manufacturer to highlight the best qualities of the kit.

When selecting your upgrade kit, take the time to read which programs are included. Competing companies offer packages that contain very similar CD-ROM drives and sound cards, but the number and quality of software packages is different. Most kits offer a few award-winning bestsellers and then bulk up the bundle with shareware and less popular programs. Check the software sections of your local retail store to see whether any of the bundled software is available on the shelves. Note the price of the software and any awards the programs may have earned. Bundled software can be a terrific bargain if you get recognized programs; likewise, it can be a needless expense if you never use it.

Regardless of which multimedia upgrade kit you decide to buy, you'll never know its real value until you've used it for a while. If you don't have to upgrade again soon, there's no dust on your software, and you wonder how you ever got along without multimedia capabilities, then you can rest easy—you've made the right decision.

Skill 8

Installing a Sound Card

In the past, audio was the neglected element in the computing world. Video, graphics, and input devices received all the attention. The addition of a mouse made communicating with your computer more enjoyable while larger, full-color screens and improved processors provided lavish visual images. When it came to audio, however, the computer often was relegated to attempting to re-create rich stereo sound through a tiny internal speaker, whose qualifications for the job consisted of a few beeps and a rare chime. Silence was a preferred alternative.

Computer audio no longer is drudgery, though. Enhanced software products, especially those found on CD-ROM discs, have given sound the same level of quality as other computing components. A sound card, when teamed with external speakers, can take advantage of the improved audio capabilities found in today's programs. If your system doesn't contain a sound card, you can buy one and install it yourself with minimal effort.

The Basics

A sound card is an expansion board for your PC that generates sound and provides audio output to external amplification devices, such as speakers or headphones. The term *sound card* is interchangeable with the terms *sound board* and *audio card.*

An *expansion board,* also called a *circuit board,* provides a base for and connection between electronic components. Expansion boards give your computer access to additional features, such as audio, communications via a modem, or a network connection. Most expansion boards are made of green plastic, and the electronic components and computer chips are attached to the plastic. The components are connected by copper etching.

You plug an expansion board into an expansion slot, which is a narrow socket inside the computer that provides a connection between the expansion board and the rest of the computer. The bottom portion of the expansion board, which looks like an insertion tab, is called the *connector,* and fits in the expansion slot. It contains small, gold pins that form a rectangle. They are responsible for exchanging data between the board and the computer.

Physically installing a sound card isn't difficult, but making your computer communicate with it could be. Your sound card package should include software the computer needs to interact with the card. The software is usually easy to install, and you won't need to make any adjustments to your system. But there are a few occasions where you might have to perform some troubleshooting to get the sound card to work.

You'll also need to remember the type of sound card you have because many programs with audio capabilities will require you to specify your sound card.

Sound Card Standards

There are three major sound card compatibility standards: Microsoft Windows Sound System, General MIDI, and SoundBlaster. You also might run across an older standard, called AdLib. You'll definitely want a board that supports at least one of the major standards (most boards on the market fit this description), and you'll be best off with a board supporting all three.

The most popular and commonplace standard is SoundBlaster, which is made by Creative Labs. Most sound cards meet SoundBlaster's specifications instead of soliciting support for their own boards. Game players should make sure they have SoundBlaster-compatible sound boards, because many game software programs list "sound board (SoundBlaster)" among their system requirements. To play music, users should be more concerned with having sound cards that are General MIDI-compatible and feature wavetable technology.

MIDI (Musical Instrument Digital Interface) sound cards allow musical instruments, synthesizers, and computers to communicate using wavetable technology, which is a form of music synthesis that uses a stored set of real instrument samples.

We installed a SoundBlaster 16 SCSI-2 AST sound card. The physical installation of all sound cards is basically the same, but the installation of the software will differ, and you'll need your user guide to perform the correct installation.

Preparing for Installation

Before you attempt any hardware installation, it's important to read through the user manual and installation guide provided with the product. You can then familiarize yourself with different components through drawings in the manuals, and you'll learn about any odd configurations. Although many user guides will spell out exactly which tools you need, a Phillips screwdriver is a must when installing a sound board.

You'll have to install some software with your soundboard. Because the software probably will make changes to your AUTOEXEC.BAT, CONFIG.SYS, and WIN.INI files, you should make backup copies of these files before installing the sound card software in case a conflict occurs.

Skill 8

You'll need free hard drive space for the sound card's software. Many sound cards ship with add-on programs, and you'll need additional space for them. The SoundBlaster software we used required 7.5MB of hard drive space. Your user/installation guide should tell you how much hard drive space you need, as well as any other system requirements.

 TIP   Keep your sound card inside its static-resistant packaging until you are ready to install it. A buildup of static electricity, as well as dirt and oil from your hands, can damage the card.

Installing the Card

When you're ready to begin the installation, move your monitor out of the way, and be certain you have plenty of cleared desk space to work on. To prepare your computer for installation, then read Skill 3 then.

Selecting an Expansion Slot

Most newer sound cards will require a 16-bit expansion slot, rather than an 8-bit slot. (The expansion slots are at the back of the computer, as shown in Figure 8.1.) You can tell which type of slot you'll need by the number of connectors on your sound card. Expansion boards requiring 16-bit slots will have two connector areas—one about 4 inches long and another about 2 inches long. If your computer has a mixture of 16-bit and 8-bit expansion slots, you'll see that the 16-bit slots are longer than the 8-bit slots and contain room for both sets of connectors. Find a free 16-bit expansion slot for your sound card. If you plan to connect a CD-ROM drive or a daughterboard providing additional sound capabilities to the sound card, make sure you place it in an expansion slot with an empty slot beside it.

After selecting an expansion slot, you'll need to remove the corresponding metal plate on the outside of the computer's case. Remove the screw on top of the plate and lift the plate out from the top. Save the screw, because you'll need it to fasten your sound card to the computer casing. The metal plate you removed protects the inside of the computer when no expansion card is installed in its corresponding expansion slot. When you install your sound card, the metal plate on the end of the card (containing the speaker and microphone ports) will replace the metal plate you just removed, so you no longer need the plate for this installation.

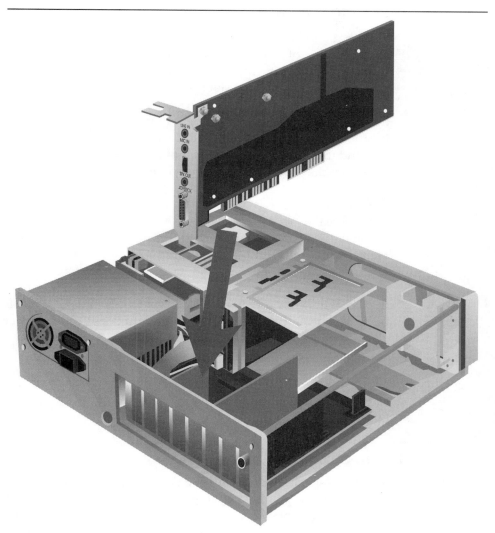

FIGURE 8.1:   The board you are installing will fit into one of the expansion slots at the back of the computer.

 NOTE   If you don't have a metal plate in the slot you've chosen, that means it has already been removed, and you'll have to find another screw to fasten the sound card. Generally, you shouldn't remove the metal plates until you're ready to install an expansion board.

Skill 8

Inserting the Card

Take the sound card out of the static-resistant bag. Touch the edges of the card so the buildup of static electricity is minimal, and so you don't damage any of the electrical components on the card. Line up the connectors on the sound card with the empty expansion slot (see Figure 8.2). The connectors should slide almost entirely into the expansion slot, leaving only the extreme top of the connectors' gold pins visible. It's a tight fit in the expansion slot, so you might find it easier to roll the card into the slot by placing a corner in the expansion slot first and then fitting the remainder of the connector into the expansion slot. Don't jam the sound card into the expansion slot because you may damage components.

If the sound card has been inserted into the expansion slot correctly, you should see the metal plate on the edge of the sound card aligned with the empty slot in the back of the computer's case. You should be able to easily connect the metal plate of the sound card to the computer's case with the screw you removed from the original metal plate. Don't use the screw to force the sound card to line up properly; it should fit properly in the expansion slot with or without the screw in place. The screw is only used to prevent the sound card from inadvertently being bumped out of place. If the sound card doesn't appear to be inserted correctly, remove the card, and try again. You can look at the other expansion cards in your computer for guidance.

After inserting the sound card, make sure the other expansion boards haven't been accidentally jostled. In the cramped quarters inside your computer, it's easy to knock a component out of place, so you'll need to use caution when installing any device.

Connecting the Cables

At this point, if you have a CD-ROM drive, you'll want to connect it to the sound card. The SoundBlaster 16 SCSI-2 AST contains a SCSI connector designed to connect to your CD-ROM drive. (SCSI is a hardware interface allowing connection of several peripheral devices.) You'll connect the sound card and CD-ROM drive via a SCSI cable (see Figure 8.3). If you have an internal CD-ROM drive, the SCSI cable will connect from the back of the CD-ROM drive to the sound card. If you have an external CD-ROM drive, the SCSI cable will connect from the external CD-ROM drive's expansion card to the sound card. Check the instruction manuals for the CD-ROM drive and the sound card for exact connection requirements.

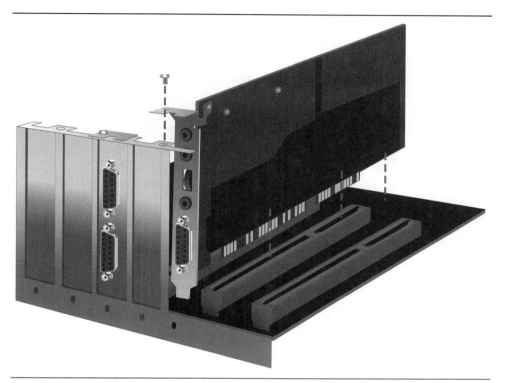

FIGURE 8.2:   The sound card fits snugly into the expansion slot.

At this point, you can replace the computer case cover if you're afraid of damaging the inside of your computer, or wait until after you've tested the sound board and have made sure that your system is working properly.

Hooking Up Everything Else

You can use the PC's internal speaker with your sound card, but using the tiny speaker is going to defeat the purpose of the sound card. You'll probably want to connect external speakers to the sound card instead. The speakers' cables will connect to a port on the metal plate of the sound card, which should be visible from the back of the computer. Different sound cards, even those of the same brand, sometimes will have different connection ports. For example, the metal plate on the SoundBlaster card we used contains (from top to bottom): a Line In port for an audio CD player or a synthesizer, a Microphone In port for a microphone, a

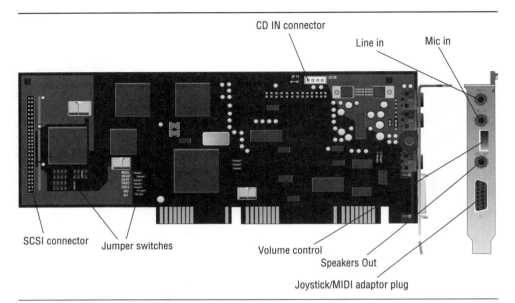

CD IN connector

Line in

Mic in

SCSI connector

Jumper switches

Volume control

Speakers Out

Joystick/MIDI adaptor plug

FIGURE 8.3: A cable connects the sound card and the CD-ROM drive.

Volume Control knob, an Audio Output port for speakers or headphones, and a Joystick/MIDI Connector port for a joystick. You'll probably want to have the drawing of the connection ports for your particular sound card handy when you are ready to plug in the speakers because the tiny writing on the sound card can be difficult to read, especially after the card is installed.

Reconnect the monitor, computer, and speakers (if necessary) to their power sources. Turn on the computer.

Installing the Drivers

You can now install the sound card's software. Make certain you've made backup copies of your system files, as we mentioned in Skill 3. The sound card's installation guide should provide instructions for installing the software that is needed to make the computer work with the sound card. Most of the time, the software will automatically make all necessary system adjustments. The software will include device drivers, which are software files that let the computer communicate with hardware devices. Sometimes the software has a program that lets you adjust the volume on the sound card; the program takes the place of a volume knob. After installing the software, you'll need to reboot your computer so the computer will recognize the changes to your system.

If you can't get any audio from the speakers, you may need to adjust the volume level. Some sound cards have a volume knob you can turn on the back of the card to adjust the volume, others require you to make the adjustments on-screen. If you still can't get any audio, you'll need to check the user guide for some troubleshooting tips. Many companies offer free technical support as well.

 NOTE   As long as you stick to a brand of sound card that supports at least one of the three major sound card standards, you should have little trouble with installation.

Installing a sound card and speakers can be expensive, but after hearing the true audio capabilities of your computer, you'll wonder why you ever subjected your ears to the beeps and chimes of your computer's internal speaker.

Installing a CD-ROM Drive

Internal. External. SCSI. IDE. Double-speed. Quad-speed. These words mean little to those who have only heard of compact disc, read-only memory (CD-ROM) drives. But as foreign as these words sound, the obvious allure of multimedia—bright lights, motion video, and resounding audio—is no surprise to anybody. Why buy a 26-volume set of encyclopedias when a few compact discs will give you just as much text plus lots of multimedia enhancements? There's no doubt that home entertainment and education haven't been the same since CD-ROMs became the data source of choice in millions of households around the world.

For those who have decided to jump on the multimedia bandwagon, there are a few things you should know before you install the CD-ROM drive.

Internal or External?

Internal CD-ROM drives, which fit inside the computer and sit just below the diskette drive, use the computer's power supply instead of their own. They also tend to cost less than external drives because they usually have an Integrated Device Electronics (IDE) interface rather than a SCSI. IDE controller electronics are housed on the drive itself, eliminating the need for a separate adapter card.

Skill 8

Even with all the advantages of internal drives, there is one major disadvantage, says Tim Meyerhoff, a Panasonic multimedia products specialist. Internal drives can't be transferred easily from one machine to another, preventing two computers from sharing one drive. External drives, on the other hand, can be unplugged and moved around without any problems.

External drives, which sit on the desk next to the computer, have several other advantages, with the most notable being that they primarily use SCSI. Meyerhoff says external drives rarely use IDE because the data transfer cable that connects an IDE drive to the computer usually doesn't extend more than 18 inches, meaning the CD-ROM drive has to be located fairly close to the computer. SCSI cables, on the other hand, can be up to three meters in length, letting users set the drive some distance away from the connected computer. Users do pay a price, however: External devices demand valuable and already limited desk space.

For serious CD-ROM users who can afford paying $50 to $100 more for the SCSI drive, Meyerhoff says "go for it." A SCSI drive can handle up to seven peripherals, while IDE limits users to four. SCSI also has faster data throughput rates when compared with IDE. Meyerhoff recommends users weigh the cost factor against computing needs in order to determine which type of drive best suits them.

Drive Speed

Users also must consider drive speed. The speed of the drive determines picture and sound quality and how quickly information is transferred between the disc and the computer. The faster the drive spins, the faster your computer can access programs stored on compact disc. The faster your computer gets the programs, the better the programs will look and sound because the pictures will appear on-screen more quickly and the sound will be less choppy.

A stereo compact disc player spins your audio CDs in single speed. CD-ROM drives don't come in this speed because the discs aren't spun fast enough for the computer to access the information. CD-ROM drives currently come in six speeds: double- (2X), quad- (4X), six- (6X), eight- (8X), ten- (10X), and twelve-speed (12X).

Another installation option consumers should consider is a multimedia upgrade kit (like those we discussed when we talked about upgrading for multimedia). These kits include a CD-ROM drive, sound card, speakers, and software.

Purchas-ing the kit means you won't have to shop around for each part, and it eliminates the risk of buying incompatible components.

Installation Preparation

Now that you've bought your drive, you're almost ready to roll. Before you begin the installation, make sure you read the instruction manual that came with the CD-ROM drive to familiarize yourself with the procedure. While the manual will tell you exactly what tools you'll need for this procedure, a Phillips screwdriver is a necessity. You also may need several megabytes of free hard drive space (your manual will tell you how much).

The illustrations of our CD-ROM drive installation may differ slightly from what you see as you perform your installation (placement of the basic components change with each brand of PC). Refer to Figure 8.4 to get reacquainted with the basic computer components. However, the components illustrated are in all computers; you may just have to look a little harder to locate each part.

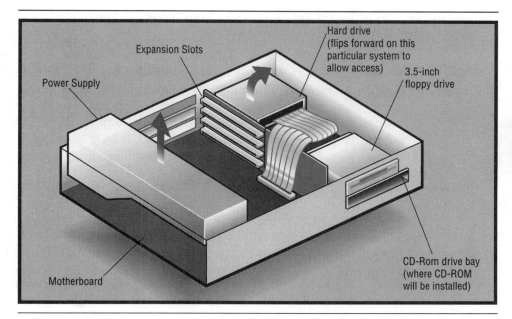

FIGURE 8.4:   This is one example of a computer's configuration (the location of computer components varies from computer to computer).

Skill 8

NOTE Keep your interface board in its static-resistant packaging until you're ready to use it. Static electricity, along with dirt and oil from your hands, can damage the board.

Installing the CD-ROM

When you're ready to install your CD-ROM, make sure your PC is turned off, and unplug the monitor and the computer from their power sources. Read Skill 3, *Taking Precautions Before You Begin*, before you start this installation.

Before handling the computer parts, ground yourself by touching the metal part of the case. This prevents electrical damage to the computer's circuits. After grounding yourself, don't move around too much to prevent the buildup of static electricity. Make sure all the parts you'll need for the installation are handy and that you have plenty of room on your desk to complete the procedure.

Checking the Jumpers

Remove the plastic and metal panels that protect the drive bay where you want to install the CD-ROM drive, and take the drive out of its plastic shipping wrapper. You should consult the installation manual to see how you should set the drive's jumpers. These jumpers are located on the back of your drive and are used to set the drive's ID (see Figure 8.5). Most jumpers already are set to the proper ID before the manufacturer ships the CD-ROM drive, but you may want to double-check these settings to prevent any installation mishaps.

Placing the Drive Inside

You're now ready to slide the new drive into the vacant drive bay. Make sure the CD-ROM drive is flush with the diskette drive (see Figure 8.6). If your computer has a diskette drive, you may need to take out the screws that hold the drive in place and slide the drive forward a couple of inches to give yourself more room to work inside the computer. Don't disconnect the drive's cables. If there are any cables in the bay where you want to install the drive, move them out of the way so you can slide the drive into the bay unimpeded.

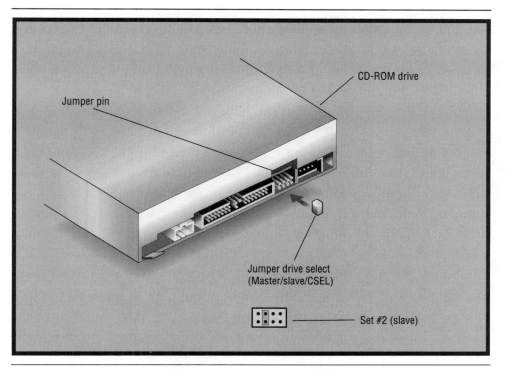

CD-ROM drive

Jumper pin

Jumper drive select
(Master/slave/CSEL)

Set #2 (slave)

FIGURE 8.5:   The jumpers on the back of the drive are usually set by the manufacturer.

Hooking Up the Cables

After the CD-ROM drive is in place, you need to hook several cables to it. First, connect the DC power cable to the back of the drive (see Figure 8.7). This cable runs from the computer to the CD-ROM drive and should be lying just beneath the hard drive. If the hard drive is in your way, you can loosen the screw that fastens it to the motherboard and move it out of the way. Next, connect the interface and audio cables to the back of the drive. Both of these cables are included with the installation kit, so don't worry about finding them.

Now that you've attached the cables, put the hard drive back in place. Make sure the interface and audio cables aren't pinched under the hard drive when you

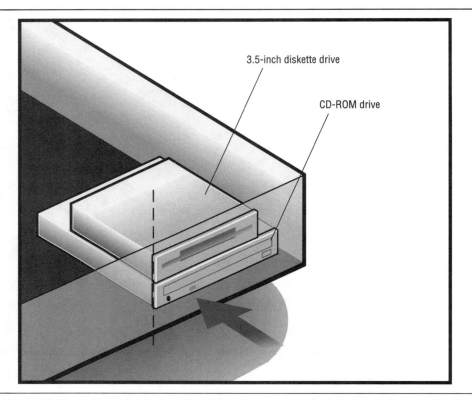

FIGURE 8.6:   Slide the CD-ROM drive so that it's flush and aligned with the floppy drive.

put it into place. These cables must have room to reach from the CD-ROM drive to the expansion slots. Also make sure the cables aren't stretched too tight; the connection should be snug and the cord relaxed. You don't want to risk damaging or losing the connection.

Installing the CD-ROM Interface

The installation of the interface board comes next. You'll probably need to locate an empty 16-bit expansion slot inside the computer. We discussed expansion slots earlier in this skill when we installed a sound card. To determine if your board needs an 8-bit or 16-bit slot, check the number of connectors on the bottom of the interface board. If the board has two connector areas instead of one, you need a 16-bit slot. Almost all recent expansion cards use 16-bit slots.

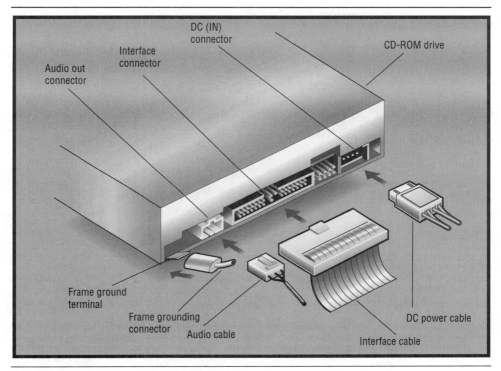

FIGURE 8.7:   The CD-ROM won't be of much use unless it's connected.

 NOTE   If you are installing from a multimedia kit, you may be working with a sound card instead of an interface card. Follow the directions in your instruction manual and see "Installing a Sound Card" earlier in this skill.

Before you can slide the interface board into the empty slot, you must remove the metal plate that covers the opening on the back of the computer. If you find that space is tight when trying to remove the plate's screw, you may be able to remove the power source located on the right side of your computer. Again, don't disconnect any cables. You won't be able to remove the power source completely but may be able to flip it over and lay it on top of the hard drive to get it out of your way. Remove the plate's screw and save it because you will need it to secure your interface board. If you don't have a metal plate corresponding to the slot you have chosen, it probably has been removed already for another reason, and you'll just need to find different screws to hold the board in place.

Grounding Yourself

Your interface board should still be in its shipping wrapper. Before you remove the board, ground yourself to prevent static electricity from damaging the circuits. Once again, you'll need to consult the installation guide to make sure the board's jumpers are set correctly. These jumpers look like little black Legos on gold connector pins (see Figure 8.8). As with the jumpers on the CD-ROM drive, the manufacturer should have set these jumpers to the correct setting; you shouldn't have to change them.

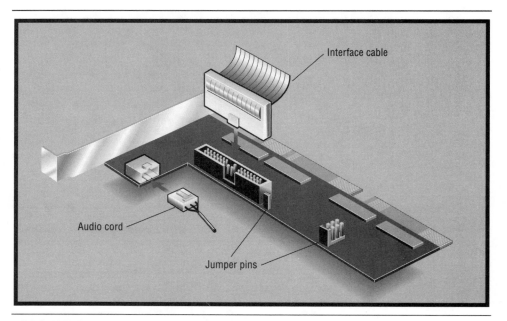

FIGURE 8.8: The jumpers on the interface board must be set correctly before installation.

Sliding In the Board

Once you have checked the settings, you're ready to slide the board into the expansion slot. You need to press firmly to get the board into place. If you can't get the board into the slot, try pushing in just one side of the board at a time, and ease it into the slot. The board should slide in easily once it's in the right position. If you have to really shove, take the board out and try again.

Once the board is in the slot, replace the screw you removed. You shouldn't have to force it into place; the board should stay in position without the screw. The screw simply keeps the board from being bumped out accidentally.

Now you'll connect the interface and audio cables to the interface board. You shouldn't have any problem figuring out where the interface cable connects because there's only one slot on the board resembling the interface cable. The audio cable may be a little more tricky, as there are three different ends on the cable, enabling it to fit into different slots on different boards. However, only one end will fit into the connection on your board, so you just need to determine which is the match. (See Figure 8.8 for the location of the cable connections.)

Adding the Software

Now that you've installed the hardware, you can put the computer's parts back where they belong, tighten loosened screws, and replace the computer case. It's okay for the audio and interface cables to be bent underneath the cover. When the case is back on, reconnect the monitor to the computer, and plug them into a power source. You can now turn on your computer, and begin the software installation.

The software installation is easy if you follow the directions in your manual. We only had one problem. We had to choose to install the software to DOS, Windows, or both. The first time we chose the Windows Only option, but the computer could not find the CD-ROM drive with this choice. So we went through the process again, this time choosing both DOS and Windows, and the installation was complete. The installation diskettes contained the driver (the software program that lets the computer communicate with a hardware device). So, besides answering some on-screen questions, we didn't have to do anything during this process.

If you've completed the installation and your CD-ROM drive doesn't work, don't panic. There are several things you can investigate before running to the phone to call technical support:

- Are all the connections between the interface board, cables, and CD-ROM tight?

- Is the software installed properly?

- Did you put the disc in the drive with the label side up?

- Are all the settings correct, both on the CD-ROM drive and the interface board?

If you've checked all these things and your drive still doesn't work, call the technical support number listed in the installation manual.

Skill 8

Most CD-ROM drives are fairly easy to install, and the manual should help you along. But don't despair if you can't get your drive to work the first time. Some drives are harder to install than others. Just keep plugging away; the results are definitely worth it.

Are You Experienced?

Now you can. . .

- ☑ prepare for a multimedia upgrade
- ☑ evaluate hardware and software based on multimedia standards
- ☑ select and install a sound card
- ☑ shop for and install a CD-ROM drive

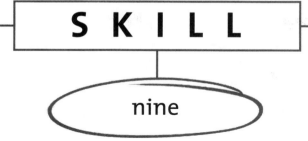

S K I L L

nine

9

Installing Video Cards and Video RAM

❑ Deciding whether to upgrade your video capabilities

❑ Installing a graphics card

❑ Upgrading your computer's video RAM

❑ Identifying and solving monitor problems

Upgrading your computer's video capabilities can do more than give it a pretty face. Sure, video and graphics will appear crisper and clearer, and you may avoid the eye strain that can come with viewing grainy images. But upgrading your computer's monitor and graphics cards also can help your machine run programs it could not run before. Have you ever picked up a great software package, only to discover it requires an SVGA monitor with 256 colors—and your VGA system displays a mere 16?

Each new generation of software adds more video and graphical elements that require better on-screen resolution. As a result, many computer users have found that the systems they bought only a few years ago fail to meet the demands of the latest software titles.

If you have a VGA system, you're not out of luck. If you're willing to spend at least $90, you may be able to upgrade your computer's video and graphics so you can run some of those spiffy new software titles.

To Upgrade or Not to Upgrade?

Before you get your hopes up, you must determine whether your monitor can support an upgrade. Monitors have fixed capabilities, says Mike Viramontes, senior product marketing manager at Diamond Multimedia, a California-based manufacturer of video cards. Monitors are equipped to perform up to a specific resolution, which is a measurement—usually given in dots per inch (dpi)—of the sharpness of an image generated by a monitor. This means a monitor is limited in how many dots, or pixels, can appear on-screen. For instance, a Video Graphics Array (VGA) monitor draws up to 640 rows of pixels by 480 lines of pixels and displays 16 colors. Another common standard is Super Video Graphics Array (SVGA), which can draw up to 1,280 rows of pixels by 1,024 lines of pixels and displays 16 million colors.

Just because your computer only displays 16 colors in a VGA mode, doesn't mean it can't perform better. It simply means the graphics card in your computer is set to work in VGA mode with 16 colors. Your monitor may be able to operate at a higher resolution. The best way to find out is to check your monitor's documentation or call the manufacturer. It's important to make sure your monitor can handle a new resolution before you upgrade. If you install a new graphics card and the monitor and card won't support each other, you'll end up with a screen that looks like a television with a faulty horizontal hold.

Still, there may be times when you don't want to upgrade your monitor to a higher resolution, even though it can accommodate it. For instance, you may not want to boost a 14-inch monitor's resolution above 800 × 600. Using more pixels will improve resolution and make the image clearer, but it also squeezes pixels together on-screen, which makes the image smaller. Using a resolution above 800 × 600 on a 14-inch or 15-inch monitor may make it seem like you are working on a small-screen television. (To review the recommended resolutions for different monitor sizes, see Figure 9.1.)

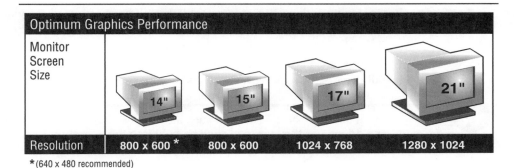

FIGURE 9.1:   The best resolution varies depending on the size of the monitor.

What You Need for an Upgrade

Once you're certain the monitor can be upgraded, you need to find a compatible *graphics controller card* (also known as a video card or graphics accelerator card) so that your computer knows the monitor can display the new colors and resolution. The graphics card is a regular expansion card, or circuit board, that you plug into an expansion slot inside the computer. The card works as the go-between for your computer's microprocessor and the monitor. The microprocessor tells the card what information it wants displayed, then the graphics card passes that information to the monitor in a language the monitor can understand.

Before you plug just any graphics card into your computer, you have to determine what kind of bus it will use. The bus is the pathway that connects cards to the microprocessor. Common bus interfaces are Peripheral Component Interconnect (PCI), Industry Standard Architecture (ISA), and Video Electronics Standards Association

Skill 9

(VL-bus or VL local bus). If your computer has MS-DOS 6.0, Windows 3.*x*, or both, using Microsoft Diagnostics is one way to learn which bus your computer uses. Type **msd** at the DOS prompt, then check the Computer section. Here you can see what bus type the computer uses. Or in Windows 95, choose Settings from the Start button menu. Then select Control Panel, then Settings, and then the System icon. Next, click the Device Manager tab, and select System Devices to see the computer's bus type.

The hardware installation for each type of card is fairly similar across the board, Viramontes says. The difference is apparent when software is involved. For instance, with an ISA card, you likely will have to install software drivers into the computer so it will know how to communicate with the new board. A PCI card, on the other hand, may automatically be recognized by the computer, especially if the card is a Plug-and-Play model. In this case, you only may have to install drivers to work with specific software programs.

 NOTE If you use an operating system such as Windows 95, you may not need to install any drivers, as they probably will be built into the operating system.

You might need additional video memory to complete your new system because better resolution and better colors on-screen will require more memory. Memory specifically allocated to video, such as video random-access memory (VRAM, also called video RAM) or dynamic random-access memory (DRAM), helps images form on-screen more quickly because it takes some of the heat off the microprocessor.

A 640 × 480 system displaying 16 colors will easily be handled by 1MB of video RAM. But display that same image at 1024 × 768 with 65,000 colors, and you're going to need at least 2MB of video RAM. When computers encounter a certain threshold of resolution and color capabilities, they require a second megabyte of video memory. (See the section later on "Memory Thresholds" to see if you need the extra megabyte.) Another rule of thumb is that if the graphics card uses a 64-bit data path (which means it can move 64 bits of information at one time), you should upgrade to 2MB. Graphics controllers over the past couple of years have used a 32-bit data path, and 1MB of video memory will likely work fine with this setup. However, the 64-bit data path moves more information more quickly, so increasing the amount of video RAM is a smart idea, Viramontes says. (See "Video RAM to the Rescue," later in this skill, for step-by-step installation instructions.)

Installing a Graphics Card

The only extras you need to install your new card are a screwdriver, the video card installation instructions, and your computer's owner's manual. You also might want to make a bootable system diskette and copy important files, such as AUTOEXEC.BAT and CONFIG.SYS, to a diskette in case anything goes wrong. (For details, see Skill 3.)

We installed a Diamond Multimedia SpeedStar 64 graphics accelerator card, which used an ISA bus. While most graphics cards require the same basic setup, your card may not follow these exact steps. Check your user's manual to be sure that the installation steps for your video card move in the same direction.

Before you begin, read Skill 3 for instructions on opening your computer.

Out with the Old

Unplug the monitor cable if you haven't already; then locate the old video graphics card and remove it. If you aren't sure which card it is, check the port where your monitor cable resides. This port will connect to the back of the card. To remove the card, unfasten and save the screw that secures the card's metal plate. Gently but firmly pull the card out of the expansion slot (see Figure 9.2). It may help to loosen one side of the card and then the other.

If the port for the monitor cable corresponds to the motherboard, you'll have a little more work to do. (The motherboard is the main computer circuit board that contains the expansion slots and the microprocessor.) You can't remove the motherboard, so you must disable its video port. Check your owner's manual for instructions. On our Hewlett-Packard Vectra computer, we had to flip a tiny switch on miniature jumpers found at another location on the motherboard. (Jumpers are little metal pins on a circuit board that can be set different ways to tell the board and the computer what addresses they will be using to communicate.) Next, locate an empty expansion slot, and remove the metal slot cover that corresponds to it (see Figure 9.3). In some machines, the expansion slots are in the bottom of the computer; others are positioned along the side. To remove the metal slot cover, unfasten a screw on the side of the cover. Don't lose the screw; you'll need it later.

Plugging in the New Card

Now you are ready to plug in your new video card. Gently push out of your way any cables inside the computer. Position the video card next to or above the expansion slot (depending on where the slots are located in your computer). One end of the card contains a video port; this end should slide into the position vacated by the

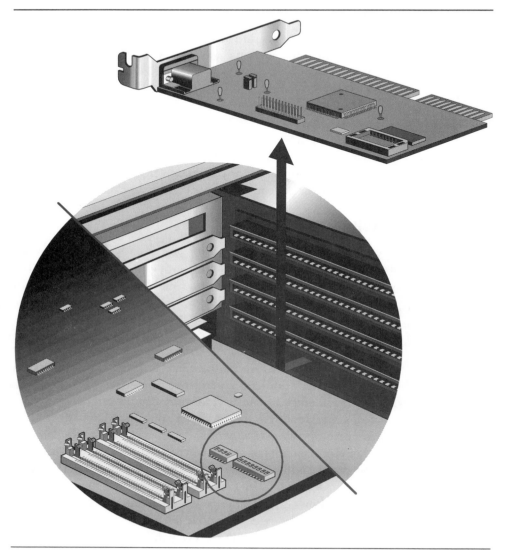

FIGURE 9.2: The video graphics card must be removed from the expansion slot.

slot cover you just removed. Be sure to line up the metal pins that run alongside the card to the grooves in the expansion slot. Gently, but firmly, push the card into the slot (see Figure 9.4). It may help to push in one end and then the other. Don't be afraid to push; it may take a bit of pressure to insert the card.

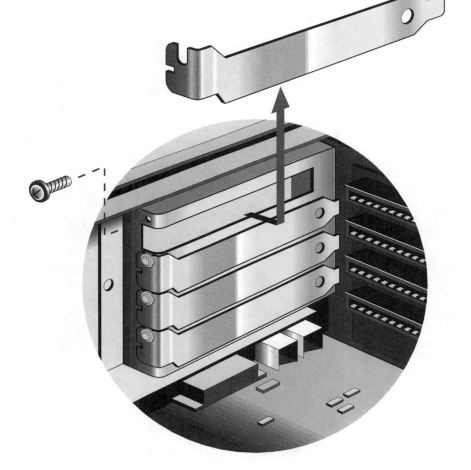

FIGURE 9.3:   The metal slot cover is removed from the empty expansion slot where the new card will go.

Screw the leftover screw into the side of the metal slot cover to firmly secure the video card. Then replace the computer case, and plug in the computer cords. Plug your monitor cable into the new port on the back of the new video card, and turn on the computer.

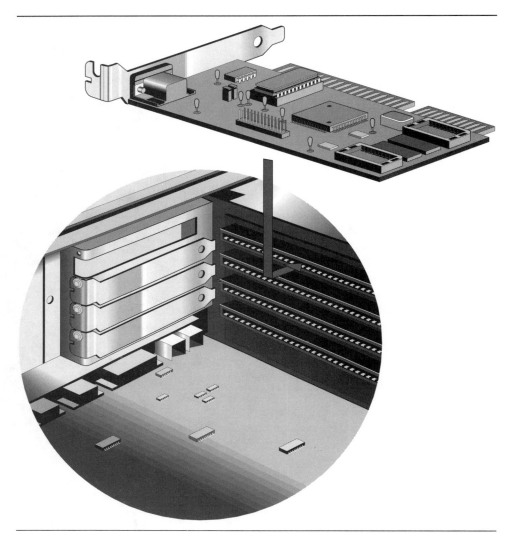

FIGURE 9.4: The new card is inserted into the vacant slot.

Installing the Driver

The next step is to install the new video card driver. If you're using Windows 95, the operating system will help you set up and walk through the driver installation, or it may take care of the installation for you, depending upon the card's bus type and if it bears the "Designed for Windows 95" logo. If you're using Windows 3.*x*, you'll probably need to install the software yourself. Start at the Run option from the File menu in the Windows Program Manager.

Following the installation, reboot the machine. If all goes well, the computer will start with its new resolution and colors. If not, you may need to adjust the jumpers on the expansion card. At the factory, these jumpers are set to conform to the majority of computer configurations, so most users will not need to adjust them. If you do need to adjust the jumpers, check the video card manual, or call technical support for assistance.

The actual hardware setup is easy and takes about 20 minutes. The hard part comes in doing your homework—whether you can and should upgrade and what kind of card you'll need. All things considered, upgrading is worth it for the better graphics and wider range of programs you can run.

Video RAM to the Rescue

Video problems can come in many forms. You might have a flickering screen, you might have a screen that scrolls slowly, or you might experience *artifacting*—the annoying tendency of some monitors to update part of the screen while another part displays old information. If you have these problems, you should think about adding video RAM to your graphics accelerator card. But read this skill carefully before you do; things can get complicated because only certain computers qualify for a video memory upgrade.

Video random-access memory (RAM) is that part of your computer's memory that supplies information directly to the video monitor. Note that this is different from your system's main RAM where program information is stored. Video RAM resides on the system's *graphics accelerator card.* Since the process of displaying graphics is bulky with data, this special circuit board is used to speed those instructions so the quarterback of your computer, the CPU, is free to perform other tasks. This speeds the entire computing process. Some RAM on a graphics card, as we'll discuss later, is faster than regular RAM chips because a monitor requires a constant, faster input than regular RAM.

 NOTE   Video RAM is often called VRAM, but we'll call it video RAM since there is a specific chip called VRAM.

You probably don't need to worry about your graphics card or the amount of RAM in it unless you're a graphic artist, play a lot of games, or create professional multimedia presentations. If you fit one of these categories and have a computer with at least a Pentium CPU, consider adding video RAM chips to your graphics accelerator card.

Later in the skill we'll provide instructions on adding chips to your graphics card. But first we'll discuss why the Pentium crowd is best-suited to add video RAM and what types of video RAM chips are available for your card.

RAM Fire

Imagine for a second that the key elements that bring an image to your monitor are like a fire truck pumping water. The truck itself might be compared to the CPU, the engine that constantly interprets and distributes information. The fire hose is the computer's *bus*, the data pathway connecting the internal sections of a computer, allowing whatever contents it carries to reach the proper destination. The nozzle at the end of the hose is analogous to the graphics card and video RAM.

This type of RAM is the temporary holding place for resolution and color data that will be used by the video monitor's grid of square dots, called *pixels*. Adding video RAM increases the resolution of your video monitor, adding to the number of colors a monitor can display. Two megabytes of video RAM provides data a grid of 1,024 × 768 pixels with 65,000 colors. Remember that if you work mainly with spreadsheets or word processing, the colors your monitor is able to display will be of little concern.

MEMORY THRESHOLDS

When should you boost the amount of video memory in your computer? It depends on two variables: your monitor's resolution and the number of colors you want to display. Ordinarily, 1MB will be plenty of video memory. Here are the three most common resolutions and the maximum number of colors you can have with 1MB:

- If you have a 640 × 480 resolution, you can show up to 65,000 colors.
- If you have a 800 × 600 resolution, you can show up to 65,000 colors.
- If you have a 1024 × 768 resolution, you can show up to 256 colors.

If you want to display resolutions that exceed these color thresholds, you will need at least 2MB of video memory.

We can see from our fire truck analogy why video RAM will only theoretically speed your computing. Obviously, many things go into the speed of water delivery. An antiquated truck won't pump with the gusto of a state-of-the-art model. Fire hoses, too, can be spindly and inadequate. So capping both of these with a shining gold nozzle will do little to produce the results you want.

This is true of computers, too. The latest video card with 4MB of RAM will do little to improve a computer equipped with a 486 microprocessor. The real culprit for users of these CPUs isn't necessarily the microprocessor, which in some cases is fast enough to provide an adequate graphics presentation. The problem lies in the machine's bus, which, as we mentioned earlier, will be designed with Industry Standard Architecture (ISA) or Extended Industry Standard Architecture (EISA). Both are considerably slower than the Peripheral Component Interconnect (PCI) bus of the Pentium-based computers. Adding video RAM (or swapping graphic cards) to a 486 system might provide a 10 percent to 20 percent speed increase. But the true gains come only on the Pentium systems with PCI buses.

Even so, no matter what type of microprocessor is running your system, adding 2MB of RAM on the graphics card can be a cheap attempt at making things run faster. A motherboard and a Pentium CPU can cost from several hundred dollars to more than $1,000; several megabytes of RAM can cost from $20 (for 2MB of DRAM) to $80 (for 2MB of MDRAM). Then again, $20 can be a lot if it produces no discernible difference from what you had before.

Types of RAM

When you go to add video RAM, you'll probably be limited to the type of RAM already in your video accelerator card. The following descriptions should help you make sense of the various types of RAM found on video cards. Before planning an upgrade, make sure your card even supports an upgrade.

The RAM on your card is probably not VRAM at all, but something called DRAM, which is an inferior technology. DRAM, or dynamic RAM, is a chip designed around tiny capacitors and transistors that quickly lose their charge and must continually be refreshed electrically.

This refreshing process is slowed because most DRAM chips have one access point, or *port,* that accepts information from the CPU. But while it's accepting that data, the DRAM chip is also trying to send information to the digital-to-analog converter (RAMDAC), which then sends a signal to the pixels in the monitor. With one port to execute these two operations, the DRAM chip is highly inefficient (read "slow") when it comes to sending data to the RAMDAC.

A more sophisticated option than DRAM is VRAM, which is a chip with two ports. This type of chip can take two forms. One is called *dual-ported,* which receives data through one port while sending through the other. The other form is called *video memory*. With this type of chip design, one port sends and receives data from the CPU while the other supplies the near-continuous feed of information that the video monitor needs.

The latest generation of video RAM architecture has been produced for a couple of years but only now is gaining prominence. Called *multibank DRAM*, this chip has begun to be installed in more capable, high-end graphics cards. The difference between MDRAM's design and the other two types has more to do with what's happening inside the chip than the number of ports on the outside. Inside a DRAM or VRAM chip are rows and columns of capacitors that hold bits of data until RAMDAC needs the information. These rows and columns form what are called banks of memory. There are 16 banks of memory in the average DRAM or VRAM chip. Table 9.1 provides an overview of the makeup of some of the more popular Video RAM chips.

T A B L E   9 . 1 : Making Sense of Video RAM

Name	Description
DRAM (Dynamic RAM)	The most common type of video RAM. Limited by design type—16 memory banks and a single port.
VRAM (Dual-ported Memory)	Two ports let data enter and exit the chip simultaneously, but 16-bank technology is beginning to become dated.
VRAM (Video Memory)	Also has two ports, but one feeds a constant stream of data to the video monitor while the other sends and receives from the CPU. Limited by its 16-bank technology.
MDRAM (Multibank Dynamic)	Usually single-ported. But technology inside the chip RAM allows for speedier and more efficient processing. MDRAM chips are called multibank because they have double the number of storage banks.

A problem that constantly arises with DRAM and VRAM chips is that switching from row to row limits the usefulness of this design. Instead of efficient switching between one row of one column and a row in another column, there's a significant delay in data sent. That leads to a corresponding delay in updating information to the RAMDAC and thus the monitor screen itself.

The engineers of MDRAM have circumvented this design limitation by using 32 smaller memory banks in their chip. The smaller rows help to decrease the amount of time it takes to switch among rows. The design also decreases the chances of bits of information being taken from the wrong column and row. Coupled with an internal bus, which helps accelerate the data to and from the chip, the multibank architecture boasts some impressive numbers. MDRAM chips are 70 percent better than DRAM chips at locating the column and row that is being accessed to send or receive data, according to MoSys Inc., a Silicon Valley company that develops and manufactures MDRAM chips.

Cracking the Case

Actually adding to your video RAM is an easy enough process that doesn't require removing your motherboard or probably even the graphics accelerator card. These are the steps we followed to upgrade our video RAM:

1. Turn off your computer and remove its cover. On many computers, the cover is removed by pushing inward two tabs located on the front and bottom of the case. Before touching any internal components, discharge any static electricity in your body by touching a metal portion of the outer case. Identify your graphics card by following the cord that connects your monitor to your computer. The card where the connection is made is your graphics accelerator card.

2. Your card should have at least one empty socket near the top of the card. (A socket is a rectangular receptacle with small silver bars on one end. It should look like your video RAM chip would fit inside.)

 NOTE   The upgrade process for your graphics card may differ somewhat from our example, but every upgrade essentially comes down to snapping on chips.

3. If you can fit your hand and fingers down near the sockets, you won't have to remove your graphics card. If the card is too close to another card, remove the screw holding the card in place and gently remove it from its socket.

4. Your video RAM chip probably has a black dot on one corner. The socket on your video card has three corners that look the same: squared-off. One corner, though, is cut or beveled. As you press the chip in place, make sure the black dot lines up with the beveled corner.

5. Repeat these steps for other chips. Some of the latest cards can handle up to 8MB of video RAM.

6. If you've removed the graphics card, it's now time to replace it. As you turn on your computer, you should see your new RAM amount listed on the screen. If the old amount shows, turn off your computer and reseat each chip, making sure the black dot is aligning with the beveled corner of the socket. There's also the odd chance you bought a bunk chip, so call the manufacturer's technical support if the problem persists.

Skill 9

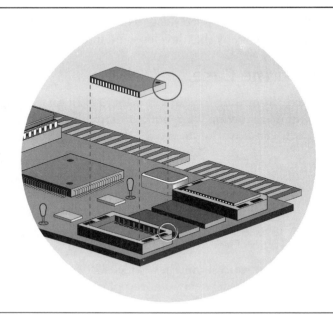

FIGURE 9.5: The RAM chip must line up precisely with the socket.

Troubleshooting Monitors

When you went shopping for that PC that now sits on your desk, you were mainly concerned with processor speed, memory, multimedia capability, a fax/modem, and a good package deal (system and bundled software). Therein lies the first, most common, and most avoidable problem that PC owners make regarding the most scrutinized piece of their system: the monitor.

In the fiercely competitive PC market, vendors are racing to win market share, which sometimes means trimming corners or, in this case, providing a monitor that doesn't match the system's performance. Unfortunately, the customer is often the last to know.

Think of the monitor as you would a pair of running shoes: They may be a bargain and look great, but if they don't feel good on your feet, the only time you might wear them is around the house. The same holds true for a monitor: If it's of poor quality, the whole computing experience will be diminished.

Bottom line: You don't want a bargain.

With the same ease that you can buy a bundled system, you can choose a separate monitor for your computer. This could mean a few hundred dollars tacked onto the total purchase price of the system, but it might mean fewer problems and greater satisfaction in the long run. The good news for users is that monitors tend to be reliable and sturdy and not the big headache they're portrayed to be. Often, the monitor is just the messenger—so don't shoot it.

Before Crying Wolf

Troubleshooting monitors is tricky because the monitor is closely coupled with the system's electronics. The easiest way to troubleshoot a monitor is to swap it with another one to see if the problem disappears. If that is not an option, follow these steps before calling technical support.

- Read the vendor-supplied users guide and "Getting Started" guides. This material is provided to help consumers set up the system, learn about the component, and keep it running.

- Always double-check your monitor's connections. An improperly plugged-in monitor won't work right, so make sure all connections are secure and snug. Other signs of a poor connection: odd colors, streaking, or on-screen flashing.

- Be patient if the monitor works, but the colors are out of alignment (say one of the three electronic color beams [red, green, and blue] seems to overlap the color in the image). What you're seeing is misregistration. Monitors take, on average, 20 to 25 minutes to reach their operating temperature. Let the monitor warm up, and the problem will likely disappear.

- Realize that the most common problem is monitor misconfiguration. Make sure the screen resolution you set is within the monitor's refresh rate (how often the screen is redrawn.)

The Basics

Monitor terminology is difficult to grasp, but it's important for any PC owner. Some of the most important monitor specifications to consider when buying hardware include resolution, refresh rates, and dot pitch. Here's what you should look for:

Resolution   This refers to the degree of detail you see on-screen, which is measured in pixels. Pixels are dots of light that comprise computer images; the more pixels, the sharper the image. Resolution is measured in strings of numbers such as 640×480, 800×600, 1024×768, and 1280×1024, which represent the number of pixels horizontally and vertically.

Refresh Rate   Measured in hertz (Hz), refresh rate is the number of times per second the monitor can redraw the screen. If the screen is not redrawn fast enough, the image will flicker. Ideally, a standard 15-inch monitor at 1280×1024 resolution has a 60Hz refresh rate or better.

Dot Pitch   This measures the distance in millimeters between the tiny, same-colored phosphors (red, green, blue) that make up the color in your image. As a general rule, the smaller the distance, the sharper the image. A dot pitch of .28mm is ideal for crisp, sharp text and graphics.

Horizontal Scan Frequency   Monitors also have a horizontal scan frequency, which is measured in kilohertz (KHz). The resolution, refresh rate, and horizontal scan rate must all be within the manufacturer's specifications for the monitor to work properly (see your user's manual).

The burden of monitor configuration with the video card is often placed on the user. Reputable manufacturers spell out their system requirements in their product documentation. Before buying a system, check its user's manual(s); poorly written materials might raise a red flag to steer clear of a vendor.

As a whole, the industry is moving toward higher refresh rates to avoid perceivable flicker. Video card manufacturers, however, are designing more sophisticated technology that not all monitor manufacturers' equipment can handle, so be sure to read all documentation.

Common Problems

If you misconfigure the monitor, you could damage it, but that's unikely. What's likely to happen can range from the mild to the extreme. For example, the monitor will be out of sync, be unreadable, display a line or lines on-screen, or emit a high-pitched whine.

Top-tier monitor manufacturers have built-in safety devices, or on-screen display (OSD) warnings, that appear as messages such as "Scan frequency outside of monitor range." Monitors without OSDs might revert to mute-mode or display a black screen where they appear to be off except for the LED (the light that indicates the monitor's power on/off status), which continues to glow. In this case, users should consult the product manual, find the information about resolution, refresh rates, and horizontal scan frequency, and reconfigure the system to correct the problem.

The industry is moving toward Plug-and-Play compatibility, which means that the computer and its components correctly configure themselves, thus taking the onus off the user. Products that follow another standard—display data channel (DDC)—will optimize themselves and send key information between the monitor and computer to set the display characteristics, such as screen size and resolution.

Another common problem occurs with the monitor's control settings, in particular, brightness and contrast. If your on-screen image just doesn't look right, check your brightness control; typically, users crank up the brightness control and end up with a washed-out picture. To properly adjust your screen, set it to black, turn the brightness control until it just begins to change the black to gray, then bring the control back to black. You then can use the contrast control to adjust the brightness of the image.

Other control adjustments include screen size and position. Most manufacturers use dial-type controls, digital push-button controls, and on-screen level adjusters. Many also offer preset screen adjustments to make it easier for the user. Preset monitor positions can be manually overridden by the user, so read the manual to learn about control adjustments.

Running Interference

Electromagnetic interference (EMI) affects monitor performance by inducing a wave-like effect or color distortion. There are several culprits to investigate if you suspect electromagnetic interference. If your computer is located near a power line, move it away from the force field (the EMI decreases by the square of the distance). Unseen electrical wires in the wall also can cause problems.

Speakers located too close to the monitor can cause EMI as well as impure colors. If you're purchasing a multimedia system, buy only speakers that are magnetically shielded (it should say so on the packaging). Again, move the speakers away from the monitor, and see if the problem is lessened. If it isn't, turn off the monitor for about 20 minutes, and then restart it to see whether the colors readjust. While turned off, the monitor will degauss (demagnetize) itself. Some high-end monitors have a degauss control that can be used to correct this problem.

Shipping also can be problematic; jarring the system during transport can loosen internal components. After you have the product at home, have tried several troubleshooting methods, and called technical support, you have no alternative but to return it to the dealer.

 **WARNING**   To avoid problems during shipping and handling, users should look at the carton before they bring the product home. Is it damaged? Banged up? If so, don't buy it. If not, handle the bulky box with care.

Video Cards

Because the monitor tends to reflect other problems in the computer system, it's nice to know there are ways to distinguish monitor problems from other component failures. Often, so-called monitor problems are actually the result of problematic video cards. Most technical support calls to video card manufacturers deal with improperly configured systems, fixed frequency monitors that users have tried to change, and poor quality monitors.

Remember that a color monitor cannot fail in such a way that it becomes a monochrome (black-and-white) device. Additionally, if you see an image that has become pixelated (looks like a checkerboard), it's not caused by the monitor.

 NOTE   Video cards are configured to run at a particular refresh rate. If you haven't configured your card and monitor to meet specifications in the user's manual, you might notice lines across the screen.

Lack of on-screen color also can be caused by the video card. A faulty autosensing feature on the video card can result in color loss. If your graphics card is an autosensor, turn on your monitor before turning on your computer.

If you've already purchased your monitor and realize it's junk, you have two options: Come to terms with it, or buy a new one. If you're about to buy a monitor, do your homework, learn the terminology, know what separates the good monitor manufacturers from the bad, and check out product warranties, vendor service, and support.

Are You Experienced?

Now you can. . .

☑ **evaluate the benefits of upgrading your video capabilities**

☑ **choose and install a graphics card**

☑ **upgrade your computer's video RAM, if you decide your monitor can handle it**

☑ **troubleshoot problems with your monitor**

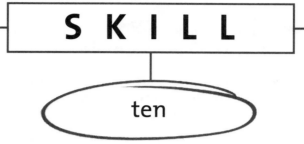

SKILL

10

ten

Installing External and Internal Modems

❑ Understanding what makes modems work

❑ Installing external and internal modems

❑ Using your modem with your phone line

❑ Keeping your modem operating effectively

While internal modems traditionally have ranked among the most difficult pieces of hardware to install, people who use a modem to go online will testify that the toils are worth the frustration. A modem-equipped computer opens a whole new world of possibilities. Here we'll provide step-by-step instructions for installing external and internal modems and provide advice for dealing with installation headaches.

NOTE   Although most external and internal modems connect to the PC in the same manner, the location and setting of COM ports and IRQs usually differ. We'll explain a common installation scenario, but you may encounter some different situations.

Modem Basics

A modem, or modulator/demodulator, lets your computer exchange information across telephone lines with another modem. It does this by converting a computer's digital signal to an analog signal that can travel over phone lines, and then converting the signal back to a digital form a computer can understand. Some modems can exchange data only; others, called fax/modems, can send and receive fax messages. Other modems add voice capabilities, letting you record messages on your computer.

Modems are available in internal and external versions. An external modem, the easiest to install, connects to a port on the back of your computer and sits on your desk. If you'd rather save the port (and desk space), you can install an internal modem, which is contained on an expansion card. (An expansion card provides additional features for your computer and plugs into a narrow socket inside the computer, called an expansion slot. By now you should be familiar with the expansion slots in your computer, if you've performed any of the installations outlined earlier in the book.)

IRQ Nightmares

Making your computer communicate with a modem, especially if it's an internal model, can be a nightmare because of conflicts with IRQ settings and COM ports. An *interrupt request line* (IRQ) is the hardware line over which devices send interrupts, or requests, for service to the microprocessor. IRQs are assigned different levels of priority, allowing the microprocessor to determine the importance of each request. Unless each hardware device has a different IRQ setting, conflicts may occur. A *COM port* is a serial communications port. Different hardware devices connect to the serial ports, and the operating system uses different COM port designations (such as COM1, COM2, COM3, and COM4) to identify the connections. Two hardware devices cannot use the same COM port.

External modems, used in tandem with software, take care of the settings for you, making them simple to install. Although internal modems have become easier to install, you still may encounter some IRQ or COM port conflicts. Many times the modem's factory settings will prevent these conflicts, but, if they don't, you'll have to correct the settings manually. The ease-of-use that comes with external modems isn't free; such modems cost $20 to $50 more than their internal counterparts.

CHANGING MODEM SETTINGS

COM1 sometimes isn't available for a modem because it may host the mouse connection. And if your modem won't work on COM2, you'll have to change the modem's settings.

Most newer modems, and those from major manufacturers, use DIP (dual inline package) switches to configure the COM port and IRQ settings. Rocker DIP switches simply need to be flipped on or off (like an electric light switch), while Slide DIP switches are slid into the on or off position. The configuration of the DIP switches—which you'll find in groups of two, four, or six, depending upon your type of modem—determines the COM port and IRQ settings.

The DIP switches can be located in various places on the expansion board. Many times, the factory settings will suffice for installation of your modem. If not, you'll need to adjust the DIP switches. The modem's documentation should show the correct settings for your modem. If your modem contains no such documentation, you have two choices: Use a trial-and-error approach or call technical support.

Skill 10

Some modems contain pins with a plastic jumper switch. You must move the jumper switch to cover various pins to change the COM port settings. Mainstream modems usually don't use these pins. If you *must* change the COM port setting of your mouse or network connection, though, you probably will find this configuration on the expansion board.

The External Modem

To install an external modem, you only need a flat-head screwdriver and a modem cable. Many external modems don't include these cables in their packaging, so check the box or directions inside; if a cable isn't included, you can find one easily at a computer store. You will not need to open your computer's case to perform this upgrade.

 **WARNING**   Make sure you have recent copies of your AUTOEXEC.BAT, CONFIG.SYS, WIN.INI, and SYSTEM.INI files on a diskette. Whenever you install a new device, its driver software will likely add entries to these files. If errors occur, you'll have a record of these files from the last time they were in proper working condition.

Connecting the Modem

First, turn off the computer. Take all the components out of the box and follow these steps:

1. Plug one end of the modem cable into a vacant port on the back of your computer and the other into the back of the external modem. On our computer, the end with a nine-pin plug went into the computer while the 25-pin plug went into the modem. To firmly attach the plugs, you may need to turn the screws on either side of the plug into the port. The screws to the port on the back of the computer were easily fastened with our fingers, but those on the sides of the modem plug required a flat-head screwdriver.

 NOTE   The port on the back of the computer that you plug your modem into will correspond to the COM port you'll be using. If you plug your modem into a serial port labeled *A*, this corresponds to COM1.

2. Locate the cord plugging into your phone line. Plug this cord into the back of the modem, at the port labeled *Line*. If you still want to use a phone on this line, take the gray phone cord that came with your new modem and plug one end into the port labeled *Phone* on the back of the modem and plug the other into the port on your phone.

3. Now, plug the small, round end of the power cord into the small, round port in back of the modem; on ours, it was labeled *AC*. Then plug the power supply into a wall outlet or into your surge protector.

You're ready to test your external modem.

Checking Your Work and Finishing Up

Next, we turned on our computer and the modem to check the connection. (On the Hayes Accura 28.8 V.34 + Fax we used, we turned the modem on by flipping a switch to the "1" position.) If the lights are working, you're ready to install the communications software.

If the lights on the modem are *not* working, there are four possible causes:

- You may not have securely connected the ports and plugs.

- You may have something plugged into the wrong port.

- There may be a problem with your modem.

- You may have the wrong kind of modem cable.

If all goes well to this point, you can turn on your computer and install the communications software. Follow the on-screen prompts. Eventually it will ask which COM port to use. We chose COM1 because we plugged the device into Port A. If you are installing the modem in Windows 95, an Installation Wizard will walk you through the process, especially if your modem is a Plug-and-Play device.

The Internal Modem

We installed a Hayes Accura fax/modem which, by virtue of being an internal device, was a little more difficult to install than the external model described earlier. A Phillips screwdriver is a necessity when installing an internal modem.

Read Skill 3 before you begin to make certain you understand the basics of opening and upgrading your computer.

Skill 10

Choosing the Right Slot

Internal modems can use either an 8-bit or a 16-bit expansion slot. (The expansion slots are at the back of the computer.) Most modem expansion cards have just one connector about 4 inches long. If your modem requires a 16-bit slot, the expansion card will have a second connector (about 2 inches long) behind the first. Your computer probably has a mixture of 8- and 16-bit expansion slots; the 8-bit slots are shorter and have room for only one connector. If possible, you'll want to install the modem in a slot that has empty slots on either side, which will help reduce electrical noise and interference that sometimes, although rarely, inhibits modem communications.

After you've selected an expansion slot, you'll need to remove the corresponding metal plate blocking the expansion slot's hole in the computer case. Remove the screw on top of the plate and lift the plate out from the top. Save the screw, which you'll need to fasten your modem card to the computer case. The metal plate you removed protects the inside of the computer from dust when no expansion card is installed in its corresponding slot. When you install your modem, the metal plate on the end of the card (containing the telephone line jacks) will replace the plate you just removed.

Installing the Modem

Remove the expansion card from its packaging, handling it by the edges as much as possible. Avoid touching the components on the card or the pins on the connector. Line up the connector on the expansion card with the empty expansion slot (see Figure 10.1). The connector should slide almost entirely into the expansion slot, leaving only the extreme top of the gold pins visible. It's a tight fit, so you might find it easier to roll the card into the slot by placing a corner in the expansion slot first and then fitting the remainder of the connector into the slot.

 WARNING   Don't jam the expansion card into its slot; you could damage the components.

If you've properly installed the modem expansion card, the metal plate on the edge of the card will align with the empty slot in the back of the computer. You should be able to connect the metal plate of the expansion card easily to the computer's case with the screw you removed from the original plate. Don't use the screw to force the modem expansion card to line up properly; it should fit properly in the expansion slot with or without the screw in place.

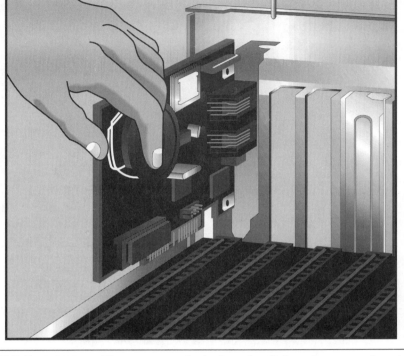

FIGURE 10.1:   The connector is designed to fit into the expansion slot.

 TIP   One way to check the alignment of the modem expansion card is by connecting the telephone line to the modem. The telephone jacks are visible from the back of the computer. If your jacks are hidden, your board is incorrectly installed. You'll need to slide it out and start over again.

Putting It All Together: Lines and Cables

Now take the phone line (connected to the wall jack) and plug it into the jack on the back of the modem card labeled *Line.* Take the additional cable that came with your modem and plug one end into the modem jack labeled *Phone* and the other into the back of your phone (see Figure 10.2).

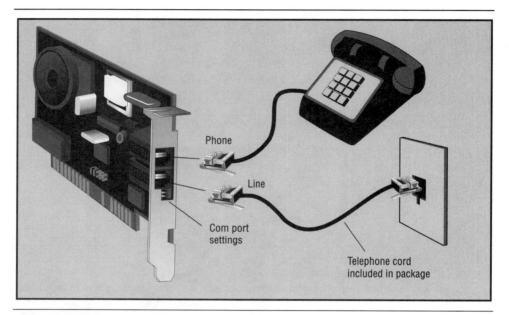

FIGURE 10.2:   The phone line is plugged into a jack on the modem card.

At this point, you can replace the computer case cover or wait until after testing the modem to ensure it is working properly.

Reconnect the cables and turn on your computer. You should notice no changes as it boots. The easiest and quickest way to check the status of your modem is the Terminal application in Windows 3.1. (If you use MS-DOS or Windows 95, skip ahead to the "Software Comes Next" section.)

In Program Manager, double-click the Accessories program group. Double-click the Terminal icon.

You should see a dialog box that lets you select a COM port for your modem. Most modems will use COM2, so choose that option. (If you don't see the dialog box and end up at the Terminal screen, your modem probably is ready to work. Type a command, such as **at,** then press ↵. If Terminal responds with an "OK," your modem is probably ready.)

If you can't type on the screen or if you receive an error message when you try to select COM2, your modem may be on a different COM port. Open the Settings menu, and select Communications. In the Communications dialog box, try selecting other COM ports one at a time. If none of them work, the factory settings on your modem won't work with your system, and you'll have to work with the DIP switches (see the earlier sidebar "Changing Modem Settings").

Software Comes Next

If it appears your modem is working properly, you can install your communications or online service software. Make sure you have handy the backup copy of the AUTOEXEC.BAT, CONFIG.SYS, WIN.INI, and SYSTEM.INI files you made before starting the installation, because the software's installation procedure will probably make changes to these files.

Considerations for High-Speed Modems

If you're installing a 28.8 Kbps (kilobits per second) or 33.6Kbps modem, make sure you have a 16550 UART. To take advantage of the higher throughput rates offered by these modems, you need a fast UART. The speed at which the computer can communicate with the modem may be as high as 115,200 bits per second (bps); with a slower UART, such as an 8250 or a 16450, you will experience data loss at these higher speeds. This is especially noticeable during file downloads, when you might experience an excessive number of retries that effectively slows or lowers the overall throughput.

 NOTE A chip with the strange name of UART (Universal Asynchronous Receiver/ Transmitter) manages the data sent from your communications software to the modem and resides on your computer's motherboard.

If you are unsure which UART type you have, run the Microsoft System Diagnostics (MSD) utility in DOS and for the COM Port section. MSD can be run under DOS by typing **msd** at the prompt.

 NOTE We don't recommend running MSD from Windows, or from the MS-DOS Prompt icon, because MSD reports are often inaccurate when generated from Windows.

If you do use an older UART, you will need to slow your software down to eliminate the data loss. You should lower the *port speed* (the term used in most packages) to 9600bps for an 8250 UART and 19,200bps for a 16450 UART. To make this change in your communications software, look for an option such as Modem Settings, which lets you adjust the modem/port speed. Even if you have a 28.8Kbps modem on your system, for example, if you change this setting to 14.4Kbps, your software will not let your modem run faster than the speed you specified.

If you buy an internal modem, an outdated UART won't be an issue because the new modem card will have an updated UART chip on it, which will override the one in your system. External modems are a different story; you will have to buy an input/output (I/O) port card, which will have new COM1 and COM2 ports and an updated UART. These cards cost about $30 and will disable the COM ports that came with your system.

I'VE GOT THE MODEM, NOW WHAT?

Many questions technical support staffs frequently hear are in one or more general, yet fairly obvious, categories. If you experience problems with your modem, run through this list. You could save yourself toll-call charges and/or technical support fees by being aware of the following:

- Are the power connections on your modem and the computer's power supply firmly placed? A not-so-tightly placed power cord can provide sporadic power supplies and confusing error messages.
- If you're using an internal modem, is the modem card seated properly in its expansion slot? If it's an external modem, is it securely connected in the proper port at the back of the computer?
- Is your connection to the telephone line secure?
- Have you properly configured the modem initialization strings in your communications software? (A common initialization string is AT&F&C1&D2S7=60.) Other things to check: dial-up procedures, special scripts, prefixes for outgoing calls (such as 9), and auto-logon settings for online services that let you bypass the usual sign-on process. (Initialization strings tell the software what to expect from the modem so they'll speak the same language during a transmission.) You can eliminate the need to enter AT strings if, during installation, you pick your modem model (or a generic one) from the software's install list.
- Most manuals have a section on frequently asked questions (FAQ); check it before calling technical support.
- Have you disabled call waiting? If not, add the prefix specified by your phone company (such as *70) to the phone number your modem will dial. Otherwise, you could be bumped offline by an incoming call.

Modem Configuration

Beyond hardware connections, there are other steps you can take to ensure good modem performance. One thing to remember: Once you install your modem, you generally shouldn't have to mess with it again.

Sam Knox, an online services engineer for Hayes Microcomputer Products, recommends picking your modem's exact name from a communications package's configuration list. If you don't see it, pick something similar. For example, if you have the external version of a company's modem, but your software only lists the internal version, try picking that; it's very likely they'll use the same initialization strings. Or, pick the generic Hayes error-correcting setting, which won't slow down your modem transmissions or prevent you from getting online. What it will do, Knox says, is send out commands that most modems use and which should be enough to get you online. From there, he says, you can contact the manufacturer's World Wide Web site or bulletin board system to see if there's something else you can use.

If you have Windows 95, expect relatively trouble-free installation, especially if you're using Plug-and-Play components. You can use these devices on a Windows 3.*x* system, but they're not as easy to configure. If you buy a Plug-and-Play device for a DOS or Windows 3.*x* system, make sure that the device is compatible with those systems. Some manufacturers don't intend for their products to support anything but Windows 95. Check the product's box; if you're still unsure, ask a salesperson or call the company.

Error-Checking

Unlike video cards, whose device drivers seem to be updated every 30 days, modems rarely have drivers.

If a modem requires a driver, it's called a *host-controlled* modem, which means error checking is done by the software, not the hardware. Because these modems use proprietary drivers, they can run into problems with operating systems; if you're not a techno-wizard, you may want to avoid these modems.

"If a product box says 'requires Windows,' it's a big tip off that error checking is done by the software," Knox says. When software does the error checking, it requires microprocessor time, which can slow down other operations; when the checking is done by the modem, it doesn't use the microprocessor. A majority of modems, though, conduct error checking within the hardware. Knowing industry buzzwords can save you grief later, so keep your eyes open and ask salespeople or the manufacturer to clarify catch phrases you don't understand.

Installing a modem can be one of the easiest hardware installations you'll perform. It also can be one of the toughest. Unless you know your computer's configuration inside and out, it's doubtful you'll know how difficult the installation will be until you're nearly finished. After you're done, though, your modem's obnoxious grinding, squealing, and whining noises will never have sounded so good.

Are You Experienced?

Now you can. . .

- ☑ understand how modems work and why they sometimes don't
- ☑ install both external and internal modems to work with your computer
- ☑ hook up a modem to your phone line
- ☑ take steps to ensure good modem performance

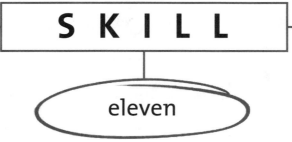

S K I L L

11

eleven

Installing Keyboards and Joysticks

- ❑ Understanding how input devices work

- ❑ Choosing and installing a keyboard

- ❑ Installing a joystick and game card

- ❑ Exploring the many types of input devices, including infrared and voice recognition

- ❑ Maintaining trouble-free input devices

In their 20 combined years working for Key Tronic, the world's largest independent manufacturer of keyboards, Senior Product Manager Norm Morse and Technical Support Representative Clark Osterson have heard their share of crazy keyboard stories. Like the famous author who uses a different keyboard and mouse for each of the three pseudonyms he writes under. Or the guy whose giant Macaw ate his key caps. Or the woman whose cat mysteriously turned on a sticky keys function that she couldn't uncode.

"People get very emotional, very attached, and a little bit weird about their favorite keyboards and mice," Morse says. Osterson adds, "We've been asked to resurrect keyboards drowned in coffee or soda, clogged up with pet hair, and all sorts of contaminants that cause keys to stick or mice to malfunction."

The Input Device Age Gap

Obviously, it's hard to let go of your favorite input device. But when you move to a system with more computing power, it may be challenging to make classic keyboards or mice work with a contemporary PC. The general tips offered here help make sense of the array of connectors and standards you'll run into when mixing old input devices with new machines. You'll also find help for similarly frustrating attempts to make the latest input devices get along with dated computers.

The latter problem, a lack of backward compatibility, arose because as computers evolved from the PC ATs of the 1980s to today's Pentium screamers, so too did keyboards and mice. The latest keyboards, like Microsoft's Natural Keyboard and Key Tronic's Lifetime Series (standard, designer, trackball, touchpad, and wireless keyboards), sport special function keys that only work in Windows 95.

Microsoft's IntelliMouse, a high-end version of the company's traditional mouse, has a tiny wheel embedded between the two standard buttons. While the mouse works with any software, when you add special IntelliPoint software, the wheel has special functions that appear in Microsoft Internet Explorer and Office 97 applications like Word 97, Excel 97, and PowerPoint 97.

Keyboard Connections

As PCs become faster, smarter, and sleeker—and older 486, 386, and 286 models are phased out—more users wonder what happens when you want to mix and match old and new hardware.

Consumers favoring function keys on the left instead of running across the top of the keyboard have already made a sacrifice in the name of hi-tech progress. Very quietly, keyboard manufacturers stopped making left-side function keys in the late 1980s. If users want to use a new Windows 95 keyboard or any of the ergonomic models in what industry analysts estimate to be a $100 million replacement market, they're forced to make what many complain is an untenable trade: new features vs. the familiar feel of their favorite function keys.

While the designs of keyboards and mice have evolved, so have their connections. Older keyboards used in the 286, 386, and 486 era have larger 5-pin DIN (a standard for various device connections) plugs. Newer keyboards have smaller mini 6-pin DINs.

To get an older keyboard to work on a newer PC—or a newer keyboard to work on an older PC—you'll need a special PS/2 keyboard adapter. These are often included with new keyboards. You can also buy just the adapter for a few bucks at most computer stores. In most cases, you can expect newer keyboards and mice to work on any older computer, as long as the computer is running on MS-DOS 3.0 or newer. The special Windows 95 function keys on that new keyboard will not work on the older system, however. Obviously, these newer keys are missing from older keyboards, so users can't take advantage of them even if they're using Windows 95. And unless Windows 95 is on your older PC, your old operating system—whether it's Windows 3.1 or DOS—won't recognize the special keys. You can press them, but nothing will happen.

A more challenging, though admittedly much rarer problem, occurs if you plug a newer keyboard into a 286 or older PC. These machines use a prehistoric BIOS that can't recognize and translate scan code signals issued from newer keyboards.

You probably don't need to worry about this problem. An estimated 90 percent of all keyboards use the current scan code and should have no problem switching between old or new PCs. Everyone else, however, faces the same problem as lovers of left-sided function keys; unless they can find an older keyboard at a swap meet, pawn shop, garage sale, on the Internet, or somewhere else, they'll have to upgrade.

Mouse Connections

Switching and upgrading a mouse is a bit more complicated than switching a keyboard, and depends on whether you have a serial, PS/2, or bus mouse.

Serial Mouse

The most common mouse is a serial mouse, sometimes called a PS-232-C mouse (a technical name for a serial port and serial protocol). You don't need to remember the fancy name, just that there are two types of serial mice. Older versions for 386 and 286 PCs have a 25-pin connector; newer models for 486 and Pentium PCs have a smaller, sleeker 9-pin connector. As PCs generally come with two serial ports—COM1 and COM2—a serial mouse can be plugged into either.

To tell which serial mouse you have, just look at the connector. Then look for the 9-pin or 25-pin serial port on the back of your PC. If your new mouse connector doesn't fit on your old PC, or your old mouse connector is too big for your new PC, don't panic. All you need is a 25-to-9-pin reduction adapter. Often, new mice come with an adapter, or you can buy one inexpensively at a computer store.

Motherboard or PS/2 Mouse

Most newer computers come with a dedicated mouse port built into the motherboard. IBM started this trend in 1982 with its PS/2 system; thus, this interface is called a PS/2 mouse interface. However, don't be fooled into thinking a PS/2 mouse only works with a PS/2 computer. As logical as that sounds, it's wrong. A PS/2 mouse will work on any PC that has a dedicated PS/2 mouse port on the motherboard. The big advantage of a PS/2 mouse is that it frees up both serial ports so they can be used to plug in devices like a modem or a scanner.

Whereas a serial mouse has nine pins, the PS/2 mouse has the same mini DIN 6-pin connector used on newer keyboards. While every computer has a serial port, not every PC has a PS/2 mouse port. A PS/2 mouse works only in a PC with a PS/2 mouse port. Adapters will not work. A serial mouse has the advantage of being able to work on both PCs with a serial port and a PS/2 port.

If you have a PS/2 mouse but your computer lacks a PS/2 mouse port, your only solution is to buy a serial mouse or what's called a *universal* or *hybrid* mouse. A serial mouse generally costs $10 to $20 less than a universal mouse, but the latter can be used in either a serial or PS/2 port.

Bus Mouse

A bus mouse was used in older PCs that did not have a motherboard mouse port or any available serial ports. To use these mice, users had to pop the top off the PC, insert a special bus interface board into a slot on the motherboard, then plug the mouse cord into the port on the back of the card. Not only was this complicated, but a bus mouse could only be used in a bus port. There are no special adapters for computers with serial or PS/2 ports, and you can't shuttle your old bus card into a new computer, because they're incompatible and can cause serious conflicts with other devices like a modem or scanner. In other words, if your favorite mouse is a bus mouse, it won't be joining you on a new PC. You'll have to buy a new serial or universal mouse for a new computer. If your old bus mouse dies, unless you can find one someplace—a slim possibility—you'll have to sacrifice a serial port on your old PC.

Warning Signs

If you're trying to keep your favorite keyboard alive as long as possible, look for signals that it's in need of maintenance. Sticky keys, throwing up extra characters, and missing keystrokes are signs that your keyboard needs to be cleaned or most likely replaced. If it's not under warranty, you'll have to buy a new one.

To extend your keyboard's life, experts recommend maintenance including vacuuming your keyboard or using a can of compressed air to blow out dust and dirt at least once a month. Be sure to turn your PC off first.

If you're having problems with your mouse (the cursor is erratic or jumpy or doesn't want to move in one direction) shut down your PC and clean the mouse. Unplug the mouse, turn it over, twist off the panel, and remove the ball. You can wash the ball in soapy water, use rubbing alcohol, or purchase a mouse cleaning kit. Be sure to dry the ball before putting it back in the mouse. For best results, use a compressed air cleaner to blow out dust and dirt inside the mouse. Then put the ball back in the mouse and close the panel.

If you still have a problem, be thankful keyboards and mice are cheap, especially compared to a hard drive or monitor. Depending on quality and features, you can buy either for as little as $40 to $100.

Keyboard Considerations

A keyboard is a basic necessity. Somehow, you've got to turn those letters into computer language. But as most computer users know, the basic keyboard has been made over—with some surprising results. It seems like keyboards have been designed for everyone and everything.

Ergonomics

The prevalence of carpal tunnel syndrome has been linked to the long hours spent at typewriters or computer keyboards. Ergonomic keyboards are designed to alleviate this injury and other conditions associated with repetitive tasks. Because people are built a little differently, the wrist and arm positions we find comfortable are going to vary. Fortunately, ergonomic keyboards come in all shapes and sizes. One ergonomic keyboard may offer a contoured wrist rest and another may set the keys on a slight incline. Many advertisements will claim that this or that keyboard is "ergonomically correct," but the most ergonomically correct keyboard for you is the one that provides the most comfort.

KEYBOARDS FOR WINDOWS 95

If you're upgrading your operating system to Windows 95, you can add a keyboard that has been designed specifically to take advantage of it. Standardized early on by Microsoft but reproduced by many companies, the Windows 95 keyboard adds three new keys to the standard 101-key line-up. These keys function as shortcuts to the Start and pop-up menus—two of the operating system's primary navigational tools. They save you the time it takes to move your hand from the keyboard to the mouse, but Windows 95 keyboards are hardly necessary to make the most of your operating system.

Installing Your Keyboard

Taking the cover off your computer is not necessary for the installation of a keyboard. Before you begin you should close any open applications and turn off your computer.

Finding the Port   The keyboard port is on the back of your computer. There are two kinds of keyboard ports. The 6-pin PS/2 port is a small round port, approximately one-half inch in diameter, that has six holes in it. The 5-pin DIN port (DIN is short for Deutsches Institut fur Normung, a German standards institute) is a larger port, approximately 1-inch in diameter, that has five holes in it.

Finding the port shouldn't be too difficult, though; your old keyboard should be plugged into it. If your keyboard is already unplugged, you'll find the port easily, as most systems have a keyboard icon above the keyboard port.

Check the connector at the end of your keyboard cord. Just as there are PS/2 and DIN ports, so are there PS/2 and DIN connectors. If your port and connector don't match, you can buy an adapter to make them fit together. Some keyboards include the adapter in the package. There are adapters to fit a 6-pin PS/2 connector into a 5-pin DIN port, and vice versa, so make sure you have the right one (see Figure 11.1). If you need to use an adapter, plug the end of your connector into the corresponding end of the adapter and plug the adapter into the machine.

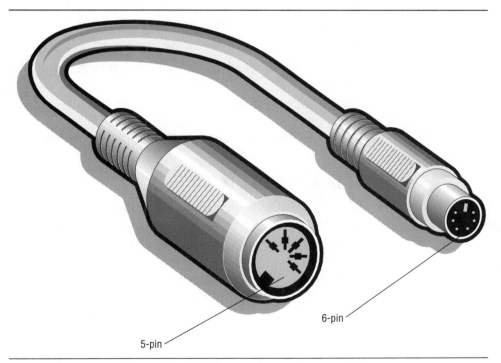

6-pin

5-pin

FIGURE 11.1:   Some keyboard installations may require an adapter.

Plugging In the Keyboard   Line up the pins, plug the connector into the port, and turn on the computer. If you're plugging the 6-pin connector into the back of the PC or if you have several cords around the keyboard port, it might be easier to plug the adapter into the PC first, and then plug the cord into the adapter. Skip to the section below titled "Installing the Software."

Kid Stuff—and More

As computer technology continues to permeate society and the PC becomes an integral part of every household, it is important to give children the chance to become familiar with a computer. Two issues must be resolved before handing over the controls: keeping children interested in the action on-screen and keeping them from destroying expensive equipment. The answer? Check out the several keyboard designs on the market that are durable enough to weather youngsters' worst treatment, but include colorful, eye-catching software products to help acclimate them to the world of new technologies.

In addition to these soon-to-be mainstream innovations, expect to see keyboards with telephones, remote control enhancements, and other unusual input devices attached to them.

Multimedia Keyboards

The push is on to transform the PC into an all-in-one home entertainment system. For applications that include sound, buying speakers and a microphone can be expensive and occupy a lot of space. One alternative is a multimedia keyboard, which incorporates those peripherals into the design of the keyboard.

Multimedia keyboards tend to have a few more cords to install because of the many functions the unit performs. Installation will vary slightly depending on the components included in the unit. Our installation was performed using a multimedia keyboard that included speakers, a microphone, and a headphone connection.

Again, there's no need to remove the cover. Simply close any open applications and turn off the computer before beginning the installation.

Cords and Ports   Take a minute to get organized. You should have one long, thick cord that splits into four thinner cords: a 6-pin PS/2 connector or a 5-pin DIN connector, which plugs into the keyboard port; two audio cords with identical ends that resemble a Sony Walkman headphone plug; and an AC adapter cord.

Locate your keyboard port on the back of the PC. It will be either a 6-pin PS/2 port, which is a small round port, approximately one-half inch in diameter, that has six holes in it, or it will be a 5-pin DIN port, which is a larger port, approximately 1-inch in diameter, that has five holes in it. Finding the port shouldn't be too difficult, though; your old keyboard should be plugged into it. You also may recognize the keyboard port by the keyboard icon located above it.

Plugging In the Connector   Check the connector at the end of your keyboard cord. Just as there are PS/2 and DIN ports, so are there PS/2 and DIN connectors. If your port and connector don't match, you can buy an adapter to make them fit together. Some keyboards include the adapter in the package. There are adapters to fit a 6-pin PS/2 connector into a 5-pin DIN port, and vice versa, so make sure you have the right one. If you need to use an adapter, plug the end of your connector into the corresponding end of the adapter and plug the adapter into the machine. Line up the pins, plug the connector into the port, and turn on the computer.

Audio and Microphone Plugs   On the back of your PC, you will see three identical, small round ports. The two about which you need to be concerned are labeled SPK OUT (for speaker output) and MIC IN (for microphone input), as shown in Figure 11.2. The two identical plugs on the keyboard cord should be labeled AUDIO and MICROPHONE, or something similar. Insert the audio plug into the speaker port. Insert the microphone plug into the microphone port.

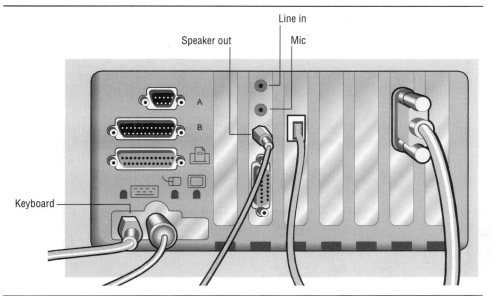

FIGURE 11.2:   The three round ports on the back of the computer should be clearly labeled.

Finishing Up   Plug the AC adapter cord into the nearest electrical outlet, and turn on the computer. You are now ready to install the keyboard's software.

Installing the Software

Now that you have the hardware hooked up and ready to go, you need to install the software that contains the new keyboard driver. A driver is a program that lets a hardware device communicate with the computer.

To install the driver in Windows 3.*x*:

1. Insert the installation diskette into the diskette drive.

2. In Program Manager, open the File menu, and select the Run command.

3. In the Command Line field of the Run dialog box, type **a: setup** or **a: install.** Double-check the prompt command in the instruction manual.

4. After installation, reboot the system to activate the new driver.

In Windows 95:

1. Insert the installation diskette into the diskette drive.

2. Click the Start button on the Windows 95 Taskbar, then select Run.

3. At the prompt box, type **a:setup** or **a:install.** Double-check the prompt command in the instruction manual.

4. After installation, reboot the system to activate the new driver.

After rebooting the system, your new keyboard should work fine. If your keyboard fails to respond to typing, if you get a sporadic response to your typing, or if strange error messages appear, you may have a faulty keyboard connection. Double-check the keyboard's connection at the back of your computer to ensure that it fits securely.

If this doesn't work, the keyboard's circuit board may have a break in it. A break may happen if the keyboard is dropped to the floor. Another possibility is that the connector may have shorted out. Don't attempt to fix these problems yourself. Contact the keyboard's manufacturer or your local computer repair technician.

Installing Joysticks

While using the keyboard is fine for some games, such as Tetris, most of the current computer games are designed to be played with arcade-like controls. Battle games, flight simulators, and other games requiring quick, reflexive movements are the ones most enhanced by the use of a joystick.

Joysticks come in many shapes and sizes, from the simple hand grip with a few buttons to a contoured command center for a full arsenal of virtual weapons. There are also special models developed for certain kinds of game play. For example, some joysticks developed for flight simulation resemble the controller in the cockpit of an airplane.

Before installing the joystick, you'll need to find a 15-pin game port to which to connect it. On most systems, the game port is located on the sound card. If your system doesn't have a sound card or the sound card doesn't have a 15-pin game port, you'll probably want to buy a new sound card and install it before you continue. (For details, see Skill 8.) Another option to consider if your sound card doesn't have a 15-pin game port or if you want maximum gaming performance is to install a game card. A game card is an expansion card dedicated to enhancing a joystick's capabilities.

Installing the Joystick

Removing the PC's cover is not required for the installation of a joystick. Just close all of your applications and turn off your computer before beginning. Then follow these steps:

1. Look at the back of your PC for the slot containing the sound card. The sound card probably will show several possible connection points: a 15-pin port, two or three audio-related lines, and possibly a network or fax connection. Locate the 15-pin port. It might be labeled *Joystick* and it might not, but it should be the only 15-pin port available.

2. Insert the joystick plug into the port and screw it down if screws are available. If you don't see any screws on the plug, the connection likely is secure enough without the extra protection.

3. Turn the computer back on and return to your operating system.

Installing the Software

Once the joystick is plugged in, you'll need to install the driver. As you've seen in earlier exercises, the driver is the program that enables a hardware device and the CPU to communicate. This software should be packaged with the joystick.

Because many of the graphic-intensive games run better from the DOS environment, the joystick's installation instructions may suggest or require that you install the driver in the DOS operating system.

To install a driver in DOS:

1. Go to your DOS (C>) prompt.

2. Your driver probably will come on a diskette. Insert the diskette into your diskette drive. Access the A: drive by typing **a:** at the C> prompt. (If your diskette drive is B:, change the instructions accordingly.)

3. From the A> prompt, type **a:setup** or **a:install** according to the instructions provided.

To install a driver in Windows 3.*x*:

1. Insert the installation diskette into the diskette drive.

2. From Program Manager, open the File menu, and select Run.

3. In the Command Line field in the Run dialog box, type **a:setup** or **a:install**. The installation manual will give you the exact command to enter in the Run dialog box.

4. After installation, reboot the system to activate the new driver.

To install a driver in Windows 95:

1. Insert the installation diskette into the diskette drive.

2. Click the Start button on the Windows 95 Taskbar, and then select Run.

3. In the prompt box, type **a:setup** or **a:install.** Check the installation manual for the exact command.

4. After installation, reboot the system to activate the new driver.

Game Cards

A game card is not essential for playing games or using a joystick, but it can make a difference in the quality of game control. The card enhances the level of control to such a degree that the joystick might seem too sensitive for less experienced joystick users. Joysticks attached to game cards also are a little more difficult to calibrate. Unless you're unhappy with the response of your current joystick setup, there is no reason to make the switch to the game card. Installing the game card and its accompanying software is a little more complex than installing the joystick itself. First, you'll need to disable the current joystick driver on your system.

> **NOTE** Before removing a driver, make sure you have the diskette from which you originally obtained the driver. This diskette should be the same installation diskette that came with your joystick. If you no longer have this diskette, contact your joystick manufacturer to obtain another one.

Disabling the Old Driver

To begin, follow the steps below that apply to your system.

In Windows 3.*x*:

1. Double-click the Main program group, then double-click Control Panel.

2. In the Control Panel window, double-click the Drivers icon. The Drivers window will list all installed drivers.

3. Locate the joystick driver. It will be labeled with a title, not a filename. It should be listed under the same name as your joystick, such as Thrustmaster or SideWinder. Look for the brand name of the sound card if a specific label isn't obvious.

4. Once you've found the driver, highlight it and double-click. You might encounter an option that lets you disable the driver. Disable the driver in this way if you are able. If your driver does not give you an enable/disable option, highlight the driver, and click Remove. This will remove the driver from your system.

In Windows 95:

1. Go into the Control Panel. You can find the Control Panel by clicking the Start button and selecting Settings ➤ Control Panel.

2. Double-click on System, and select Device Manager from the tabs at the top of the screen.

3. Click the icon that reads Sound, Video, and Game Controllers. All of your current sound, video, and game controller drivers, including your joystick driver, will be listed under this heading. Double-click the Gameport Joystick option.

4. In the Properties window, select General. At the bottom of the window is a box labeled *Device Usage*. That smaller window will contain the configuration status. Click the box so there is no checkmark in it.

Installing the Game Card

You are now ready to install the game card. Before beginning the hardware installation, make sure you have read and understand Skill 3.

1. When your computer is open, find an open expansion slot. If necessary, remove the corresponding plate at the rear of the case.

2. Line the card up so the tab with the metal connectors can slide into the internal expansion slot. Make sure the ports are exposed through the slot in the rear of the case. Slide the game card into the slot, pressing gently but firmly. Do not force the card. If the card is being stubborn, try inserting one corner into the expansion slot and easing the card into it.

3. Plug the joystick cord into the 15-pin port on the game card (see Figure 11.3). Some cards are equipped for two joysticks. If you have only one, make sure you plug the cord into the first port (either on top or to the left).

4. Replace the cover and turn on the PC.

FIGURE 11.3:   The 15-pin joystick cord plugs into the matching port on the game card.

Installing the Device Driver

When your joystick expansion card is installed and your computer is running properly, you can install the new device driver.

To install the driver on a DOS system:

1. Go to your DOS (C>) prompt.

2. Into your diskette drive, insert the installation diskette that contains the driver.

3. Access the A: drive by typing **a:** at the C> prompt. (If your diskette drive is labeled B:, change the instructions accordingly.)

4. From the A> prompt, type **a:setup** or **a:install** according to the instructions provided with the diskette.

To install the driver on a Windows 3.*x* system:

1. Insert the installation diskette into the diskette drive.

2. In Program Manager, select File ➤ Run.

3. In the Run dialog box, type **a: setup** or **a: install.** Check the installation manual for the exact command.

4. After installation, reboot the system to activate the new driver.

For Windows 95 systems:

1. Insert the installation diskette into the diskette drive.

2. Click the Start button, and select Run from the Start menu.

3. In the prompt box, type **a:setup** or **a:install.** Check the installation manual for the exact command.

4. After installation, reboot the system to activate the new driver.

Joystick Calibration

Once you have installed the joystick, the final step is calibrating it for game play. You can do this once the game is loaded and ready for play. Most games give you the calibration option in the same group of commands as Save Game, Load

Game, and Exit. There are many ways to do this calibration, depending upon your setup and software, but they should be similar to these basic instructions:

1. Select the Calibrate Joystick option from the game's menu. You will see a bar with a wavering line on it. At this point, the line does not need to be centered and probably won't be.

2. The instructions will prompt you to move the joystick to the upper-left corner and click a button. Depress the joystick's primary firing button, such as the trigger. After you let go, the joystick usually settles into a stationary spot. You then will be prompted to do the same for the lower-right corner. As you move the joystick to the far corners, the cursor should move to the corresponding corners of the screen. When you're finished, the cursor should be holding steady close to the middle of the screen. If it's still wavering, repeat the above steps until it evens out.

If the installation proves problematic, double-check the troubleshooting guide in the instruction manual. There are many joysticks from many manufacturers on the market; these generic instructions may not include an important step for your particular installation. If the problem persists, contact the company's technical support line.

Other Input Devices

Your computer system probably came equipped with the standard keyboard and a mouse. Undoubtedly, you installed them at the time you set up your computer. But times change, and you may find that you would like to try a new mouse or an alternative input device.

An input device is any tool you use to enter information into your computer. In this section, we're only addressing the smaller input devices: mice, trackballs, touchpads, light pens, and pointing sticks. We've already talked in detail about two other types of input devices: keyboards and joysticks. With the exception of the light pen, all of these devices install in the same manner and use the same kinds of ports.

First, let's look at what these input devices are and how they work.

Mice

A mouse is the most familiar input device for most users. This device is so named because it remotely resembles a mouse. For those who have trouble with this analogy, imagine that the cable connecting the mouse to the computer is a tail.

There are, however, both cordless mice and mice in other shapes. The least rodent-like mouse may be the pen-shaped mouse, designed for people who are more comfortable using a writing instrument than a computer. There are also novelty mice, shaped like cars, rocks, footballs, other animals, and so on.

A user moves the entire mouse, gliding it across a flat surface. A ball in the bottom of the device rolls when the user moves the mouse across the desk or mousepad. The cursor position on the screen is related to the movement of the rolling ball. The amount of cursor movement relative to the mouse's movement is adjustable.

A mouse usually has two buttons that allow you to interact with a graphical user interface (GUI). A GUI, such as Windows, lets you interact with the PC using menus and icons—symbols that represent programs, files, or actions—to open files, carry out commands, and select options. A GUI is the opposite of a text-based interface, such as DOS, that requires the user to enter text commands. To select an icon or menu item in the GUI, users press the left mouse button. The right button is less often used, but it is assigned special functions, especially in the Windows 95 operating system.

Trackballs

Trackballs look a bit like mice turned upside down. They have a roller ball on top instead of on the bottom surface. Rather than move the entire unit, you use your fingers or thumb to move the roller ball. Trackballs have buttons just as mice do, but they usually have more than two. The trackball that we installed had three buttons, one for the thumb and two for the last two fingers of the hand. The thumb button is used just like the left button on a mouse. The remaining buttons can be programmed for other functions, such as double-clicking.

Touchpads

Touchpads, in a sense, use the most basic pointing device of all—your finger. You move your finger across a touch-sensitive pad, and the movement of your finger directs the movement of the cursor on the screen. To click on something on your screen, you tap on the pad instead of pressing a button, as you would with a mouse or trackball.

Light Pens

Instead of being used on the desktop, light pens are used in contact with the computer screen. These are not to be confused with pen-shaped mice, which have a roller in the tip and work just like regular mice.

Pointing Sticks

These devices, which have become common in laptop computers, look like eraserheads and function much like joysticks—you move the stick in the direction you want the cursor to go. In fact, one of the pointing sticks that we used for this article referred to itself as "The One-Touch Joystick for Your Desk." The main difference between joysticks and pointing sticks is their size; you use only one finger to move the pointing stick, instead of gripping it and moving it with your whole hand, as you would a joystick. Because of their small size, most pointing sticks are embedded in the keyboards of laptops. However, it is possible to purchase one for use with your desktop computer. A pointing stick is usually accompanied by two buttons, one on either side of the device, that function just like mouse buttons.

Infrared

Imagine your life without infrared technology. No remote controls. You would actually have to stand and walk to the television to change a channel. Operating many stereos and VCRs would be quite different, too. You wouldn't be able to print or connect to your network from your portable computer without using a rat's nest of cords and connectors. And forget beaming confirmation of a transaction from your handheld, electronic checkbook to the merchant's cash register.

Your response: "Whoa. Back up. Those last two aren't familiar. Infrared can do that?"

Yes, it can. Infrared technology, because of its ease of use, quick and accurate data transfer ability, and inexpensive implementation, will undoubtedly establish a solid hold in the computing world. Exactly when that will happen is up for debate. But infrared (IR) is beginning to make inroads. According to the Infrared Data Association (IrDA), 80 percent of all new portable computers sold in 1996 contained built-in infrared ports. Several new printers contain built-in IR ports as well. Many companies sell connectors to give other devices infrared capabilities. And infrared device drivers will be available for all major PC operating systems, including Windows 95, Macintosh, and OS/2.

"Infrared's biggest stumbling block now is educating PC users," says IrDA executive director John LaRoche. "We have to make people aware of the feature," LaRoche says. "The notebook providers—and I can understand why—haven't really taken ownership of educating their buyers that there is an IrDA feature. We need to make sure we allow the consumer to realize that not only do they have that smoky glass on the back of their new notebook, but it can do some things, and (we need to) inform them how to do those sorts of things a little bit better."

LaRoche says system providers need to ship written material with their products so end users can learn what IR can do for them and their computers.

What Is IR?

Infrared is a series of wavelengths in the electromagnetic spectrum, which is energy that encompasses all wavelengths. Different wavelengths produce different types of energy. Visible light is part of the electromagnetic spectrum, but it's only a tiny part. Infrared is just beyond the visible spectrum, with wavelengths longer than those of red, visible light (see Figure 11.4).

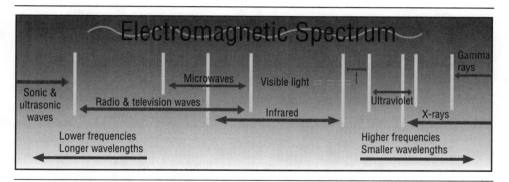

FIGURE 11.4:   Infrared is a part of the electromagnetic spectrum that can't be seen.

Direct infrared beams are able to carry data between devices, allowing them to turn electricity on and off, as long as an unbroken, direct line of sight is available. Infrared is used in your television remote control, and the IrDA standard uses technology that is similar to what is found in your remote control.

"First of all, it uses the same type of technology because it's infrared diodes," says LaRoche. "It's very inexpensive. It's directional. It's like the remote control where you're supposed to point one device at the other device. It's not diffuse, where it floods the room with the signal. You're actually pointing something at something else, and it makes the link and sends something across. It's a high-speed data link, and it's two-way, so it can discover whether it's pointing at a printer or at another computer, or perhaps at a pay telephone. It'll be able to understand what it's doing."

IrDA Information

The Infrared Data Association (IrDA) is made up of more than 130 members that have set the standard for the use of infrared data transfer in computing. The IrDA standard is extremely technical, but it basically guarantees that devices of different brands will make connections and transfer data easily, use very little power to prevent battery drain on portable computers, require a low rate of error during transmission, and allow data to be transferred at the touch of a button.

In devising its standard, the IrDA wanted "to create an interoperable, low-cost IR data interconnection standard that supports a walk-up, point-to-point user model that is adaptable to a wide range of appliances and devices." According to the IrDA, implementation of IR should be inexpensive and easy to use on a variety of devices.

The standard is widely compatible, and is supported by a large sector of the computer industry.

If you would like more information about the IrDA or its standard, you can contact the association through its World Wide Web site (http://www.irda.org), by e-mail (info@irda.org), or by postal mail (Infrared Data Association, P.O. Box 3883, Walnut Creek, CA 94598).

Point and Shoot

Current infrared use is limited because it is being implemented slowly. "We're hoping to have lots of (products) that can use this kind of link for two-way connections," LaRoche says. "Although the promise is quite significant, right now there's not an awful lot of support. If novices buy a brand new notebook, they're going to see one or two IR ports on there. And they're going to wonder, 'What am I supposed to do with this?' "

Depending upon your setup, you can do quite a bit. A few printers, such as Hewlett-Packard's 5P and DeskJet 340, have built-in IR capabilities. You then can print a file, just as if you were connected through cabling, as long as the infrared ports on the printer and portable computer are lined up properly. You also can exchange data between two portable computers, as long as your data transfer software supports IR. Various companies make IR adapters that connect to desktop PCs, portables, printers, and network computers lacking built-in IR capabilities, and allow you to make an infrared connection (see Figure 11.5).

Infrared eliminates the need for cabling and, because of the strong IrDA standard, makes connectivity among products from different manufacturers much easier. Infrared data transfer is fast, too, working at about 115 kilobytes per second (KBps) (similar in speed to accessing data from a diskette drive) with eventual expansion to 4MB per second.

FIGURE 11.5:   The JetEye series of products from Extended Systems provides infrared attachments for desktops, printers, and networks.

Upgrading to IR

Adding IR capabilities to any device is fairly easy. All you need is to connect an infrared adapter to a free serial port, which is a connector on the back of a computer to which you can attach input devices. According to IR industry experts, the hardware requirements for infrared capabilities are minimal. Virtually any type of computer can use infrared, regardless of its microprocessor speed or random-access memory (RAM) capabilities.

Before you make a quick purchase of an infrared adapter, though, make certain you really need IR and can take advantage of its benefits. For example, adding an infrared adapter to your desktop computer may not benefit you much. Your desktop computer rarely moves from its position on your desk, meaning connecting to a printer or to a network with cabling isn't a hassle. You can hook up cables once and ignore them.

If you use a portable computer with built-in IR in tandem with a desktop computer, though, you might find a desktop infrared adapter useful. You then could synchronize files between the two computers without the hassle of creating a cable connection each time.

"With (IR on) a desktop, a user plops his portable down, and automatically synchronizes the files he wants," says Mark Willnerd, product manager for the infrared product line of Extended Systems of Boise, Idaho. "The two key ingredients of IR are the ease of use and the quickness with which it happens. There's no messing around. You just set it down and make the connection."

Infrared and portable computing form a more natural team than desktops and IR because of the nature of portable computing. If you're using a portable, you're likely making various connections to many types of computers, printers, and networks, all while on the move. Finding the proper cables can be a hassle. The main avenues for IR are the portable market and the personal digital assistant (PDA) market, says Willnerd, whose company builds IR adapters for printers, networks, and desktops. Use of infrared in printing is "probably more predominant than desktop PCs. The reason being is that 50 percent of the people who are buying portables today are replacing their desktops. They're no longer using the desktop, and they're exclusively using the portable."

Because most new portables contain built-in infrared capabilities, using IR with it is relatively easy and fast, Willnerd says, and many people prefer making connections with infrared rather than cabling.

Microsoft Connects Infrared to Windows 95

When introducing Windows 95, Microsoft touted the solid portable computing features found in the new operating system. With its emphasis on helping mobile computer users, it's no surprise Microsoft decided in 1995 to add support for the IrDA standard in Windows 95. Newer versions of Windows 95 include an IrDA device driver, which let users make easy connections between infrared-equipped devices. For people with versions of Windows 95 shipped before the IrDA device driver was included, the driver can be downloaded from the Microsoft home page (http://www.microsoft.com) or from the IrDA home page (http://www.irda.org).

With the Plug-and-Play feature included in Windows 95, recognizing infrared peripherals is simple, and all necessary drivers are automatically installed and configured.

When using the Windows 95 IrDA driver, you'll be notified in the Desktop's Taskbar when you've made a connection and when the data transfer begins. If the connection is broken, you'll again be notified with a status bar message, and you'll have 40 seconds to re-establish the connection. After the connection is made again, the transfer picks up where it left off when the break occurred.

Using Voice Recognition Technology

One of the more idealistic goals for computer users is perfect voice recognition. We imagine our PCs being able to respond to our commands, render our spoken words as text, and even make intelligent replies. Voice recognition has come a long way since its inception, but it is still by no means perfect.

In order to become widespread, voice recognition software must have four qualities:

- It must be easy to "train" so that it is able to respond correctly to different voices. Ideally, repeating just a few words or sentences should be enough.

- It must take dictation with near-perfect accuracy. Rapid dictating could be an incredible time-saving tool, but if it requires the speaker to redo every 10th or 20th word, it's not rapid.

- The user must be able to personalize it effortlessly. The needs of all PC users are different. If voice recognition can't help everyone meet their individual needs, it's useless.

- It must be inexpensive—perhaps even integrated into an operating system or other software.

We decided to see if we would be able to run our PC using only our voice. In this section we show you how to install, configure, and run a typical voice recognition package, and see if voice recognition is finally here.

What Is Required?

We tested one of the most popular voice recognition systems currently on the market: Dragon Systems' DragonDictate for Windows Personal Edition version 2.5. This low-end (about $400) version of DragonDictate comes with a 10,000-word vocabulary and is packaged with all the extras. It comes with a monstrous 220-page manual, a headset, and a quick reference card. Its requirements are fairly steep. To run DragonDictate, you need a 66MHz 486 or higher CPU (Pentium is recommended), 12MB of RAM (16MB recommended), 36MB of free hard drive space, at least a 16-bit sound card, and Windows 3.*x*, Windows 95, or NT.

Installing the software wasn't really difficult. We were guided by the typical Windows setup wizard that held our hand through the installation, but it still turned out to be a bit of a project. By the time we put DragonDictate's ninth disk in, we thought we'd installed a new operating system. The microphone headset was no problem. It just plugged into the back of the sound card—the red microphone wire into the slot labeled *Microphone,* and the black headphone wire into the slot labeled *Out.*

Testing Our Voice

After we finished the installation, we fired the program up, and another wizard led us through the process of creating a new user. After asking us to enter a name and gender, DragonDictate ran the microphone headset through a series of tests to ensure there were no hardware problems with either the microphone or the sound card. We also had to provide enough information about our voice that the program would be able to recognize our commands. This was done by repeating a simple series of words and phrases.

DragonDictate comes with a 20-minute tutorial that serves as an introduction to voice recognition software in general and DragonDictate specifically. For our initial test of the software, we said, "Quit Tutorial." This saved us time that we were glad to have as we began training the software to recognize our voice.

The DragonDictate Quick Training is not quite that quick: It takes about a half hour to complete. But the software lets you complete just one of the four segments at a time if you want, then save the results and return later. The training was simple. DragonDictate would pop a word or phrase up on-screen and we would say it once. If DragonDictate didn't understand us, we would have to repeat it a second or third time.

Repeating letters, numbers, and words until we were hoarse (not to mention the stares we garnered from around the office) quickly became mundane, and it was readily apparent that DragonDictate began to attune itself to our voice. We didn't even have to completely finish two of the training sessions because DragonDictate had adapted so well to our speech patterns.

Voice Applications

After we completed the training, we decided to see if a hands-free approach to computing was really practical, by experimenting with DragonDictate's Command Mode. The Command Mode is the state of the program in which it is able to control the desktop and applications. We found most actions can be performed at least as quickly by using voice commands instead of commands from the keyboard and mouse. Simple maneuvers, such as opening, closing, minimizing, and maximizing windows can be done just by speaking a word or two.

DragonDictate is capable of more complex activities, but in many of the more difficult instances we learned it was less efficient to use voice commands. For example, DragonDictate can resize an open window, but in the amount of time it took us to say, "Size Window," "Move Right," "Stop," "OK," we could have tried eight window sizes with the mouse.

You can move about the desktop and between windows in three ways, but they are all a bit awkward and take some getting used to. First, you can use arrow movement commands by moving the highlighted cursor from point to point by issuing directional commands such as "Move Up," "Move Right Three," "Move Down Five," and so on. We learned this isn't much faster than using the Alt key combinations on the keyboard.

A user also can move the mouse pointer with voice commands. By saying "Move Upper Right," "Stop," and then "Button Click," for example, a window can be minimized. But this mouse movement is not even close to the speed and accuracy achieved through physical movement of the mouse.

A more effective, but more complicated manner of desktop and application manipulation is achieved by using a mouse grid. When a user says, "Mouse Grid," a matrix of nine numbered boxes appears over the screen. Then you can pick one of these boxes by saying "Number X," where "X" is 1 through 9. This shrinks the grid to the box you selected, and you can pick one of the smaller boxes by choosing another number. After the mouse pointer is over the selected item, you can say "Button Click" or "Button Double-Click" to open it. This isn't as complex as it sounds and was actually fairly quick after we got better at it.

After we had an open application, we discovered that we could access any menu by saying the word we would normally click with the mouse, such as "File" or "Edit." After a menu has popped up, we could access any of the commands that appeared by saying them. The accuracy wasn't perfect, but it improved after we completed the entire training and corrected some of the misunderstandings (more about that later).

In general, maneuvering about the desktop and through applications was slower than if we used the mouse and keyboard, but with patience and training, it improved. Once DragonDictate warms up to the user, the interface runs quite smoothly.

Say "Dictate Mode"

Well, it's called DragonDictate, so how does it do with dictation? Not bad, but not perfect. The commands for dictating are very simple. After the user says, "Dictate Mode," DragonDictate will render everything it hears into text until the utterance of "Command Mode" returns it to its controlling interface. Everything else is fairly straightforward. If you want to insert a comma, say "Comma." If you want to start a new paragraph, say "New Paragraph."

When we first started in Dictate mode, the results were pitiful. Between one in five and one in 10 words were misunderstood. But a Choice List appears after each word we said, letting us enter the correct word, and giving DragonDictate a chance to learn from its mistakes. If we didn't enter the correct word, Dragon-Dictate would learn the wrong word and be more likely to bring it up the next time. After we got rolling (and after we corrected a lot of words), the dictations were much more accurate. It was never perfect, but the accuracy level did surpass 95 percent.

The adaptability of DragonDictate makes us optimistic about the future of voice recognition. It was easy to teach the program new words. If improvements can be made, such as implementing grammatical recognition so the program can realize when it makes a mistake and then teaches itself, dictating to a computer could become efficient enough to be worthwhile.

Customizing

Probably the most important aspect of voice recognition software is its ability to be tailored to specific needs. In addition to being able to learn new words and correct its mistakes, DragonDictate has some exceptional macro abilities. (A macro is a keystroke or key combination that holds an entire series of keyboard and mouse actions.) In voice recognition, a macro is a single spoken word or phrase that holds several lines of text or several commands.

There are many reasons to create macros in Dictate mode. Commonly used addresses, letter openings and closings, or any phrase or sentence that is repeatedly used are some of the most prevalent macros. Macros also can be highly useful in Dragon-Dictate's Command mode. To open frequently used files, you can create a macro that will let you automate all the required steps into one simple voice command.

There are other options a user can activate, depending upon how advanced he or she has become. If the choice list pops up too quickly when you are dictating, you can increase the delay. And if you become really adept at your dictation, you can turn on an option that allows DragonDictate to change the previous word based upon the context of the current word (we never got that good).

Apart from changing words in the choice list, most of the customizing wasn't very easy to do, but it addressed a variety of user needs. Again, with improvements that allow the software to recognize these needs—perhaps creating new macros automatically—or other ways to make them easier to achieve, voice recognition could gain a wider audience.

DragonDictate demonstrates some of the major leaps that voice recognition software has made in recent years. The length of time it takes to train a system, while still too long, has decreased substantially. The actual recognition of spoken words has, with new adaptive abilities, become that much closer to 100 percent. Customizing has become a reality and is beginning to become simpler. Unfortunately, with a price of just less than $400, cost is still a factor to consider.

The long and short of it is that computers are getting more adept at listening, but it still may be a while before the technology is perfected.

Skill 11

TALK CAN BE CHEAP

Purchasing voice recognition software doesn't have to mean giving up sending your children to college. Verbex Voice Systems has provided a useful and relatively inexpensive alternative with their Listen for Windows 2.0.

At the time of this writing, Listen For Windows listed for $99, but if you download it from the Internet, you could pick it up for less than $60. It requires 4MB of RAM, 14MB of free hard drive space, a sound card, a microphone, and Windows 95. We chose to download the software.

After we ran the executable files that set up Listen on our computer, we chose the applications we wanted it to work with and created a new user. We entered a name, indicated our gender, and were ready to go. One of Listen's features is Speaker Independence, meaning it can understand you as soon as you begin using it. We had some difficulty getting it to understand our speech, so we decided to go through the optional training.

Listen's training is not as intensive as DragonDictate's, but it still requires you to run through 330 phrases. You can complete a portion of the training, and Listen will save what it has learned and let you continue later. Listen also allows you to customize the training, so you can decide which phrases are most important for the program to learn. For example, if you frequently work with numbers, it also features a short digit training exercise so it can learn to recognize numbers with greater accuracy. You can personalize Listen by creating voice macros, which allow the program to carry out a series of commands with only one vocal prompt.

Another customization feature, called Command Editor, is a tool that lets you modify existing commands or add new ones. With the Editor, a user can personalize Listen for use with almost any application. This is fortunate, since the list of applications with which Listen is initially prepared to work is extensive, but far from complete.

continued ▶

We found Listen to be a useful voice recognition program. It was incapable of receiving dictation, but was adequate at desktop navigation and application manipulation. If you're interested in trying out voice recognition for the first time, take some time out to Listen. (Verbex can be reached at http://www.verbex.com.)

General Input Device Installation Tips

This section serves as a general guide to the various installation procedures for several input devices. Our instructions will be based on the products we installed. The instructions will vary somewhat from one product to another.

NOTE   You should refer to the manual included with the input device you have purchased, and use it in conjunction with our directions.

In preparation, turn off your computer and make sure you understand the information covered in Skill 3. Follow the steps outlined there before you begin your upgrade. Whether you'll need to work inside your computer case will depend upon which device you are replacing or adding to your system. Check your user's manual before opening the case to see if it's necessary.

If you are installing a new device to replace your current mouse, unplug the current mouse so you can use that port for the new device.

NOTE   If the input device you're installing doesn't require a bus expansion board, skip ahead to "Connecting the Cables" now.

Expansion Board Installation

A few input devices will require the installation of a bus expansion board, either because of special needs or because all of your existing ports are being used for other devices. Such boards, which are installed in expansion slots inside your computer case, create new ports at the back of the computer so you can add new input devices (see Figure 11.6).

The light pen we installed also required us to install a light pen board. We installed this board, which came with the pen, into an Industry Standard Architecture (ISA) slot. ISA is an unofficial designation for the bus design of the IBM PC/XT expansion slot. Installing this card is similar to installing an expansion board for an input device if you don't have open ports.

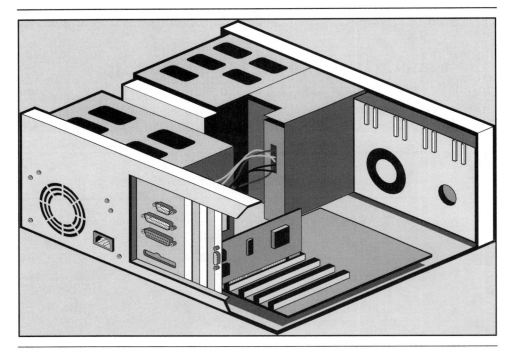

FIGURE 11.6:   Installation of a bus expansion board is required before some input devices can be added.

First, make sure the base input/output (base I/O) address through which the computer will talk to the card is different from those used by other cards in your computer. (To check the base I/O address of a board, check its manual.) If there is a conflict, the manual should offer alternative settings and explain how to set the switches on the new board to one of these alternatives.

Before installing the board, you need to set the jumpers. Jumpers are small plugs or wires used to alter an aspect of a hardware configuration by connecting different points in an electronic circuit. These settings must be correct for your input device to work properly with the computer and any other peripherals. Instructions included with the input device will explain the various settings and how to change them if they conflict with another device.

Find an empty expansion slot, remove the slot cover, and keep the screw from that cover handy. You'll need it to secure the metal retaining bracket of the board.

 NOTE   In the case of the light pen, using the slot closest to the video card will make connections easier.

Line up the board's connector with the slot socket, press the board firmly into place, and then secure the board with the screw from the expansion slot cover. Put the cover back on your computer.

Adapting to PS/2 and Parallel Ports

Locate the port you will be using for the device. If you have installed an expansion board, the port on that board can be accessed from the back of the computer. Most input devices come with an adapter that lets you connect the device to either a PS/2 port or a serial port. A few, however, don't come with adapters and only fit into one port. Check to be sure that your new device is compatible with an available port on the back of your computer.

PS/2 ports (also called mouse ports) are small and round; the connectors that fit into them are round with six pins. Serial ports are trapezoidal and generally have nine pins. Figure 11.7 shows examples of each type of connector. The connectors for serial ports often have thumbscrews to secure the connection of the cable to the computer. These screws can be tightened by hand. While most input devices are designed to fit either a PS/2 or a serial port, you can order adapters that let you plug the devices into a 25-pin serial port. Although these adapters aren't included with most retail packages, you usually can request one from the manufacturer.

If necessary, connect the adapter to the device's cable before connecting the cable to the port. This is done by matching the end of the adapter to the cable connector, pressing the two firmly together, and tightening thumbscrews, if there are any.

Skill 11

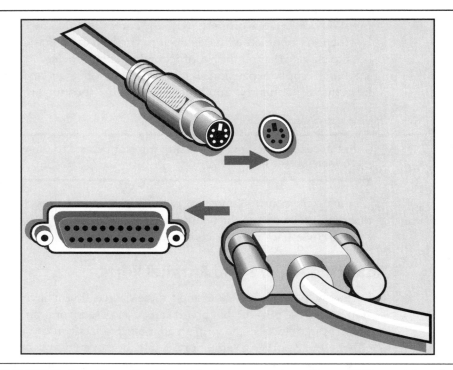

FIGURE 11.7:   Most input devices connect to either a PS/2 port (above) or a serial port (below).

Next, connect the cable (with adapter attached, if needed) to the port on the back of your computer. Again, as with the adapter, match up the connector and the port so that any pins line up correctly, and press in firmly. Note that the connector will only fit in the port one way. If it doesn't seem to fit, don't force it. Look closely at the connector and port to be sure that they are compatible and that you have them lined up correctly. In most cases, it is very easy to determine how to line them up. Many connectors have arrows or flat sides indicating the top.

The light pen we used had two cables: a three-way serial cable to connect the light pen expansion board to the monitor and the video card, and a cord with a connector similar to a telephone jack to connect the pen to the board. Connect both of these cables now.

Once you've plugged the device into its port, you're ready to reconnect all of the cables and turn your computer on.

Input Device Software Drivers

Some input devices require software drivers. Many of those that require a driver will use one that's already in your operating system. Your manual will tell you whether you need to install a driver. If you do, the instructions will be included with the device, and the installation usually is guided by on-screen directions for each step. In Windows 3.*x*, you ordinarily begin the installation process by opening the Program Manager File menu, choosing Run, and typing an installation command such as **a:\install**. The specific command will be provided in your manual. In Windows 95, software is installed by clicking Start, pointing to Settings, clicking Control Panel, and then double-clicking the Add/Remove Programs icon and following the prompts. Input device drivers also can be installed in DOS. To do this, you usually insert the diskette containing the software, type **a:\inst_DOS** at the DOS prompt, and press ↵. The installation program will begin, and from there you just follow directions. Check the installation manual for the specific command to type at the DOS prompt.

 NOTE   No matter which operating system you're using, you will need to restart your computer after installing the software for the new settings to take effect. Some installation programs automatically perform a reboot (restart) for you; others will prompt you to do it at the appropriate time.

You may need to adjust some settings to make your new input device work the way you prefer. For example, the tracking speed (how much the cursor moves on-screen in relation to how much you move the input device) may need to be adjusted if a device is significantly more or less sensitive than the one you've used previously. Another change some users, especially those who are left-handed, will want to make is to switch the buttons so that most actions use the right mouse or trackball button instead of the left. If you do that, you must use the opposite button from the one given in instructions. For example, if the program directions say to click with the left mouse button, you must use the right one. Some devices, like the trackball we installed, let you choose functions for various buttons.

To adjust these settings in Windows 3.*x*, open the Main program group in Program Manager, double-click Control Panel, open the Settings menu, select Mouse, and make your changes. In Windows 95, you get to the Control Panel by clicking Start, then choosing Settings ➤ Control Panel. From that point, the process is the same.

Skill 11

If the input device you're using required software installation, there may be a control panel for that specific device. If this is the case, the custom control panel will be found in your Control Panel program group. These custom control panels offer the same kinds of options as the mouse control panel that is part of Windows: motion speed and sensitivity, double-click speed, acceleration, and button swapping.

Troubleshooting Input Devices

Input devices help you communicate with your computer and give directions to the microprocessor. We discussed the most common input devices, the keyboard, mouse, and joystick, as well as a few less well-known alternatives. A keyboard and mouse are indispensable; a joystick is essential only if you play computer games. Regardless of the input device you choose, it will require proper care to provide trouble-free service.

In the days before PCs, computer operators fed cryptic messages on keypunched data cards into their mainframes (data input). The computer responded by ejecting cryptic messages into data card bins (data output). The earliest computer input device was the key-punch machine. The concept is the same as today's primary input device for the PC—the keyboard.

Keyboards come in three design types. The most common is the standard 101-key model that's about 20 inches long. Some manufacturers ship compact designs that are slightly shorter but have the same number of keys, though the keys are closer together. The third design type is the ergonomic keyboard, which has the keys turning toward the outside between the F6 and F7 keys. This design lets the user's fingers work at a more natural angle than with a regular keyboard because the wrist is forced into a straight position over the keys.

When people used DOS-only computers, the mouse wasn't very important. The four arrow keys on the keyboard provided a fast way to move the cursor through on-screen text. The popularity of graphical user interfaces, such as Windows and OS/2, has made a mouse essential to navigating text, toolbars, and menus.

There are three types of mice:

- The most common device for home PCs, the mechanical mouse needs a spacious, flat desktop surface so the ball on its underside can roll freely as you move it to locate the on-screen pointer. If the mechanical mouse crosses foreign objects such as dust or a paper clip, the on-screen pointer will bounce.

- An expensive alternative to the mechanical mouse, the optical mouse uses a laser light beam instead of a rolling ball. The mouse measures its light's path and location on the grid of a special mouse pad.

- The optomechanical mouse uses a ball to track its path, but it also drags a perforated disc that emits light that is read by the pad.

The alternative is an upside-down mouse called a trackball. Instead of moving the pointer by rolling the mouse, you use your thumb to turn a larger rolling device. To track a path with the pointer, roll the ball in its place. Trackballs are ideal for cramped desk areas and portable computers because they don't need to be moved around a flat surface. Some full-size keyboards have a trackball built into them, and many portable PC keyboards have trackball units that clip onto the side.

We've already discussed joysticks. They take the basic concept of a mouse and make it more like a steering device. To make on-screen selections, you move the joystick up, down, and side to side within its base. Joysticks usually are used to play computer games.

 TIP   All three input types have distinctive plugs that fit into specific sockets on the back of the computer. Never plug or unplug any input device while the computer is running. Doing so may disable the input device until you restart the computer. It also can damage the circuitry in the input device itself or its connection.

Keyboards

Make it a rule to never have food or drink near the keyboard. Accidents do happen, despite precautionary measures. Spilling liquid on the keys can short out the keyboard and one or more components in the computer. Likewise, crumbs can get underneath keys and damage contact surfaces.

Similarly, smoking around the computer is a bad idea—hot cigarette and cigar particles can mar the surface of the keyboard or, worse yet, burn the contact centers beneath the keys. Smoke from cigarettes and cigars also forms a film in diskette drives and on the computer's internal surfaces. A fan inside the computer blows air across the motherboard (the main circuit board of your computer) to control heat buildup. This same fan draws smoke into the box, adding to the wear and tear of the system.

Skill 11

Keyboards usually come with a clear plastic cover. When you aren't using the computer, keep the keyboard covered to prevent dust and dirt from getting under the keys. Occasionally, you should remove excess dust from the keyboard by blowing canned air over the keyboard itself and around the keys.

If you connect a keyboard that doesn't work, it may be designed for more than one type of computer. Some keyboards have a small selector switch with positions for XT and AT computers. Look for this switch on the bottom or back edge of the keyboard. (The XT position is for older computers having microprocessors lower than a 386. Make sure the selector switch is positioned to match your computer.)

Sometimes when you start the computer, you will get a message announcing a keyboard error. Keyboard errors are most often caused by a connection that has been loosened when the PC or your desk was jarred. To fix the problem:

1. Turn off the computer.

2. Remove the keyboard plug from its socket in the back of the computer.

3. Plug it back in, making sure it's pressed as far as it will go into the socket.

If securing the connection doesn't solve the problem, the keyboard may have a break in its printed circuit board. This can happen if, for example, the keyboard is knocked to the floor. Do not take the keyboard apart in an effort to fix it. There are no serviceable parts inside; if you tinker with it, you could short out the connecting port or damage the other electronic circuits in the computer. If another keyboard is available, try switching it with the non-working device. This will confirm that either the first keyboard is damaged or the connector is shorted out. A damaged keyboard can be easily replaced by a new keyboard; a damaged connector will require repair by a trained technician.

Mice

Two problems can affect a mouse's operation: the cable and the roller. A bad cable makes the mouse act strangely, such as an on-screen cursor that won't move or mouse-clicks that don't receive a response. If your mouse isn't working, but you see sporadic movement from the on-screen pointer when you move the cable, the mouse cable is probably worn and the mouse will need to be replaced.

The mouse cable's path from the computer should be clear of obstructions; the computer or other heavy objects shouldn't sit on the cable. Also, avoid keeping the cable in a stationary position other than straight; if the cable bends around other equipment on the desk, it may develop a crease or break.

A second mouse problem—lint buildup in the roller's compartment—is easy to fix. Mice should be cleaned periodically to ensure that they remain trouble-free. Lint builds up on the roller and wraps around one or more of the three directional control arms that rest against the ball; the pointer eventually loses its smooth movement and won't go where you want it to without repeatedly repositioning the mouse. To solve this:

1. Locate the circular cover plate on the underside of the mouse. Rotate this cover counter-clockwise until it is unscrewed.

2. Pop the ball out into your hand.

3. Clean the ball with a cotton cloth. Spots can be cleaned with gauze pads dipped lightly in rubbing alcohol.

4. Let the ball dry—outside of the device—in a well-ventilated room for a few hours.

5. Use a clean pencil eraser to remove lint from the control arms. (Cotton swabs work well, too.)

6. Blow out stray matter from the mouse shell with compressed air.

Joysticks

The design of joysticks leaves little to maintain—the only moving part is the pivoting arm. Accumulated dust and dirt in the "ball and socket" can be blown out with canned air. Occasionally, you may have to adjust the joystick. There are two thumbscrews on the bottom surface that calibrate the movement. Check the manufacturer's instructions for the specific method to use with your model.

If you already have a mouse attached to the computer, adding a joystick usually doesn't pose any problem because the joystick uses the mouse driver that's loaded when the computer starts. (Drivers are programs that facilitate communication between a PC and a hardware device.) Otherwise, you have to install the mouse driver by listing its location in the CONFIG.SYS file, which helps the PC recognize its components upon startup. If you run Windows 95, the Plug-and-Play process should install the necessary drivers.

One final word of caution if you run Windows 95: This new operating system doesn't load a mouse driver for DOS applications, so neither the mouse nor the joystick will work when you run DOS software. Check with the product manufacturers for details on how to work around this situation.

Skill 11

Are You Experienced?

Now you can. . .

- ☑ understand how input devices work and which is best for your needs
- ☑ select and install a keyboard
- ☑ install a joystick, and a game card to get it working
- ☑ comprehend the pros and cons of using input devices, including infrared and voice recognition
- ☑ troubleshoot and maintain your input devices

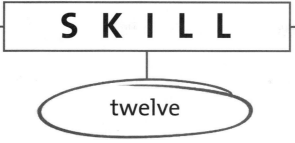

SKILL

12

twelve

Installing a Printer

- ❑ Understanding how printers work

- ❑ Installing a laser printer

- ❑ Installing an inkjet printer

- ❑ Troubleshooting printer problems

Despite nearly two decades of hype about the paperless office, the need to get words and pictures on paper remains with us. That means printers are an essential part of any personal computer installation, whether it be for home, home office, small business, or corporate giant. Those big guys have an edge—they have someone on staff to make their printers work. On the other hand, you may find yourself on your own.

To make printers work, it's helpful to have some idea of how they work. There are literally hundreds of different printing technologies, all of which transfer a character or a graphic from the computer to the paper: these are far beyond the scope of this book. We are concerned here with how printers work from a software point of view. And to keep things simple, we'll focus on printing text.

Printing A to Z

Your computer stores text information in the form of numbers. For example, the letter z is represented by the number 122 and Z is represented by 90. There's nothing magical about those numbers; long ago, in the days of telegraphy, somebody decided on a way of encoding which eventually evolved into a standard called ASCII. Every make and model of printer for a personal computer understands this basic code, so if your computer sends the number 122 to your printer, it will print z on the paper.

The z will appear using the defaults built into the printer by the manufacturer. Most printers default to a font such as Courier, which is ideal for printing columns of numbers and acceptable for text. It's important that printers have such defaults and can understand ASCII because it means that you can get a printer working at a basic level with very few steps and no added software. And it means that if you can't get the printer working with those few steps, the printer may be broken.

Now let's get your printer working.

Before You Buy

There is one technical issue you must address before you carry your new printer home. Does your PC have an available printer port?

Your computer probably has at least one parallel port and one serial port built in. Current systems usually have one parallel and two serial ports. The parallel port is most often used for a printer. A parallel port is the one with the larger connectors; it has 25 pins in two rows. The computer's printer port has a female connector. If you see a 25-pin male connector, it's not a printer port, and your cable will not fit it properly.

If you don't see such a port on your computer, you will need to buy one. The good news is that they are very inexpensive, probably less than $25. The bad news is that you will have to open the PC to install it and will need an available expansion slot. (See Skill 14 for a step-by-step introduction to installing ports.) If you have any concerns about that, your local computer store can do it quickly and, hopefully, cheaply.

If you already have one printer and are adding a second one, there are two ways to go. The first is to buy cabling and a switch box so you can alternate between the printers as needed. This will probably cost about $100 total (as much as $200 for the higher-quality switches and cables). If you are still using MS-DOS, you will probably have fewer setup headaches with this method. The second method is to buy a second parallel port. This is cheaper and recommended in most cases.

At the Store

There is one important technical issue to consider. When buying parallel cables and printer ports, be sure to ask for bidirectional capability.

In the past, the computer talked to the printer but the printer could not talk back, thus the interface was unidirectional. With bidirectional communication, printers have the ability to talk back to the PC, which can be very helpful in getting the software to tell you about printer problems and in having the software understand the capabilities of the printer.

Back at Home

Printer manufacturers, especially Hewlett-Packard, have become much better at including helpful and understandable unpacking and setup instructions in their printer boxes. Take the time to look at this information and follow the instructions carefully. After you have the printer out of the box, loaded with paper, and plugged in, run the printer's self-test as described in the manual before plugging the printer into the PC. If the printer works at this stage, you will know that the printer is not to blame if it won't print later.

The next step is to make sure the parallel port is working properly. There is a very simple way to check this out from the MS-DOS command line. If you are using MS-DOS, you're ready to go. If you're using Windows 3.*x*, exit to DOS or open a DOS Window. If you're using Windows 95 or Windows NT, select the MS-DOS Prompt from the Start menu. At the prompt type **copy con: lpt1**.

The system will respond by moving the cursor to the next line and waiting for you to type **Hello, World.** Then press ⏎. Press Ctrl+N and release both keys, then press F6. The system will return to the DOS prompt and your printer should print a page that says "Hello, World."

 NOTE   If you have more than one parallel printer port, use the name of that port in the first command. For example, if you've added a second port, you would type **copy con: lpt2**.

This is a quick test, so it might be dirty. As long as you see "Hello, World." on the printed page, consider the test a success. After the test, turn the printer off and then back on to reset the printer.

Now for the hard part. Making your printer work with your software can sometimes be a challenge. The steps you must follow are different depending upon the operating system you are using.

What Does the Driver Do?

If you've read the earlier skills in this book you've become familiar with the term *driver*. A driver is a piece of software that provides a connection between a hardware device and the operating system. The purpose of a driver is to standardize the method used by the operating system to communicate between applications and a class of hardware devices.

Printer drivers perform this function for, obviously, printers. But there are also drivers for other kinds of devices, such as modems, sound cards, diskette drives, and monitors. Because there are many makes and models of printers there are many printer drivers.

MS-DOS

DOS is certainly the simplest environment to deal with. Because DOS is a text-based operating system, and because printers default to ASCII, many DOS-based programs will print without requiring any form of setup.

The trick with DOS is that the operating system itself provides no printer support. Each DOS application must provide its own printer drivers. Most major DOS applications come with extensive libraries of the most popular printer drivers. The king of the DOS printer-driver hill was WordPerfect; its DOS printer-driver library supported nearly 3,000 printers in its heyday.

If an application doesn't support your printer out of the box, you might be able to get the driver you need by calling the software vendor, dialing into the company's bulletin board system, or downloading one from the Internet. If you can't get a specific driver, you might be able to find another driver that will operate your printer. For example, there may be few DOS drivers available for a printer such as the HP DeskJet 870cse. A DOS driver for the HP DeskJet 500 will probably operate the DeskJet 870cse, but new features of it will not be available.

 NOTE   Many vendors, software and hardware alike, believe that DOS is dying, if not already dead. Thus, fewer and fewer new printer models will come with DOS drivers. It's just a fact of life; there's not much you can do about it.

Windows 3.x

You don't hear much about versions of Windows earlier than 3.1, and for good reason. Printing got a major overhaul in Windows 3.1 and the face of the printer industry changed as a result.

Microsoft included a remarkably long list of printer drivers in Windows 3.1, a tactic that immediately put printer manufactures on the defensive. In less than a year, just about every printer manufacturer started including software drivers for their printers in the box. This made it easier than ever to get a printer working with Windows.

Getting a printer working is very similar in both popular versions: Windows 3.1 and Windows 95. If you are using Windows NT 4, you will find the Windows 95 installation instructions that follow a suitable guide.

There are two common methods for installing printer software into Windows 3.1. One is to run the Windows Control Panel, and the other is to use a vendor-supplied installation utility.

The Control Panel can be launched from the Main group in the Program Manager. Double-click the Control Panel icon. The Control Panel window will appear. Double-click the Printers icon to display the printers dialog box. You will see a list of printers already installed. To begin installing the new printer, click Add. Scroll down the list to try to find your printer or, if you don't see an exact match, choose something close.

If the printer is in the list already, Windows will also know where the driver is. When you click Install you will see an Install Driver window. If the driver is located on one of its own diskettes, insert the diskette, click OK, then follow the instructions. If you can't find the right diskette, click Cancel or Close in each window until you get back to the Control Panel, and then close it.

To use the driver diskette that came in the printer box, the process is almost exactly the same except for a few small things. Select Main from the Program Manager. Double-click the Control Panel icon, and then double-click again on Printers to display a dialog box. Double-click Install Unlisted or Updated Printer from the list. You will be asked to locate the driver.

At this point Windows will look at the spot you designate, trying to find a special setup information file that describes which drivers are available. If that file, called OEMSETUP.INF, is found, you will see a list of printers from which you can select. Often there is just one printer in the list. Select the correct printer, click OK, and follow the instructions.

Windows 95

Like Windows 3.1, the release of Windows 95 dramatically improved the printer situation. The number of drivers supplied with Windows 95 is huge compared with Windows 3.1. With years of experience behind them, printer vendors were ready for the improvements in Windows 95. Today the Windows 95 drivers are in almost every printer box and can also be obtained quickly via the Internet.

The Windows 95 process is easier than Windows 3.*x* to get started. Click the Start button, select Settings from the menu, and then select Printers. Double-click the Add Printer icon to display the Add Printer Wizard screen.

 NOTE   A nice feature in Windows 95 is that you can back up when using wizards. If you suddenly realize that you've done something wrong on a previous wizard dialog box, just click the Back button until you get to the point where you can make a correction.

The first Add Printer Wizard dialog box just welcomes you. Click the Next button to begin the installation process. You may see a screen that asks if the new printer will be attached locally or if it is on a network. You may see this even if your computer is not attached to a network but you happen to have an

Internet browser. If the screen appears, select the proper answer and click the Next button.

The next wizard dialog box shows lists of all manufacturers and printers from that manufacturer. Say, for example, you have a Hewlett-Packard DeskJet 560C, select HP from the manufacturers list and DeskJet 560C from the printers list. Windows 95 has been around for a couple of years, so although it has newer models than Windows 3.*x*, it still doesn't know about a printer introduced in late 1995 or after. If your printer is not listed but you have a disk from the vendor, click the Have Disk button. You will be prompted for the location of the files, usually a diskette. The wizard will look on the diskette for an information file and, if it finds one, will display a list of drivers provided on the diskette. If you see the printer you need, select it.

The next wizard window will ask you which port will be used to connect the printer. All ports, whether in use or not, are listed. Usually you will be connecting the printer to LPT1 or, if it's a second printer, to LPT2.

Windows 95 next offers you the chance to give the printer any name you like. It will propose the name it found in its files. You can accept the suggestion or you can use any name you like. This wizard dialog box also asks if the printer is to be designated the default printer, that is, the printer Windows 95 will use by default unless instructed otherwise. If your printer is the first one installed or is the only one, then it automatically becomes the default printer and you will not see this box.

The wizard will then ask if you want to print a test page. If you've already confirmed that the printer is working, you might be inclined to ignore this suggestion. Don't; it's a worthwhile test to find out if everything is set up correctly. When Windows 95 has finished printing the test, it will display a dialog box asking if the test completed. If the page doesn't print, or if it doesn't look quite right, answer No. At that point, Windows 95 will launch a printer troubleshooter that will recommend actions and ask about the result. The printer troubleshooter is fairly good and can help you find most common setup problems.

If the installation and the printer test go without a hitch (and they usually do), you will eventually be returned to the Printers Explorer window, where you will see an icon for the newly installed printer.

 NOTE   If you are using Windows NT, don't expect Windows 95 printer drivers to work. You need to find a printer driver specifically designed for NT. Microsoft has plans to eliminate this problem with the next versions of Windows and Windows NT.

Skill 12

WHERE TO FIND PRINTER DRIVERS

If you get a printer that doesn't come with drivers (perhaps you've purchased a used printer), and neither Windows 95 nor Windows 3.x has the printer in its list, there are two things you can do to find it. One is to simply call the manufacturer. Driver diskettes are often supplied for free; competition is brisk in the printer business and the companies like to make friends.

A faster method is to look on the Internet. Most printer vendors have World Wide Web sites. The Web address will most likely be included somewhere in the literature that came with the printer. If all else fails, search for the company's name using one of the search engines in your Web browser. Once there, most vendors have something right on the home page that directs you to drivers.

Setting Up a Laser Printer

It feels just like opening a present. You rip off the tape and pull the new laser printer from the box. You throw the instruction book aside, knowing you'll be able to set up your new laser printer without any help from that stupid book, right?

But what do you do when you push the toner cartridge in backward? Or you forget to remove the plastic packing tape from the toner cartridge? You scramble for that book, wondering how you could have messed up that simple process. Any time you add new hardware, especially new printers, you will want to have a few tips and tricks at your fingertips—and that user's guide—when problems arise.

Going Over the Parts Checklist

The first step is exactly what you have done already: open the box and pull out the laser printer and all the other contents. You will want to make sure you have all the necessary parts before you begin setting up the printer. Many companies will include a checklist of items to have on hand and tasks to do to set up your new printer. Usually, the first few pages of the user's guide are devoted to setting up the new machine.

Many times, manufacturers don't include the necessary printer cable, so it's likely you will need to visit your local computer store to pick one up. The best cable to have is an IEEE-1284 cable, which allows for bidirectional communication between the printer and your PC, according to Cindy Greiner, a product manager for Hewlett-Packard (HP). It typically costs about $20 and can be found in most computer or office supply stores.

Next, pull the plastic cover off the printer and find a suitable spot on your desktop. Try to make sure the printer is close to its power source and relatively close to your computer.

N **NOTE**

> Printer cables usually come in 3-foot or 10-foot lengths. Communication between the computer and printer is more stable when it travels a short distance. Couplers are available to expand the length, but you may experience broken signals at lengths of more than 10 feet.

In most cases, the moveable parts of the printer will be restrained with packing tape and cardboard. Remember to remove all packaging materials before turning on the printer. The packaging will usually be inside the front cover and inside the paper-loading tray. The user's guide should tell you right away if there is internal packaging that must be removed.

The next step is to install the toner cartridge. Because toner is the substance that forms the text and images on a page, it's an important step that should not be overlooked. Each printer accepts toner cartridges in a slightly different manner; consult your user's guide for instructions specific to your printer. The toner inside the cartridge will likely have settled during shipping. Therefore, you will want to remove the cartridge from the package and gently shake it to evenly distribute the toner. Usually, the cartridge is shipped with a plastic seal holding the toner in place that will need to be removed before it's ready for use (see Figure 12.1). Refer to the instructions on the toner cartridge's package about how to remove the sealing tape.

Next, you'll want to open your printer and install the toner, following the instructions included in the user's guide (see Figure 12.2). Remember to check that the correct toner cartridge came with the printer. The model numbers on it should match the model number printed in the user's guide. Some laser printers

Skill 12

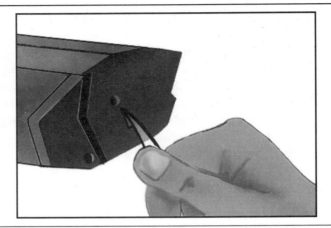

FIGURE 12.1: Most toner cartridges come with a plastic seal that must be removed before installation.

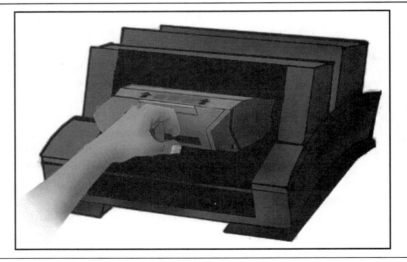

FIGURE 12.2: The toner cartridge slides into place in the printer.

we reviewed for this issue had a variety of problems, including the wrong toner cartridge included with one of the printers.

As we followed the installation instructions, we noticed that the cartridge would not slide into place. When we cross-referenced the cartridge's model

UNLIMITED RESOURCES

FOR LIMITED TIME

SUBSCRIBE NOW!

24 issues for just   **12** issues for just

$48* or $29

Smart Computing is written for all experience levels, whether you're a novice or an expert, you'll find articles and information written with you and your interests and questions in mind. *Smart Computing* grows with you as you gain experience.

Fewer ads means more room for step by step information and instructions, in-depth tutorials, editorial reviews, and helpful glossary of terms, written in plain english so they're easy to understand.

Each issue is delivered directly to your home, before they appear no the newsstand, and at a 61% savings from newsstand prices.*

We're so sure you'll love *Smart Computing*, we've made subscribing **RISK FREE**. If you decide to cancel your subscription at any time, you'll receive an immediate refund for all unmailed copies--no questions asked. You have absolutely nothing to lose.

Order  **Smart Computing** IN PLAIN ENGLISH today!

number with the suggestion in the user's guide, they were not the same. We immediately returned the cartridge to its packaging and notified the company. If major problems arise during your installation, immediately stop and notify either the printer retailer or the manufacturer. They should be able to talk you through the problem.

The toner cartridge comes in a dark plastic package because it is extremely sensitive to light. Don't leave it in the light for more than a few minutes. If you experience problems and have to remove the toner cartridge from the printer, remember to put it back into the plastic package for safe keeping.

 TIP   Here's how to extend the life of your toner cartridge. When your toner is running low, you will notice streaks and light shades in your printing. Take the toner out and shake it gently (much like the first time you installed it). This will let you print about another 100 pages.

Plugging In

The next few steps supply the power and the information pathway to your printer. First, shut down your computer and prepare to attach the parallel printer cable. There is only one port on the printer that the cable will fit into. Gently push the cable into the port and secure it using the small clasps on the side of the port. Next, attach the other end of the cable into the parallel port on the back of your computer. There usually will be only one port the cable will fit into. Insert the cable into the port and secure it with small screws on the sides of the connector.

Next, attach the power cord to your printer. Make sure you plug the power cord into the printer before plugging it into a wall outlet. For peace of mind, you might want to plug your computer into a surge protector, which can protect electronics from high-voltage surges or spikes in electrical current. This little device can save your system if it gets hit by a surge of energy, such as lightning or a power outage. After you plug in the printer, you're ready to fire up your computer and finish the installation.

Installing the Software

After the printer is connected to the computer, you're only one step away from being able to print. You now need to install the drivers that make the computer communicate with the new printer. Your new printer should have come with software that included the necessary drivers (If you are missing the drivers, refer to the earlier section "What Does the Driver Do?"). Use the following directions for the operating system you're using.

Windows 3.x

Installing the Windows 3.x software isn't as difficult as you might think. Actually, it's quite simple. Turn on the computer. Unlike Windows 95, Windows 3.x has no idea the new printer is there. It will not recognize it on startup. To install your new printer, close all open applications on your desktop. Open the Control Panel and double-click Printers. Click Install on the lower-right side of the dialog box. Insert the driver diskette into your diskette drive. In the command line, type **a:\setup** (if the A: drive is your diskette drive) and click OK. The computer should then recognize the new printer.

It's a good idea to print a test page to make sure everything is working properly. Open any document and send it to the printer. If it prints properly, you're ready to go. If not, it's time to go back and figure out what went wrong. For example, after setting up one of our review printers, we printed a test page. The text printed off the left side of the page. To correct the problem, we changed the document's margin settings. Our next test page printed properly. Your user's guide and troubleshooting guide will come in handy at this point.

Windows 95

Windows 95 installations are even easier because of Plug and Play (the feature we described in Skill 1). When you start your computer, it will recognize the new hardware and build a driver base for it. The New Hardware Found dialog box will appear and present you with four options for installing the drivers. You can choose to use the pre-installed drivers in the operating system, or you can install the drivers from the diskettes that came with the printer.

If you choose to use the drivers from the diskettes, you will be prompted to insert the diskettes in sequence until the installation is complete. Then you will be prompted to restart your computer to complete the setup. Restart, and the job should be finished.

After Windows 95 is restarted, you will be prompted to complete the setup of the new printer by printing a test page. This will help you identify the nature and severity of any problems with your printer. Windows 95 will then run a test page verification in a dialog box after the page is printed. Some troubleshooting tips can be attained from here.

SOLVING A COMMON PROBLEM

Whether you are using Windows 3.*x* or Windows 95, if your test page printed properly, you are ready to print. If it did not, let's look at some simple solutions. HP's Greiner says a common problem is installing the wrong printer drivers or installing them incorrectly. Most printers comes with a driver diskette in the box, but some people choose to ignore that software.

In some newer operating systems, such as Windows 95 and Windows NT 4, some printer drivers come pre-installed. But in Windows 3.*x*, no drivers come pre-installed. That's where the driver diskettes come in. It's a good idea to use the drivers that come with each individual printer so you can be sure you have the correct drivers. When we installed our review printers, we always installed the drivers provided on diskette.

In Times of Trouble

Every new printer should come with a user's guide. You may find it handy when setting up your new printer. Also, many laser printers we reviewed came with smaller, handy troubleshooting guides. If the problems you are experiencing aren't covered in the troubleshooting guide, the technical support telephone number can usually be found in the user's guide.

Most printing problems don't require technical support to fix. You should be able to fix most problems yourself with the help of your user's guide. If you've purchased the right printer cable, installed the factory drivers properly, and shaken the toner cartridge before installing it, you should be ready to enjoy the thrill of printing with your new printer.

Skill 12

GETTING YOURSELF OUT OF A PAPER JAM

Paper jams are common when using laser printers. There is no need to panic: Paper jams are easy to fix, and printing can resume rather quickly. It's important to remember, especially with today's top-loading laser printers, that paper is drawn from the front of the stack, not the back. By drawing the paper from the front, it is easily jammed when you have loaded more paper without taking out the paper already in the printer tray. When you put new paper in your printer, take out the paper sheets that are already in the printer and stack them together. Then, put all the paper back in and let the printer draw in the first sheet.

At some point on the paper's journey through the printer, a fold or small tear in the paper could get snagged on a gear pushing the paper through. The paper will keep feeding normally on one side and then become jammed. Each laser printer is different. Some will have mechanisms to remove the jammed paper. Look for a piece of the paper and slowly, gently pull out the paper.

We jammed a couple of different lower-end laser printers, and here's what we encountered. In the worst case, the paper jam took us more than 30 minutes to clear. The best case took us only a matter of seconds. To remove the jammed paper, open the front of the printer and find where the jammed paper is. Slide the toner cartridge out and place it in the dark until the job is finished. With the front of the printer open, identify where the jam is. Try gently pulling out the paper. If the paper tears while pulling it out, stop and get a better grip.

When paper tears, there often is no place to pull out the rest of jammed paper. You need to remove all jammed paper before starting the printer again. Even the slightest corner of paper left can cause problems later. In our case, the paper was wrapped around the rollers that push the paper through the printer. The paper ripped before it all came out of the printer, so the problem worsened. Most of the sheet came out, but the corner was wrapped tightly around the roller.

continued ▶

Our job required some small tools to remove the paper. The best tools for this operation are tweezers and a screwdriver. Use the tweezers to grab a small portion of the paper and gently try to remove it. If you are lucky, that will take care of the problem. If you are unlucky, like we were, you will need to loosen the roller to pull out the paper. Take the screwdriver and loosen the roller. Use the tweezers to grasp the paper and gently remove it. Tighten the screw back down and slide the toner cartridge back in. Be patient. Removing the paper jam the right way will keep your new investment working properly for a long time. Removing it the wrong way will ruin your printer and frustrate you further.

When all of the paper is removed, close the front of the printer. It should recognize that the jammed paper has been removed and reprint the page.

Setting Up Your New Inkjet Printer

When the personal computer craze first began in the early 1980s, outputting documents was both expensive and sketchy. Early dot matrix printers produced dotty silhouettes. Those sketchy pages gave way to better quality printing as dot matrix technology advanced from nine-pin printers to 24-pin printers. Even better quality printing resulted from two major advances in printer technology: inkjet and laser. Inkjet printers have become increasingly popular because of their laser-like quality, low cost, and compact size. You also will find they are easy to install and use. There is, however, a standard setup process you must complete before you can use your new inkjet printer. But before setting up the printer, it's important to understand the differences of output quality between inkjet printers and other types of printers.

Comparing Printer Quality

Dot matrix printers use a series of pinpoints that push against an ink ribbon, similar to a typewriter hammer striking the ink ribbon to create an impression. Inkjet printers form an image by spraying ink through tiny jets onto the paper. Because only the ink touches the page in this process, the inkjet produces a sharper image

Skill 12

and makes much less noise when printing. Inkjets also can work with more fonts than a dot matrix. Because of its printing process, dot matrix printers are limited to only a few resident fonts, which can often appear amateurish. Inkjet printers can work with a variety of fonts and can produce clearer text and graphics at resolutions of 300 to 600 dots per inch (dpi) or better, which rivals the quality of laser printers.

Laser printers approach the quality of commercial offset printing. Professional print shops produce pages with text and graphics at resolutions of at least 720dpi. And most laser printers produce text and graphics at resolutions starting at 600dpi. Some high-end inkjet printers also can produce pages at resolutions that are as good, while less expensive inkjet printers usually produce pages with a standard output of 360dpi.

A major consideration is price. Laser printers can cost from about $400 to more than $2,000, while inkjets start at about $150. The printer you choose should be determined by the output quality you need. For all but the most demanding business needs, attach an inkjet printer to your computer, and you will get eye-pleasing printed pages at a great price. Before you can enjoy these state-of-the-art printing features, however, you must set up the printer properly to work with your computer. So roll up your sleeves and prepare yourself to get to work.

Preparing for Installation

Printers need little assembly before they are ready to be installed. Depending upon the model you choose, you may have to perform simple tasks such as inserting paper trays. You also will have to insert the ink cartridges after the printer is powered up the first time.

Before you start installing the printer, make sure all the required parts are in the box. These usually include the software disks, print cartridges, and the power cable. Manufacturers usually include a small startup booklet that tells you what parts should be in the box, a little bit about the printer, and how to set it up. Also look for a larger user's guide that acquaints you with all of the printer's features and maintenance needs.

Printers generally come packaged with their moveable parts restrained by tape, cardboard, or both. After unpacking the printer and its supplies, make sure you remove these restraints. Powering up the printer with these items still in place can damage the printer.

You also will need a special parallel printer cable. Many manufacturers do not include cables, so it's likely you will have to go out and buy them. If you are connecting the printer to a DOS or Windows computer, you will need either a standard parallel cable or the newer IEEE cable. Many older inkjet printer models still being sold use the standard parallel cable. But many newer models require the IEEE cable. The standard cable isn't bidirectional and can't handle the increased communication the latest inkjet printer models need. The standard parallel cable costs less than $10, and the IEEE cable sells for about three times that amount. Both of these have a wide connector that fits into the printer. Before heading to the store, make sure you consult the user's guide to find out exactly what kind of cables you will need.

The next step in preparing to install the printer is to find a good location for it. Ideally, you will be able to place the printer next to the computer. If not, place it as close to the computer as possible. What we said about printer cables and laser printers applies to inkjet printers as well. Printer cables are limited in how far they can carry data signals from the computer. Printer cables come in 3-foot and 10-foot lengths. Although printer cables can be linked together with a special coupler to increase the distance, this is not a good idea because the signal breaks down frequently when traveling more than 10 feet.

Putting the Pieces Together

So, you have the correct printer cables and have found the best place on your desk to put the printer. It's time to start connecting the pieces.

Start with getting power to the printer by plugging it in. We recommend plugging the printer into a wall socket rather than to a power strip. Inkjet printers have their own built-in shut-down procedure that is activated when the printer's power button is turned off. If the printer is plugged into a power strip, which is also used to turn off the monitor and computer simultaneously, the printer will lose power without shutting itself down first. This shut-down process involves returning the print cartridge to its storage location and clearing the printheads of excessive ink. To ensure that the printer isn't damaged when the power is unexpectedly shut off, plug the printer into a single socket power protector. This will provide protection against power surges without the inherent danger of accidentally bypassing the printer's on/off switch.

 NOTE   Don't be concerned with noises and motions the printer makes when it powers up or shuts down. It's just moving the printhead into position, priming the ink, and aligning the paper in the paper tray with the rollers.

When you've determined that the printer's power is working properly, turn it and the computer off. Now you're ready to connect the printer cables.

You will notice that the parallel printer cable will only fit into the parallel printer port socket on the computer's rear panel. Gently push the connector into the socket and pull the fasteners into place. Then connect the other end of the cable to the computer in a similar fashion.

Next, install the ink cartridges. Depending upon the printer model, there are three possible configurations. Some printers hold both the black and color ink cartridges in side-by-side cradles. Others take only one ink cartridge at a time. To print in black-and-white, insert the black cartridge, and to print in color, insert the color cartridge. The third configuration, which is not very common, uses five separate cartridges in five separate cradles.

Remove the cartridges from the foil wrapping. Then carefully peel off the tape that covers the metal contacts (see Figure 12.3). Make sure you don't touch the contacts because this can damage or ruin them. The cradle must be in the correct position to receive the cartridge. You will probably need to turn on the printer's power switch before installing the cartridge. The process varies slightly with each manufacturer, so check the user's guide for instructions.

After the cradle is ready, insert each ink cartridge so that the metal contacts line up with the metal receptors in the cradle (see Figure 12.4). When the ink cartridge is properly in place, return the cradle to its printing position. This usually means closing the cover; however, other steps may be required depending upon the printer. Refer to the user's guide for specific instructions on your particular printer.

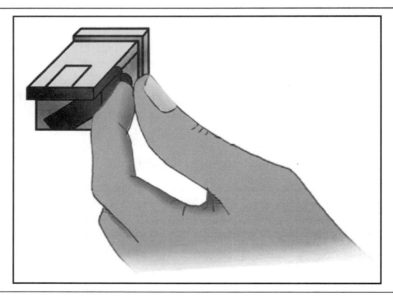

FIGURE 12.3: The protective tape that covers the printer cartridge must be removed before use.

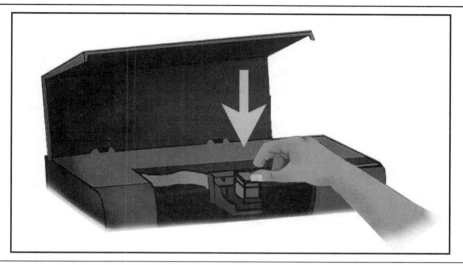

FIGURE 12.4:   Each ink cartridge is inserted into a cradle in the printer.

 **WARNING**   Do not force or slide the cradle manually as that will damage the mechanism.

When all the pieces are connected, it's time to install the software that will make them work together.

Software Setup

Locate the software package that came in the box with the printer. The software package will include the printer drivers needed to make the printer work with your applications, as well as special programs designed to maintain the printer, online help files, and troubleshooting guides that help you solve printing problems that may arise.

The procedure for installing the printer software varies depending upon the type of computer, operating system, and printer you use. Follow the procedures below that match your equipment. In all cases, you'll need to turn on the printer before starting the computer and installing the software.

Before you begin, turn off any utility programs on your computer, such as Norton Utilities, First-Aid, WinCheckIt, as well as any antivirus programs. These programs may interfere with the installation process.

Skill 12

Windows 95   When Windows 95 starts to load, the Plug-and-Play feature should detect the new printer and run the installation wizard. A screen will appear and ask you to confirm the printer port's location. Most likely there will only be one parallel port connector on the computer's rear panel, the port location is COM1. Another screen will ask you to confirm the printer's manufacturer and model. If Windows 95 doesn't list your new printer, it will ask for the manufacturer's installation diskette. Insert it in the diskette drive and click OK. Then click Finish and the installation will be completed.

If Plug and Play doesn't automatically start the installation process or you don't have the Plug-and-Play feature, you'll need to start the installation process yourself by doing the following:

1. Click Start and then Settings.

2. Select Printers from the Settings menu.

3. Double-click the Add Printer icon.

4. Click Next until you see a list of manufacturers and printer models.

5. Click the Have Disk button, insert Disk 1 into the computer's diskette drive, and follow the instructions on the computer's screen.

Windows 3.x   Because Windows 3.x does not have the Plug-and-Play feature, you will need to start the process manually by inserting Disk 1 into the computer's diskette drive. Then follow these steps:

1. From Program Manager's File menu, select Run.

2. In the Command Line box type the letter for your computer's diskette drive (usually **a:** or **b:**) followed by Setup (**a:\setup**).

3. Click OK and follow the instructions on the computer's screen.

4. Restart Windows 3.x at the end of the installation.

To Print or Not to Print

After all the cables are connected and all the software is installed, you'll want to test your new printer to make sure everything is working together properly. If you can't get the printer to print, go back and make sure your cables are all firmly plugged into the appropriate ports and that the software reflects those port selections. Also, make sure that the power is turned on, all the shipping tape and cardboard is removed from inside the printer and that there is paper loaded into the paper tray. If you still can't get it to work, you may have a problem with the drivers. (See the section that follows for tips on what to do when your drivers aren't working.)

Each time you print a document, there are some adjustments you will have to make depending upon what you are printing. If your printer only uses black ink, there are no other adjustments to make. However, if your printer has only one cartridge cradle that exchanges color and black ink cartridges, you must select which cartridge you want to use. You can print black with the color cartridge loaded, but the black quality isn't as sharp as it would be if it were produced from the black ink cartridge. That is because it is using a combination of all the colors to produce black.

If your printer has cradles for both black and color ink cartridges, there is nothing to select regardless of whether you print in black only or black and color. These dual-cartridge printers, however, need to have the print heads aligned each time you change them. This process provides a sharper output. Check your user's guide for instructions specific to your printer.

Many printer manufacturers include a set of utility programs in the software installation to align the ink cartridges and clean the inkjets if the output gets blurry. These utilities can be found in the printer folder on Windows 95 computers or in the printer's directory or program group on Windows 3.*x* computers. Run the appropriate utility and follow the directions on the screen.

After you get your new inkjet printer set up and working, you can add color and life to all your documents. And don't stop there. Experiment with some of the specialty papers to really make your documents flashy. Happy printing!

What to Do When the Printer Won't Print

Having a little trouble printing documents? Don't panic. When it comes to printers, the situation is simple. There are only two possible solutions: the easy ones and the expensive ones. This section will help you determine which is which.

There are three types of printers commonly used with home computers: dot matrix, inkjet, and laser. Regardless of the printer type, there are only three types of problems that you're likely to experience:

- It won't print at all.

- It prints—but badly.

- It prints correctly—but it's printing the wrong thing.

The "it won't print at all" class of problems has common roots, so we'll look at this one first. For the others, we'll look at the causes (and solutions) separately.

Common Problems

It won't print. In fact, it looks dead. No lights, no activity. For this problem, there are two easy solutions and one expensive one.

Easy Solution #1   Check the power cord at both ends. It might have been pulled out of the wall when you vacuumed last week, or the end that plugs into the printer might have come loose. If it did, plug it back in. If this is a new installation, make sure you didn't plug it into a power outlet that's connected to a wall switch. If the outlet is mounted upside down (the ground plug or "third prong" is at the top), it's a switched outlet.

Easy Solution #2   It might be a blown fuse on the power supply. All dot matrix printers have fuses, and on most printers, the fuse is located next to the power cord under a small black cap that you turn slightly and then pull off. If it is the fuse (you'll see a melted piece of metal inside), replace it with the exact same fuse type. Radio Shack and your corner electronics store will have them.

If there is no fuse cover, the fuse is inside the case. Now you need to make a decision. It's not hard to open the case and check the fuse, but there are a couple of things you need to know first.

 **WARNING**   There are things inside the case that can kill you, even when the printer is unplugged.

The power supply has devices called capacitors that can store thousands of volts of electricity for hours after the printer has been unplugged. If you don't know what a capacitor is and can't recognize one by sight, don't open the case. Take the printer to the local repair shop or send it to the factory for warranty repairs. Don't be a hero for a $40 repair job or a $2 fuse.

The Expensive Solution   You replaced the fuse, and it's still dead. That means the power supply has died. If it's a dot matrix printer that's no longer under warranty, give it a decent burial because it's probably going to be cheaper to buy a new printer than to have this one repaired. You can confirm that by calling the repair shop and asking how much it would cost to have a new power supply installed on your printer. Most repair shops charge $30 to $50 to diagnose problems, and with new dot matrix printers costing $200 or less, that usually isn't a worthwhile investment.

If it's an inkjet or laser printer, you'll want to take it to a repair shop. Power supplies are expensive, but these are nowhere near as expensive as replacing the printer. Another option is to mail it to the factory repair center, but some of these printers are quite heavy and the freight will cost you a bundle. It's much better to find a local source for repair.

The Dot Matrix Dumps

Dot matrix printers are the simplest printers and the ones most likely to break down because they have more moving parts than other printer types, and they're often made more inexpensively. The good news is that many of these problems can be solved easily or inexpensively on your own.

Dot Matrix Problem #1   It works, but the printouts are either too light or really dark and smeared.

The problem's the ribbon. If the printout is too light, replace the ribbon. If it's still too light, there's a lever on the left side of the printhead that adjusts the distance between the printhead and the ribbon; push that lever towards the ribbon. If the printout is dark and smeared, check that the ribbon is installed properly, and that the printhead distance lever is pulled out at least part of the way.

Dot Matrix Problem #2   It works, but there's a white line that runs through each line of print.

This one is easy to diagnose. One of the print wires has either burned out or become jammed. There are three possible solutions; before you try any of them, unplug the printer. First, dip a cotton swab in rubbing alcohol. Rub the swab gently across the front of the printhead where the wires emerge. Don't rub too hard, or you'll get cotton in the printhead and jam other wires.

If that doesn't work, get a spray can of WD-40, and spray the printhead. Wait five minutes, then turn on the printer and try to print. If neither of these actions work, you need a new printhead. Printheads cost $50 or less (typically $30) and you can install them yourself in 15 minutes with a Phillips-head screwdriver.

Dot Matrix Problem #3   It prints, but the output looks like gobbledygook.

There are three possible causes here. First, your software is incorrectly configured, and you're sending commands for a different kind of printer. Your printer sees these commands, tries valiantly to comply, but ends up confused and spouts nonsense.

Skill 12

Verify the program settings. For Windows, use Control Panel's Printers icon to verify that the default printer is the right type. If not, click Install, and install the correct printer driver (software that lets your computer communicate with the printer). You'll need your Windows installation diskettes to do this.

Second, if the printer settings are correct and the problem still exists, you need to ensure that the printer thinks it's the right kind of printer—many dot matrix printers can emulate other printer types. Check your printer manual to learn how to verify and/or change this setting.

Finally, if you've done all of the above and the problem persists, the printer's logic board is the source. Again, if the printer's warranty has expired, observe a minute of silent respect for the newly departed, then go buy a new printer. The cost of repair will outweigh the cost of a new printer.

Icky Inkjets

Inkjet printers have one slight advantage over dot matrix printers: There are fewer moving parts, so it's often easier to diagnose problems. However, there are fewer things that you can fix yourself.

Inkjet Problem #1   The print is too light, too dark, or too smeary.

Inkjet printers don't have adjustment levers, so we're going to have to solve this one with our brains. First, have the printer clean itself. All inkjets have a cleaning cycle, and there's a Clean button on the control panel. They're supposed to clean themselves, but, as with little children, they sometimes forget.

If that doesn't work, you'll need to grab the printer manual. There's a setup program built into the printer, and it can be used to increase or decrease the print density. If output is too light, increase the density; if it's too dark or smears, decrease it.

If that has no affect, there are two other tricks. Smearing can be caused by using cheap paper; try printing the same document using good letterhead paper or high-quality bond. If that solves the problem, toss the old paper and buy some good stock. If it doesn't solve the problem, try a new ink cartridge. The cartridge includes the printhead, so you're really replacing the entire front end. This often solves the problem quite nicely.

Inkjet Problem #2   It prints, but there are parts missing and it looks splotched.

Try putting the printer through a cleaning cycle. If that doesn't work, replace the ink cartridge. That should solve it.

Inkjet Problem #3   It prints, but it seems to be printing in Martian.

Double- and triple-check the printer configuration in your software. Inkjet printers are not known for logic board insanity, so misconfiguration is almost certainly the problem. If the printer settings are correct and the printer is still speaking a language never heard on Earth, take the printer to your local repair shop. Since inkjet printers are (comparatively) expensive, a $200 repair job does make sense in this case.

Laser Lunacy

Laser printers are fairly complex devices, but there are only a few simple things that you can do to correct problems. Luckily, those few simple things cover about 80 percent of the possible problems, so let's see what we can do. By the way, they're called laser printers for a reason; LASER is actually an acronym for Light Amplification by Simulated Emission of Radiation. The key word is Simulated. It does get hot inside a laser printer, but only in terms of temperature. You can leave the lead gloves for handling Aunt Martha's meatloaf.

Laser Problem #1   The output's too light or too dark, but there isn't any smearing.

If your printer uses a cartridge that includes the drum and toner in a single unit (all Hewlett-Packard LaserJet printers, Canon Laser printers, and some others, but not Panasonic laser printers), try the following step first. Open the printer, remove the drum/toner unit, and shake it gently from side to side to redistribute the toner inside the cartridge. Don't do this over a bare floor or carpet because some toner will fall out; spread some old newspapers regardless of the floor type (unless you really enjoy vacuuming).

Replace the unit, wait for it to warm up, and try printing again. If this had little or no effect, try adjusting the print density. On some printers, this is a knob or slide lever inside the printer case; on others, it's a software setting that you change from the front panel. Check your printer manual for details.

If this doesn't work, put in a fresh drum/toner unit. That should fix the problem because you've just replaced the "heart" of the printer.

Laser Problem #2   Printouts are smeary or streaky.

There are a couple of possible causes for this problem. First, check the corona wires. Inside the printer case along the paper path is a set of very fine wires, usually right in the middle. These wires are extremely hot if the computer has been running, so don't touch them. Grab some cotton swabs and run them gently along each wire. This should dislodge any debris clinging to the wires.

If that doesn't work, the drum is probably used up. Regardless of the printer type, try replacing the drum unit. This solves about 90 percent of problems, and you should keep your fingers crossed that it will solve yours. If it doesn't, that means the fuser unit is bad, which means a trip to the repair shop and a $300 to $400 bill.

Laser Problem #3   It prints, but you get Error #20 and the documents print out messy after that happens.

For some reason, almost every laser printer manufacturer uses error #20 to mean the same thing: out of memory. Laser printers must be able to hold the image of an entire page in their onboard memory before the printing process starts, and the page image your program just sent was too big to fit into the printer's memory in a single gulp.

There are two easy ways to fix this problem. The cheapest one is to change your printer settings to a lower resolution. Default resolution for most programs and for Windows is 300 dots per inch (dpi), but you can reduce that to 150 dpi or even 75 dpi if you don't want really sharp printed images. Most people can't see the difference between 200 dpi and 150 dpi when two pages are laid next to each other, but cutting the resolution to 150 dpi cuts the printer memory requirement in half.

The other solution is to add memory to the printer. Almost all laser printers can have 2MB, 4MB, or more of internal memory. Some (such as the Hewlett-Packard LaserJet 4) can use standard single in-line memory modules (SIMMs) to upgrade your PC. (SIMMs are small circuit boards that accommodate memory chips while occupying less space on the motherboard.)

Laser Problem #4   It prints garbage.

Are you thinking driver mismatch? Good—that's almost certainly the case. With laser printers, there's one more thing to watch out for. There are two different languages that computers use to talk to laser printers: PCL and Postscript. Often, your program produces one when the printer expects the other, and interesting things happen. If the garbage looks like...well, garbage... you probably have a Postscript printer that's receiving a PCL printout. If the garbage looks like programming code, you have a PCL printer that's getting Postscript output.

Go into the program's printer settings or Control Panel, make the necessary correction, and that should solve it.

There are many other problems that can occur, but the ones we've discussed are the most common. Always keep your printer's manual handy; it can be your friend in times of crisis. Virtually all manuals have a "troubleshooting" section that lists the common problems for your printer type and tells you what to do about most of them.

Are You Experienced?

Now you can. . .

- ☑ understand the basics of printer functions
- ☑ install an inkjet printer and print in color and black and white
- ☑ install a laser printer and keep it running
- ☑ troubleshoot printer problems by decoding error messages and adjusting hardware

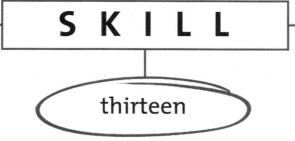

SKILL

thirteen

13

Installing a Scanner

- ❑ Evaluating the different types of scanners
- ❑ Understanding optical character recognition (OCR)
- ❑ Installing your scanner

Optical scanners let users enter entire documents into their computers with little effort. A scanner passes a light beam over a document and picks up patterns of light and dark, or color, by the amount of light reflected or absorbed by the page. It then converts the patterns into digital form and enters them into the computer. Once a document has been scanned into the computer, it can be printed, sent by fax or e-mail, or edited in a word processor.

Types of Scanners

There are three basic types of scanners: flatbed, sheetfed, and photo. *Flatbed scanners* look like miniature photocopiers—you place a document on a glass panel and close a hinged lid before beginning the scanning process, repeating the process for each page you need to scan (see Figure 13.1). Some flatbed scanners have optional attachments that automatically feed the sheets through the scanner for you.

The price and size of flatbed scanners make them impractical for many home users. Prices start at about $200. A compact flatbed scanner is 12 inches wide and 17.5 inches deep; regular-size flatbed scanners start at 15 inches by 22 inches.

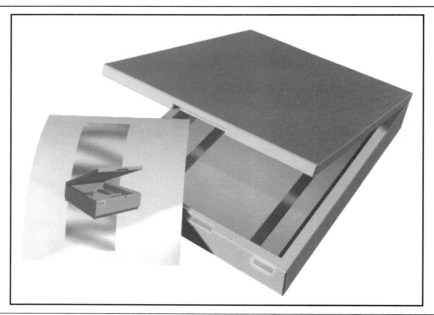

FIGURE 13.1: Flatbed scanners resemble photocopiers.

Sheetfed scanners, as their name implies, take in documents and pass them through the scanning mechanism. These scanners, which usually cost between $200 and $399, take up considerably less space than flatbed scanners, making them much more practical for use in homes and small offices. For example, the sheetfed scanner we installed measured only 3 inches by 12.5 inches, taking up only slightly more space than a three-hole paper punch would.

Photo scanners have only recently emerged on the market. Photo scanners provide less image for the buck when compared to other scanner models that scan text as well as graphics. But if your needs dictate a lot of image scanning and not much text scanning, they provide great quality without taking up half your desk. You might even find photo scanners, which are only about the size of a Polaroid camera, built into some new computers.

Only time will tell whether these unique scanners will survive in the scanning world. Their specialized—and limited—abilities make them the perfect scanner for users who are only interested in digitizing pictures.

SCANNING ON A SMALL SCALE

Handheld scanners usually cost between $70 and $150, but they can only scan part of a page at a time. These are best used for scanning small images, such as logos, clip art, business cards, and signatures. Most handheld scanners cover a width of 3 to 4 inches at a time, and come with stitching software that digitally rejoins the columns to re-create the full page on the computer. Handheld scanners work well enough, but are inconvenient for users who need to scan large volumes of full-page material.

There's a subcategory of handheld scanners, called *pen scanners,* that scan one line of text at a time. They're used like a highlighter pen, moving across the text—just as you would read it—to enter it into your computer. These scanners are best for people who need to scan individual lines of text, perhaps to enter direct quotes from other printed material into an article or paper.

OCR: Translating the Image

When you scan a block of text, what is actually stored in your computer is an image of the text, not the text itself. This image is a graphic that is not recognized by the computer as text, and therefore it can't be edited the way regular text can. Optical character recognition (OCR) is the process that takes the scanned image and translates it into text that can be used and edited in word-processing applications. It's also the name of a category of software that performs this image-to-text translation. OCR software, which is included with scanners, has evolved from older versions that only recognized one font, to today's versions that recognize most common fonts with a high degree of accuracy.

In a few cases, handwriting is recognized by the software, although it usually only works in a very limited context. Handwriting recognition is not nearly as accurate as recognition of fonts, but industry experts expect that one day OCR software will be able to scan any handwritten document into a word processor, where it can be edited.

If the OCR software package that comes with your scanner fails to meet your needs—for example, if it doesn't support the format you need for entering data from scanned material into a certain program—don't despair. You're sure to get a custom fit from one of the many OCR software packages available.

Installing Your Scanner

Once you've made your scanner purchase, the hardest part is over. Scanner installations usually are fairly simple. The process may vary slightly from one scanner to another, but all three types follow the same basic process.

 NOTE The instructions provided here are meant to illustrate the installation process; they do not replace the directions that come with your scanner. Manufacturers' instructions may vary from ours. Use this section as a guide to clarify anything that is confusing in your manual.

Before beginning make sure you've read and understood Skill 3. Although some scanners won't require you to install any parts inside your computer's case—which means you won't need to remove the computer's cover—you should still turn off your computer before beginning the installation process.

Next you should read the documentation included with your scanner. There should be a packing list, either in the owner's manual or on a separate sheet of paper. Check to be sure you have all of the necessary parts. If you are missing anything, call the manufacturer or the store where you purchased the scanner to obtain the missing part. Carefully read through the installation instructions in the owner's manual to familiarize yourself with the process before beginning. These instructions will clarify whether you need to work inside the computer during installation.

Then clear a space on your desk for your scanner. The manual or box should list the dimensions of the scanner you've purchased. Make sure the scanner has plenty of room around it. If it's a sheetfed version that ejects the paper to the front or side of the device after scanning is completed, be sure there's enough room for those papers. Also make sure that the necessary cords will reach from the scanner to the computer and the power source.

NOTE If your scanner doesn't require the installation of a scanner controller board inside the computer case, skip to "Plugging into the Serial Port" now.

If your scanner requires the installation of a scanner controller board, install it now. Follow the instructions in Skill 3 for removing the computer cover and grounding yourself before proceeding. Then follow these steps to install the scanner controller board:

1. Once you have the computer open, choose an empty expansion slot for the board. Remove the expansion slot cover. Hang on to the screw that attached the slot cover to your computer. You'll need it to secure the scanner controller board in the expansion slot.

2. Carefully remove the controller board from its antistatic bag. To prevent damage to the board, hold it by the edges, and avoid touching the board's components.

3. Locate the jumpers (small pins, some covered with a plastic block) on the controller board. They will be set to the default address setting. If this setting is being used by another board in your computer, you'll need to change the setting on the scanner board before installing it. The setting is changed by moving the plastic block so that it covers different pins. Instructions on how to change the board to different settings will be included in your scanner's manual.

4. Insert the board into the expansion slot, making sure that the gold-striped edge at the bottom of the board is firmly seated in the slot (see Figure 13.2). Use the screw that held the expansion slot cover in place to secure the board in the slot.

5. Plug the scanner cable into the port on the back of the controller board (see Figure 13.3). It should only fit in the port one way. Many cables have an arrow or other mark to show you which side is the top.

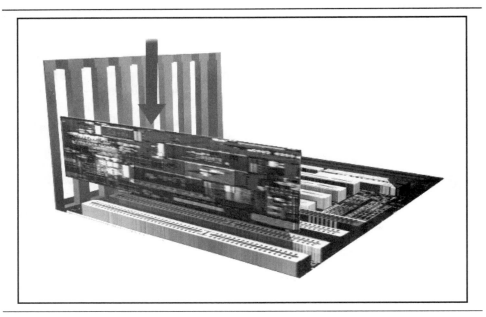

FIGURE 13.2:   The scanner controller board fits snugly into the expansion slot.

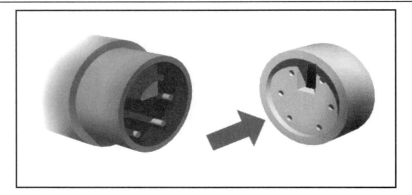

FIGURE 13.3:   The scanner cable fits into the port on the back of the controller board.

6. Replace the computer's cover and plug in the computer, but don't turn it on. Skip to "Taking Care of Power and Security" now.

Plugging into the Serial Port

Plug the PC end of the scanner cable (the end with a serial connector) into an empty serial port. Most serial ports have 9-pin connectors, and the scanner is likely to have a cable that is ready to attach to a 9-pin serial port. However, some serial ports have 25-pin connectors (see Figure 13.4) and will need an adapter to accommodate a 9-pin serial cable. The sheetfed scanner we installed came with an adapter. If you need it, attach the adapter to the scanner cable, and then to the serial port. The pins in the connector (either on the cable or the adapter) and the holes in the port will only fit together one way. Press the connector firmly into the port. You shouldn't have to force them together. If they don't join easily, examine them to be sure you have them aligned properly. Most cable connectors for serial ports have thumbscrews to secure the connection between the cable and the computer. If your scanner's cable is equipped with them, tighten them after you've pushed the connector and the port together. Most thumbscrews can be turned by hand, but a few may require a small screwdriver.

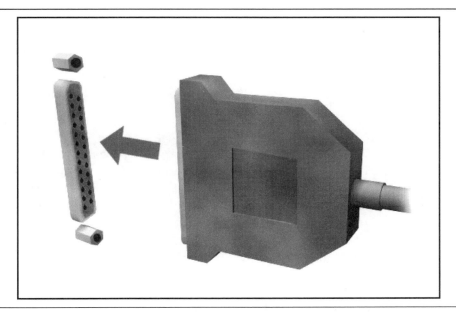

FIGURE 13.4:   A serial port with 25-pin connector requires an adapter.

Taking Care of Power and Security

If the other end of the cable isn't already attached to your scanner, plug it into the port on the back of the scanner. There probably is only one way it will fit. If it doesn't attach easily, you may be trying to insert it incorrectly. Don't force the connector into the port. Take it out, and check to be certain it's aligned properly.

Some scanners need to be plugged into a power source, while others only plug into the computer. If your scanner has a power adapter, plug the power adapter's cable into the power jack on the scanner, and then plug the power adapter into a power source. Listen for a slight hum, indicating that the scanner is receiving power. Some scanners have power buttons; some sheetfed models start automatically when a page is inserted into the scanner.

 NOTE As with all of your computer equipment, it is best to plug your scanner into a surge protector rather than into an unprotected outlet. Surge protectors won't prevent damage from lightning, but they can prevent harm from minor power surges.

Some scanners have security connectors that lock them down to your desk with a steel cable. Ordinarily, one end of the cable (usually purchased separately) locks into the connector on the scanner, and the cable wraps around a desk leg or other immovable object so the scanner can't be removed.

Installing the Software

Once you have the scanner set up, you'll probably need to install some software. Turn on your computer, and insert the software into the drive. The software should include a setup program that installs all the necessary files to your hard drive. During the setup process, you'll likely need the scanner's serial number. To begin the setup process in Windows 3.*x*, open the Program Manager File menu, choose Run, type the setup command, which will be something such as **a:\setup** or **a:\install** (check the manual), and click OK. To begin the setup process in Windows 95, click Start, choose Run from the list of commands, type the setup command in the Command Line box, and click OK. From there, the setup process takes over.

 NOTE The exact procedure you should follow will be listed in your scanner's manual and possibly on the setup diskette(s) or CD-ROM.

Skill 13

Testing the Scanner

Once you've installed the software, it's a good idea to test the scanner to be sure everything works correctly. Following your scanner's instructions, scan a test page into your computer. Some scanners come with a test page or calibration card that you may have been directed to scan at some point during the software installation. If your scanner doesn't include one, use any document you have handy. You may want to test it with text and graphics—and with color if it is a color scanner—just to see how it performs each task.

After you've scanned a document for the first time, play around with the different features of your OCR software to see all the things you can do with the digital version of the document.

Once you have the scanner up and running, you're ready to start using it for all kinds of projects. Scan in that photo you've been wanting to e-mail to your sister. Scan in the diagram that will make tomorrow's presentation to your boss just perfect. Just don't admit how easy it was, or how much fun you had doing it.

Are You Experienced?

Now you can. . .

☑ evaluate the different types of scanners and what they have to offer

☑ understand how scanners work through the use of optical character recognition (OCR)

☑ install a scanner and get it up and running

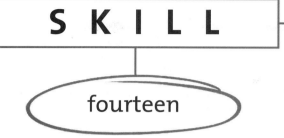

SKILL

fourteen

Installing Serial and Parallel Ports

- ❏ Assessing your need for additional ports

- ❏ Assigning addresses to your ports

- ❏ Putting your ports to optimal use

- ❏ Installing an I/O card

If you've ever installed additional hardware to your computer—or if you've completed some of the installations outlined in this book—you've probably run across instructions that require you to plug the device into one of the ports on the back of your computer case.

But what happens when you have more peripherals than ports? Most computers come with only a few ports for devices such as mice, modems, and printers. But, when you want to add another device, maybe a second printer or a scanner, you can find yourself left holding the plug.

You can add a few more ports to your computer for about $50 to $100 each. We installed the I/OAT55 Serial/Parallel Adapter card by Boca Research Inc. and will be using it as an example to demonstrate the basic steps most cards require.

 **NOTE**   If you purchase an I/O card from a vendor other than Boca, you may have to install additional software or complete steps other than those detailed here. Be sure to consult the installation manual before you begin.

Before You Buy

Before making a trip to the computer store to purchase an I/O (input/output) card, take a minute to determine which kind of ports you need.

Ports come in all shapes and sizes. Usually your computer will come equipped with one *parallel port*. Parallel ports commonly feature 25 holes, let data flow through the cable at a high speed, and often are referred to as LPT1 or LPT2. Most often, they are used by peripherals such as printers.

Your computer probably will offer two other ports. These *serial ports* may feature nine pins or 25 pins. Commonly referred to as COM1, COM2, (and, in DOS 3.3 and newer, COM3 and COM4) these ports connect input devices that operate at slower speeds, such as mice and modems, to the computer, although most computers now include special round PS/2 ports designed especially for mice.

Which of these ports do you need? That depends upon what you want to connect to your computer. Maybe you have an external modem or a scanner that requires a serial port or an additional printer that requires a parallel port.

The peripherals you will be using determine which port combination you want. Perhaps you want an expansion card with one parallel port and two serial ports (as we will be using here). Or, perhaps you just want one of each. I/O cards are available with a variety of combinations.

Addressing New Ports

After you have determined the kind of port you need, the next step is to determine if the computer has the room to address that port.

All your hardware devices are connected to your microprocessor through wires called interrupt request lines (IRQs), which let a hardware device request its share of attention from the microprocessor. All hardware devices are assigned I/O addresses, which let the microprocessor determine where devices are located.

But your computer only has a limited number of these settings. On top of that, the serial and parallel ports can only use specific IRQ lines and I/O addresses. So before you can add more ports, you need to be certain there will be locations available to accommodate them.

The Microsoft Diagnostics (MSD) program, found in Windows 3.1 and MS-DOS 6.0 and later, is one way to learn which ports your computer is using. (For more information about Microsoft Diagnostics, see Skill 2, *Using MSD to Learn about Your PC*.) Type **msd** at the DOS prompt (make sure you have completely exited Windows first), and press ↵.

When the program opens, select the LPT Ports button and/or the COM Ports button to determine which serial and parallel ports are being used. Then select the IRQ Status button to find out which addresses are already occupied.

 **WARNING**   Although you may not have any devices plugged into the serial ports on the outside of your computer, that does not mean the COM ports are idle. Some devices, such as your modem, may use internal connections.

A Little Give and Take

As we stated earlier, your serial and parallel ports operate at specific IRQ addresses. Refer to Table 14.1 to determine which ports generally correspond to which I/O and IRQ addresses.

By default, your computer is aware of which COM ports and LPT ports correspond to which IRQ addresses. There are times, however, when you can change and tinker with these settings if you want to add more ports. For instance, two peripherals occasionally can share an LPT port, and two LPT ports can share one IRQ address, especially if the peripherals are two printers you won't use at the same time.

However, it's not a good idea for devices to share a COM port or an IRQ address. (In Table 14.1, COM1 and COM3, as well as COM2 and COM4, share the same IRQ

TABLE 14.1: Port Types and Their Corresponding Addresses

Port Type	I/O Address	IRQ Address
COM1	03F8	IRQ4
COM2	02F8	IRQ3
COM3	03E8	IRQ4
COM4	02E8	IRQ3
LPT1	0378	IRQ7
LPT2	0278	IRQ5

address.) You don't want your mouse on COM1 with an address of IRQ4 and your modem on COM3 with the same IRQ address. Your mouse is almost always communicating with your computer, and it could confuse your system if you tried to dial up an online service while you were using your mouse.

Does this mean you can never use COM3 and COM4 if you plan to use COM1 and COM2? Not necessarily. If your port and your software are flexible, and if you are willing to do a little give and take—such as giving up a second LPT port—you can use one of those extras. Read the I/O card's box or the installation instructions. If they indicate that the jumpers (more about these later) can be set to IRQ3, 4, 5, or 7, you are almost there. Then check the software that operates the hardware.

For instance, if you plan to operate a modem on COM3 via IRQ5, check your communications software or your online service software. Most let you determine which port to use, but do they also let you determine the IRQ setting? If so, then you are in business. Or, is the software a Windows-based program? When you set the port and IRQ settings in the Port application in the Windows Control Panel, the Port application ensures all Windows programs will use the correct settings.

I/O Installation

Now you are ready to roll up your sleeves and get started. You will need a screwdriver, the instruction manual, the I/O card, and the extra serial port assembly (if applicable).

Configuring IRQs and COMs

Configure the Boca card, and tell it and the computer which ports and addresses they will be using by setting jumpers, which control the way the card operates. Jumpers are little metal pins, mounted side by side on the circuit board. Settings are changed by moving a little plastic block that contains tiny electrical connectors over specific pins. This is probably the most difficult part of the installation.

On our circuit board, there are three lines of jumper pins, each with two plastic blocks (see Figure 14.1). The top line controls the parallel port while the bottom two control Serial port A (which is the port on the main I/O card) and Serial port B (the additional port assembly that connects to the main card through a cable). Tackle the parallel port first. The left three pins control which LPT port is best to use: LPT1 at 0378 or LPT2 at 0278. Make sure the parallel port you choose is not already being used and that you use the corresponding I/O address.

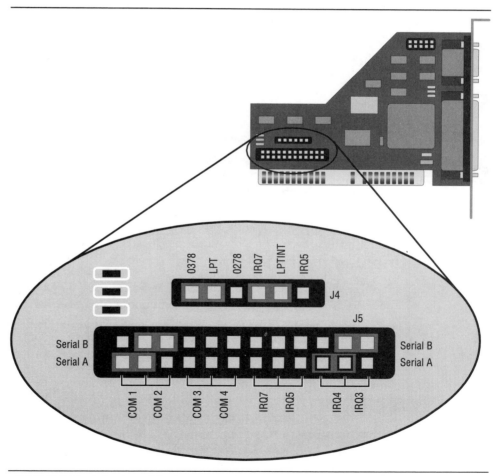

FIGURE 14.1:   The jumpers are set to use LPT1 at IRQ7 in the first line of pins. Serial A will use COM1 at IRQ4 and Serial B will use COM2 at IRQ3.

Place the plastic block over the pins labeled *0378* and *LPT* to select LPT1, or over the pins labeled *0278* and *LPT* to select LPT2 (the pins are next to each other). Set the second plastic block in the corresponding IRQ setting: over *IRQ7* and *LPTINT* for LPT1, or over *IRQ5* and *LPTINT* for LPT2. When removing a plastic block, pull straight up from the card. To insert a block, line up the holes in the block with the pins, and push down until the bottom of the block is flush with the base of the pins. Now move on to the serial port settings.

 NOTE We set our COM ports to COM1 and COM2 as an example. Your system may already be using these port settings. Be sure to check which ports are available and adjust your jumper settings accordingly.

The six pins on the left of both serial lines control the COM ports, and the six pins on the right control the IRQ settings. It's not hard to set up these jumpers because each of the settings is labeled. For example, we wanted to set Serial A on COM1 at IRQ4 (see Figure 14.1). So we set the first block over the first and second pins to the left (labeled COM1) and the second block over the 10th and 11th pins (labeled IRQ4). Then we set Serial B on COM2 at IRQ3. The first block went over the second and third pins to the left (labeled COM2) while the second block went over the last two pins to the right (labeled IRQ3).

If you don't want to use Serial B at this time, you can disable the port so the system won't recognize it. Disabling a port is as simple as removing the plastic blocks from the Serial B line of pins.

Unplugging the System

Unplug the system and the monitor from the electrical outlets, then disconnect the monitor from the computer. Move the monitor out of your way, and remove the cover from the computer case. You may need a Phillips screwdriver to remove screws from along the edge of the case, or you may have to unclasp hooks to slide the top off. See the information on working inside your computer in Skill 3 before you proceed with the rest of this installation.

Opening It Up

Locate the expansion openings at the back of the computer. You will need to remove one, or two (if you are adding all three ports), metal expansion slot covers. It's best to choose a slot consecutive to other expansion cards. This will make it easier for you to add more expansion cards in the future and avoid being "wedged in."

To remove the slot covers, you may need to remove the screws holding these covers in place (see Figure 14.2). If necessary, gently move aside any cables, cords, or even the power supply to access the screws. Put the screws aside for safekeeping, and slide out the metal covers.

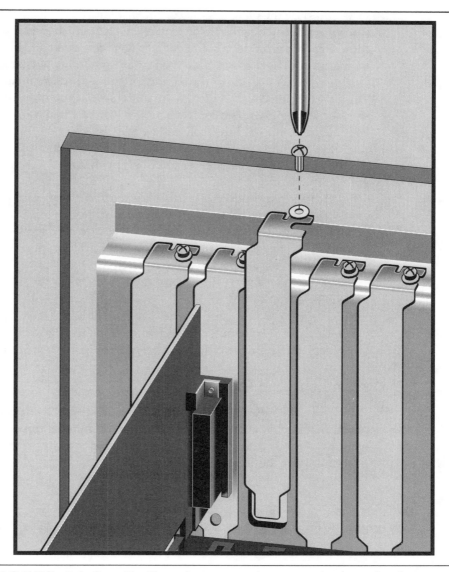

FIGURE 14.2:   You'll need to remove the screws that keep the slot covers in place.

Installing the Card

Remove the expansion card from its antistatic bag. The back of the expansion card has a metal plate that will slip into the place of the metal slot cover that you have just removed.

As you slide the plate into place, you also must slide the edge of the card (the side with gold etchings) into an expansion slot, which is a long socket inside your computer that provides a connection to your computer's main circuit board, the motherboard. The slots will be located either on the bottom (so the cards are installed vertically) or on the side of the computer (so the cards are installed horizontally). The gold etchings on the side line up with metal contacts inside the expansion slot (see Figure 14.3). The contacts, in turn, connect to pins on the motherboard and tell the computer how it should be addressed.

It may take some pressure to get the card into the slot. If you have trouble, push one side of the card in at a time, and don't push too hard. It will go in eventually with a little effort.

If you are adding both serial ports, slide the additional metal plate into another empty opening at the back of your computer. Although this add-on does not require you to install anything in an expansion slot, you do need to plug the interface cable that runs from this port into a plug on the I/O card. This plug is located in the corner diagonal to the jumpers (see Figure 14.4).

Using the screws you removed from the metal plate covers, screw the new plate(s) tightly in place.

Replace any cords or components you may have moved to get to the expansion cards. Replace the computer's cover, and clasp any hooks or secure any screws you removed. Reconnect your monitor, and plug in everything.

Getting Up and Running

Reboot your computer. At the DOS prompt, restart MSD or Boca's Com-Check program. Check that you have the appropriate number of ports. If you often work in Windows, go into the Ports application and make sure your new COM ports are using the correct settings.

If these new settings don't appear, turn everything off, reopen your system, and check that you have set the jumpers correctly.

If you've configured your system to use COM3 or COM4 and the settings don't appear, your system may be unable to recognize any ports past COM2. This happens occasionally in some name-brand computers.

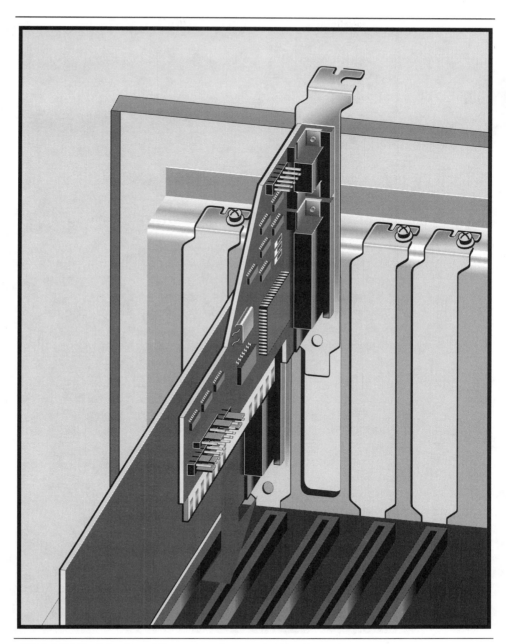

FIGURE 14.3:   The expansion card slides into place.

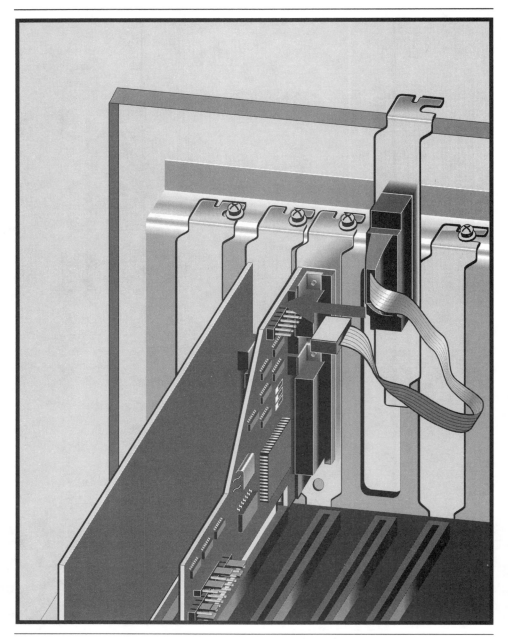

FIGURE 14.4: The interface cable runs from the second serial port to a plug on the I/O card.

The BIOSs these systems use try to avoid conflicts by not recognizing these ports. (The BIOS is a set of routines that work with a computer's hardware to support data transfers between various elements of a system.) If this is the case, you may want to use the free fix-it utility called DOSPORTS.EXE that Boca offers on its bulletin board system that lets your computer see the additional ports by adding another line to your AUTOEXEC.BAT file.

There's Nothing to It

The actual installation of Boca's I/OAT55 Serial/Parallel adapter was a snap, although initially it was difficult to figure out how to set the jumpers and to push the expansion card into the slot. In fact, the whole installation probably will take you no more than 15 to 30 minutes.

Installing ports is worth the time, effort, and money when you consider all the different kinds of new hardware you can add to your computer. It's also a handy process to know if you plan to add faster ports for faster modems or other more advanced devices.

Are You Experienced?

Now you can. . .

- ☑ **determine whether you need additional ports depending on what you plan to connect to your computer**
- ☑ **assign addresses to your ports without causing conflicts between devices**
- ☑ **take advantage of the most your COM ports have to offer by choosing the best settings**
- ☑ **install an I/O card from start to finish**

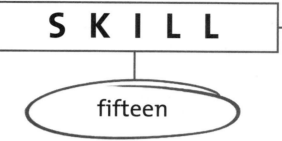

S K I L L

fifteen

15

Installing a Motherboard

- ❏ Understanding what can be upgraded
- ❏ Considering the pros and cons of an upgrade
- ❏ Installing a motherboard
- ❏ Testing and troubleshooting a motherboard

Just because a computer manufacturer claims its PC is "upgradeable" doesn't mean that all of its parts can be swapped out for more advanced models. Upgradeability can suggest a lot of things. Does it mean the processor can be changed, or is it implying that the PC simply has plenty of expansion slots?

With improved sound, video, and three-dimensional effects making their way into many new software titles, computers need a boost to keep up with the times, and just adding more RAM may not be the answer. Upgrading may involve changing more complicated components, such as cache or a system's BIOS.

Confusing matters is the fact that there aren't any set rules for motherboard design. Not only are components in different locations on the motherboard, but some manufacturers allow components to be removed easily while others solder the components right into the board. These soldered components can be dislodged only with a soldering iron.

Candidates for an Upgrade

Unless you look under the hood of a new computer, you take a gamble on what can be updated. Table 15.1 shows that the checklist of common upgradeable features varies, depending upon the computer manufacturer and the type of motherboard.

TABLE 15.1: On the Board or Upgradeable? If the component can be changed, its original type is listed.

Company	Microprocessor	RAM	L2 Cache	Graphics Card	Sound Card	BIOS
Acer	Intel	EDO	on motherboard	on motherboard	on motherboard	flash
Apple	Power PC RISC	EDO	512 KB on board 256 KB upgradeable	on motherboard	on motherboard	masked ROM
AST	Advantage: Intel; Adventure; Intel, AMD, and Cyrix	Advantage: EDO; Adventure: DIMMs and EDO	on motherboard	on motherboard	on motherboard	flash
Compaq	Intel, except Cyrix on 2000 models	EDO, except on 4000 and 8000 models	upgradeable, except 2000 models	separate, except 2000 models, 3000 N/A	separate, except 2000 and 3000 models	flash
Hewlett-Packard	Intel	EDO	on motherboard	on motherboard	on motherboard	flash
IBM	Intel	SDRAM	upgradeable	on motherboard	on motherboard	flash
Sony	Intel	EDO	on motherboard	on motherboard	on motherboard	flash
Toshiba	Intel	EDO	on motherboard	on motherboard	on motherboard	flash

The Mighty Microprocessor

When most computer manufacturers indicate that their PCs are upgradeable, the microprocessor is one of the first components on the upgrade list. "Upgradeable" chips usually reside in Zero Insertion Force (ZIF) sockets on the motherboard. These sockets include little levers that you use to quickly remove the old chips and insert the new ones. Without a ZIF socket, you may have to pry out the chip on your own. But most new computer owners don't have to worry about this; their new PCs should include ZIF sockets, which help prevent pins from breaking off the chips when removed. Very few systems actually solder the chip right into the motherboard (see Figure 15.1).

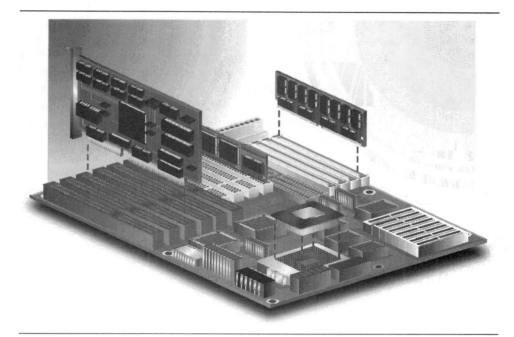

FIGURE 15.1:   Most computer manufacturers try to make their products upgradeable.

Just because you can remove your old chip doesn't mean you can replace it with a new Pentium processor, however. First of all, there are voltage issues to consider. When microprocessor manufacturers, such as Intel, improve chips and make them smaller, they often reduce the amount of volts the chips require to operate, says David Pistone, technical marketing manager at Intel. You can't replace a 486 microprocessor running on 5 volts with a Pentium processor operating at 3.3 volts. You need to use a chip replacement designed to overcome this hurdle, perhaps one equipped with a voltage regulator to take the 5 volts from the system and change it to the 3.3 volts the new chip can handle.

"If (consumers) try to do it another way, it may work for a few hours or days, but eventually, they'll burn up the processor," Pistone says.

Also, each microprocessor generation has its own pin configuration, so new chips simply may not fit into the older socket configurations.

Intel has developed a replacement for its own chips. Intel OverDrive processors can take care of all these problems for you, but the chips are limited as far as which processors you can upgrade. For instance, you can upgrade a 50 MHz 486 processor with an OverDrive processor that will boost your system to a 63MHz Pentium. Or you can upgrade a 66MHz 486 to an 83MHz Pentium. But that's about as far back as Intel goes.

You also can upgrade newer Pentium processors with Intel's MMX technology. This technology lets PCs take advantage of redundancies when reproducing graphics and audio, increasing performance in multimedia applications. However, the chips are available only for Pentium processors. For instance, you can upgrade a 100MHz Pentium with an OverDrive chip to operate at 166MHz with MMX. This would improve performance by approximately 150 percent when running audio, video, imaging, and 3-D software.

If you purchased a consumer system from a popular computer manufacturer, you'll want to consider OverDrive chips; almost all of the manufacturers we talked to use Intel chips. (A few, however, do use chips from Cyrix or AMD.) But Intel isn't the only manufacturer making upgrade chips. Other companies, such as Evergreen Technologies, also make generic chip replacements.

Boosting Your RAM

Another popular way to improve computer performance is to increase its "horsepower" by adding more random access memory, or RAM. Although many manufacturers solder RAM directly onto the motherboard, almost all motherboards include additional slots so you can add more memory. Most memory modules are in the form of single inline memory modules, or SIMMs.

Upgrading RAM, however, isn't as simple as it used to be. Advances in memory have widened the choices of RAM available. For instance, some RAM is now available as dual inline memory modules, or DIMMs. DIMMs have a different pin configuration than SIMMs and won't fit into a SIMM's slot. Likewise, there is a higher-performance memory called Extended Data Out (EDO) RAM that may not be compatible with some motherboards and systems. Many 486 systems won't support this kind of memory.

You should check your computer's manual or call the manufacturer to find out which type of RAM will work with your system and if there are any limitations. (For more information on buying RAM, turn to Skill 3.)

Caching In

Prepare for things to get sticky when you think about upgrading your cache, which holds in memory bits of data that are used often by the microprocessor. Adding more cache space, can speed up how quickly your computer operates, but it can be upgraded only in some forms on some systems.

Cache comes in two types. Level 1 (L1), also referred to as internal cache, usually is located in the microprocessor and normally isn't something you can tinker with. It's contained in small amounts, such as 8KB, 16KB, or 32KB. The other kind of cache, Level 2 (L2), is external cache and may be upgradeable. Common sizes of L2 cache are 256KB or 512KB.

On most motherboards, L2 cache is soldered into the board, and you usually buy a system with a certain cache configuration. However, a few computer models actually put L2 cache into a socket on the motherboard. On those systems, upgrading cache would be similar to adding more RAM.

In a very few instances, you can upgrade L1 cache if you upgrade your microprocessor. For example, if you upgrade to some OverDrive chips, you'll double the amount of L1 cache in the system. Some OverDrive processors can increase cache to 16KB or 32KB. If you operate applications that are small enough to stay resident in the processor and don't require RAM to run, Pistone says the upgrade will make a phenomenal difference in how quickly those applications work.

Getting Graphics and Sound

Displaying graphics and producing sound are two other integral parts of the motherboard's job. They are so integral that some computer companies build graphics cards and sound cards right into the motherboard, taking up one less expansion slot and leaving more room inside the PC. Most cards, however, are the basic graphics and/or sound cards that take up one of those valuable slots. The capabilities of these cards are probably sufficient for most home or small-business users' needs.

But if you want a "hot-rod" system to play games or make multimedia presentations, you'll want a setup that can efficiently create high-performance graphics.

The basic capabilities built into the motherboard may not cut it. Therefore, you'll want a graphics or sound card that can handle more data bits at a time. In addition, you may need a graphics card with more video RAM (which is usually built into the card). For instance, you may want to install a 64-bit graphics card with two megabytes (MB) of video RAM and a 32-bit sound card with three-dimension sound.

Before purchasing an expansion card, you need to learn what type of bus the computer uses to transfer information. Common bus types include Peripheral Component Interconnect (PCI), Industry Standard Architecture (ISA), Small Computer System Interface (SCSI), and Video Electronics Standards Association (VL-Bus).

Once the bus type is determined, you can begin the upgrade. To upgrade the graphics or sound card, you must first disable the old card on the motherboard before installing the new one into an expansion slot. This may be done in several ways, such as through the BIOS or by physically changing jumpers on the motherboard. (A jumper is similar to an on/off switch that is used to alter hardware configurations.)

Although some users have no choice but to make room for graphics and sound cards, these users will have an easier upgrading experience. Once they find an expansion card that is compatible with their computers' bus, they just pop out the old card, pop in the new one, and make a few software changes.

Changing Clocks

You should *never* consider upgrading the system clock. This clock, which coordinates all timing applications, is usually a crystal oscillator that's on the motherboard, and if you mess with it, you can do irreparable damage. In the rare event your system clock breaks down, you should take your computer to the manufacturer or a computer repair shop so it can be fixed by a professional. However, because computer repairs are so costly, it may be more economical to buy a new motherboard or even a new computer.

Keep in mind that system clock replacements won't necessarily speed up your system. To increase system performance, you should replace the microprocessor.

Altering the BIOS

Your computer's BIOS controls the startup process of your computer, as well as other basic functions, such as working with the hard drive or monitor. Even though many people refer to the BIOS as software, it's actually firmware, a set of instructions encoded in the hardware's circuitry.

Ordinarily, you wouldn't worry about upgrading the BIOS from the motherboard. At one time, however, the BIOS was contained in a physical component on the motherboard. In systems older than 486s, the BIOS was usually contained in Erasable Programmable Read-Only Memory, or EPROM. Since the BIOS is in read-only memory, it isn't erased when the computer is turned off.

The only way the contents of EPROM could be changed by the consumer was by taking out the component and replacing it with a new one. Users commonly sent a nominal fee to the BIOS company or the manufacturer to receive a replacement EPROM BIOS chip.

In newer systems, the BIOS is contained in flash chips, known as flash BIOS. Upgrading flash BIOS happens through software, meaning you can replace the old BIOS without having to physically tug a chip out of the computer.

Updating your BIOS comes in handy if your computer won't recognize hard drives with capacities more than 528MB. You also can change the BIOS if you want a new hardware component, but the existing BIOS doesn't understand the new hardware.

Adding Ports, Slots, and Controllers

Occasionally, you need to upgrade your computer—not to increase performance, but to add more capabilities to the system.

One way to expand your computer's upgradeability is by adding more ports. This isn't a simple job, but it can be done. Special expansion cards are available to equip your computer with additional ports, known as serial or parallel. (Serial ports are communications ports that connect devices such as modems to the computer. Parallel ports commonly connect devices such as printers to the computer.) The expansion cards plug into slots on the motherboard and extend additional ports out the back of the computer.

Of course, your computer will need addressing locations, available through the operating system, to add more ports. If your computer doesn't have any available interrupt request lines (IRQs) to address the new ports, upgrading may be a useless task.

Expanding your system internally by adding more expansion slots is really not an option, experts say, because the motherboard is only designed to accommodate a fixed number of slots. However, some expansion/adapter cards can plug SIMM sockets into the motherboard, so users can take advantage of older, lower-density memory rather than throwing it away and buying higher-density modules. This could also allow the user to access different size memory modules in the same system (such as a 30 pin in a 72-pin slot).

A few users may want to expand which types of components they can work with by adding another disk controller. The disk controller handles the operations of your diskette drives and other storage drives. Although most users will never need to change their disk controller, some drive upgrades may require a new controller card.

Most consumer computers use Integrated Drive Electronics (IDE) controllers, unless they are high-end systems. IDE is capable of handling most hard drives and diskette drives. But if you want to add a high-performance 6GB SCSI hard drive, a high-speed CD-ROM drive, or another disk drive to the computer, you may first need to install a new SCSI controller card into an expansion slot.

Planning for Obsolescence

Simply installing physical components can be difficult enough. However, there are additional considerations the average consumer should take into account. For instance, is the option you want to upgrade easy to get to? The processor may be positioned under other components you need to remove in order to replace the chip.

Also, as technology advances, upgrading gets stickier. True, the industry has established standards over the years, so installing a new video card or sound card is painless. But there will always be exceptions when technology advances. Take, for example, SIMMs, DIMMs, and EDO RAM. With quantum leaps in technology, some users and systems are sure to be left behind in these areas.

To avoid such problems, always check your manual to find out if, for example, that 16MB of EDO RAM will work in your 486. Upgrading won't be as difficult if you've considered all the options beforehand.

Motherboard Installation

As we've said, most of today's computers are put together in ways that let people make them faster, bigger, or generally better in the eyes of the person footing the bill for the upgrade. All you need to upgrade the computer's motherboard (also called the system board or the main board) is the motivation, the money, a few simple tools, and a plan.

Some motherboards cannot be installed in some compact desktop computers because many compact PCs use motherboards specially designed to save space. Always tell the vendor supplying the new system board about the make and model of your PC before you buy to avoid this problem.

Considering an Upgrade

There are many reasons to upgrade your PC's motherboard. Here are a few:

- You want a faster 486- or Pentium-class processor.

- You want more memory capacity than your current system board provides.

- You want to take advantage of faster bus technologies such as VESA or PCI.

- You want the advanced features and performance of the latest motherboards.

- You want to be able to use more, or different, types of expansion boards.

- That aging Model T of a PC may become a real race car with a new motherboard/processor upgrade.

The list goes on and on. Your reasons for performing a motherboard upgrade may be uniquely your own, but when you actually perform the upgrade, you're not alone.

Upgrading your PC's motherboard can be fun, but not carefree. This type of upgrade is not a task for a beginner. We cannot emphasize enough the difficulty of a motherboard upgrade. Even if you are confident, bring a lot of patience to the task. To do it without creating errors requires a lot of documentation and careful thought.

 **WARNING** If the idea of removing your computer's cover makes you squeamish, you should not consider doing this upgrade.

Before you start, there are some things to consider. Most importantly, make sure any system board you buy has a BIOS dated no earlier than June 1995. Refer to the date on the BIOS maker's label, not the date on the BIOS chip. Having an older motherboard could lead to compatibility problems with Windows 95 and chipset hardware. Users also should buy a motherboard with a BIOS made by one of the top three companies so they can upgrade it; having a BIOS that was manufactured by a no-name company that flees in the night could leave you stranded should you decide to upgrade. The companies to look for are American Megatrends Inc. (AMI), Phoenix, and Award; these companies sell their BIOS chips direct.

Your motherboard stores vital information about your computer. You should make an effort to write down every CMOS setting in your current motherboard. Many computer and motherboard manuals provide a place to keep these settings noted and organized; if not, record them on the inside cover of your manuals so you'll always know where they are.

 NOTE   CMOS, or complementary metal-oxide semiconductor, is a high-speed, low-power-consuming device that is generally used for random access memory (RAM) and switching applications.

Most motherboards made after 1994 can automatically identify your hard drive type as well as other significant settings. Just in case, write down your hard drive parameters so you can enter them should your hard drive not identify itself properly when you test your new motherboard. Your current motherboard's manual or your PC's manual should detail how to find these settings.

Getting to Know Your Motherboard

Here's a quick rundown of terms that you'll come to know quite well during a motherboard installation (see Figure 15.2):

- **Anchoring screws:** Fasten the motherboard to the chassis in the computer's case in such a way that the board cannot be moved. (Compare to *nylon standoffs*.)

- **BIOS:** Basic Input/Output System. Controls the startup process of a computer as well as other basic functions such as the keyboard, display, and disk drives. The BIOS is stored in read-only memory (ROM), which is not erased when the computer is shut off. Newer computers store BIOS on flash ROM, which can be erased and rewritten if the user needs to update the BIOS program.

- **Cache slot:** A location on the motherboard into which a cache card can be inserted. A cache card holds memory into which the PC places data that is frequently accessed.

- **Clock:** A circuit that generates a series of pulses that pace the electronic system within the computer, thus pacing, synchronizing, and coordinating the operations of the computer's circuits.

- **COM slots:** Locations on the motherboard into which you can insert input/output cards that contain physical ports to your computer. In this instance, these slots service your COM1, COM2, COM3, and COM4 ports (also known as communications ports).

- **CPU:** Central Processing Unit. The computer's control unit. Made of silicon that is enclosed in plastic casing, this chip interprets and carries out instructions within a computer. In layman's terms, this chip is often referred to as the "brain" of a computer.

- **Diskette drive controller:** The location on the motherboard into which you plug the ribbon cable owned by the diskette drive's expansion board. The controller manages the flow of information between a computer and a device by relaying information between them.

- **IDE slots:** Let you insert expansion cards that comply with the Integrated Device Electronics standard for hard drives. Under the IDE specifications, controller electronics are on the drive itself, thus allowing you to connect the drive directly to the motherboard.

- **ISA slots:** Allow you to insert expansion cards that are built according to the specifications of the Industry Standard Architecture bus. ISA slots allow users to install 16-bit expansion cards into the motherboard. Though ISA is outdated, most PCs still include ISA slots to accommodate the large number of ISA-compatible expansion boards in existence.

- **Keyboard slot:** The port into which the keyboard's plug is inserted.

- **LED connections:** Provides electricity to the light-emitting diodes (LEDs) on the front of the computer, which are used to indicate hard drive activity or power supply to the computer.

- **LPT:** Line Printer Terminal. The parallel port that connects a printer to the computer. DOS assigns the names LPT1, LPT2, and LPT3 to the first three parallel ports on a computer.

- **Nylon standoffs:** Attaches motherboard to tracks in the computer case's chassis while still allowing the user to slide the motherboard in and out of the case.

- **PCI slots:** Lets you insert expansion cards that comply with the Peripheral Component Interconnect bus standard. The PCI specification allows for faster communication between the CPU and peripheral devices, effectively speeding up a PC's operations.

- **Power slot:** The point at which you plug in the ribbon cable that connects the computer's power supply to its motherboard.

- **RAM (SIMM/DIMM) slots:** Places on the motherboard where you can insert single inline memory modules, which are small circuit boards that have random access memory chips soldered to them. RAM slots typically accept SIMMS with either 32-pin or 72-pin connectors.

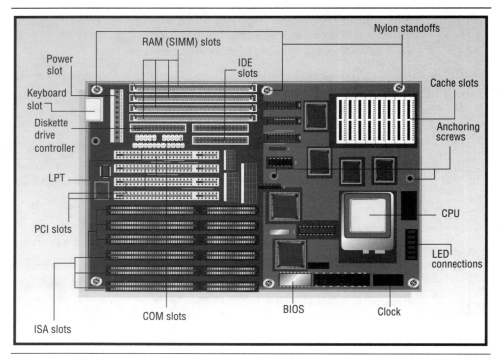

FIGURE 15.2: It's a good idea to become familiar with the different parts of a motherboard before beginning installation.

The Installation

When you're ready to begin the motherboard installation, open your computer's case (see Skill 3 for details on how to do this). Look at the interior, and learn where things are. First, locate the four major parts of your system: the power supply, the disk drives, the motherboard, and any expansion boards.

Your PC may be a little more crowded and complex than the one illustrated on these pages (we used an Infolink 6×86). There are so many PCs out there, that we couldn't possibly give you a definitive view of every PC. You also should locate the following items:

- **The microprocessor:** This chip should be the largest on the motherboard.

- **The BIOS:** This chip should exhibit a printed label.

- **The expansion slots:** The connector sockets that accept expansion cards such as the drive controller card, internal modem, and video card.

- **RAM:** Will appear probably as one or several tiny circuit boards holding small chips. These boards are usually placed in tandem next to each other in small, long, white sockets.

- **Jumpers:** Small plastic devices used to change settings.

- **Power connectors:** Usually two white connectors harnessing eight wires each.

- **Keyboard connector:** A jack that accepts the plug on your keyboard's cable.

- **LED or switch connectors:** On the front panel, LEDs are usually used to show the on/off (power) status of your hard drive, and other wires connect to the Turbo, key lock, and power switches.

- **Speaker:** Usually located at the front of the PC.

- **Battery:** Slightly weird-looking, you won't need to fuss with this item. Do your best to avoid touching it with any computer components during the upgrade.

Next, disconnect the power supply connections to the motherboard and all of the various devices. Be very careful when removing these connections; many are seated very tightly. Don't yank them out or try to pull them out by holding onto the power cords running into the connectors. Exercise a little patience, and maneuver them gently to ease them out. Note which connections went where; in some computers, the connectors will have alphanumeric characters printed on them that will help you identify them later.

Removing the Expansion Cards

Remove the expansion cards from their slots. To do this, first remove the screws that fasten the cards to the computer's case. Don't bother with the blank covers that aren't attached to an expansion board; they're only there to keep out dust. Once the screws are out, you're ready to remove the expansion cards. Be sure to handle each card by the mounting bracket and green circuit board edges to avoid damaging the card's components (see Figure 15.3).

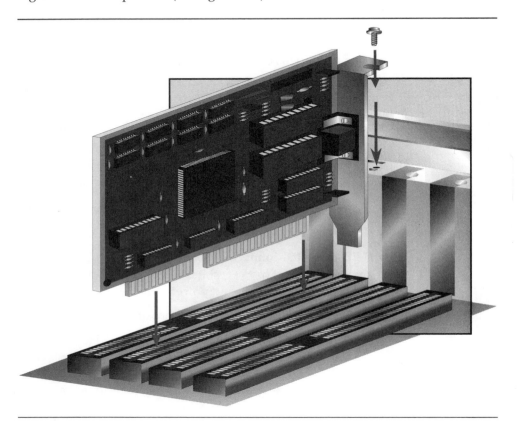

FIGURE 15.3:   Expansion cards must be handled carefully.

Most expansion cards will have cabling of some sort running from the card to the device it controls. Note that some cables (like the gray ribbon cables) are polarized with a marked conductor on either edge of the cable. These marked conductors must mate to the end of the connector (on the expansion card) that is marked with the number 1. You can write down (or sketch) each cable, where it comes from, and how it's plugged in, but avoid removing the cables if you can help it. Reconnecting the cables after the upgrade is complete can be a very complex task. Do everything you can to leave all wires and cables attached to expansion cards, and only disconnect cables attached to the motherboard.

Slipping Out the Motherboard

In some computers, your hard drive, diskette drive, and CD-ROM drive may be sufficiently out of the way. You should be able to remove the motherboard without any trouble. If this is the case, you can skip to the next paragraph. Sometimes, the drive bay carriage in some computers cannot be removed, as was the case with our system. Fortunately it was not a hindrance. If you can remove your drive bay carriage, and your upgrade will be impeded by leaving it in, remove it now. The drive bay carriage will be held in place by screws attaching it to the side and bottom of the computer's case (see Figure 15.4). In our computer, however, the hard drive was fastened to the side of the drive bay carriage and was hanging over the motherboard, which left us no choice but to remove it. We removed the two screws fastening the drive to the computer's drive bay, then set aside the drive and its screws. Remove any ribbon cables running from drives to the motherboard. Note beforehand what goes where. You do not need to disconnect cables from the drives themselves.

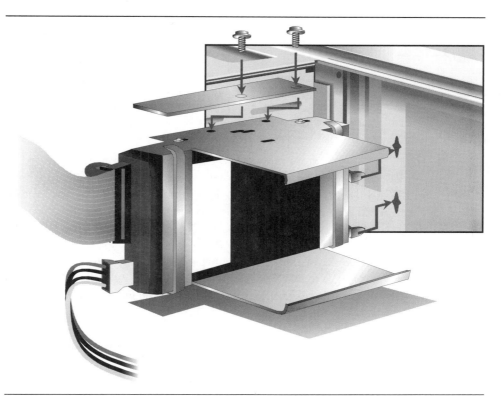

FIGURE 15.4:   The drive bay carriage may be removable.

Disconnect the small, thin wires at the front of the computer that power your LED lights (usually for power, hard drive, and Turbo), as well as your Turbo and Reset buttons and key lock. Note where each wire was connected onto the motherboard. Many motherboards in our offices actually had the slots for these connections labeled on the motherboard, and some of the connectors on the wires are labeled as well. It's not possible, however, to list all the names in full on the motherboard, so manufacturers also use alphanumeric codes. Check your new motherboard's manual for these codes and their assignments. Do not disconnect the wires from the front of the computer.

Taking Out the Screws

Now look for the screws holding the motherboard to the bottom of the computer's case. Remove them and set them aside. Do not put them in the same location as other screws; while the screws should look different from the others you removed, you could get them confused if you aren't paying attention.

 NOTE   Before you begin the actual disassembly, be sure to check the holes in your new motherboard to make sure the standoffs (nylon fasteners) in the board will line up with the holes in the computer's chassis. Standoffs keep your motherboard from accidentally touching the computer's chassis and then shorting out. If the standoff holes don't match up very close, your new board may not fit into your PC's chassis, and you'll need to call your computer dealer.

Once the screws are removed, you can slide the motherboard out (see Figure 15.5). In our system, there was only one side through which we could pull out the board. Take a moment to determine your most likely exit route for the motherboard. In our computer, there were standoffs in each of the four corners of the board. Slide the motherboard until the standoffs feel free of the PC's chassis, and gently ease the motherboard out of the computer. Be careful when handling the motherboard; there are some very sharp edges underneath the board. Handle the board by its edges to avoid scratching your hands.

As you remove the motherboard from the PC, be careful not to disturb any other wires. You also need to make sure that you don't accidentally remove any jumper switches with rough handling. Correctly set jumpers are crucial for proper operation of the motherboard and must not be disturbed during the upgrade. If the new motherboard is defective, you may have to reinstall your old system board—and you'll want that board to be in its original condition so you can use your computer while you arrange to replace the new-but-defective motherboard.

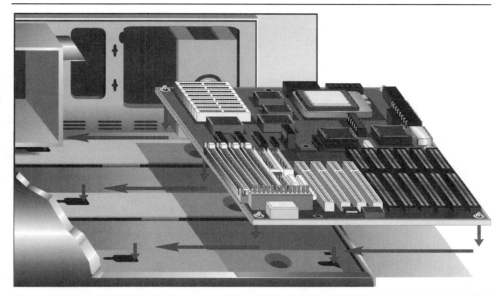

FIGURE 15.5:   With the screws out, it's time to remove the motherboard.

Removing the Single Inline Memory Modules

Set the motherboard in an area where you can work. Locate your single inline memory modules (SIMMs). You'll want to remove these regardless of whether you'll install them on your new motherboard, because you can sell them to a used computer parts dealer. Use the manuals for both your old and new motherboards to determine how to remove and install memory modules. On the motherboards we used, there were clasps at the end of each SIMM slot. Using your thumbs (or thumbnails), unsnap the clasps. Tilt the SIMM back to a 45-degree angle, then carefully remove it from the slot (see Figure 15.6). To install a SIMM in these slots, slide it into the slot at a 45-degree angle. Once it's seated properly, push it gently into a 90-degree angle until the clasps snap into place.

 NOTE   Some older memory modules require an adapter in order to be used on newer motherboards. If your memory modules don't fit into your new motherboard, don't force them! See your motherboard's supplier for a handy SIMM adapter, which should cost you less than $10.

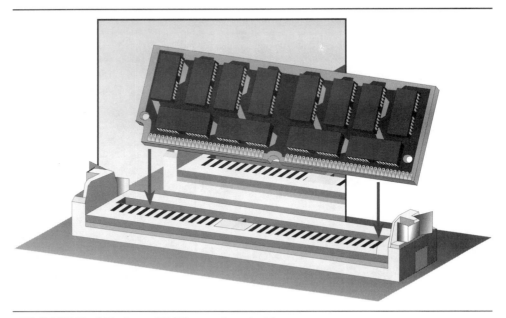

FIGURE 15.6: SIMMs are detachable.

The nylon standoffs are meant to be collapsible so that they can be removed. To remove the nylon standoffs from your old board to be inserted into your new board, you'll need a pair of needle-nosed pliers. Grip the standoff with the pliers about three-quarters of the way down the standoff's post. This distance is important; if the pliers are too far down the post, they'll impede your progress. If they aren't far enough, you can't get enough leverage. Squeeze gently with the pliers, then push the standoff through the board. To insert the standoffs into your new board, just pop them through the appropriate holes.

Putting It All Together

You're now ready to put in the new motherboard. Ease the standoffs into their connectors on the PC's chassis, then push the board away from you until the motherboard is in place. Be careful not to upset any jumpers or other components on the new motherboard by touching them directly. In short, try to handle the motherboard by its edges, and avoid touching anything on the motherboard's surface that you don't need to touch.

Before reinserting the screws that fasten the board to the bottom of the computer, check the placement of your expansion slots in relation to the holes in the back of the computer. The expansion slots should be in perfect alignment with the holes in the computer. If not, try placing the board again. Replace the screws.

 NOTE   Be careful of where you put the screws and standoffs. You do not want to put a standoff in a screw hole or vice versa.

Consulting your new motherboard's manual, reattach the wires for the buttons and LEDs on the front of your computer to the motherboard. Be patient. The quarters in this area of the motherboard are rather cramped, and fingers larger than those of a child may have trouble grabbing hold of the connectors. Remember, you are looking for the hard drive lamp wire connector, the speaker wire connector, the Turbo wire connector, the CPU clock speed wire connector, key lock, and any wires to the LEDs on the front of your computer.

If you had to remove your hard drive, replace it now. To do so, screw it back onto the drive bay carriage. Reconnect its ribbon cable to the Primary IDE controller slot on the motherboard. (Our motherboard had this slot labeled. If yours doesn't, consult the manual.) Since you're working with drives, this would be a good time to reconnect your diskette drive to the diskette drive controller on your board. (Again, this should be marked either on your motherboard or in its manual).

You now can plug your expansion cards into your new motherboard. Find your notes detailing which cards went where and, if cables had to be detached, which cables were attached to them. Be careful that you install the cards into the right slots. Slots differ, especially if you have a motherboard that lets you use ISA, VESA, and/or PCI expansion boards on the same motherboard. Make sure that you don't stretch your drive cables so taut that they unplug themselves or obstruct the installation of future expansion boards in any free slots.

Using the mounting screws you removed earlier, secure any expansion cards to the computer's case. If you put the screws aside in a manner that will make them easily identifiable, this should be a quick process.

Now perform a last cable/connector check on your motherboard, the expansion cards, and drive cables as they attach to the rear of the disk drives. Each cable should feel well-seated as you place gentle pressure on it. You also should make sure you didn't upset the memory modules during the installation. If you've had to use a memory module adapter device in order to use older memory modules, that adapter can unplug or unseat itself during handling.

You now can reconnect your power cables. Before reconnecting any of the power supply's cables to devices in your PC, consult your notes to confirm what was connected where and how. Be extremely careful when plugging the power supply cables into the motherboard. A mistake here can fry your new motherboard. Use

Skill 15

the manual that came with your new motherboard to identify each of the two power cables, and the way they should be plugged in.

Rebooting the Computer

It's time to plug the computer's power cable back into the wall socket and the power connector on the back of the PC. Now plug every other cable into your PC that was in place when you started the upgrade. This will include your mouse, keyboard, phone cable, printer cable, and so on. Don't put your computer case's cover back on just yet, though.

Turn the power on, and watch your computer boot. Note that the Turbo switch may not be engaged at this point. If the machine seems to load very slowly, try hitting the Turbo button and see if that makes a difference. A lot of PCs are set at the factory to run within very safe-but-slow parameters. Don't be alarmed if things aren't zinging along. We will address performance a bit later.

At this point, your new motherboard should be functional in your PC. Let's look at some of the ways you can troubleshoot your upgraded PC should trouble arise.

Testing the Configuration

It's always advisable to stay away from upgrading more than one piece of hardware at any one time, just to make troubleshooting easier if things go wrong. Do any single upgrade, then turn the system on to make sure it works properly before you proceed to another installation. If your PC does not start normally after you upgrade a hardware component, such as a motherboard, the most likely culprit is an unconnected or misconnected cable. Check your cables and connections against your manuals and notes to assure proper cable installation.

The first time you start your PC with a new motherboard, make every effort to be patient and let the PC go through its complete startup routine before making any changes to settings or cables. Most modern motherboards use the safest and lowest performance settings to ensure upgrade success. Refer to your motherboard manual for settings changes that will enhance performance once the upgrade proves successful. Here we'll walk through a very generic motherboard setup process.

If the PC seems to be in good working order, reboot the PC by simultaneously pressing the Ctrl, Alt, and Delete keys, then invoke the Setup program. This program is the way you manage the CMOS settings used to identify your computer's components to your motherboard. To activate the new motherboard's setup process, you'll be prompted to either press Delete or another key (or keystroke combination) while the computer is starting up. If you see the message *Starting MS-DOS* or *Starting Windows 95,* you've missed your queue to enter Setup. If you've missed this prompt, reboot the machine, and try again.

Once in the Setup screen, you'll need to define what kind of drives are located in your PC. Follow your motherboard's documentation to describe the installed drives. If you haven't kept a good record of your hard drive's parameters, your new motherboard should be able to automatically identify your existing hard drive(s). (Most modern hard drives identify themselves quickly and effectively when you use this part of your Setup utility. This automatic identification is preferable to entering manual parameters because it eliminates simple typing mistakes that can render a drive inoperable.)

Once you've identified your diskette and hard drives and set the date and time, you can proceed to the next level of Setup. These mid-level settings are usually set to factory defaults. Review your manual to learn about each of the settings offered and how to change them to improve system performance. It's impossible for us to review individual settings here because the variety of available settings for various motherboards is almost infinite. Refer to your new motherboard's manual or call your dealer for assistance with changing these settings.

If you feel you're up to changing some Setup settings that you suspect will enhance your PC's performance, please consider doing it the slow but safe way! Make only one change at a time, logging each change before saving your settings and rebooting your PC. If you make several changes at once to save time and hassle and then have trouble running your PC, it will be difficult to figure out which of the changes caused the problem. A lack of patience here can force you to return to square one, which means resetting your new motherboard to the manufacturer's idea of "fail-safe" settings just to get the PC to run. Then you'll have to start all over again!

Are You Experienced?

Now you can. . .

- ☑ **understand which parts of your computer can be upgraded**
- ☑ **evaluate the pros and cons of an upgrade**
- ☑ **move step by step through the installation of a motherboard**
- ☑ **test and troubleshoot a new motherboard**

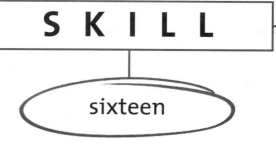

SKILL

sixteen

16

Installing a Power Supply

Of all the components that make up your computer, the one least thought about—but most likely to fail—is the internal power supply. If you plan to expand your system, a weak or inadequate power supply can quickly hinder your plans. If you purchased your computer with all the bells and whistles, its power supply is probably fine. If you are starting out with a bare-bones system, however, the power supply might be unable to cope with all the power-hungry devices you want to attach to it.

Making the Decision to Upgrade

A faulty power supply can leave "footprints" that signal problems, including consistent overheating of your system, intermittent powering up or system startup failures or errors, intermittent parity errors, electrical shocks from the case or connections, and noisy operation.

Though not inclusive, this list gives you an idea of what to look for. A power supply is not meant to be repaired by a beginner. When troubles arise, take it to a technician, or replace it with a new one.

How Power Supplies Work

Your computer's power supply converts the electricity coming from your wall socket to power suitable to run your computer. The power supply takes the 120-volt, 60 hertz AC current and converts it to a DC current of 5 and 12 (plus and minus) volts. Usually, electronic components such as the motherboard, disk drive cards, adapter cards, and most 3.5-inch diskette drives use the +5-volt supply leads, while the hard drive motors and cooling fans use the +12-volt output. Your computer depends upon a clean, steady supply of both types of current to operate properly.

Power supplies also act like electronic power sentries, assuring the system that there is adequate power for it to operate properly. A special signal called the "Power-Good" signal is sent to the motherboard (the circuit board that is the foundation of your PC's system). If the motherboard does not receive this signal, your computer will not run. This prevents your computer from harming itself when a power outage occurs.

The power supply's internal fan cools the power supply and helps maintain a consistent temperature in your computer's case. An improperly designed case and power supply combination will cause intermittent errors.

 **WARNING** Removing the lid from a computer can have the opposite effect from what you might expect. Instead of allowing more air to circulate, removing the lid stops air flow created by the power supply fan.

If you experience intermittent problems, including hard drive data loss, your system might be overheating. Don't leave any empty motherboard slot positions without their filler brackets inserted. If you remove a card, reinsert the filler bracket to ensure correct air flow in your computer.

Loading

A power supply is designed to operate with an electrical load. This type of load-only operation is called *switching*, and this type of power supply uses an oscillator circuit to generate different output voltages. This makes the power supply more compact, and it weighs less than its linear counterpart that uses a transformer to supply current.

A switching power supply must be plugged into a load that is drawing +5 and +12 volts, or the power supply will not operate. If you plug in a power supply without a load, it will not run, and you might actually damage some cheaper power supplies by burning up the overload protection circuit.

Better power supplies have a built-in load resistor that lets them run even in a no-load situation. This protects them from being damaged when plugged in without having any of the power leads attached.

Ratings

Power supplies are rated in output wattage. Early PCs had power supply outputs of less than 70 watts. Today, power supplies come in a variety of outputs up to 500 watts. The typical power supply averages about 200 to 300 watts. Most power supplies have their capacities clearly marked on their shells. Also, you can check your computer manual for the power supply's wattage rating.

As wattage increases, the available amperage at +5 and +12 volts increases. For example, the +5- and +12-volt outputs 20 and 8 amps, respectively. A 250-watt power supply outputs 25 amps at +5 volts and 10 amps at +12 volts.

Estimating Your Power Needs

Before your computer starts balking at an inadequate power supply, there are some calculations you can make that will help determine when it is time to upgrade your power supply. The +5 volt devices, such as motherboards and cards, consume a wide range of power. A motherboard can use from 3 amps to 5 amps, and adapter cards also have a wide range of power requirements, although they typically require 1 amp to 3 amps. Check your computer and interface card manuals to find the electrical specifications.

If you do not have any data on your motherboard or cards, it is best to use maximum amperage consumption when estimating. Your computer's bus type affects maximum amperage draw, or power consumption. (A bus is the hardware wires used to transfer data among a PC's components.) The following list shows average amperage draw per voltage for common bus types:

- **VL-Bus and ISA:** +5 volts, 2.0 amps; +12 volts, .175 amp

- **EISA:** +5 volts, 4.5 amps; + 12 volts, 1.5 amps

Each of these values represent the maximum amount allotted to each slot, but because different cards have different requirements, they may not need the full amperage set aside for them to use.

The next power consideration is the hard drive. Today's typical 3.5-inch hard drive uses about 1 amp of +12-volt power and about .5 amps of +5-volt power for the onboard *logic circuit*. Largely because of their mass, the larger 5.25-inch drives require an average of 2 amps of +12-volt power to operate. (A logic circuit is an electronic circuit that processes information.)

A 3.5-inch diskette drive runs on +5 volts, and uses about 1 amp to supply power to the motor and logic. A 5.25-inch drive uses about 1 amp of +12-volt supply for its motor and about .5 amps of +5-volt supply for its logic.

Following is an example list for estimating the 5-volt and 12-volt needs for a typical system with a 200-watt power supply.

5-Volt Power

Motherboard: 4.0 amps, estimate

Video adapter (actual spec): 1.2 amps

Drive controller (VL-Bus): 2.0 amps

Sound card (ISA): 2.0 amps

Serial/parallel (ISA): 2.0 amps

Two 3.5-inch diskette drives: 1.0 amps

3.5-inch hard drive: 0.5 amp

CD-ROM drive: 1.0 amps

Total used: 13.7 amps

Total available: 20.0 amps

Remaining available: 6.3 amps

12-Volt Power

Three ISA slots: 0.53 amps

3.5-inch hard drive: 1.0 amps

CD-ROM drive: 1.0 amps

Fan: 0.1 amps

Total used: 2.63 amps

Total available: 8.0 amps

Remaining available: 5.37 amps

This system is currently not taxed, and there are empty slots that can use additional power. Adding a second hard drive and tape backup unit would start to put a strain on the system.

Skill 16

THE CASE FOR POWER SUPPLIES

In an ideal world, everything fits. Since we haven't achieved computing utopia, power supplies come in different sizes and shapes. Some power supplies are generic, and some are proprietary to the computer manufacturer. There is a loose industry standard for case styles such as PC/XT, AT/Tower, Baby AT, and Slim, and for their power supplies.

Do not associate power supply output with the size of your computer's case. Just because you see a full-size tower case, don't assume it has a 300-watt power supply.

When swapping out your power supply, measure the power supply's outside physical dimensions to find which category it falls into. The dimensions are displayed in metric measurements and should provide an idea of which type of power supply you are working with.

To find an appropriate power supply, you can contact your computer's manufacturer, who can sell you a replacement or direct you to an appropriate vendor. Sales publications listing computer parts are also an excellent source.

Upgrading a Power Supply

If you decide to upgrade your power supply, you can follow the steps in this section to remove your old power supply and replace it with a new one.

First, you'll need to open your computer's case to reach the power supply. For instructions on opening your computer's case and preparing for installation, read Skill 3.

As you work through the installation process, note how and where various components in your computer case are plugged in. You might consider drawing a rough sketch of how your system looks. Improperly connecting components, especially the motherboard, could irreparably damage the whole computer system.

Most power supplies are located at the back of the computer case on the right (as you face the computer), as shown in Figure 16.1. Your computer's fan at the back of the case is on the power supply. If you have trouble locating your power supply, your manual can help you.

To replace a power supply follow these steps:

1. Move any ribbon cables that might be tucked under or around your power supply to a less crowded area in the computer case. You can detach these cables if you need to, but if you can avoid unhooking them it will save you the trouble of reconnecting them later.

2. Some computers will have a bracket around the power supply. This must be removed. Remove the two screws that connect it to the bottom of the computer case. Then remove the two screws that fasten the bracket to the back of the computer case.

3. Electrical cords that connect your power supply to various computer components must be disconnected. When disconnecting power supply cords, pull the connectors. Do not pull on the cords themselves. (On our computer, green-, blue-, and cream-colored cords from the power supply were connected to a large white connector to the motherboard, which was on the base of the computer case.) We pulled the white connector to disconnect the power supply from the motherboard.

 NOTE   Our computer had unconnected cords and connectors attached to the power supply bracket with a plastic tie. We had to cut the tie with scissors to free the cords from the bracket.

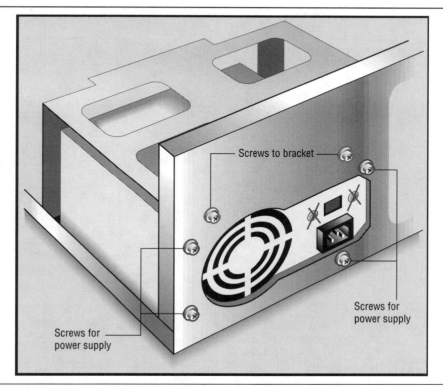

FIGURE 16.1:   The power supply is usually at the back of the computer on the right side.

4. On our computer, red, black, and yellow cords connected the power supply to a diskette drive, a CD-ROM drive, a hard drive, and a drive controller card (see Figure 16.2). Unhook these and any other connections by pulling on the plastic connectors to these components. Be patient; these connections are often extremely snug.

5. Disconnect the cable from the power supply to the power (on/off) switch at the front of the computer. Remove the screw fastening the on/off cable to the computer's case (see Figure 16.3). Lift the bottom of the bracket from the small slot holding it to free the cords. Remove the two screws that hold the power cable's bracket in place. A small, differently colored cable branching off the main cable to the power switch also must be disconnected by removing a screw. Set the bracket and screws aside.

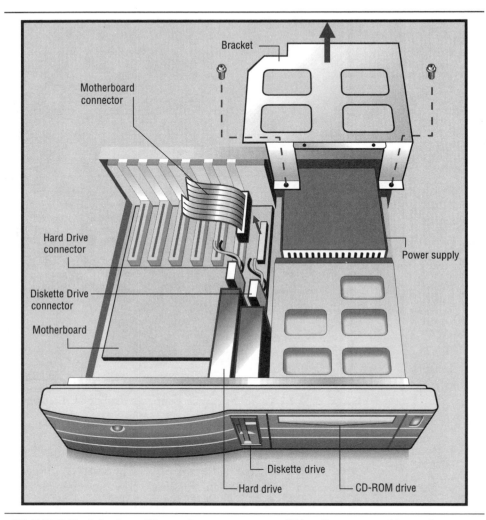

FIGURE 16.2: The main components will be disconnected from the power supply.

6. Now that the power supply is disconnected from all internal computer components, remove the four screws that connect the power supply to the back of the computer case (see Figure 16.4). Do not remove the screws near the AC outlet, which is underneath the volt setting.

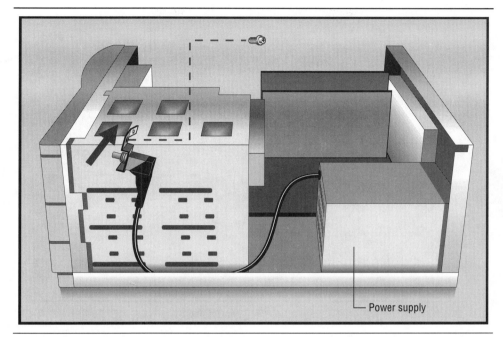

Power supply

FIGURE 16.3:   The on/off cable is detached from the computer's case.

7. The power supply now can be safely removed from the computer case (see Figure 16.5).

8. Remove the new power supply from its packaging. Line up the power supply so its screw holes match up with the screw holes on the back of the computer case. Reinsert the screws that attach the power supply to the computer case.

9. Attach the new on/off cable to the bracket you removed in Step 5. Reattach the smaller, colored cable.

10. Insert the bracket into the computer's slot below the power switch, ease the bracket into place, and attach it to the front of the computer case.

11. Reconnect your computer components (diskette drive, CD-ROM drive, hard drive, drive controller card, etc.) to the power supply.

12. Reattach the white connector to the motherboard.

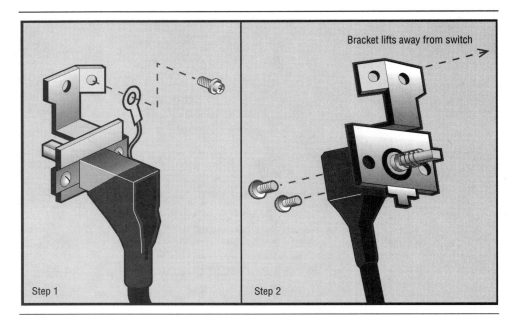

Step 1

Step 2

Bracket lifts away from switch

FIGURE 16.4: The screws near the AC outlet remain in place while the others are removed.

 NOTE   Some computers have two connectors to the motherboard. These plugs are designed so that wires of the same color sit next to one another when installed correctly. To prevent faulty installation, consult the notes and sketch you made earlier.

13. Put the power supply bracket back in place (if applicable). Line up the screw holes on the back of the computer case, and reinsert the screws. Then reinsert the screws that connect the bracket to the bottom of the computer case.

14. Unused connections on your new power supply can be placed on top of the bracket or the power supply itself, or they can be attached to the bracket with some sort of tie.

15. Move the ribbon cables to approximately their original location. Reconnect them if necessary.

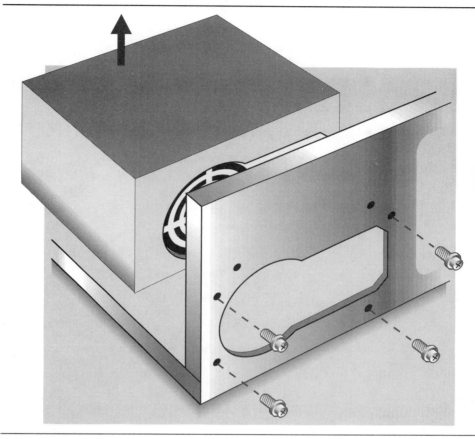

FIGURE 16.5:   Remove the screws and lift the power supply from the computer case.

16. Replace the case cover, and reinsert all screws.

17. Plug in your computer and hardware. Turn on the computer to see if it is operating properly with your new power supply.

If you have any of the faulty power supply symptoms mentioned earlier—or maybe ones that occasionally crop up for seemingly no reason—consider replacing the power supply. A good power supply not only can help your system last longer, it can also protect your data by keeping your system running.

Are You Experienced?

Now you can. . .

- ☑ decide whether it makes sense to upgrade your power supply
- ☑ understand what makes power supplies work
- ☑ evaluate what you need in a power supply
- ☑ install a power supply from start to finish

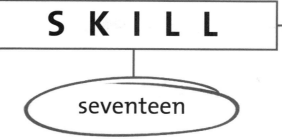

S K I L L

seventeen

Upgrading Your Portable Computer

- ❑ Understanding how PC Cards work

- ❑ Using the many types of PC Cards

- ❑ Upgrading your portable's processor, RAM, and hard drive

- ❑ Making sure your upgrade is cost effective

You may have noticed that funny little slot in the side of your laptop computer, lurking under the flip-down door. It's not the serial port, you found that on the back. It's not for a hard drive, there's already a hard drive in there. What's it for?

That slot is your PC Card interface adapter socket. Because laptop and notebook computers don't have the expansion slots that desktop computers do, there has to be a way to add capabilities to the road warrior's machine. PC Cards offer that ability.

What kind of expansion capabilities do PC Cards offer? It might be simpler to list the things that you can't add, because the list of what you can add is almost endless. A partial listing of capabilities includes:

- Random access memory
- Internal modems
- Hard drives
- Multimedia sound capabilities
- Controllers for external CD-ROM or optical drives
- Network adapters

What's a PC Card?

A PC Card is a circuit board using the latest in electronic miniaturization, enclosed in a protective metal case with an industry standard connector on one end, and whatever connector type it needs on the other. The connector that plugs into your computer works the same regardless of what type of PC Card it is, and runs from the same set of software drivers.

There are three official types of PC Cards: Type I, II, and III. The only difference in the types is how thick they are. Type I cards are only 3.3 millimeters (mm) thick, not much thicker than a credit card. Type II cards are 5mm, and Type III cards are 10.5mm. (See Figure 17.1.)

You can use a PC Card in any socket as long as it physically fits. Most notebook computers have two PC Card slots, one right above the other. You put a Type I or a Type II card into either or both slots; if you have a Type III card, it will only fit into the bottom slot and blocks the top one. If your computer only has a single PC Card slot, the odds are that it's a Type II slot, which means you can only use Type I or II cards.

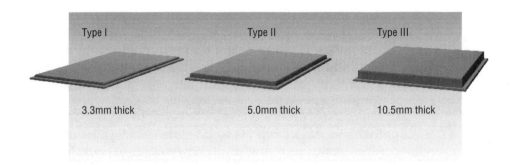

Type I   Type II   Type III

3.3mm thick   5.0mm thick   10.5mm thick

FIGURE 17.1:   The three types of PC Cards vary in thickness.

In most cases, all you have to do is stick a PC Card in the slot. The reason for this ease of use is called *Card Services*. PC Cards really have two components: the hardware (whatever PC Card you bought and the slot it fits into) and the software. When your computer boots up, it loads special programs called Card Services drivers, which control, manage, and manipulate PC Card sockets and devices.

We'll examine Card Services later, but in summary there are drivers that activate the socket, drivers that manage the socket especially in terms of how much power it uses, and drivers that hook up PC Cards with software that needs them (such as PC Card modems and communications programs).

PC Cards vs. Other Devices

In almost all cases, you'll want to choose a PC Card over an equivalent external device, even if it costs more. There are a number of good reasons for this. First, they're smaller and lighter, so you don't have to load yourself down, and you can take more of them (and, thus, more features and functionality) on the road with you.

Second, because they're internal devices, you won't need cables or external power supplies. This further lightens your load and makes setting up and breaking down the computer much easier.

A third reason is reliability. PC Cards are either entirely solid state (no moving parts) or the moving parts are extremely durable (much more so than desktop equipment). They're built for the road, and for the punishment that occurs while you're traveling.

The fourth reason—we'll call it "swap-ability,"—is the best one of all. You can buy a hardware/software combination for your desktop computer that fits into a standard 5.25-inch drive bay and adds PC Card capability to your home machine. That way, you can switch cards and, therefore, features between your desktop and laptop PCs. Why, for instance, buy two modems if you're only going to use a modem wherever you actually are? It's better to buy a really good PC Card modem and move it back and forth between systems.

Once you've made the decision to add a PC Card adapter to your home or office PC, a huge list of options opens up. For example, you could create a PC Card hard drive with your word processing program and all your documents on it and simply slide it in wherever and whenever you need to work. No more fussing with whether a program is installed, what version of the program is installed where, or which diskette a file is on.

One of the nicest things about PC cards is that they're "hot swappable." In other words, unlike reconfiguring a home computer, you can plug PC Cards in whenever you feel like it. As soon as you plug in a card, the Card Services software takes over and initializes the card for you.

If you're working under Windows 95, that's all there is to it. Windows 95 is fully PC Card-aware, so even if the card requires additional drivers to work, Windows 95 will recognize that and put the drivers to work for you.

If you're working under DOS or older versions of Windows, you might have some work to do. Some PC Card modems, for instance, need their own initialization program to tell them which serial port they should pretend they are, whether to "tweedle" at you as the connection is made, and so forth. The modem manufacturer will provide a utility program, which you'll usually need to run right after plugging the card into your laptop computer.

Another thing to consider is that the Card Services software is very power-management sensitive. If you have a PC Card modem in your computer and the computer goes into "sleep" mode because you went for a cup of coffee, the modem goes into sleep mode, too, and likely will have forgotten the things you told it with the startup program. Therefore, you'll probably have to rerun the startup program when the computer comes out of sleep mode.

Types of Cards

There are many types of PC Cards. We'll run through the most commonly available ones and describe their form and function.

Random Access Memory Cards

Be careful with these. They're an easy way to add additional memory to your computer, but there are a couple of "gotchas." First, this is not the most cost-effective way to add memory to your PC. All desktop computers and most laptops have dedicated RAM sockets for adding memory without using up one of your PC Card sockets. Second, PC Card RAM is often twice as costly as socketed SIMM memory.

 NOTE   This is the only type of PC Card that has to be present when you start up the computer, or the computer will refuse to recognize and take advantage of the additional memory. That means you have to reboot every time you add or remove a RAM card.

RAM cards are almost always Type I and even the weird ones aren't any bigger than Type II, so if you've got the slot, they've got the RAM.

Flash RAM cards

Flash RAM is treated like a hard drive made entirely from chips. Typically available in 10MB, 20MB, and 40MB sizes, you can think of Flash RAM as a hard drive that operates at the speed of light.

Flash RAM is used to make programs work incredibly fast or to access data hundreds of times more quickly than from a normal hard drive. Even though it's RAM, it really does work like a hard drive and maintains your data even when the card is unplugged. Inside the card is a trickle-charge battery that keeps the memory refreshed even if the card is left unplugged for up to a year. When you plug in the Flash RAM card, the battery gets recharged and the whole cycle can start again.

There are two negative aspects to using Flash RAM cards. The first is that they offer very limited capacity compared to hard drives. Typical hard drives for portable computers start at 250MB and exceed one billion bytes of storage, but the Flash RAM card doesn't store more than 40MB (70MB or more if you use compression software). The other negative is that these cards are very expensive. A 40MB Flash RAM card will cost you a cool $1,000.

Flash RAM cards are always Type II, so they'll work in any PC Card slot.

Modems

Modems are always Type II PC Cards, and they're certainly the most popular PC Card devices. Why carry around a bulky external modem with a serial cable and power supply when you can plug a PC Card modem into the laptop, attach a phone cable, and be online in moments?

PC Card modems are available in 14,400 bits per second (bps) and 28,800bps models, and are also capable of acting as fax machines with the appropriate software. Several manufacturers have also introduced Integrated Services Digital Network (ISDN) modems that operate at 128,000bps over special digital circuits.

A NOTE ON USING PC CARD MODEMS

If you're using a portable as a fax machine, remember that the computer is going to want to turn itself off after a period of inactivity, so the computer could be snoozing soundly when that fax finally comes through. You'll need to attach the computer to a wall outlet and disable the power management features. If you're not using Windows 95, check your computer manual for instructions on doing this. If you are using Windows 95, go to the Control Panel and select the Power icon. Some manufacturers also provide a Power Management icon for older versions of Windows. Check your computer manual to be sure.

Network Adapters

There are PC Card adapters for Ethernet and token ring networks with all the popular network operating systems. LANtastic is a notable exception, but you can use software designed for Novell NetWare networks with some LANtastic networks. Your local computer expert will know how to set this up.

Getting on the network is as simple as plugging in the PC Card, attaching the network cable, and running some programs that log you in to the network. Once on, you can do anything you could on a desktop PC, and just as quickly (assuming your portable is as powerful as your desktop PC). Network adapters also are Type II PC Cards.

Hard Drives

These are incredible little devices. When you look at a PC Card hard drive, it doesn't seem possible that there are several hundred megabytes of information stuffed into a box almost the exact size and shape of a pack of matches. There is, though, and that extra capacity and portability can make a PC Card hard drive worth far more than its minuscule weight in gold.

When you first install a PC Card hard drive, also called an AT Attachment (ATA) drive, a drive letter will be reserved for it, and as soon as you plug it into the card slot it will be ready for action. If your portable already has a C: drive, the PC Card hard drive may be named D:. Card Services watches disk requests, and if you ask for access when the drive isn't plugged in, you'll get the traditional *Drive Not Ready* error message.

Hard drive PC Cards are Type III, so they're not for everyone. They're also not cheap—at around twice the price of traditional, permanently installed hard drives—but the convenience factor may make up for that very quickly. Remember, you can move a PC Card hard drive from notebook to laptop to desktop with the same programs and information installed. Plug it in and you're right back to work.

Small Computer Systems Interface (SCSI) Controllers

There are a lot of devices that, no matter how hard you try, just won't fit into a portable computer. Take tape backup units, for example. Many tape backup drives, external hard drives, and CD-ROM drives use the Small Computer Systems Interface to attach to personal computers.

If you had a desktop computer, this wouldn't be a problem, as you would just drop a SCSI controller card into an available expansion slot and you'd be done with it. Portables are another matter. Recognizing the need, manufacturers have created Type II PC Card SCSI controllers.

There's another reason to add PC Card slots to your desktop PC. As hard drives get larger, getting a good backup copy of your data on diskettes gets harder. Why not purchase a SCSI-based external tape backup drive that you can use with your portable and desktop PCs?

Multimedia Cards

There are a few portable computers on the market now that do everything but the dishes. They have built-in CD-ROM drives, speakers, full-motion video, and sound capabilities. Most of us aren't lucky or rich enough to have one, because these things are expensive. So what do the rest of us do? Add some or all of those capabilities with a PC Card multimedia adapter.

Multimedia adapters typically include the capability to:

- Generate sounds from either FM Synthesis or tables of recorded sounds stored on the card.

- Record sounds from a microphone or other source.

- Record and play music with special musical instruments using the Musical Instrument Digital Interface (MIDI).

The latest adapters also include an Enhanced Integrated Device Electronics (EIDE) connector to allow you to attach yet another kind of external CD-ROM drive.

Multimedia adapters can be used to spice up business presentations and allow you to listen to audio CDs while you're working. Many users get these adapters so that they can play computer games.

Combo Cards

You'd think these tiny cards would be hard pressed to have just a single function built in, wouldn't you? Through the miracle of miniaturization, manufacturers have managed to pack several functions into some cards. This is really useful for subnotebooks with only a single PC Card slot. Modem+Network cards are the most common combo cards, but there are others, including Video+Modem and Video+Network. Combo cards can be any type, but Modem+Network cards are usually Type II.

Wireless

Motorola and a couple of other smaller manufacturers have introduced PC Card and software combinations that turn your portable (or your desktop, if you have PC Card slots) into an alphanumeric pager. If you sign up for the ARDIS digital radio network, you even can have two-way paging that lets you type messages that are relayed back to the sender.

This is a new technology and, as with anything else that's new in this industry, it's expensive. The PC Card will cost up to $500, and you can very easily spend $200 a month in messaging costs.

 NOTE　Even though this feature will impress your customers and competitors, a cellular phone might be a better option.

Wireless PC Cards are weird-looking devices. They fit in a Type II slot, but there's a huge "bulb" that sticks out in order to have space for an internal coil antenna (see Figure 17.2). The card also juts out several inches, which means the slot cover door has to stay open.

There also are PC Cards for wireless local area networks, but it's an unusual application, so we'll just note that they do exist.

FIGURE 17.2:   The antenna-equipped AllPoints PC card offers wireless features.

Putting It Together

As with any electronic device, a PC Card is just a lump of circuits when you plug it into your computer. It's the software—in this case, Card Services—that brings the chips to life and lets them do what they were designed for. Your portable computer came with Card Services software, and if you buy a PC Card kit for your desktop it will come with Card Services, too.

There are three companies that write Card Services software, but the biggest by far is CardSoft, so we'll look at how they do what they do.

Here's a sample section from the CONFIG.SYS file of a portable computer with Card Services installed (in this case, a Gateway Handbook with one Type II slot):

```
Devicehigh=C:\Cardsoft\Cscirrus.exe
Devicehigh=C:\Cardsoft\Cs.exe /irq  a
Device=C:\Cardsoft\Csalloc.exe  Devicehigh=C:\Cardsoft\Cardid.exe
```

```
Devicehigh=C:\Cardsoft\Atadrv.exe
Devicehigh=C:\Cardsoft\Sramdrv.exe
```

In this case we've loaded everything but the kitchen sink. Cscirrus.exe is the Socket Services program. This program watches your PC Card slots and notifies the next program, Cs.exe, when a new card is inserted or a card is removed.

Cs.exe (Card Services) and Csalloc.exe (Card Services Allocation) work together. The first program controls and talks to devices that are installed in PC Card sockets through the hardware channel or interrupt reserved, in this case interrupt A. Card Services Allocation keeps track of which memory addresses and other hardware resources the PC Card has requested so there aren't any conflicts if you try to fire up an additional card or device.

Cardid.exe is the program that identifies system requests and routes them into Card Services when they're destined for a PC Card device. It works very closely with whatever version of DOS you have installed.

The last two programs are optional depending upon what PC Card devices you're going to be using. Atadrv.exe is the program that controls PC Card hard drives and Flash RAM cards, and Sramdrv.exe is the program that controls RAM cards you might have installed.

Each of these programs is very small. As you can see from the DEVICEHIGH statements in our example in the previous column, they can be loaded into memory above what your DOS programs normally use in order to minimize the space required.

It's in the Cards

Or at least attached to them. As you can see, PC Cards add a wonderful variety of options to your portable or desktop computer, and are easy to install and configure. With PC Card accessories, your computer can be bigger, better, stronger, and sometimes faster, so don't ignore them when it's time to think about upgrading.

Adding Muscle to Your Mobile

You've had that portable computer for a year now, and as your skills have grown, so have your computing requirements. You've added new programs, upgraded a couple of existing ones, and have started to notice that your new desktop computer can run circles around your take-along. What can you do to improve your portable?

Depending on the make and model of your computer, the answer ranges from "just a few things" to "how much money have you got?" Most late-model portable computers, commonly called *laptop* computers, have a host of options available to make them nearly as brawny as their desktop counterparts. There are three ways to make your portable pack a bigger punch: make it faster, make it bigger, and make it better.

Unless you have a computer workshop in your basement or at work, your kitchen is the best place to perform the upgrade activities described in this section. Why? The kitchen is probably the best-lit room in the house, it's usually one of the only rooms in the house without carpet, and there are probably lots of waist-high electrical outlets.

Good lighting is obviously important. You're going to be working with small pieces in tight spaces, and it makes sense to be able to clearly see what you're doing. Not having carpet is also important, but for a less obvious reason. Static electricity is the enemy of computer components, and your body builds up a static charge every time you shuffle your feet on a carpet. A linoleum floor minimizes the amount of static electricity that you'll pick up as you work on your computer.

Waist-high electrical outlets are important because they make it easier to plug in your portable computer when you're ready to test your additions and changes. They also are handy because of the little screw that holds the face plate of the outlet in place. The screw is attached to the frame of the wall socket, which is attached to the ground wire. To rid yourself of any static electricity that you're carrying—a process known as *grounding*—just touch the screw with your index finger.

Once you're in the proper surroundings, you're ready to upgrade your portable computer.

Making It Faster: Processor Upgrades

The first part of making your portable faster is looking at which processor is already installed.

There are three basic ways to upgrade your processor: replace the existing processor with a faster model, add an additional processor that complements or takes over for the existing processor, or exchange the entire motherboard for one with a faster processor. (The PC's motherboard is the circuit board that forms the foundation of your computer's system. See Skill 15 for more on motherboards.)

Processor upgrades come in many shapes and sizes. If you have a portable based on the Intel 80386 processor, it's possible to change it into the equivalent of a 486, assuming you can remove the existing chip. Cyrix, Texas Instruments, and Advanced Micro Devices (AMD) all make replacement 486-compatible processors that fit into 386 sockets. Cyrix's is even clock doubled, which means it runs internally twice as fast as your old processor did.

If you have a 486, a number of upgrade paths are available. Intel makes OverDrive processors that will turn your 486SX into a true 486DX or even into a special version of the Pentium processor. Owners of older 486DX machines can choose faster 486DX2, DX4, or Pentium OverDrive chips. Check with your computer's manufacturer to see which chips will work with your computer, but take the advice with a grain of salt. After all, the manufacturer would rather have you buy a whole new computer and give this one to your nephew Joey. Double-check by calling upgrade chip manufacturers directly. Intel, Cyrix, AMD, and Texas Instruments all have toll-free upgrade hotlines that can advise you on the best chip upgrade for your portable.

Is Upgrading the Processor an Option?

It's possible that you won't be able to upgrade the processor on your portable computer. To simplify the construction process and cut costs, many portable computer manufacturers designed their systems with processors that either are glued to the main circuit board with electro-conductive glue or are permanently mounted to the board by a process called wave soldering. In either case, you can't remove the processors from these computers.

To find out if your computer's processor is upgradeable, review the user manual or call the vendor's technical support telephone number. Either one will tell you if the processor is removable and how to remove it, if an OverDrive socket is available and where it is located, or whether you'll have to call customer service to get a price on exchanging your motherboard. Your cost can range from a few hundred dollars for a brand new processor to several thousand for a complete motherboard.

If the processor is upgradeable, the first thing you'll need to do is find the processor inside the computer. Some manufacturers have made it easy by providing a small door on the bottom of the case that gives direct access to the processor. If you're not that fortunate, you'll probably have to remove the entire bottom of the case. Before attempting a "case-ectomy," read on. You may decide to take the computer to your local computer repair shop rather than do it yourself.

Once you have uncovered the processor, you'll find that it sits in a socket. You'll also find that it is held in place by as many as 200 gold pins that extend downward into the socket and cover the entire underside of the chip. Even with a special tool called a pin lifter, it takes a lot of patience and a very steady hand to remove a processor without damaging it or the socket.

Installing an OverDrive Processor

If you've been living right, you won't have to worry about any of this. After checking your manual or calling the manufacturer, you may discover that your portable has an OverDrive socket. Instead of removing the processor, all you need to do is put a second processor into that socket. Contact the manufacturer's technical support staff and find out which OverDrive processor (also called an *exchange processor*) would work in your computer and where you can purchase the chip. Now you're ready to install it.

The installation manual should tell you where to find the socket and how to access it.

 NOTE   Before you open the computer, and especially before you open the case that contains your new chip, you need to make sure you're not carrying a static electricity charge. Touch that screw in the middle of a convenient electrical outlet, grab a metal object, such as a handle on a cabinet or drawer (be sure to touch a bare metal surface, not a painted one), or shake hands with someone in the room. This dissipates or neutralizes any static electricity you've picked up.

Now you're ready to open the computer case or access panel. Use an empty cup or coffee mug to store any screws or fasteners you remove. Once you've located the socket, you'll need to figure out how to put the processor chip in it, and this isn't as easy as it sounds. The chip and socket are both square, but it's crucial that you put the chip into the socket so that Pin 1 aligns with Socket Hole 1. Look at the socket and the area around it. There should be a big silk-screened "1" on the circuit board at one of the socket's corners. If there isn't one, look at the socket to see if one corner has a beveled edge, so that the socket isn't perfectly square. If there's a bevel, that corner has Socket Hole 1. Now open the case that contains your chip, and take a close look at it. There should be a "1" or a white dot on one corner of the chip. That's where Pin 1 is.

Skill 17

Align the chip with the socket, and with one finger on each of the four corners of the chip, press gently and evenly to insert the chip into the socket. Never press directly on the center of the chip: that's where the delicate electronics are located. You could easily kill the chip just by pressing your finger on the center of the chip package.

As the processor begins to slide into the socket, you can begin pressing more firmly. The processor will go about an eighth of an inch into the socket before it stops. You won't hear a click or any other noise to tell you when the processor is fully inserted, so be careful. Look around the edges of the socket to make sure the processor is evenly seated all the way around. Close the case, turn on the computer, and revel in your newfound speed.

If your computer requires a new motherboard, here's what you do: Put the computer in a well-padded box. Write a well-padded check. Put the well-padded check in the well-padded box and mail it to the manufacturer. Wait several weeks. The well-padded box will eventually return with your computer but without the check. Take the computer out, turn it on, and have a blast.

Adding RAM to Your Portable

Sometimes, you don't need to replace the processor to get a faster computer. If you're running any version of Windows on your computer and your computer has less than 4MB of random access memory (RAM), you probably need to increase the amount of memory on your motherboard. Windows 3.*x* chugs slowly with 4MB or less, especially when it tries to run almost any of the programs released in the last year. Windows 95 needs at least 8MB of RAM. Both Windows 3.*x* and Windows 95 will benefit tremendously from additional RAM. Many of the latest computer games require 16MB of RAM and most new computers are sold with 24MB to 32MB of RAM. Another reason to add RAM is that it has become one of the cheapest and easiest upgrades to perform. In one year ago the price of 16MB of RAM dropped from $500 to less than $250.

So how do you add RAM to your computer? Again, it depends on the individual manufacturer. A few manufacturers (mostly clone manufacturers) put the RAM directly on the motherboard, so it's not upgradeable. Fortunately, such machines are very rare.

Most portables have one or two special sockets for adding RAM. Because of the small size of a laptop, sockets are often nonstandard, and you might have to buy your upgrade from the manufacturer. If you have a well-known brand, such as NEC, Texas Instruments, Epson, IBM, or Toshiba, you can probably purchase RAM from a third-party manufacturer.

The upgrade sockets are often accessible through a door at the top or bottom of the computer, but on some brands they lurk under the keyboard. The owner's manual can help you locate these sockets.

TIP   When selecting the size of your RAM upgrade, always buy the maximum that you think you'll ever need. A lot of portables only have one upgrade socket, so each time you upgrade your RAM, you have to replace the old module completely.

Making It Bigger: Hard Drive Upgrades

One of the most amazing developments in an industry filled with amazing developments is the growth in hard drive memory capacities. Just five years ago, a hard drive that could store 80 million characters (80MB) of information was considered jumbo, and most people had hard drives of 40MB or less. A couple of years ago, 230MB drives were the jumbos, and most of us squeezed by with 120MB. Today's standards are quite a bit loftier. A jumbo drive stores at least 1.6 billion bytes, or 1.6GB, of information, while many of us make do with dinky 540MB drives. The growth of hard drive capacities corresponds to a decrease in price-per-megabyte for storage devices.

At the same time, the size of the programs that you're likely to use has been growing—a lot. Version 1 of that word-processing program that you bought four years ago only took up a few megabytes of storage. Imagine your surprise when Version 6 arrives in the mail and the box says it requires 10 times as much! Of course, you haven't exactly been inactive during that time. Odds are that you've added a program here and a program there, and you've probably produced some useful work with these programs, which means that you also have a lot of data files. As a result, your hard drive is probably stuffed fuller than Dad after a Thanksgiving dinner, and it's time to think about a hard drive upgrade.

Before you reach for your wallet, check one thing. Are you using a disk compression program on your hard drive? If you're not, you could have 50 percent or more additional storage space for free! If you're using MS-DOS 6.22 or Windows 95, you already have a perfectly serviceable disk compression tool, built right into the operating system.

NOTE   If you're using a version of DOS 6.21 or earlier, do not mess with the disk compression program built into the operating system. It has problems, which is why 6.22 was released in the first place. Either purchase a third-party compression program, such as Stac Electronics' Stacker, or upgrade your DOS to 6.22.

Skill 17

If you're already using a compression utility and you're still running out of space, it's time to think about purchasing a larger hard drive. Depending on the make and model of your computer, you'll have a few options with this upgrade, as well.

Installing a hard drive can be performed easily and safely, but buying and setting up an appropriate hard drive can be daunting. There are a few questions to consider.

First, with which type of hard drive is your portable compatible? Some older laptops can't recognize the newer, larger hard drives that are currently available, and there's nothing built into your system's Setup program that will let you tell your computer to recognize them. You can get around this with a special program called a BIOS extender. The BIOS extender works with another chip, called the complementary metal-oxide semiconductor random access memory (CMOS RAM) chip, to carry information about how the laptop is configured. As we mentioned, you could use a BIOS extender—but it is a real pain.

The second issue to consider is the physical size of the drive. Is it a 3.5-inch drive, a 2.5-inch model, or one of the super-small 1.8-inch drives? And last, but certainly not least, does the drive use a nonstandard connector and cable that you must purchase from the manufacturer and that may not be available anymore?

That last scenario poses a sticky problem. Nonstandard equipment is out there, and you may not know that you have acquired some until it's too late. The hard drives made by Conner Peripherals for the Compaq LTE 286 are one example of nonstandard equipment. These hard drives use a nonstandard connector and the original drives aren't available anymore. IBM's ThinkPad 700 and 720 (but not the 701) are other examples. Because these computers use micro-channel architecture for transmitting data, most hard drives, which conform to the industry standard IDE interface, just won't work with them. But let's put all that aside and assume that your computer is in fact upgradeable, and that you can purchase and install a new hard drive that will fit, connect, and be recognized.

How do you do install a hard drive? Many portables, such as those made by IBM, NEC, and Dell, have a removable hard disk that plugs into the side of the computer. This makes upgrading your hard drive easy: You upgrade a hard drive by sliding the old one out and sliding the new one in. You can keep both hard drives, putting your most commonly used applications on one hard drive and the more infrequently used applications on the other. Then, just trade them back and forth as needed.

Unfortunately, your options for actually purchasing that second hard drive are limited. You can go back to the manufacturer and pay the often inflated prices for the upgrade packages. You can hunt for a third-party manufacturer, but unless you own a portable from one of the major manufacturers—IBM, Compaq, Toshiba, Epson, or NEC—the odds of finding a third-party manufacturer are slim.

TIP One company that can help you is Road Warrior International, which specializes in upgrades and enhancements for portable computers. You can reach them at (800) 274-4277, or at http://www.warrior.com on the World Wide Web.

What if there's no package available for your computer? If the portable supports new drive types and uses a standard interface, and you can locate an appropriate drive, then you can replace the existing hard drive yourself.

First, make absolutely certain that you have your operating system setup diskettes. You'll need them to load the operating system on your new hard drive once it's installed in your computer. Second, you'll need to make a complete backup of the existing hard drive, so get lots of blank, preformatted diskettes, and use the DOS or Windows 95 backup program to make your copy.

Before you open the computer, take a look at the new hard drive's documentation. You'll need to write down the drive's geometry, or the number of tracks, cylinders, sectors, and read/write heads. Most laptop BIOS Setup programs will require you to enter this information before the computer will recognize the drive.

Now it's time to open the computer case. Following the manufacturer's directions, open the hard drive bay or computer case. If your manual doesn't provide these directions, call the manufacturer's technical support department. They'll have information they can mail or fax to you.

WARNING Remember to ground yourself frequently, and keep all screws, washers, or other small pieces in a cup so you don't lose them. Take your time, make sure of each action, and be careful. You'll be working near the circuit board; one slip with the screwdriver can gouge the board and turn your lovely laptop into an expensive doorstop.

Once the new drive is installed and the computer case is buttoned up again, you'll need to put your first setup diskette in the drive and turn on the machine. For most laptops, it'll take longer to boot than usual, and the first thing you'll see is a *Hard Drive Failure* message. That's normal because the new drive has different parameters than the old one. Remember the geometry information you wrote down earlier? In a moment, it'll be time to enter that information.

If your laptop bypasses this step, don't worry. What happened is that the BIOS has a special setting called Auto Identify that automatically reads the geometry information off the drive. Although this setting has become standard on most new desktop computers, there are lots of laptops that still don't have it.

At this point, you should find yourself in the System Setup program, where you can enter the geometry information on the line marked Hard Drive 0 (or Hard Drive 1). Flip through the options on that line until you see the item Drive Type, and change it to User. You can then move across the line entering the geometry information you collected. There might be a couple of items for which you don't have information, such as Write PreComp and LZ. Don't worry about them; new drives perform those functions automatically. After you have entered the geometry information, exit the Setup program, and the system will start from the diskette drive. The operating system setup program will walk you through the process of formatting the drive and setting up the operating system.

The last step is to use a Restore program, such as the DOS RESTORE command, to place all your programs and data from the diskettes onto the new hard drive. The Backup program lets you store the system data your computer requires, including the AUTOEXEC.BAT and CONFIG.SYS files, and the Restore program adds this data to your new hard drive. When it's done, restart the computer one more time, and you're back in business.

Making It Better: Adding New Components

This type of upgrade depends on which accessories are available for your specific brand and model. This can be divided into three categories: better screens, exchangeable modules, and PC Cards. See "What's a PC Card?" at the beginning of this skill for more information on PC Cards. In this section, we'll discuss screens and modules.

For most portable computer owners, doing a screen upgrade yourself may be out of the question, but let's not rule it out completely. If you have a monochrome Liquid Crystal Display (LCD) and are hankering for color, call the manufacturer. It's likely the manufacturer will offer to upgrade your computer or exchange it for a model with color display. The price, while steep, is usually only a fraction of the cost of a new laptop.

You may have a color display on your laptop already, but you may be unhappy with the resolution. Until recently, laptops were only available with standard VGA monitor resolution of 640 x 480 dots, called *pixels*, measured horizontally and vertically on a screen. There's nothing wrong with this resolution, but because most home computers now use a resolution of 800 x 600, you'll notice the lack of clarity when you hit the road. Portables are now available with a resolution of 800 x 600. They're pricey, but the quality is a quantum leap over what you're used to.

Before performing a screen upgrade, talk to the manufacturer. If you have an NEC Versa series notebook computer, you have it made. Move a clip on either side of the display, and the whole panel lifts right off the computer. This lets you perform your own screen upgrade, wallet permitting.

The last upgrade option we'll discuss is expansion modules. Some portable computers let you choose what to stick into the bays in the side or front of your computer. You might have a diskette drive in there now, but flick a lever, give a yank, and out it comes. Once the bay is empty, you might pop in a second battery for those long, boring flights, or a CD-ROM drive to run programs or listen to audio CDs, or a Motion Picture Experts Group (MPEG) player that allows you to watch digitized movies in full-screen mode.

 NOTE The manufacturer is your best resource regarding expansion modules. Don't assume that just because these options weren't available when you originally bought the computer, they aren't available now.

Skill 17

The Bottom Line

A wealth of options are available to stretch the useful life of your portable computer. If anything, there may be too many options, so listen to the advice of a good vendor, and double-check what the manufacturer's representatives tell you. When deciding to upgrade your portable, don't be hasty. Consider your options, and when you're ready to upgrade, take your time and be thorough.

Are You Experienced?

Now you can. . .

- ☑ **understand how PC Cards work and what they can do for your laptop**
- ☑ **evaluate your options for using the many types of PC Cards of the market**
- ☑ **upgrade your portable computer's processor, RAM, and hard drive**
- ☑ **make upgrading decisions that make financial sense**

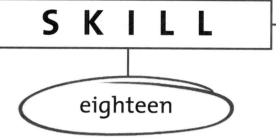

S K I L L

eighteen

18

Setting Up an Ethernet Network

- ❑ Understanding the nuts and bolts of networks
- ❑ Making hardware and software choices
- ❑ Avoiding common network problems
- ❑ Installing an Ethernet network
- ❑ Getting the most from your network

Networking is a word we hear everywhere these days. But how many people really understand the term? Getting to know networks doesn't have to be difficult. With just a bit of education, you'll be able to throw around words like LAN and token passing with the best of 'em.

Getting to Know Networks

A *network* is a group of computers hooked together, usually by cables or telephone wires, for the purpose of sharing information and resources.

A decade ago, the main reasons for buying a network were that several cheaper PCs (with no hard drives) could all share a single, large, expensive hard drive on the server PC; all PCs could print on one printer attached to the server; and all PCs shared one copy of expensive software purchased only for the central server PC. Today, these are usually not primary reasons to network.

Today's networks are more about getting people and information together and allowing teamwork. A network can let people work together more smoothly and create a sense of group identity, helping an organization become greater than the sum of its parts.

For example, in most word processors, several people on a network can review one draft of a document, each leaving "sticky-note" comments and marked changes and suggestions scattered within it. This is all possible with no one leaving a desk, attending meetings, or photocopying multiple copies and coordinating everyone's comments. Also, keeping individual and company-wide calendars on a network can eliminate telephone tag when everyone is checking who is available for meetings.

So, usually the main reason to use a network is to share identical, live data (information, numbers, files, letters, etc.) that is constantly available to, and modifiable by, different people at the same time. A good example is an inventory database or spreadsheet that must be kept current, yet must be seen by several people from their own workstations at any time.

Simple networks also prove handy for home users who want multiple PCs to share a single peripheral, such as a laser printer.

In order to work well, the network must be set up to provide the best performance between the most distant network workstations. A *local area network*, or *LAN*, operates primarily over a small area, such as an office building. The connecting cables used to hook it together are owned by the user. A *wide area network*, or *WAN*, on the other hand, covers a large area, such as all the branches of a state bank. It's usually connected through leased telephone lines and satellite hookups. The Internet is the ultimate WAN, spanning the globe and connecting millions of computers.

These network types operate in similar ways. Classifying a network as LAN or WAN is a good first step in understanding networks.

Hardware

To create a network, several essential components are needed. In its simplest form, a network consists of computers connected together using network interface cards, networking software, and network cabling.

Each networked PC is called a *node* and has its own unique network address and name that sets it apart from other network devices. The network address is permanently "burned" in a *network interface card* (*NIC*) or a network adapter. The NIC is a small circuit board plugged into an adapter card expansion slot in each node.

The network adapter works with the networking software, telling each node how to operate as part of the network and controlling the data exchange between every hardware component. Based upon user-supplied setup information, the networking software helps determine how the node will act on the network and provides the network name to help users easily identify the node.

Another crucial element in creating a network is a medium to hook the nodes together. This is usually done with copper or fiber-optic cabling. Wireless LANs can be created using infrared or radio waves. Because of their slower data transfer rates and smaller range of operation, wireless LANs are normally used only when cabling is impractical.

Every network device has one or more connectors, called *ports*. Network cables plug into NIC ports to provide high-speed data transmission. The type of network adapter plays a big role in determining what kind of network it will be, how fast it operates, and how far down the cables a signal can be transmitted without extra hardware to help it. There are four popular types of NICs available. They include *ARCnet* cards (*Attached Resource Computer Network*), which are fading from use; the wildly popular *Ethernet* cards; *token-ring* cards, which are also fading in popularity; and *ATM* (*Asynchronous Transfer Mode*) cards, which are quickly becoming more widely used.

 NOTE   A cable's primary function, besides providing connections between every node on a network, is to transmit data in the safest possible manner. This means the data should be transmitted over a network and end up in the right place without errors.

Network data is sent as a series of ones and zeros. Each one or zero is called a *bit*. A group of bits sent out on a network is called a *frame* or a *packet*. A frame or packet normally has all the address and error-control information it needs to complete a transmission. As with the NIC, the type of cable selected affects how far apart computers can be located, how easy the network is to run, and how susceptible to interference the cable will be.

Cables

There is no network without cables. As you become familiar with the basics of networking you'll learn the pros and cons of different cabling options. (For a concise list describing the types of cables and connectors, see the sidebar on "Network Connections" later in this skill.)

Coaxial Cabling   *Coaxial* cable, known as coax, is the original networking cable, much like the cable used for cable television. Coax is a copper wire center surrounded by a screen of fine braided wire, which is then coated in plastic. It offers substantial protection from electromagnetic interference.

The downside to coax is that it's expensive, stiff, fat, and hard to run through walls. It's also finicky about kinks and often is set up in a "daisy chain" (computer-to-computer-to-computer) manner that's vulnerable to having one link break and bringing the whole system down. That said, coaxial cable does offer a modest form of security because of the braided copper shielding. The shielding also lets network signals run farther distances before they have to be amplified.

Twisted Pair Cabling   By far the most popular cable in use today is *twisted-pair* cable. Twisted pair contains two insulated copper wires spiraling around each other in opposite directions, a basic electronics trick that keeps interference at a minimum. It comes in two types: shielded and unshielded. *Shielded twisted pair (STP)* is surrounded by a braided copper and metal foil shield. *Unshielded twisted pair (UTP)* is not shielded and is more prone to interference. Both are pretty much universally used because of their flexibility and low cost.

Twisted-pair cabling uses standard telephone connectors and patch panels to set up the network wiring. This helps greatly in organizing the wiring for large LANs. Currently, the RJ-45 style connector that can handle up to four wire pairs is favored instead of the two-pair JR-11 connector.

Fiber Optics   The next generation in network cables is *fiber-optic* cable, which is made of glass or plastic thread. It is the most protected, and most expensive, cabling available. Instead of transmitting electrical signals through metal, it transmits light pulses that carry voice, data, and video through the threads. While plastic thread fiber-optic cables are easier to install, glass thread fiber-optic cables can transmit network signals a much longer distance.

Because light pulses are used, there is no risk of electromagnetic interference or accidental transmission of electromagnetic radiation. Fiber-optic cables are also used when security is a top concern, because they are not like other cable types, in that you can't use a radio receiver to record a network transmission from some distance away.

Other Network Devices

Cables sometimes need a little help to do their job correctly. A *router* helps out by sorting data and sending transmissions over the fastest possible route. It is often used to link a LAN with a WAN through phone lines.

A *repeater* amplifies a transmission so that it can travel farther, and is used in a campus setting to help join LANs between buildings. Normal transmissions are diluted as they travel, but repeaters make sure that the signal stays strong throughout its journey. Repeaters are also used to translate network frames from one type of medium to another. For instance, a fiber optic to copper repeater translates a light pulse into an electrical pulse, letting you join fiber-optic networking equipment with copper cable network equipment.

Clients or Peers?

Once the hardware has been gathered, it's time to decide what type of network hierarchy to operate under. There are two options: client/server or peer-to-peer.

On a *client/server* network, one computer, called a *server*, handles nearly all the storage needs of the entire system. It's normally a larger computer than the others, with more operating speed and lots of storage space. The server can be *dedicated*, meaning its sole purpose is to function as the network server, or *nondedicated*, which means it can also perform other tasks.

The computers connected to the server are called *clients*. Clients are workstations or nodes where users can do their work by harnessing the power of the server. The server acts as a mediator, letting the clients get the files and data they need to accomplish a task. This formation is popular with offices that have dozens of computers.

 NOTE Servers also offer a measure of security. In most network operating systems, a user must have an ID and password in order to gain access to the network.

The second network hierarchy is *peer-to-peer*. Unlike a server-based network, in a true peer-to-peer network, each computer can "see" and access every other computer on the network (with the proper access privileges, of course), and can use the data, programs, and printers on any other computer on the network. This formation is less expensive than a client/server setup and, though it can be used for very large networks, is used primarily in smaller networks of 10 or fewer computers, since peer-to-peer networking software limits the number of users attached to any one shared resource. Today, large companies often find that a hybrid network consisting of, say, several Windows NT or Novell-type servers (each with several smaller Windows 95 peer-to-peer networks attached to them), provides the advantages of both approaches.

"When it comes to putting things into a single manageable location, server-based operations are better suited for that sort of thing," says Samm DiStasio, product marketing manager for Novell Inc. From a server, all information can be backed up at once, instead of having to work with several different PCs to take care of scattered data. By the same token, however, if you have flaws in your backup system or the system goes down, you're completely down.

In either formation, the basic process of network operation remains the same. A node requests data from the server, which then retrieves that information and sends it to the node. The node performs whatever work it needs to and perhaps returns data to the server to be put into storage again. (It's kind of like a trip to the library, except there isn't a late fee.)

Topologies

The manner in which network cables are connected is called the *network topology*. This topology doesn't determine how the nodes and servers are physically positioned in a building, but it does determine how the cables hook everything together. There are three main network topologies—bus, star, and ring.

Bus Topology

The *bus topology* involves one line of communication and is arranged in a line with all nodes connected with a single cable. The network has two distinct ends. All nodes have the same access to the network. If one node wants to communicate with the server, a broadcast is sent out through the bus in both directions. All the nodes read the broadcast to determine whether the information is meant for them. When the message reaches the correct node, that computer accepts the message and processes it, while the other nodes ignore the message.

In a small network, this works well. But in a large network, the fact that cable travels computer to computer to computer (in a daisy chain) becomes a weakness. The routing of the cable can suddenly get convoluted when, say, you need to add one new computer several hundred yards away from the center of the existing cable run. And if one part of the cable is interrupted, by, say someone jerking their desk too far from the wall, the entire network can go down.

Star Topology

The *star topology* has a distinct central switching device called a *hub*. From there, each node is connected with a cable so that the formation resembles the spokes on a bicycle wheel. In a star topology, every node has its own connection to a central hub. Typically, each spoke on the wheel can act as a hub making a pattern of stars within stars, etc. When one node sends a message to another node, the message first goes to the hub where it is processed and then is forwarded to the correct node.

 NOTE   Client/server networks are often set up on a star topology.

The star topology is fairly stable. If a node goes down, the whole network won't be affected. If, however, the hub goes down, the network will crash as well. More network cabling is required for a star topology than for a ring topology, but changes and additions are easier to make. Furthermore, troubleshooting is centralized and can be simpler.

Ring Topology

The *ring topology*, as you might guess, takes the shape of a circle. Each node is connected with small pieces of cable, making each node dependent upon the next. Messages sent from one node move around the ring until they reach the right one, moving in one direction only. Peer-to-peer networks work well on a ring topology. Because each node is connected only to the ones directly beside it, if one computer goes down, the network goes down as well, although it's possible to program the network to pass over a node that is not functioning. The number of PCs included in the loop is sometimes finite because once a ring network is set up, it's not easy to expand. Also, if there is a need to add additional PCs, the entire network must be taken down. Not much cable is required, on the other hand, bringing costs down a bit.

Skill 18

Collisions and Controls

What happens when two friends want to say something at the same time? One has to pause and let the other go ahead, or they risk interrupting each other. The same thing occurs on a network. Each node is trying to communicate with other nodes or trying to get through to the server. As you can imagine, there could be quite a problem with PCs interrupting each other, which is called a *collision* in network jargon.

Networks deal with collisions based upon the type of protocol, or access method, they use. *Protocol* is the set of rules followed by all communications between nodes and devices. Protocols control format, timing, error correction, and running order.

Two primary protocols are used to control traffic and interruption on a network: *carrier sense multiple access/collision detect (CMSA/CD)* and *token passing*. The Ethernet network adapter uses CMSA/CD while the Token Ring network adapter uses the token-passing protocol.

The CSMA/CD protocol requires that before a node is allowed to transmit a signal to another node, it must check the line to see if it's in use. If no other node is using the line, the node can go ahead and send its message. But if the network is already in use, the node will wait a short, random period of time and try again until the line is free.

The second network control protocol is token passing. In this case, the node waits for permission to use the line. A special packet called a *token* is passed around the network, stopping at each node to see whether it has any messages or requests to transmit. Only the node for which the packet is addressed answers the token "call." All other nodes ignore the packet.

Once the token has taken the packet where it's supposed to go, it then travels back to the original node that sent the message. The token informs the node that its request was processed and goes back to traveling around the network looking for jobs that need to be done. This ensures that two nodes will not try to speak at the same time.

Both of these collision control processes seem rather complicated and lengthy, but in actuality, the whole process is nearly instantaneous. Without one of these control methods, traffic on the network would be backed up worse than a Los Angeles freeway at rush hour.

Operating Systems

The software that handles all these protocols, provides the screens users see, monitors passwords, and does all the other things needed to make a useful network is called the *network operating system*. Some examples include Windows NT, Novell's NetWare, and LANtastic. Microsoft's Windows for Workgroups and Windows 95 are often thought of as single-user software, but with a group of computers with cables and NICs, they actually are complete peer-to-peer network operating systems in themselves.

"Essentially, the goal of a network operating system is to augment the client workstation but not change the way you do things," DiStasio says. "So you file things the same way, you print things the same way, you launch applications the same way. The real benefit is the ability to manage things."

Each node on the network needs its own operating system as well. On a client/server network, the operating systems do not need to match up. For instance, you could have Windows 95 machines with Macintosh machines using the same Windows NT server. Generally speaking, on a peer-to-peer network, however, the operating systems must be the same.

THE NEED FOR NETWORK SECURITY

Control of who can do what and use what (and when and where they do it) is called *network security*. The amount of this which is available, or even desirable, varies widely with the network operating system. On a three-user peer-to-peer network consisting of a family-owned business, there may be no need for *any* security. In other cases, complex levels of access (high, middle, low) and groups (accounting, production, editorial) all with different things they can access may be needed and desirable. Probably the most neglected form of network security, however, is backup. Failure to create adequate backups on networks causes far more losses than security breaches.

Networking has come a long way. It's matured into user-friendly setups designed to make your life easier. And with its growing use in nearly every part of our lives, understanding the technology will pay off.

NEW NETWORKING TRENDS

The following is a sampling of emerging trends for the (not-so) distant networking future:

- **Wireless networks:** These transmit signals in the air. They're becoming a viable option when there are problems hooking up networks because of space and wiring conflicts. Wireless networks are flexible but also fairly slow (at one to two megabits per second).

- **Desktop video conferencing:** Once an option only for Fortune 500 companies, desktop video conferencing may be a reality for the average user in the near future. New technology using the Internet makes live communication easier, and, more importantly, affordable.

- **Intranets:** The newest office networks combine the Internet with traditional networking technology to create an office communication setup that rivals the easiest network architecture. World Wide Web browsers provide a user-friendly interface with e-mail, file sharing, and conferencing. The setup is very similar to a wide area network except it's much cheaper because no leased lines are needed. An Internet hookup provides the cabling.

- **Home Integration:** Almost everything has a computer chip and copper wiring in it these days; networks can take advantage of that technology by connecting home devices to one centralized network. One day, users may be able to manage household functions through their computers, says Novell's DiStasio. He predicts that smart set-top boxes for television will be the earliest innovation, allowing users to navigate the Net through their TV.

Installing an Ethernet Network

The great and terrible moment has arrived. You've decided to network your office PCs. You've realized that by pooling the computer resources in your small office, the staff can work more efficiently and save money by sharing expensive peripherals. The only remaining question: How are you going to do it?

Although networking still depends on too many acronyms and technical terms for most users, manufacturers are working to make it easier to understand and accomplish. In the meantime, there are a few important concepts that will help you figure out how to create a LAN.

A Network Primer

As we saw earlier in this skill, at the heart of every network scheme is the notion of sharing a computer resource such as a file, directory, or printer with at least one other user. This can be accomplished in two major ways discussed in the earlier section, "Clients or Peers."

First, you could give everyone the ability to share their computer resources with everyone else via peer-to-peer networking. In this type of network, every computer can act as a host (the computer with the resources other people want to access) or a workstation (a computer trying to obtain resources from a host). Novell's LANtastic and ArtiSoft's Personal NetWare are examples of DOS-based, peer-to-peer networks. Windows 95 and OS/2 Warp Connect are examples of advanced operating systems that provide peer-to-peer networking.

Between the DOS-based network software and the advanced operating systems lies Microsoft Windows for Workgroups 3.11 (WFW). While claiming to offer 32-bit networking services similar to Windows 95 and OS/2, it is still based upon MS-DOS. This operating environment helped make peer-to-peer networking a popular network blueprint for small numbers of users.

Peer-to-peer networking bogs down, however, when one resource becomes heavily used. The extra workload slows down the host PC, usually irritating the user who is working at its keyboard. At this point, it might be wise to switch to another method.

Heavily used resources can be placed on a computer dedicated to sharing these items with other users on a client/server network. A server sits in a corner of the office, sharing its resources with other users and is not used as a workstation. PCs that access and use the server's resources are called network stations or requesters. Banyan Vines, IBM OS/2 LAN Server, Microsoft Windows NT, and Novell NetWare all offer server-based networking.

Server-based networking helps handle heavy demand for resources such as a customer order database or a laser printer. Provided the server software is compatible, it also can be used with a peer-to-peer networking solution to let users access the server while still occasionally sharing low-use files or peripherals.

There are two major protocols, or methods, of doing business on a PC network: Novell's interpacket exchange (IPX) protocol, and the network basic input/output system (NETBIOS) family of protocols are used in products such as LANtastic, WFW, and OS/2 LAN Server. There are several flavors of NETBIOS; the most advanced version is NETBEUI. This has been used in WFW and Windows 95.

While Microsoft has tried to provide support for Novell's NetWare products with its Windows products, NetWare has the reputation for being more difficult to set up under Windows. That said, NETBIOS-based networks are supposed to be slower than IPX networks and don't use network resources as efficiently.

Should you elect to use Windows 95 or WFW as your network software solution, these programs by default use NETBEUI as the LAN protocol. There's nothing wrong with this, provided all the computers you're going to network are Windows-based machines.

If your office has a Macintosh computer in addition to PCs, you'll most likely be working with either Novell or Farallon solutions. Novell has long had a Macintosh NetWare client that lets Macs share the same resources as PCs. Timbuktu 3 by Farallon lets PC users share files and run Mac software by remote control.

Although WFW and Windows 95 have good peer-to-peer services, these products won't work on your office 286 and may not perform well on your 386SX machines. Personal NetWare or LANtastic offer a good solution for networking old and new PCs. You can find both of these products bundled with network cards and cabling.

Choosing a Network Card

When networking was the domain of large businesses and universities, only a handful of manufacturers provided network interface cards (NICs). Today, many manufacturers offer network cards that fit within nearly everyone's budget.

The Ethernet network interface is a widely accepted standard, which can be likened to polite conversation around the dining room table. When one person is speaking, everyone is supposed to listen. Ethernet uses something called carrier sense multiple access (CSMA), or the "contention method," to broadcast data to another network station. If two cards try to broadcast at the same time, both stop and then attempt to broadcast again after a random period of time. For small office networks, simple Ethernet cards are reliable and affordable.

Ethernet cards range in price from less than $50 to about $200, and they are available in either Industry Standard Architecture (ISA) or Peripheral Component Interconnect (PCI) models. ISA Ethernet cards are usually 16-bit, so if you're still using PC or XT computers, you'll have to do some shopping. Look for cards that automatically sense if they're plugged into an 8-bit or a 16-bit expansion slot. Addtron offers such a card for as little as $30. (ISA allows adapters to be added to a system by inserting plug-in cards into expansion slots on the motherboard. PCI is a standard design for motherboards and expansion slots that can transfer 32 or 64 bits of data at one time.)

PCI bus Ethernet cards make 32-bit networking a reality. They are more expensive than their 16-bit ISA bus counterparts, but usually cost less than $100. Because computers that support PCI bus cards also support plug-and-play automatic hardware configuration, setting up a PCI bus Ethernet card is quick and easy. If all of your computers are Pentiums, get this card if you can afford it.

Also look for manufacturers who offer installation software that simplifies the task of configuring the network card. Kingston Technology offers the EtheRx LC line of ISA and PCI cards. Using Kingston's DOS-based QStart installation program, users can set up their Ethernet cards without changing settings on the card itself. Users can either automatically set up their cards for NetWare or answer a series of simple questions. Before running Qstart, read the 14-page manual and the README.DOC and QSTART.DOC files on the EtheRx LC driver diskette. Incidentally, Kingston is expected to field an Ethernet card that automatically sets itself up in Plug-and-Play PCs without the aid of installation software.

3COM markets the high-performance EtherLink III parallel tasking adapters, which let you send and receive data from the network simultaneously, thus offering more efficient operation. These cards also offer automatic installation in Plug-and-Play PCs or by using the AutoLink configuration utility.

EtherLink III models are available for the Extended Industry Standard Architecture (EISA), ISA, and PCI standards, and PC Cards. (EISA describes expansion cards that can transfer 32 bits of data at a time.) Advanced features such as the McAfee ROMShield antivirus firmware utility provided with the card and parallel processing make the EtherLink III cards some of the best on the market. Expect to pay from about $100 for a basic ISA model up to about $240 for advanced models.

All-in-One Solutions

Artisoft, Microsoft, and Novell bundle their network operating systems as part of a "LAN starter kit." These kits contain everything you need to network two 10Base-5 Ethernet cards together.

Artisoft has a starter kit for the LANtastic Power Suite and LANtastic for Windows 95. Both kits come with 10Base-5 cards, T-connectors, *terminators*, and 25 feet of BNC (British Naval Connector) coaxial cable. The Power Suite kit costs about $200 for a single user. The LANtastic for Windows 95 kit costs about $300. (A terminator is the last physical device in a daisy chain.)

LANtastic add-on kits are available for 10Base-5 and 10Base-T cards and include one copy of the software. The 10Base-5 kits also come with 25 feet of cable, a T-connector, and a terminator.

Microsoft bundles WFW with a single Ethernet card that supports either 10Base-5 or 10Base-T connectors. A T-connector, terminator, and 25 feet of coaxial cable are included. The price is about $140.

In its Personal NetWork Select starter kit, Microdyne includes two of its NE2000-plus cards, cabling, and connectors with a two-license edition of Novell's Personal NetWare and a five-license version of DaVinci's e-mail application. The cost is about $250. NetWork Select expansion kits contain a single-license version of Personal NetWare, one NE2000 plus Ethernet adapter, cabling, and connectors. These cost about $150 each.

Farallon markets an EtherWave Personal NetWare kit that includes a copy of Novell Personal NetWare, the EtherWave card, and transceiver). The price is about $250 for one kit.

Ethernet Cabling Standards

Before buying a network card, consider which kind of cabling you will need to connect your network cards.

There are two common Ethernet cabling standards that are used in small offices: 10Base-2 and 10Base-T. Some cards even come with connectors for both types. All modern network operating systems support Ethernet regardless of the cabling method. We'll also take a look at the 10Base-5 method.

10Base-2

In the 10Base-2 method, also known as Thin Ethernet or ThinNet, network cards are connected using 50-ohm coaxial cables with female BNC-style connectors on either end. The BNC female connectors easily twist on their male counterparts and lock in place.

If you've ever connected your VCR to a cable TV converter, you already know what coaxial cable looks like. A single wire runs through the center of the cable. This is covered with a plastic sheath, which, in turn, is covered with a flexible, braided wire mesh. The mesh is covered with the outer insulation sheath.

There are many types of coaxial cable, which have different physical and electrical properties. These are known by their military specification (MILSPEC) numbers. The correct type of coaxial cable for networking is RG-58A/U (also called RG-58). You shouldn't have to worry about this unless you're buying cable in bulk or trying to ensure a custom-made cable works with your Ethernet cards.

There are three styles of BNC connectors: bolt-on, crimp-on, and screw-on. The bolt-on and screw-on are the easiest to install because they don't require special tools, but they do tend to work themselves loose. Crimp-on connectors are regarded as the best type for making a reliable connection.

 NOTE

Bulk coaxial cable, crimp-on BNC connectors, BNC connector crimpers, and coaxial stripper tools are sold by mail-order firms such as Black Box, Data Comm Warehouse, and Inmac. If you aren't going to make your own cables, you can buy 10Base-2 cabling in standard 10-, 25-, 50-, and 100-foot lengths.

A three-way T-connector, with two male ends and a single female end, is used to link the BNC coaxial cables to the Ethernet card. The cables connect to the T-connector's male ends while the T-connector's female end connects to the network card's BNC connector.

Computers on either end of a 10Base-2 LAN segment must have a special 50-ohm resistor called a terminator to mark the boundaries of the LAN. If either terminator is removed, the network will not work. Likewise, if you disconnect one of the cables from a T-connector on a simple 10Base-2 network, then the entire network will not work.

While the 10Base-2 cabling standard is simple to understand and construct, it does have some limitations. First, the maximum combined length of cabling for a group of computers (called a segment) is 607 feet. The minimum cable distance between T-connectors should be no less than 1.6 feet. You can't connect more than 30 computers per 10Base-2 segment. You must connect the T-connector's female connector directly into the network card without using cabling between the card and the T-connector's female connector.

The 10Base-2 cabling standard works best if you have a few computers in a common work area. You can cheaply and easily connect them using 10Base-2 cabling, T-connectors, and two 50-ohm terminators.

10Base-T

The 10Base-T, or twisted-pair Ethernet, method uses standard RJ-11 and RJ-45 modular telephone connectors. The RJ-11 connector has two to six wires and the RJ-45 connector has up to eight wires. Some catalogs and manuals might refer to 10Base-T as UTP (unshielded twisted-wire pair). The RJ-11 connector is commonly used with three-pair unshielded telephone wire, which is called category three

Skill 18

cable. The RJ-45 connector is commonly used with category five cable, which has four twisted wire pairs.

The 10Base-T standard does not require coaxial cabling, T-connectors, or terminators. Instead, it uses standard telephone cabling and modular telephone connectors. If more than two machines are linked together using 10Base-T, a special automatic switching box called a network hub is used. Hubs come in four-, eight-, and 12-port models. Hubs can be daisy-chained together using a variety of cables.

Like 10Base-2, 10Base-T has some shortcomings, namely a shorter segment length and a higher price tag. The total cable length of all machines on a 10Base-T segment is 328 feet. While 10Base-2 cabling allows machines to be daisy-chained together with only a few inexpensive parts, 10Base-T machines are connected using four- or eight-port hubs that can cost more than $200 for a single hub.

In office buildings with many LAN connections, network lines share wall duplex jacks with telephone lines. The lines are then concentrated in "wiring closets," with telephone equipment and network hubs.

10Base-5

Ethernet's original wiring standard, 10Base-5 or Thick Ethernet, uses a much heavier type of coaxial cable. In this scheme, a device called a transceiver connects the "Thick" (RG-63A/U) coaxial cable to Ethernet adapters that use a 15-pin, attached unit interface (AUI) cable. In addition, transceivers act as traffic cops, detecting the collision of Ethernet packets.

Although 10Base-5 networks are not ideally suited for small offices, Ethernet transceivers can come in handy. Newer model transceivers still use the 15-pin AUI male connector and can have a 10Base-5, 10Base-2, or 10Base-T connection. You should expect to pay $25 to $40 for an inexpensive transceiver. Common brands include Addtron, Allied Telesyn, and Intellitron.

Transceivers can be a valuable aid in connecting AUI-type Ethernet cards to a 10Base-2 or 10Base-T network. For instance, Macintosh Quadras and Power Macs come with built-in Ethernet ports that have the Apple attached unit interface (AAUI) connector. A special AAUI cable is used to connect the Mac to a transceiver and then to the rest of the PC network. With some transceivers, such as the Allied Telesyn transceivers, you can plug the transceiver directly into the Mac's AAUI port, eliminating the need for a cable.

 NOTE　Transceivers on a 10Base-5 segment should be no closer than 1.6 feet. This is also the minimum distance between T-connectors. The AUI cable length can be up to about 119 feet.

You can buy special transceivers with two or four AUI connectors and a single BNC or RJ-45 connector. Marketed by Black Box in 10Base-5 and 10Base-T models, they let you connect two or more Ethernet AUI devices to a single BNC or RJ-45 cable. These transceivers cost about $300 to $430. These are useful, but you can buy an inexpensive 10Base-T hub for the same amount or less.

Farallon's EtherWave for the PC lets you daisy chain up to seven computers to a single network hub port (see Figure 18.1). The EtherWave 10Base-T card is based upon 3COM's EtherLink III parallel processing architecture. The EtherWave transceiver can connect two 10Base-T devices and one AUI or AAUI Ethernet device.

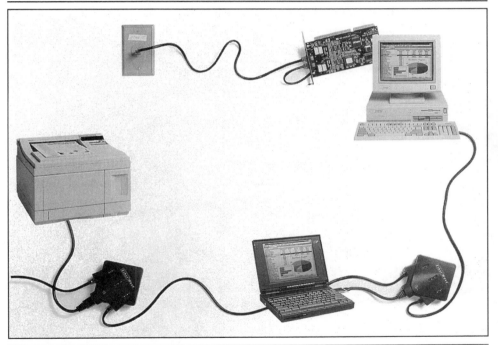

FIGURE 18.1:   Printers, PCs, and laptops can all be linked to a single wall jack connecting the equipment to the rest of the network.

Mixing Cable Standards

If your office uses a 10Base-T network with a four-station hub, and the boss adds an extra computer to the office down the hall, you don't have to run out and buy a new hub.

NOTE Similar to telephone switchboards, hubs usually allow eight to sixteen connections and let you connect and disconnect workstations from the network. These devices can be stacked atop each other and daisy-chained using a variety of cables; daisy-chaining hubs lets you add more workstations to your network.

First check your hub to see if it has a 10Base-5 male connector, which is intended to hook up two 10Base-T hubs to one 10Base-5 LAN segment. But in a pinch, you can use it to network an additional PC if the PC has an Ethernet card that supports 10Base-5 and 10Base-T. The 10Base-T connector will let you connect the same card to a hub should you add more PCs down the hall. Figure 18.2 shows an example of a workgroup hub.

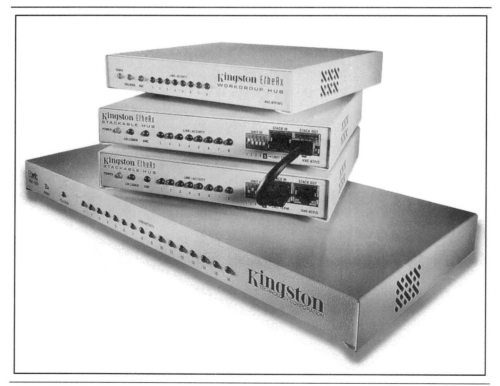

FIGURE 18.2: Kingston's EtheRx workgroup hubs allow eight to sixteen connections.

Plug in a T-connector with a terminator resistor on it to the card's male BNC connector, and then attach a BNC cable to the other arm of the T-connector. On the other end, put on a terminated T-connector and attach it to the hub's BNC connector (see the sidebar on "Network Connections").

NETWORK CONNECTIONS

This list defines some of the common terms you'll come across when looking at options for connecting your network:

- **Unshielded Twisted-Pair Cable:** Made of two uninsulated, braided copper cables. Although the twisting of these individual pairs of cables minimizes electromagnetic interference, the lack of insulation makes the transmissions more susceptible to interference than shielded cable. Because this cabling is ordinary telephone wire, it's the least expensive transmission media and is the easiest to install and work with. Unshielded twisted-pair cabling is the most common type of cabling used for local area networks (LANs). It's generally used for 10Base-T networks.

- **Shielded Twisted-Pair Cable:** Also made of two braided copper cables, this version is insulated with a metallic braid or sheath to make it less susceptible to electromagnetic interference than unshielded twisted-pair cabling. This transmission media provides better performance, but it is very expensive and is more difficult to work with than unshielded twisted-pair cabling.

- **Coaxial Cable:** A wire conductor surrounded by a cylindrical conductor and either insulating rings or dielectric material; the entire cable is covered with a shield that blocks interference. Extremely durable,

continued ▶

Skill 18

coaxial cabling lets users simultaneously transfer voice, data, and video signals. Available in thin (for 10Base-2 networks) and thick (for 10Base-5 networks) versions, thin coaxial is the most commonly used cabling. Providing more capacity than twisted-pair cabling, coaxial cable is also more expensive.

- **Fiber-optic Cable:** Made of three sections: the core (innermost layer consisting of at least one glass or plastic fiber), the cladding (glass or plastic coating with a different composition than that of the core), and the jacket (outer layer made of plastic and other materials to protect the cable from damage). Uses light to transfer voice, data, and video at high speeds. Commonly used for wide area networks (WANs) because it can send data across longer distances and isn't affected by "cross-talk," or disturbances caused by radio waves. Still fairly new, fiber-optic cable is still too expensive to make it a feasible solution for home and small office networking needs.

- **RJ-45 Connector:** Used in data transmissions across telephone wire, this eight-pin connector is used on 10Base-T networks using twisted-pair cabling. The wider end of the connector fits into the external end of a network card through the back of a computer's case.

continued ▶

- **BNC T-connector:** A metal connector in the shape of the letter T. One end plugs into the external end of a network card on the back of a computer's case. The ends that form the top of the T connect with network cables. This connector is used with coaxial cable on 10Base-2 networks.

Repeaters

Ethernet networks requiring long lengths of cable need a repeater. Data signals traveling across a network fade after a certain distance; repeaters refresh these signals so they can continue to their destination. The distance signals can travel depends upon the type of cabling used (such as coaxial cable). Before heading to the computer store, consider the type of network you're building and the type of cabling you're using. Then check with your dealer to determine your cabling's limits and place the repeater just short of its maximum allowable distance.

Repeaters can link two or more Ethernet segments together and extend the range between network stations. Multimedia repeaters support two or more wiring standards. Some do this by using removable cards or a number of different connections that are hard-wired. A small office LAN normally will not need a repeater unless one or more of the networked PCs is at a remote location at the same site (such as in a different room).

Fax Servers

If your staff is tying up too much phone time by sending faxes out on their voice lines, you can use your LAN to win back phone lines for your customers. You can create a fax server to route the fax messages across your LAN to modems attached to your fax server.

As a first step, identify a machine that will be solely responsible for managing your fax messages. Identify which voice lines you can devote to incoming and outgoing fax traffic. Then take one (or more) of your fax/modems and attach it to your fax server.

Symantec's Delrina Communications Suite 2.1, featuring WinFax PRO and WinComm PRO, lets you use your fax/modem server for regular modem traffic. The Communications Suite 2.1 starter kit costs about $350 for licenses for two users and a server. A five-user license with one server kit costs about $550.

 **WARNING**   Some network packages, such as WFW or LANtastic Power Suite, have the software to share a fax/modem. Be aware that sharing a fax/modem on a peer-to-peer network workstation can be frustrating. If your computer plays host to a shared fax/modem, every incoming and outgoing fax call can cause your work to grind to a halt. For this reason, we recommend using a PC dedicated to hosting fax/modems.

File Servers

File servers are computers that are reserved for holding either programs or database files. You can use peer-to-peer machines as servers, but you may want to upgrade your peer-to-peer server machine to a full-blown server to increase network performance.

If the server is an application server, users link to the server to run such common programs as word processors or spreadsheets. Users can save files either to their own machines or to a network drive. Application servers offer the advantage of updating only one copy of the programs that are used by a number of users.

If the server is a database server, users link to the server to access data that is shared by several users. Users can update the information or may have read-only access, thus preventing modification. Applications that use this data may be on user machines or located on network drives. Database servers ensure that everyone is working with the same information. For this reason, special care should be taken to protect and back up the information.

If you'll be using a file server, make sure the server has one or more large, fast hard drives, preferably with a Small Computer System Interface (SCSI) connection because of its high capacity. Give the server as much memory as possible, a CD-ROM drive for quickly updating software, and a PCI Ethernet adapter. Install a tape drive large enough to handle the drive capacity. Back up your server often.

Print Servers

Print servers are boxes that offer network connections and printer connections without connecting the printer to a network PC's parallel or serial ports. Most print servers support 10Base-5 and 10Base-T wiring.

Hewlett-Packard offers its JetDirect line of print servers for use with DeskJet, LaserJet, and PaintJet printers. The JetDirect EX Plus external print server supports all parallel printers for a wide variety of network operating systems. Three types of JetDirect internal print server cards are used for specific DeskJet, LaserJet, and PaintJet models.

The JetDirect external print server costs about $290. The JetDirect internal print server cards range in price from about $330 to $380.

Some other companies offer print server solutions. Pacific Data Product's DirectNet EX II print servers, which cost about $400 each, and Intel's NetPort II and Express NetPort print servers use standard NetWare print queues and can control two printers at once. Four models support AUI (attached unit interface), BNC, and UTP (unshielded twisted-wire pair) connector options. Prices range from about $400 to $460.

CD-ROM Servers

CD-ROM servers connect external CD-ROM drives to the network without using a PC as the go-between. Use a CD-ROM server if you find yourself using more than one CD-ROM drive simultaneously, or if your coworkers are complaining that their shared CD-ROM drives are bogging down their machines.

Axis Communications makes the Axis 850 (about $800), which supports 10Base-T and 10Base-5 connections for MS-DOS, Unix, OS/2, and Windows-based systems. Up to seven CD-ROM drives can be connected via a SCSI-2 connector. The Axis 950 (about $2,200) contains four out-of-the box, networked four-speed CD-ROM drives. Up to seven CD-ROM drives can be connected with the SCSI-2 connector.

JES Hardware Solutions offers networked CD-ROM drives using MicroTest's Disk-Port CD-ROM server box. Models with seven quad-speed CD-ROM drives cost about $3,600, while the 14-drive, quad-speed model should cost about $9,700.

Out the Door, Across the Street

If your business has several branch offices, you can link these office LANs into a wide area network (WAN). A router serves as the go-between for the office LAN and telephone lines. If you want to run a very fast data connection at speeds of 56,000 characters per second or better, you'll need to lease a data line from your telephone company. Leased lines are more expensive, so you won't be paying for this out of the coffee fund. Call your phone company for more information.

If your company must have a direct connection to the Internet, contact a local Internet service provider (ISP). Farallon offers a high-speed, Integrated Services Digital Networking (ISDN) Internet router called Netopia. Designed for branch offices, Netopia works well with Farallon's EtherWave networking solution. Through the "Up & Running, Guaranteed" support option, Farallon will even contact your phone company and local ISP, and remotely configure your Netopia router.

Microsoft has a similar program for Windows 95 users called "Get ISDN for Microsoft Windows." Through Microsoft's World Wide Web page (http://www .microsoft.com/windows/getisdn) users can request an ISDN connection. The ISDN Accelerator Pack, which is special ISDN software for Windows 95, will be provided by ISPs, ISDN hardware manufacturers, and participating phone companies.

NOTE   If you contact Farallon or Microsoft, don't expect ISDN connections to be available through your phone company. ISDN is often unavailable in rural areas served by smaller, independent phone companies or by telephone cooperatives that don't have the equipment to offer this service.

If you're not ready for a WAN, but need to connect to a branch office to transfer files or make printouts, Black Box offers the Async Router for about $1,700. This option lets you use voice-grade lines for LAN traffic. After your LAN has stopped sending data to the remote location, the Async Router's built-in modem breaks the connection. An installation diskette helps you configure the router through a five-step installation procedure. You'll need one Async Router at each branch location.

Fitting It Together: A Case Study

How does all this tie together? Consider the following scenario.

What started out as a retirement hobby has bloomed into a small, successful mail-order business. Supplying hard-to-find, miniature train accessories and restoring train sets, Grandpa Johnson works hard to offer quality service. Grandpa's model railroading fever has always been high, but now his grandchildren have caught the bug. They spend after-school hours working as part-time shipping and stock clerks. Grandma, a retired accounting clerk, handles the books for "Grandpa's Choo-Choo."

The business has five computers ranging from an AT-class clone to a Pentium computer. Only three of the PCs can run Windows. The company has two dot matrix printers used for mailing labels and shipping invoices. An inkjet printer connected to Grandma's Pentium is used for correspondence. Grandpa's 486SX PC has a fax/modem that he uses to contact vendors, track shipments, and send e-mail to customers via an online service.

The three older computers are located in the basement, the Pentium is in the family den, and the 486SX is in the backyard shop. Grandma and Grandpa found they were spending too much time running to the basement to check on stock or hunt down orders. After learning that their DOS-based database software had a network version, they decided to set up a network.

Grandpa eventually settled on 10Base-5 BNC cabling, Kingston EtheRx LC cards, and a Novell Personal NetWare five-user license. Starting with two of the basement machines, he configured the cards with Kingston's QStart utility and installed the software.

After connecting the T-connector to Grandma's Pentium, however, his fledgling network crashed. He discovered that there was a terminator that should have gone on the Pentium's T-connector. He set things right, and with the help of his electrician buddy, ran a short length of cable from his home to his shop.

What Do You Need?

Now that you're familiar with networking hardware, you're almost ready to head to the store. Before you go, assess your needs to ensure you buy what you need. See Figure 18.3 for a comparison of the different products that can be used to set up a LAN.

Before purchasing hardware, ask yourself these questions:

- How many workstations do I need now? How many will be added?

- Will my network be in one room, one building, one city? Is it likely to be expanded?

- What equipment do I have now?

- How will I get from Point A to Point B (under the floor, above the ceiling, in the walls)?

- Do I need a server for storing programs and data files? Or will users only occasionally share resources?

- Who will set up the network?

- Who will administer the network and troubleshoot it? If you have a "guru" onsite, you can build a more complex network than if a less-experienced person runs the network.

Armed with the answers to these questions, you'll be ready to pool your staff's resources and increase their productivity.

Skill 18

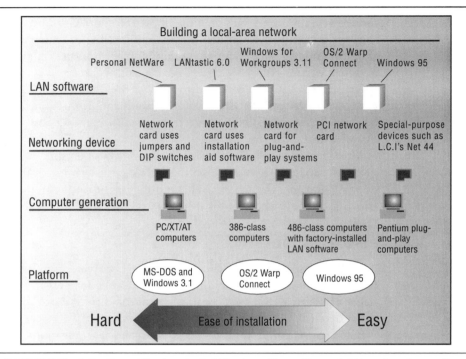

FIGURE 18.3: The level of difficulty of installing a LAN varies depending on the platform and products used.

Are You Experienced?

Now you can...

☑ understand what makes a network function, including topology, cabling, network cards, and operating systems

☑ choose hardware and software to meet your networking needs, for either a local area or wide area network

☑ avoid the problems that plague many networks, and troubleshoot those that occur

☑ install an Ethernet network

☑ keep your network in good working order

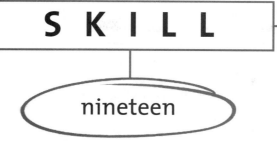

S K I L L

nineteen

19

Building a PC

❑ Considering the benefits of building your own PC

❑ Evaluating your needs and selecting components

❑ Assembling the computer

❑ Testing the results

❑ Installing the mouse, modem, and CD-ROM drive

I think I would like to build my own computer.

Not so long ago, a statement like that from the average computer user might have brought questioning stares from coworkers, worried glances from loved ones, and quips about flying pigs. But talk of building a computer isn't always the delusional ranting of a PC user gone mad. It really is possible, even if you aren't a computer genius.

Building a computer, once the territory of only hard-core computer enthusiasts, has become accessible to the masses. Improved technology, intense competition among manufacturers, and a growing population of computer users who aren't afraid of their machines have made building a computer a viable alternative to buying one off the shelf or through the mail. And when you come right down to it, who better to create your dream machine than the person who plans to use it?

In this skill we discuss the reasons a normally sane person might endeavor to build a computer. We also take a look at what you'll need to build your masterpiece and how much it will cost you.

Reasons for Building Your Own

Anyone who has successfully built their own computer can usually rattle off a mile-long list of reasons why it is better to build your own than to buy one at the nearest computer-chain megastore. Then again, if you talk to somebody who has tried and failed, or who has never opened up their computer, they can probably argue a pretty convincing case for buying a manufactured model.

Most people decide to build their own computer mainly because they can put it together exactly as they want it, it is easier to repair, and it makes future upgrades a breeze.

The real beauty of building your own computer is that you pick out exactly what you want, and you don't have to pay for features you don't need. For example, if you have no desire to join the millions of people herded onto the Internet each year by online companies and Internet service providers, you can leave out the modem. Or maybe you do want to visit the World Wide Web, but you want to wait until the prices on the faster modems drop down a bit. When you build your own, you make the call.

Another reason you might opt for building your own machine is that when something breaks down, you are in a much better position to fix it. You put it all together and you know where everything is. If you know the problem is with the video card, you can go directly to that card and decide what to do. If you still have a warranty on it, you probably can get it repaired, or get a new one, for free. If not, you can choose from the wide range of video cards available, spend as much as you see fit, then install the new one. You can complete the whole process within a day—if you can get a video card locally—and move on with your life.

Repairs aren't always that simple when it comes to a computer manufactured by a name-brand company and sold off the shelf. For starters, you probably wouldn't dare try fixing it yourself, especially if it is still under warranty. Unfortunately, you probably can't simply take your machine back to the chain store where you bought it. Most often, the store will tell you to contact the manufacturer or the local shop authorized by that manufacturer to work on the PC. Once you've finally found the right people, you may find out that the video card—like most of your computer's components—is proprietary, which means you must replace it with a part from the same company. That doesn't sound too bad until you find out the card could cost quite a bit more than your average video card or is nearly impossible to find.

Even worse than that, many manufactured computers have components such as the video card built into the motherboard. The motherboard is the heart of the computer and houses the central processing unit (CPU), which is the brain of the operation. If you have a motherboard with a dead video card, you may have to replace the whole package, and that isn't going to be cheap. (For more detailed information on motherboards see Skill 15.)

Whatever the final scenario, you could end up losing your computer for days, weeks, or even months as you ship it off to the manufacturer, your local shop waits for the right parts, or you start over with a new motherboard.

Out with the Old...

Another reason to build your own computer is that it will give you a great deal of flexibility when it comes time to upgrade in a few years. Yes, even with your souped-up ultra machine, you'll have to add memory or more disk space to keep up with the constantly evolving software out there. With your custom-built computer, upgrading is as simple as replacing a bad part. You take out the old stuff, put in the new stuff, and away you go.

Unfortunately, again, it isn't that simple with most manufactured machines. As with repairs, when you upgrade, you may face the high prices of proprietary parts and the liabilities of components built directly onto the motherboard.

Dollars and Sense

In recent years, if users opted to build their own computers, they could expect to save some serious money. But with competition for the computer buyer's dollar increasing all the time, many new computer systems are selling at incredibly low prices.

Today's average first-time computer builder will probably spend about the same amount of money to build a computer as they would to buy a comparable one off the shelf. A custom-built computer usually will cost about 10 percent more because of labor charges and added support.

We should point out that this nonscientific cost comparison comes from figuring in the cost of using good components from established manufacturers. If you buy a bunch of no-name brands from fly-by-night companies, you probably can build a pretty cheap machine and save some money. That's fine until things start to go bad and you find out that these companies are no longer in operation. It can be pretty difficult to get a nonexistent company to honor its one-year warranty on your hard drive.

Our price comparison also hasn't accounted for the possibility that you might have some components already available to you. If you have an old keyboard or diskette drive that does everything you need it to do and it is compatible with your new components, then use it. Or maybe you have a friend who wants to sell some components off her old machine. Maybe you can use them and save a few dollars.

Before giving our final plug for building your own computer, we'll mention one other option apart from doing it yourself or buying a PC off the shelf. You can always order a system from a mail-order company.

Buying a complete computer system through most mail-order companies is something of a cross between building your own and buying off the shelf. Most mail-order companies build their machines like a custom computer, with few proprietary parts. This makes them easy to repair and upgrade. The bad news is that if you aren't careful, you might find yourself repairing and upgrading often because you bought a computer loaded with low-quality parts. A cheap purchase price can cost you more money in the long run. If you do go with a mail-order package, stick with a company that will tell you exactly what goes into each machine. Make sure you are getting exactly what you want and read the fine print in those magazine ads.

Convinced Yet?

We believe that building your own computer can be the right way to go. Anyone who has some experience with installing computer hardware or working with electronics, and who has a healthy store of self-confidence, should be able to pull this off. Even so, it might be a good idea to find a friend or relative who knows their way around a motherboard *before* you get started.

If you're a little nervous about taking the lid off the computer you have now, or if the concepts of a hard drive and a diskette drive are still a little fuzzy, you might not be ready to tackle this. Don't feel bad; the big computer companies still love you.

Shopping Around

Once you choose to build, you face another set of decisions. The first involves determining what components you need and want in your machine and how much you are willing to spend for the whole package.

The best place to start your list is with a set of minimums. Set the bottom limits of what you will accept in terms of components and their performance. Then set a budget. As you begin to compare prices, you may decide that you can afford a larger hard drive or a better monitor, and you can make those adjustments before you buy.

Once you're ready to buy, you must decide whether to purchase your equipment from your local computer store or through a mail-order company. Each approach has its advantages.

When you buy components from a local store, you will probably pay a higher price. In exchange for the extra money, however, you can expect more personal service and greater accountability should anything go wrong with the part. If your video card stops working a month after you install it, it's much easier to take it out and run it over to the local store than to send it off to a company halfway across the country. And it is almost always easier to get the results you want when you can talk to someone in person instead of on the phone.

The greatest advantage to buying from a mail-order company will be a lower price, and it can be a substantial savings. While dealing with a salesperson or customer service representative over the phone and through the mail can be a hassle, a reputable company will do its best to take care of any problems you encounter. The key to a successful mail-order experience is to ask around and find out who your friends and coworkers have had the best luck with, then ask plenty of questions—including the cost of shipping and handling—when you get ready to place your order. If the salespeople on the phone are rude or act as if you are taking too much of their time, take your business elsewhere.

 NOTE   Wherever you decide to buy, make sure you know exactly what you are getting and beware of any company that has prices that look too good to be true.

Regardless of whether you choose a local store or mail order, try to buy the majority of your components (especially your motherboard, CPU, and memory) from the same company. This can help cut down on compatibility problems later. Some companies will even install the CPU and memory chips on the motherboard for you, which can save you some time and frustration. Also, buying most of your equipment from one place can save you shipping costs on mail orders, and it's easier to keep track of where to call if there is a problem.

We decided to use a mail-order company: Computer Craft Inc. in St. Petersburg, Florida. They carried a good selection, had very competitive prices, and the salesperson we talked to was very knowledgeable and courteous. They impressed us.

The prices listed in Table 19.1 give an idea of the cost of putting together a fairly standard computer. These prices were current at the time of this writing but like the prices of all computer components they are subject to rapid—and unpredictable—change.

TABLE 19.1: The Cost of Building Your Own Computer

Item	Price
Motherboard, pipeline cache, and Pentium processor	$302
16MB RAM	$160
Monitor and video card	$374
Hard drive	$209
CD-ROM kit with sound card and speakers	$219
28.8Kbps modem	$119
Diskette drive	$22
Case and power supply	$65
Mouse and keyboard	$24
Shipping and handling	$58
Total Cost	**$1,552**

The Basics

There are some components that you simply cannot build a computer without. We'll discuss the necessities first and the fun stuff later.

CPU and Motherboard

We don't recommend skimping on these two items because if they fail, you're out of luck. Spend your money on quality, and you won't be sorry. For us, quality means buying an Intel Pentium CPU.

NOTE   Anything less than a Pentium will be obsolete before you even get your new system booted up.

Stick with an Intel motherboard as well to ensure quality and complete compatibility. We like the peripheral component interconnect (PCI) bus over the rest because it gives you the speed you need and full Plug-and-Play capabilities. While you should avoid a board that has too many built-in items, we like the ones with the integrated drive electronics (IDE) interface.

TIP   You don't want to get stuck with a board with a built-in video or sound card. It might make your life a bit easier now, but you'll probably regret it in the future.

We opted for the Intel 100MHz Pentium CPU on an Intel Triton Pentium 75-133MHz PCI motherboard. The board includes an IDE interface, 256KB pipeline cache, fan, flash BIOS, three PCI slots, and four industry standard architecture (ISA) slots. There are faster CPU/motherboard pairs out there, but this unit seemed like a good price/speed combination for our needs. We can always upgrade down the road.

Memory

You can't run a motherboard without random access memory (RAM), and the more you have, the better. If you don't plan to run Windows 95 or much of the software that is coming out now, you probably can get by with only 8MB of RAM. However, we suggest at least 16MB.

RAM comes in the form of single inline memory modules (SIMMs), which you can purchase in many different configurations. Your motherboard should have at least four slots for SIMMs, so if you want 16MB, you can buy four SIMMs with 4MB each, two with 8MB each, or even one with all 16MB.

NOTE   If you plan to use only one SIMM, make sure your motherboard will run off a single SIMM; some require pairs.

When you buy your SIMMs, make sure they have the same number of contacts (usually 72) as your motherboard. Since you will probably want to add memory in the future, choose a configuration that leaves your options—and at least two slots—open. Also, most SIMMs come in speeds of 60 nanoseconds (ns), 70ns, or 80ns. The lower the number, the faster the SIMM and the better your RAM performance.

We opted for a 16MB package at 60ns. We purchased two Texas Instruments 8MB, 72-pin SIMMs for a total cost of $250. In addition, the folks at Computer Craft installed the RAM—along with the CPU—on the motherboard for us and ran a test to make sure everything worked before they shipped it. Not all companies will do this; we recommend you find one that will.

Hard Drive

When it comes to choosing a hard drive, size is important. Not very long ago, a 340MB hard drive was considered huge. But the newest software continues to demand more room, and the drives just continue to get bigger. We recommend at least a 1GB hard drive with an access speed of 11 milliseconds (ms) or lower. Make sure you get one with an IDE interface if that is what you have on your motherboard.

 NOTE   Don't go cheap on the hard drive; it is too important. Stick with the big names such as Western Digital and Seagate. And remember: You just can't have too much hard drive.

We chose the Caviar 21200 from Western Digital. It is an extended IDE hard drive with 1.2GB of storage and an 11ms access speed.

Disk Drive

Disk drives are cheap, even the good ones. Unless you are looking for a special drive that can run both 3.5- and 5.25-inch diskettes, you should be able to find a 3.5-inch wide, 1.44MB drive with an IDE interface for relatively little cash. We picked a Mitsumi 1.44MB drive.

Monitor and Video Card

Monitors can be a tricky proposition, since what sounds good on paper doesn't always look good in person. Also, postage can be pretty high for shipping a monitor. In the interest of quality and cost control, consider trying to find one locally, even if you are buying most of your components by mail order. Either way, when you buy a video card to operate the monitor, make sure the two are compatible. Again, it is probably best to buy both from the same dealer and ask to make sure the two work well together.

We recommend a 15-inch, noninterlaced, SVGA monitor with digital control and a dot pitch of .28mm or less. Monitor manufacturers measure screen sizes diagonally, so a 14-inch screen doesn't really have all that much space. A 15-inch screen is better, while a 17-inch screen is excellent.

The best test of a monitor is for you to examine it in person, view it with both text and graphics on the screen, and consider what kinds of programs you will be viewing. Then just decide what looks the best and what you can afford.

Don't bother to buy a good monitor if you plan to use a poor video card. Make sure your card is at least 64-bit and that it has 1MB or 2MB of RAM. You should also consider whether you want a card with *Motion Picture Experts Group (MPEG)* capabilities. MPEG is a video compression format that makes it easier for your computer to show full-motion video. It comes in software or hardware versions, and we recommend the software version because the hardware could limit your ability to upgrade later.

We chose a 15-inch Samtron SC-528UXL monitor with .28mm dot pitch and digital control. Computer Craft offered a package deal with the monitor that included a 64-bit Video-57P card with 1MB (upgradeable) of RAM and software MPEG capabilities for $85.

Case and Power Supply

You can buy either a desktop or tower case. Most come with a power supply already installed. Be sure you buy one with enough bays to let you expand your system in the future. Before you buy, be sure to ask if you also receive all the interior carriage parts you need. Cases are another item that can be pretty expensive to ship, so ask about cost before you order by mail.

We purchased a Pro Case brand mid-tower with seven bays that included a power supply and everything else we needed on the inside.

Keyboard and Mouse

You can spend a little or a lot for these items. If you want a high-quality keyboard, you can spend upwards of $80, while a cheap brand can run you as little as $15. The same applies to the mouse. Since the low-end products are so cheap, you can buy them now and help keep down your initial cost. You always

Skill 19

can go back and buy a better keyboard later; that way, you will have a spare in case one of them has a run-in with a can of soda. We went with a no-name keyboard and a low-end mouse from Genius.

The Fun Stuff

Let's continue our shopping spree by purchasing some items that cannot strictly be classified as essential, but that add a lot to a computer in terms of enjoyment.

Multimedia

Most computer users today wouldn't dream of buying a new computer without multimedia capabilities. When it comes to putting multimedia into your own computer, you have a number of choices. One way is to buy the CD-ROM drive, sound card, and speakers separately. That way, you can spend as much money on each item as you want. The second option is to buy a kit that contains everything you need. While buying separate pieces allows you more flexibility, buying a kit can help guarantee compatibility between the components (plus you usually get a stack of CD-ROM software titles). We don't recommend buying anything less than a 4X (quad-speed) CD-ROM drive.

We chose a kit from Creative Labs called the SoundBlaster Value CD 4X. The kit contains a 4X CD-ROM player with an IDE interface, 600KB per second transfer rate, and a 250ms access rate. The sound card is a 16-bit SoundBlaster that is upgradeable to wavetable synthesis. The speakers are decent, but nothing too fancy.

Modem

If you decide you want a modem as part of your computer setup, your first decision is whether to buy an internal or external version. An internal version slides into one of the slots on your motherboard like the other cards listed earlier. An external modem has its own case and plugs into one of your computer's ports. The advantages of an internal modem include less clutter on your desktop, a free computer port, and a lower overall cost. The benefits of an external modem include easy installation and removal and the ability to see what the modem is doing through its set of blinking external lights.

Once you have decided on internal or external, you have to pick the speed. The faster the modem, the less time you have to wait for Internet connections and data transfers. The modems most commonly sold transmit data at 28.8 kilobits per second (Kbps). The next lowest transmits at 14.4Kbps. The cost of 14.4Kbps modems dropped as the 28.8Kbps modem became the standard, and modem speeds continue to rise. Shop around before you make your decision. We picked a 28.8Kbps internal fax/modem from Rockwell.

There are a number of other items that some people will decide they don't need, at least not right away, while others will insist they can't live without them. The biggest item in this category is probably a printer. If you plan to use your new computer primarily for word processing, you'll probably want a printer from day one. If you plan to use your new machine mostly for Internet access, you can probably do without. A tape backup is another must for some people. If you can't afford the losses that can occur if your computer crashes, you should install a tape backup drive when you build the computer. If a crash doesn't mean the end of your world, you can probably wait.

NOTE   The chance to decide what is or isn't important is one of the most exciting things about building your own computer. You decide what goes in, what stays out, and what can wait until later. And you decide just how much you want to spend on each part.

The total cost of equipment ordered for our computer was $1,777, including shipping and handling. We should point out that this doesn't include any software, which you normally find in relative abundance in most store-bought computer packages.

Putting Together the PC

Now that we've gathered all the components, all we have to do is build the computer.

The Motherboard

The first order of business is the motherboard. When we removed our motherboard from its protective bag, it was pretty much ready to go. That's the beauty of purchasing most of your components from one store. We had the people at Computer Craft, Inc. (where we bought most of our equipment) install our Pentium CPU and fan, pipeline cache, and random access memory (RAM) onto the motherboard. They took care of all the necessary jumper settings and made sure that everything worked before it left their shop. You can do this all yourself, but if you can find a good store to do it for you, we highly recommend it.

If you insist on buying these parts separately, however, installing them on the motherboard is the first thing you need to do. If your motherboard came with a protective sponge mat stuck to its underside, leave it there when you set in down at your workspace. Otherwise, make a bed of newspapers to set it on to protect the underside of the board as you work. When you do handle the board, make sure you hold it by the edges and try not to disturb any of the chips or electronic gizmos that populate the interior of the board. Check the documentation for your CPU and motherboard and find out whether you need to set any jumpers to accommodate your components. Once you have done that, you can install the brains of the operation.

Installing the CPU

Installing a CPU isn't difficult, but if you do it incorrectly, the whole project is a bust. First, determine whether your CPU has a cooling fan (Pentium CPUs require their own fan) and whether you need to attach it. The CPU fan requires a power supply to operate, so don't forget to plug it in later when you are connecting power supply cables to your drives. Once you get the fan mounted, examine the CPU socket on your motherboard and determine whether it is a zero-insertion force (ZIF) socket with a lever attached or a low-insertion force (LIF) socket with no lever.

To install your CPU in a ZIF socket, lift the lever to about a 90-degree angle, align the pin number one on your CPU with the pin number 1 designation on the socket, put the CPU down into the socket, and lower the lever down alongside it. You should see the CPU lock into place. If your socket is of the LIF variety, again you need to align the two pin number one markings, then push the CPU down into the socket until it is seated securely.

Sliding in the RAM

To install your RAM SIMMs, you first must find the correct sockets on the motherboard. Your motherboard's documentation should show you where the RAM sockets are and how to line up the SIMMs correctly. Different sockets accept SIMMs differently, so be sure to read your documentation.

Most of the time, you can simply slide the SIMM in at about a 45-degree angle, then pop it up into a vertical position (see Figure 19.1). There should be a post or clamp at each end of the socket to hold the SIMM in place. Once the SIMM is in place, it should not move around. If it does, you need to try again.

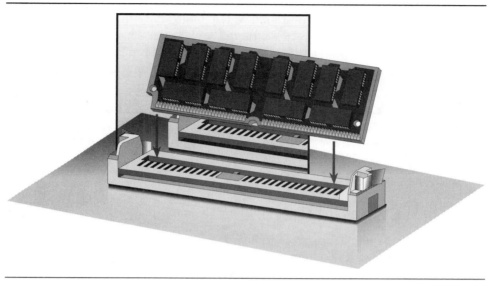

FIGURE 19.1:   Most SIMMs slide into the socket at an angle and then pop up to sit vertically.

Pipeline Cache

The pipeline memory module should have a designated socket that accepts the module with little effort. Check your documentation and follow the instructions given.

Port Connections

While you are working on the motherboard, you might as well take a moment to plug in the two COM port cables and the parallel port cable. See your documentation to find where the connections are on the motherboard and make sure you line up the colored edge of the ribbon with the number 1 pin on each connection. After you have the cables installed, set the actual ports and their metal brackets off to the side of your motherboard. Never set anything on top of your motherboard.

Once you have all the essentials loaded onto your motherboard, you need to connect it to the power supply. To do this, you must remove the case lid and set the case with the open side of the internal framework facing toward you. In the tangle of colored wires extending from the power supply box at the back of the case, there should be two white, flat connectors (they're usually labeled P8 and P9) with six multicolored cables each. This is the link between your motherboard and the power supply. Find the 12-pin power supply connector on your motherboard and insert the two sets of connectors with the double black wires side by side in the middle.

WARNING   It's very important that you connect the power correctly or you can damage your new motherboard. Make sure there are four black wires in a row in the center when you finish.

The Essential Drives

Now that your motherboard is mostly ready to go, you need to give it something to work with. First on our list of components is the diskette drive.

Diskette Drive

To identify the ribbon cable used for the diskette drive, look for a cable that splits into three parts; the middle strand has a twist in it. Connect the cable to the back of the diskette drive, making sure that you line up the colored edge of the ribbon with pin number 1. Though you might have to look hard to see the pin number marking, it's there. Be sure to push the connector in all the way. Now run the cable to the IDE interface on your motherboard (check your documentation if you can't find it) and connect it. Be sure to line up the colored edge of the ribbon with pin number 1.

The diskette drive needs power, so go back to your power supply box at the back of your case. Grab one of the standard power supply lines (it should have two plastic connectors, a big one and a little one) and run it to the back of your diskette drive. The drive should take the smaller of the two connectors, and it should only accept it one way. Be sure to seat the power connector fully on the diskette drive pins and set the drive down on the table off to the side of the motherboard.

Hard Drive

Next on our list is the hard drive, which is installed almost exactly the same way as the diskette drive. Find your second ribbon cable (the one without a split) and attach it to the drive, making sure the colored edge of the cable lines up with the number 1 pin, on both the drive and the IDE interface on your motherboard (see Figure 19.2). Be sure to push both ends of the cable in all the way.

When you're ready to plug in a power supply cable, remember the CPU cooling fan we talked about earlier and insert its power cable between the cable from the power supply box and your hard drive. (The power supply cable connects to the fan cable, which connects to the hard drive.) Be sure to seat the cable firmly onto the pins on the drive.

Monitor and Video Card

If everything is going as planned, you should now have a basic functional computer. But to test that theory, we have to see what the computer is doing. To do that, we must get the monitor and the video card operating.

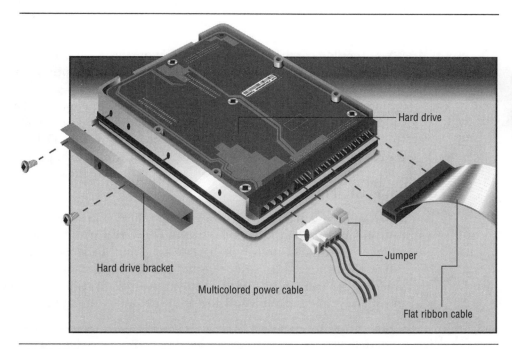

FIGURE 19.2:   Most computer cases require some type of hard drive bracket to secure the drive in the bay.

To install your video card, pick an appropriate slot on your motherboard (check your documentation if you're unsure which to use). Line up the card so that the metal bracket that houses the monitor port on the card hangs off the side of the motherboard. Gently but firmly push the card into the slot. Be sure to push the card all the way in, then connect the cable from the monitor to the port.

Test Run

It's almost time to give your new computer a test run. But first, find the keyboard connector on your motherboard (a short round connector located on one of the corners) and plug in the keyboard. Next, look at the diagram for your case and find out how to connect the power switch on the front of your computer to the power supply at the back of the case. There should be a long, thick, black cable that runs out of the power supply. On the end of that cable should be four smaller colored cables. Your documentation should show which prongs each of those four cables connects to behind the power button. Now plug the power cords into the back of your case and monitor and the surge suppressor, cross your fingers, and push the power button.

You should hear the power kick on and your system begin to operate as the hard drive and fan start spinning. You also should see information appear on your monitor. So far so good.

Now press the setup key on your keyboard. Different motherboards assign this function to different keys, so check your documentation (or possibly the screen in front of you) to see which one applies to you. Ours was the Delete key. Pressing the correct key should cause some type of setup screen to appear.

Configuration

When you arrive at the system setup screen, you should have some type of menu. Choose the Standard CMOS Setup (or your version of it) option and type in the time and date, the diskette drive type (1.44MB), and the video type (VGA or SVGA).

If you're using an old hard drive and you know all of the drive's vital statistics, you can type them in here. If you have a new hard drive, follow the instructions in your documentation on how to run the autodetection utility.

TIP   Hard drives can be tricky beasts, but if you have new equipment, it shouldn't be that difficult. Just be sure to read all about your hard drive before you get started.

Return to the main menu and work your way through the rest of the categories, reading everything carefully and making changes only where you need to. If you are unsure about a category or listing, leave it at the default setting. You can always come back and change it later.

Save and exit the setup screen, and turn off your computer. Now it's time to install your operating system.

The Big OS

As we mentioned before, we recommend Windows 95 for your new machine. We admit Microsoft's baby is far from perfect, but most new applications are written for Windows 95, and the operating system can help make your hardware installations easier. Some users are staunch OS/2 Warp supporters, but IBM's operating system has a vastly smaller marketplace following.

Since we don't have a CD-ROM drive installed yet, we used the diskette version of Windows 95 to install the operating system on our machine.

NOTE   This process takes some time, so as you wait for the signal to insert one diskette after another into your diskette drive, occupy yourself with some necessary tasks. These include separating and identifying the various types of screws included with your case and brushing up on your knowledge of Windows 95 hardware installation tactics.

Once you have Windows 95 up and running to your satisfaction, close the operating system; shut off the PC; unplug the power cords, monitor, and keyboard; and prepare to transplant your computer's guts inside the case where they belong.

The Case

If you are careful, you can move your motherboard and drives into the case without having to unplug anything.

The first thing you need to install is the motherboard itself. In a tower case, the motherboard rests on the left side of the case, inside the internal frame but behind the framework for the drive bays. Insert the pegs into the appropriate holes in the back of your motherboard. Carefully slide the motherboard in and up into the appropriate position (see Figure 19.3) with the keyboard connector and the monitor connector on your video card in line with the openings in the back of the case. Be careful not to unplug your drives or to dislodge your video card.

Skill 19

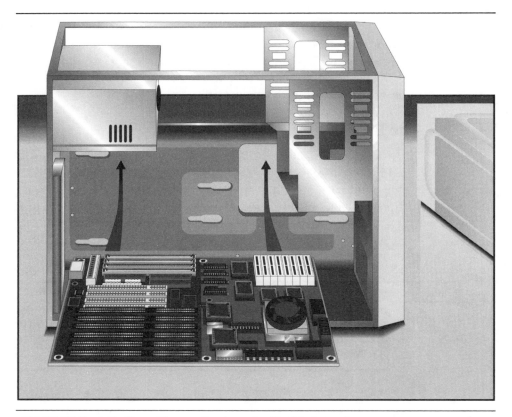

FIGURE 19.3:   The motherboard will slide into place.

Gently insert the pegs into the slide holes in the back of the internal frame, being sure to keep the bottom of the motherboard from actually touching metal. Find the aligned screw holes in the motherboard and the frame and secure the motherboard, being careful not to tighten the screws too much. Attach the metal bracket on the video card to the back of the case using the appropriate screw. Now attach the serial port and parallel port brackets to the back as well.

Once you have the motherboard in place, you can take a moment to attach the wires that lead from the case's front display to the motherboard. These are the wires that make the reset button work and the hard drive light flicker, among other things. Consult your case and motherboard documents to find out which wires go where.

Once you have completed this monumentally tiny task—the connectors are really small—move your hard drive into the bottom 3.5-inch drive bay. You may have to attach a metal extender to one side of the drive (most cases include them) to make it fit properly in the bay. Then simply slide the drive into place and secure it using the appropriate screws. Take a moment to make sure the plastic cover is in place on the front of the case to protect the hard drive.

Installing the diskette drive involves essentially the same procedure. When you get ready to slide the drive into place, be sure to remove the plastic cover on the case and mount the front of the drive flush with the front of the case. Secure the drive to the internal frame.

Once you have the motherboard and drives in the case, we recommend plugging the power cords, monitor, and keyboard back into the surge suppressor and making sure it all works. If you did knock something loose now is the time to find out, before you start putting in more boards and drives. Once you've determined that everything is working (or have taken steps to make it so), unplug the power cord again and get busy with the last few items on your list.

Finishing the Job

There are a few more details that need to be taken care of before your computer is fully up and running.

Mouse

The next order of business should probably be your mouse, since it will make the rest of your installation tasks a bit easier. If you installed Windows 95 as your operating system, its Plug-and-Play capabilities should make mouse installation pretty easy. Shut down your computer and plug your mouse into the serial port. Now restart your computer. When we did this, Windows 95 realized that we had added a mouse to the mix and asked whether we wanted to install it. Hopefully, you'll have the same luck we did, and the installation will be as easy as following the instructions on the screen.

If Windows 95 doesn't detect the new mouse during the bootup, use the arrow keys to select My Computer. Click the Control Panel icon. Then select the Add New Hardware icon and follow the instructions there for detecting a new piece of hardware. If Windows 95 doesn't detect the new hardware, follow the instructions on the screen to manually install your mouse.

NOTE   If you continue to have problems, consult your Windows 95 documentation or the instructions included with your mouse.

Once you have your mouse up and running, you can move on to your modem.

Modem

Installing an internal modem is pretty simple. Shut down your system, unplug everything, and find an open slot on your motherboard. Insert the modem card in the same manner that you did the video card, using steady force to push it in all the way. Then secure the bracket to the back of the case using the appropriate screw.

Again, follow the procedure for detecting new hardware. If all goes well, Windows 95 will make this job an easy one. Then simply install your modem's software following the instructions in your documentation.

CD-ROM Drive

We expected the CD-ROM drive installation to be among the more difficult parts of our project, but it proved to be as simple as the rest. That probably had a lot to do with the fact that we bought a kit. We purchased a Creative Labs Sound-Blaster Value CD 4X kit from A+ Computer and avoided the possible pitfalls of piecing together a separate CD-ROM drive and sound card. In the Creative Labs kit, the CD-ROM drive operated off the sound card through a ribbon cable and an audio cord.

Connect the ribbon cable and audio cord to the SoundBlaster card and insert the card in a slot in your motherboard. Make sure the metal bracket with your speaker and joystick ports lines up with an opening in the back of the case. Secure the bracket with the appropriate screw. Then attach the ribbon cable and audio cord to the back of the CD-ROM drive. Install the CD-ROM drive in one of your 5.25-inch bays and secure it to the internal frame. Now connect a power supply cable to the drive.

Plug your power cables back into the wall outlet and restart your computer. Windows 95 should detect your new card and drive. Follow the procedures on-screen and install the necessary device drivers and other software. Once you have the CD-ROM drive running, and the speakers plugged in and working, turn off your machine again.

Tuck all cables and cords neatly into the interior of the case. Slide the lid back on, replace the screws at the back of the case, and you're finished.

Start up your new machine, sit back, and admire your work. You now have a one-of-a-kind computer that should be easier to upgrade and repair than any manufactured model. You didn't have to buy anything you didn't want, and you didn't have to settle for somebody else's idea of a dream machine. And you did it all by yourself.

Are You Experienced?

Now you can. . .

- ☑ **decide whether building a PC is really for you**
- ☑ **evaluate your needs and the cost, and select the best components for the job**
- ☑ **put together your computer**
- ☑ **configure, test, and troubleshoot your computer**
- ☑ **install the mouse, modem, and CD-ROM drive**

Skill 19

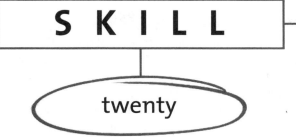

SKILL

20

twenty

Increasing Space on Your Hard Drive

- ❑ Increasing your hard drive's capacity
- ❑ Getting ready to compress your drive
- ❑ Compressing your drive under DOS and Windows 95
- ❑ Using file compression utilities
- ❑ Avoiding time-consuming compression mistakes

New PC users quickly learn this axiom: Enough space is never enough. New computer owners often stick with computer functions they find familiar, such as a word processor. But they soon discover new programs that quickly gobble up hard drive real estate.

So how do you create more space? You could use Windows 3.x's File Manager to delete some files or programs, but that's like using a teacup to empty a swimming pool. You also can load seldom-used programs onto diskettes to free more space, or you can buy a bigger hard drive.

These are some logical solutions to help solve lack of storage problems. But you also can create more space with a software solution known as disk compression. There are three types of disk compression:

- Item-by-item, manual compression utilities such as PKZIP

- On-the-fly transparent compressors for a total drive such as DriveSpace and Stacker

- Hierarchical storage management compressors such as Infinite Disk, which takes infrequently used files on your hard drive and compresses them onto the hard drive or onto diskettes or tape drives.

Creating Space on Your Hard Drive

You can expect to perhaps double your hard drive's capacity through disk compression, depending upon the compression program and options you choose. Your 400MB drive, previously crammed to capacity, suddenly has up to twice as much storage. When you compress, you are recoding information in a more efficient way relative to storage. Without compression, information is encoded with efficient retrieval as a priority. This does not mean compression will slow performance. In fact, performance might be better if you have a fast central processing unit (CPU) or a large hard drive. Generally, the higher the compression, the slower the performance. It varies, but not noticeably. If your computer is fast enough, you may never notice the difference and be happy with maximum compression.

Newer on-the-fly compression programs let you fine-tune the balance between compression and performance (see Figure 20.1).

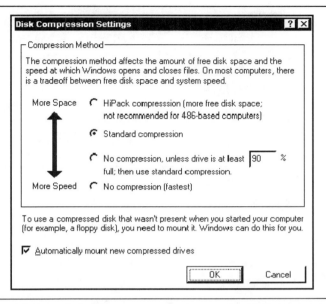

FIGURE 20.1: Selecting a compression method offers a trade-off between compression and performance.

DriveSpace 3, which comes with Microsoft Plus!, has three options: Standard (equivalent to the compression capabilities of Windows 95's DriveSpace 2), HiPack, and UltraPack. HiPack and UltraPack may yield 10 to 30 percent more space. The time it takes to open and save a file increases, however, as it is more highly compressed. A less powerful version of DriveSpace is found in MS-DOS 6.22 and Windows 95 without the Plus! pack. MS-DOS 6.21 does not have a compressor; MS-DOS 6.20 has DoubleSpace.

How Compression Works

The term "disk compression" is misleading, because it is data that is compressed, not your hard drive. On a smaller scale, you can cut the size of a single program in half with a file-compression program. If you want to double the available diskette drive space or send a file online, you might use a file-compression program, such as PKZIP.

Disk compression programs take the contents of your hard drive and package them as a single file. Imagine a bag full of dry leaves. Wetting the leaves will eliminate air in the bag and free up more room. But there's still more space to be saved. Let's say you were able to zap all duplicate leaves and keep only one representative of each type of leaf. Eliminating the duplicate leaves would create considerably more room in the bag. Disk compression programs complete this process mathematically, freeing space used by repeated (redundant) data as shown in Table 20.1.

T A B L E   2 0 . 1 : File Compression Ratios

File Type	Typical File Extensions	Range of Probable Compression Ratios
Executable programs	.EXE, .COM, .OVL, .OVR, .DLL	1.4 to 2 times
Word-processing files	.DOC, .SAM	2 to 4 times
Plain text files	.TXT, .ASC	2 to 8 times
Database files	.DBF, .DAT, .NDX	2.5 to 8 times
Spreadsheet files	.WKS, WK1, .XLS	2 to 4 times
Graphic images	.TIF, .PCX, .GIF, .BMP, .WPG	2 to 8 times
CAD/CAM	.PTL, .DXF, AutoCAD	3 to 8 times
Previously compressed files	.ZIP, .ARC, .JPG, and some games	0.95 to 1.1 times
Typical combination of file types		Most users would expect compression to be about doubled (2 times).

The disk compression process, developed in the late 1970s, is known as *lossless compression,* which means the process can be reversed. Any data compressed can be reliably decompressed. Although you need be no more concerned for your data than you ordinarily would be, precautions are still in order. Disk compression is not dangerous, but when you add complexity to a system, problems can occur. Therefore, you should back up important data before compressing your drive. We suggest backing up your entire hard drive before compressing. At the very least, you should back up important files such as documents, spreadsheets, and graphics. (See Skill 3 for more on creating backups.)

Prepping for Compression

Before compressing your hard drive, you'll want to rid your hard drive of useless files and applications. Any uninstall program can automate this process. If you're using Windows 95, CleanSweep for Windows 95, Remove-It, and Uninstaller 3, all of which also work on Windows 3.*x*, are useful for finding duplicated and unused system and application files.

Taking out the trash isn't all you'll want to do. You'll also need to scan the surface of your hard drive for bad sectors, and run a virus scan program to find and remove any computer viruses. We recommend ScanDisk (part of MS-DOS or Windows 95) or third-party programs such as Norton Disk Doctor or WinProbe, all of which will scan the drive's surface for errors and fix them. These programs also will check for other problems such as lost clusters, cross-linked files, and related problems with the File Allocation Table (FAT). Although most disks won't have any problems, it's the PC user who doesn't take this precaution to whom fate seems to be unkind.

Defragmenting is the next order of business. Defragmenting puts pieces of files and programs "separated" during computer operations back together. This improves your PC's performance considerably. You can use any third-party program such as Norton Speed Disk or the supplied Microsoft program. The compression programs have their own defragmentation programs (once you've completed compression) to keep the disk optimized. DriveSpace 3 lets you set a schedule for automatic defragmentation.

 NOTE   If you are using Windows 3.*x*, you should do a little system tweaking, or you may regret it later. If you are using Windows 95, you'll be glad to know it manages memory for you, so you can ignore this directive.

Windows 3.*x* users should check their virtual memory settings to be sure they are set at a permanent swap file before compressing their drive. Go into the Control Panel, and double-click the 386-Enhanced icon. If the information already indicates a permanent swap file, click Cancel. If your disk is too full already, it may not be possible to set at this point because contiguous sectors are needed. You cannot set a swap file after compression unless you leave a considerable amount of uncompressed space on your drive; swap files must reside on an uncompressed area.

DriveSpace

For disk compression, you'll probably use DriveSpace, which comes with MS-DOS 6.22 and Windows 95. We have been using it with DOS 6.22 for several years on a notebook computer with no problems. DriveSpace cannot, however, compress a full drive; you need to have several megabytes free before running it.

Stacker, a popular commercial product, was the first, fast, reliable disk compression solution. Stacker 4.1 is the current version. Earlier versions of DOS have either no compression or DoubleSpace. DoubleSpace in MS-DOS 6.0 is of questionable value, but the version that comes with MS-DOS 6.20 is a solid product; DOS 6.21 doesn't have a compression utility.

 TIP   Don't shop for compression program bargains. Use the most current version available.

Compressing Your Hard Drive

Now that you understand the principles behind compression, you're ready to try it on your computer.

To run Drive-Space from a DOS prompt, exit all programs including Windows (go to Program Manager's File menu, select Exit, and click OK). Do not merely click the MS-DOS icon; it loads a second copy of DOS with Windows still running.

When you are at the C> prompt in DOS and are running DriveSpace for the first time, type **drvspace** and press ↵. The installation program will run; follow the prompts. We recommend using the Express Setup. Depending upon how much data you have stored and how fast your CPU is, the process lasts from 30 minutes to several hours.

Compressed Volume Files

All your programs and files will look the same, but they will be in a single packaged unit file—called a *compressed volume file* (CVF)—labeled by the program that performed the compression. Your computer reads this file as a complete hard drive. The compression will create a host drive name for every drive (or partition) that you compress. If you compress just a C: drive, the host is called H:. On that host drive, it will store a few uncompressed system files, a Windows swap file (if one existed beforehand), and a hidden .CVF that contains all your "real" files. This is a huge file with a .CVF extension masquerading as your hard drive (C:). DriveSpace sets up a FAT especially for this file to make it act like a disk drive. When you boot your computer, your original C: drive will be renamed H: by the DriveSpace program, and the .CVF will be referred to as C:. Several hidden files can be found in the root directory of H: after you boot your computer by typing **dir h:/a** at a C> prompt.

WARNING   Whatever you do, never tamper with the hidden files found in the root directory of H:, or you may lose some or all of your data.

To see how much space you have left, type **dir/w** at a DOS prompt. To see the compression ratio for each file in a directory, change to the directory and type **dir /c /p.** The compression ratio will be listed to the right of other file information.

Windows 95

To run DriveSpace from Windows 95, click the Start button, choose Programs ➤ Accessories ➤ DriveSpace. Choose Drive on the menu bar, then click Compress to start the process.

If you didn't activate DriveSpace when Windows 95 was installed, go to the Control Panel, click Add/Remove Programs, choose Windows Setup, and click the checkbox for Disk Tools.

NOTE   With Windows 95, you don't have to adjust swap files, virtual memory, and renamed drives. Windows 95 adjusts the storage space for you as it needs it.

You can change the drive letter and adjust the amount of space on the compressed/uncompressed drive with a simple slide switch (see Figure 20.2). DriveSpace for Windows 95 will not create another drive letter if you compress a drive other than the booting drive.

DriveSpace lets you compress a drive, change the drive letter's specifications, and set the size of each of the drives. You even can create a separate drive letter from the free space (that is, without compressing the data or programs) on the drive.

You can decompress your drive, but remember why you compressed it in the first place. Do you have the space to decompress? If not, you must move or remove enough programs to free the needed space. You cannot exceed the capacity of your drive before you decompress.

After your drive is compressed and optimized by the compression program, just use your computer as before. You should look around, however, to understand what has happened to your drive.

When you install a compression program, it will report the compression ratio it has achieved. If you have predominantly text and database files, you'll get better compression than with program files and games. Also, if you store a lot of .GIF (graphics) files, you won't be able to compress them because .GIF files are already compressed. Files with the .ZIP and .ARC extensions are also already compressed.

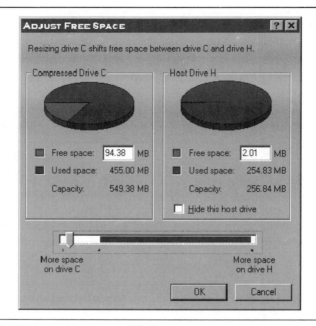

FIGURE 20.2:   A slide bar adjusts the available space between the host drive and the compressed drive.

File Compression Utilities

Programs that compress individual files (archiving programs) also can store one or several selected files inside a single file. This is different from full-disk, on-the-fly compression because such archiving utilities:

- Work on a case-by-case basis
- Don't affect your computer's basic startup operations
- Don't automatically decompress the files when you need them.

However, the archive that is produced may be copied, moved, or transmitted like an ordinary file, while retaining its compression. The recipient of the file must have the companion decompression program unless you create self-extracting archives, which will decompress files when the recipient runs them.

CARE AND FEEDING OF YOUR COMPRESSED DRIVE

You should occasionally use ScanDisk to check the integrity of your compressed drive and to fix errors. ScanDisk knows about DriveSpace, but it might not know about third-party compression software. If you install third-party compression software, use the utilities provided with it and follow those instructions. In Windows 95, ScanDisk can be scheduled into regular sessions when you're not working.

When you purchase new applications, read the box to see if the software is compatible with your compression software. The information might indicate that certain versions are required. If not, there should be no problem. But surprises, sadly, are not uncommon. If you're using DriveSpace, you should activate DoubleGuard before installing and using a new program. After using the program for several weeks, you may want to turn off DoubleGuard because it may affect performance and use up memory unnecessarily.

If you don't need full disk compression, but have a lot of data you want to keep handy on a drive with little space, file compression may be a pragmatic solution. Unlike on-the-fly disk compression, with file compression you must manually decompress files before you can access the data. You will indicate the path (drive and directory name) to which you want the files to be decompressed.

Skill 20

Using PKZIP

PKZIP has become the de facto standard for file compression. It is a command-driven, DOS-based program, although "shells" are available to simplify its use. There also are variations for Windows. The two main components of the program are PKZIP (to compress files) and PKUNZIP (to decompress files). Document files and utilities are also included.

Basic Commands

Most users only need to know how to create a .ZIP file and to unzip (decompress) it. For example, suppose you have two files, FILE1.DOC and FILE2.COM, that you want to compress into one .ZIP file. From the same directory where the two files are located, type:

pkzip -a myfiles file1.doc file2.com

This creates a file named MYFILES.ZIP. The -A tells PKZIP to add the files that follow in the command, and Myfiles is the name of the .ZIP file to be created. Most beginners will use only the -A option.

These archival programs are extensive, and other options exist. You can use the archival program for backups, spanning disks, and updating (useful if you update some files frequently). You need to be proficient with DOS to use the program successfully, and the program documentation contains many examples of how to use commands.

For example, to decompress the .ZIP file MYFILES.ZIP, type:

pkunzip myfiles

Most files you will decompress will be downloaded from BBSs or online services. The procedure is the same in DOS; you put the compressed file into its own directory before decompressing. You can use File Manager to create directories and move the .ZIP file. Then you can unzip it by going to the File menu, selecting Run, and typing **pkunzip** *file name*[**.zip**]. This means the .ZIP extension is optional here.

A slicker alternative is available if you frequently decompress files. In File Manager, select File ➤ Associate. Then type **.ZIP** in the extension box, and in the program list type the full path name to PKUNZIP.EXE. After this association is created, double-clicking any .ZIP file will automatically unzip it without typing any commands.

In Windows 95, highlight the file using your right mouse button. You will be given a menu of choices, which include ZIP and UNZIP.

Using WinZip

WinZip is a shell for .ZIP and other archive programs such as .ARJ and .LHA. It can handle them within one program as a point-and-click operation if you have the DOS versions installed properly. You can get WinZip from the same sources as PKZIP. WinZip and PKZIP can also be found on some CD-ROM utility collections.

The compression process with WinZip requires several steps, but it does the same thing as the DOS version, which is completed with one command. The difference is that in Windows, it's a more visual process. To run WinZip, simply follow the on-screen prompts.

Using Microsoft Plus!

To use the Windows 95 compression agent in Microsoft Plus!, you'll need to upgrade to DriveSpace 3, which can get you up to 50 percent more compression.

We used DriveSpace 2 to compress a drive containing mostly games, which usually can't be compressed much. We achieved an overall 1.6-to-1 compression ratio, which isn't bad considering an average computer should get a 1.9-to-2.1 ratio. Then we installed DriveSpace 3. Recompression took hours (we tested it on a 33MHz 486SX computer), and it increased the ratio to 1.9. Consider this a worst-case scenario; you will do much better (see Figure 20.3).

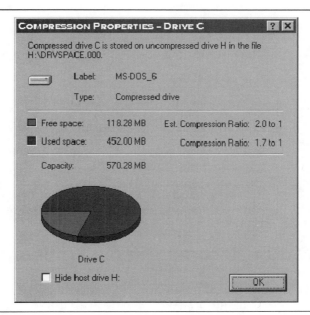

FIGURE 20.3:   In this scenario, compression has doubled the capacity of the hard drive.

Heading Off Trouble

Remember that you are working with a compressed drive. We know of one user who bought a copy of Stacker 4.0 and tried to install it over a drive that had

Skill 20

already been compressed by DoubleSpace. As a result, neither program could access the data. It took days of high-tech tweaking to unearth the data. No data, however, was lost, showing the stability of the decompression process. To avoid such catastrophes, always use the newest versions of programs. This lets them detect older versions.

The DRVSPACE.BIN file is loaded into memory and requires about 50KB.

 TIP If you find that some programs do not have enough memory to run properly, or at all, you may want to run MemMaker after installing DriveSpace to tell DRVS-PACE.BIN to load into upper memory.

Here are some tips for working with a compressed drive:

- Don't delete or tamper with hidden system files, especially Drvspace files.
- Stay off host drive H:.
- Exit programs properly, or reset them first with a soft boot (Ctrl+Alt+Del).
- Cold boot as a last resort, then run ScanDisk.
- Make a "rescue diskette" of compression files to access the hard drive. We suggest Norton Utilities.
- If you change operating systems, make sure the new system recognizes your compression scheme and supports it or updates it.

Preventing Incompatibility Problems

To help prevent programs from damaging your compressed volume because of incompatibilities, enable DoubleGuard safety checking. In DOS, type **drvspace/ doubleguard** to change the setting. DoubleGuard will check its memory for damage caused by another program.

 NOTE If you are installing Windows 95, do not install it on a compressed drive. Compress your drive after installing Windows 95.

On-the-fly disk compression can be problematic, but for most users, it's a sensible solution that helps efficiently use system resources.

Are You Experienced?

Now you can. . .

- ☑ increase your hard drive's capacity by compressing it

- ☑ prepare your drive for trouble-free compression

- ☑ compress your drive from DOS and Windows 95

- ☑ use file compression utilities such as PKZIP, WinZip, and the compression agent in Microsoft Plus!

- ☑ avoid compression mistakes that can damage or destroy your data

Skill 20

S K I L L

21

twenty-one

Using Memory Managers

- ❑ Understanding how memory works
- ❑ Evaluating the potential for improving performance
- ❑ Comparing memory management utilities

Every computer needs as much memory as it can get. No matter how much money you spend on a PC, if you skimp on memory, you'll be sorely disappointed in the computer's overall performance. There are two rules that should govern every computer purchase:

1. Get the fastest processor you can afford.

2. Have as much memory installed as you can afford.

If you followed the first edict but ignored the second, take heart. You can double your memory by installing software that promises to increase system memory by compressing what you already have. At least that's what the software developers want you to believe.

This memory compression technology, in theory, works like hard disk data compression programs that let you store up to 65 percent more data than the hard drive's size should permit. Are these claims about memory doubling software credible? Sometimes yes...to a degree. But user tests continue to show that the only real substitute for a short memory supply is more memory—the hardware kind. Still, you might see some improvements after installing the right memory management software.

Memory managers were common tools in the days of DOS. The only way to add more memory beyond the design limit of 640KB was to use special drivers with add-on memory boards. As DOS became more powerful, Microsoft and IBM included memory management software to handle additional memory that was needed to get more productivity out of the PC.

Windows 3.x managed system memory itself because it needed larger chunks of memory than DOS alone could provide. But early versions of Windows had a design flaw that caused it to hold on to memory after a program was finished with it, thus forcing users to frequently restart Windows to reset system memory or else suffer a General Protection Fault (GPF), a fancy name for a memory crash. A new breed of memory management software helped solve that problem somewhat by taking the memory controls away from Windows.

While Windows 95 incorporated some of those memory management techniques to make memory use much more stable, other software developers found new ways to provide enhanced memory management within the Windows 95 environment.

The Basic Concepts of Memory

There are two types of memory. The first is found on video boards, and handles the transfer of graphics data to the monitor. The other type of memory is generally referred to as random access memory (RAM), which holds instructions for the operating system, instructions for running each program you start, and data you use in each program.

Conventional Memory

The first 640KB of the computer's RAM is called *conventional memory*. Think of conventional memory as the first floor of an office building you are designing. You can cram people, furniture, and supplies within its walls and below the ceiling. How much will fit depends upon the size and shape of the contents. If you need more room to fit all the furniture and people you need for your business, you'll have to hire an architect to expand the plans to include a second story; the town's zoning laws require you to build up rather than out. After more room is added, you now need a way to get people from the upper floor to the ground floor where they would work with you. The first floor of your office building is just like conventional memory, you only have 640KB to work with, no matter how you reassign the work space. When the early PCs were first built around DOS, computer engineers never dreamed anyone would need more than 640KB of RAM. Back then, that much memory seemed like a space so large it would never be filled. We have been stuck with that limit ever since.

Extended and expanded memory is like the second floor you added to squeeze in more workers and equipment (see Figure 21.1). After you've added the second floor, you have to constantly regulate who enters and leaves each floor and how they get back and forth. If your traffic flow gets congested because your workers don't follow the rules you establish, your work routine comes to a sudden halt.

Engineers bypassed the 640KB memory limit with a few memory management tricks. The second floor is divided into two key areas. One lets your most essential workers from the first floor enjoy more spacious office space than they would have downstairs. The other area is a work location that houses your newer employees because the first floor is crowded with more experienced workers. This arrangement lets you expand your business operations by spreading out your workers until you need them to work more closely by your side.

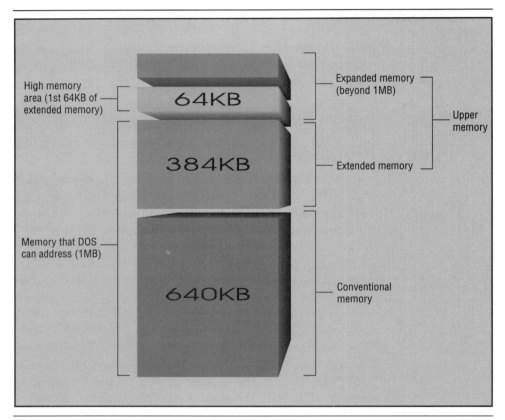

High memory
area (1st 64KB of
extended memory)

64KB

Expanded memory
(beyond 1MB)

Upper
memory

384KB

Extended memory

Memory that DOS
can address (1MB)

640KB

Conventional
memory

FIGURE 21.1:   Conventional and upper memory are like the floors of a building.

Extended and Expanded Memory

Memory above the 640KB limit is stacked in two layers in much the same way. The first layer is called *extended memory* (XMS), which gives the operating system more room to work because the management program runs as many programs as it can in extended memory. But the extension is limited to 1MB. The second layer is called *expanded memory* (EMS). This is all the installed memory beyond 1MB. Expanded memory uses a programming trick to get beyond the memory barriers;

a service door of 64KB of RAM is set aside so program code can be moved in and out in 64KB chunks. When the computer requires a 64KB chunk not currently paged in, expanded memory software finds and inserts it into the service doorway. This memory swapping is called *bank switching*. It occurs so fast the computer appears to have more than 640KB of memory.

Extended and expanded memory sound fairly similar, but they aren't (although they both are included in general reference to "upper" memory). There is one key distinction between them. Extended memory is RAM above 1MB, is found on the motherboard, and is directly accessible to the microprocessor. Expanded memory isn't directly accessible; it gets around the 640KB barrier through the bank switching trick. A bank of conventional memory is set aside to be swapped in and out as needed, providing up to 8MB of apparent RAM. With extended memory, a program must wait until the memory circuits swap the correct bank of memory into conventional memory. This gives slower access times than extended memory.

It is baffling for computer users with 2MB or more of added memory to get error messages when they try to start programs that need more memory. Although the computer has enough physical memory installed, the program isn't able to access it because it can't find enough contiguous space in conventional memory and doesn't know how to find room in upper memory.

Later versions of MS-DOS and PC DOS include built-in memory managers that load special drivers that "trick" the operating system into loading extended memory with many items that should go into conventional memory. A combination of the memory management drivers and the DOS LOADHIGH command lets computers place programs beyond conventional memory. By placing a large portion of the operating system files into the upper memory area, applications such as games and productivity packages can find room within the first 640KB of RAM.

This is an important development because many older programs weren't designed to use extended or expanded memory and can't run if conventional memory is used up. Before Windows, in order to free up enough RAM to run a variety of programs, users could configure the DOS memory managers to create separate settings to run specific programs. When users started their systems, they could select a certain AUTOEXEC.BAT file to set up the computer's memory for their specific needs during that session. Software programmers eventually started designing programs to run in expanded memory so users could keep a standard AUTOEXEC.BAT configuration to run most of their programs.

Skill 21

Advanced Memory Issues

Windows 3.1 somewhat improved the memory situation. Although it needs at least 4MB of RAM, it is better at managing the way the PC gives memory space to programs in conventional and upper memory. Despite this fix, Windows 3.1 (and Windows for Workgroups 3.11) is plagued with a fatal design flaw. The more users open and close applications, the less memory is available for reuse. Thus, the computer loses efficiency and slows down considerably after several hours of use. Eventually, the shortage of available memory causes programs to crash, locking up the computer and forcing users to reboot.

In addition to DOS memory, Windows 3.*x* (and Windows 95) divides the memory allocation into two crucial areas: User and Graphical Device Interface (GDI). Collectively, they are referred to as system resources. The User area controls objects such as buttons, scrollbars, and list boxes. GDI handles display issues such as fonts, icons, bitmaps, pens, and other output. The information managed by User and GDI is stored in chunks of extended memory called *resource heaps*, which Windows 3.*x* limits to 64KB each.

The heaps fill up easily with continued use and can't be cleared without restarting Windows. Although there is enough physical memory in the PC, Windows cannot let programs that need the memory access it, so you get *Out of Memory* messages. Several retail and shareware products step in to more efficiently assign programs to expanded memory; some of these programs can even free up available memory in the heaps.

Windows 95 hasn't completely solved the problem related to system resources, but with its 32-bit structure it has made huge improvements over the 16-bit structure of Windows 3.*x*. Windows 95 takes many of the data items stored in the 16-bit GDI and User heaps and places them in larger 32-bit heaps, creating more room for the remaining data elements.

After this overview about how computers manage memory, it's easier to look at what benefits can be achieved by memory managers designed for Windows. These utilities fall into two categories. One category promises to increase memory performance without adding more physical RAM; products in this category are generally called *RAM doublers* (although "RAM Doubler" is a trademarked name). The other category includes utilities that claim success in improving memory management; these are called *resource managers*.

Testing the Software

We tested four leading memory utilities—SoftRAM, RAM Doubler, MagnaRAM2, and Hurricane—on a variety of PCs. We ran each program on the same set of test computers and compared the performance of each PC's use of system resources and RAM gain. The test computers included:

- A clone 486SX with 8MB RAM
- A clone 80MHz 486DX with 8MB RAM running Windows 3.11
- A Digital Starion 100MHz Pentium with 24MB RAM
- A generic 166MHz Pentium with 32MB RAM
- A Sharp PC-9000 notebook with 16MB RAM
- A WinBook FX 133MHz Pentium with 32MB RAM

Clearly, most of this test hardware is not memory-starved; we were interested in seeing if the RAM doubling features of the software actually boosted the PCs' already strong performance. It didn't in most cases. If any change occurred, it was a slight loss of speed in loading programs. A few of the programs, however, did let us load one or two more programs before showing system resources too low for comfort.

 NOTE   Generally, during the testing the computers performed their tasks with less vitality than when they ran fewer programs unaided by the management software.

Our testing procedures loaded the same software in the same order on all computers:

- Microsoft Word 7.0 (version 6.0 in Windows 3.*x*)
- Gator Editor, a 16-bit text editor
- America Online and CompuServe software
- MS Paint (16-bit version on Windows 3.*x* systems, 32-bit version on Windows 95 systems)
- Paint Shop Pro, a graphics viewing utility (16-bit version on Windows 3.*x* systems, 32-bit version on Windows 95 systems)

Skill 21

The computers were already running virus and installation monitoring utilities. We used system monitoring utilities that are bundled with Windows to compare results.

SoftRAM   Installation was easy, but some of the settings didn't work from the control panel and had to be tweaked in the WIN.INI file. This utility loaded one more program in Windows 3.11, but had no effect on overall speed. It had no effect at all in Windows 95, even though a memory gauge showed that twice as much RAM was available. In fact, on the computers with 24MB and 32MB of RAM, performance actually slowed down. An upgraded SoftRAM95 was recalled last year in conjunction with a consumer lawsuit, as company officials said they had to redesign the utility to work with last-minute changes in Windows 95. That release is still pending. SoftRAM cost $56 at the time of this writing. It is available from Syncronys Softcorp.

RAM Doubler   Though the name is misleading, RAM Doubler does let you open one or two more applications than you may have been previously able to open, but you pay the price in sluggish response. This utility does stretch the limits of GDI heaps so overall memory management is improved, more so in Windows 3.*x* than Windows 95. Installation was a no-brainer that didn't require the user to make complicated settings. At the time of this writing RAM Doubler was available for $56 from Connectix.

MagnaRAM2   This package doesn't claim to double RAM; instead, it uses a RAM compression scheme to squeeze more memory room into the amount of RAM installed in a PC. RAM compression is a questionable process, but this utility seems to have it working better than most competitors. We couldn't load any more programs than we could without Magna-RAM2, but after we loaded several and started working, system performance sped up somewhat, even in our memory-rich test computers. Installation was quick and simple. MagnaRAM2 cost $28 at the time of this writing. It is available from Quarterdeck.

Hurricane   This package was the most successful in extending the capabilities of installed RAM. Depending upon the test computer, we loaded two to four more programs than we could without Hurricane, but there was no apparent increase in system speed. The most striking benefit appeared on the computer running Windows 3.11. System resources had the least degradation of any of the memory management products we tested. The impact upon system resources was not as great in Windows 95, but was still evident. Installation was fairly easy, but we had trouble installing it on two of the Windows 95 computers, the Digital desktop and the Sharp notebook; we had to enter Windows in Safe mode and adjust memory addresses manually. This isn't recommended for inexperienced users. We also had a problem uninstalling Hurricane from all the computers; the uninstall option didn't fully remove the program. We had to use a boot diskette to reinstall previous settings. Helix Software was selling Hurricane for $52 at the time of this writing.

Memory Management vs. Adding RAM

Overall, you'll get better results by installing more RAM. Memory prices fluctuate, but when they are reasonable adding 8MB or 16MB of RAM will cost less than $200—a small price to pay for the improved performance you'll get. If adding RAM isn't an option, then settle for memory management software. Just don't expect it to double your physical RAM: It won't.

Are You Experienced?

Now you can. . .

- ☑ **understand why memory is so important, how it is allocated, and how it works**

- ☑ **get a realistic idea of how your computer's performance might be improved by memory management**

- ☑ **weigh the benefits and disadvantages of several memory utilities: SoftRAM, RAM Doubler, MagnaRAM2, and Hurricane**

Skill 21

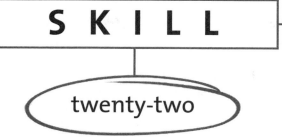

SKILL

twenty-two

22

Upgrading Operating Systems

- ❏ Installing a newer version of DOS

- ❏ Upgrading from DOS to Windows or OS/2 Warp

- ❏ Upgrading from Windows 3.1 to Windows 95 or OS/2 Warp

- ❏ Running two operating systems

The operating system can be thought of as the software floor of the computer—all other software runs on top of it. This is what allows different applications to share information in an operating system such as Windows. The OS sits in the background, managing the information flow among open programs and presenting a more comprehensible user interface.

Upgrading from DOS to Windows lets you run the entire library of Windows-compatible software. Windows can be noticeably slower than DOS in some instances, because the computer must keep track of more information at one time. Windows 95 is another leap above Windows 3.*x*, and offers better multitasking and more reliable operation.

Various versions of the DOS text-based operating system (including MS-DOS) are the mainstay for 286-based computers. While 386-based computers can handle the upgrade to Windows 3.*x*, 486s and higher are suitable candidates for Windows 95 and OS/2 Warp. In this skill, we'll explore the options for upgrading your operating system and discuss the benefits and pitfalls.

Upgrading Your MS-DOS

If you like MS-DOS, and your computer runs on MS-DOS 5, you should consider upgrading to version 6.22. Many newer applications will not run on releases previous to version 5.0, and version 6.22, the latest version of DOS, offers better memory management and features than 5.0.

If you are unsure which MS-DOS version is installed on your computer, type **ver** at the command prompt, then press ↵. The message *MS-DOS Version x.xx* is displayed.

NOTE   When upgrading from 5.0 or older, be sure you purchase the full 6.22 upgrade package. Microsoft also has a "step-up" version for users with 6.0, 6.2, or 6.21 already installed.

Preparing Your System

Before you upgrade MS-DOS, disable any disk cache, antivirus, and delete-protection programs. These programs load from either the AUTOEXEC.BAT file or CONFIG.SYS file in the C: root directory. Placing a REM (remark) command before the command lines used to start these programs is the easiest way to disable the programs. To do this, load the AUTOEXEC.BAT or CONFIG.SYS file in any ASCII text editor, and place a REM in front of any command calling out these programs. For example, if you are using Norton's SpeedDrive as your disk cache program, the line in your AUTO-EXEC.BAT file might appear as

```
c:\speedrv\speedrv install
```

After placing the REM before this line, it appears as

```
rem c:\speedrv\speedrv install
```

To re-enable the command lines, remove the REM command.

 **WARNING**   Before upgrading any system, make a complete backup of all data files. See Skill 3 for more on backing up your files.

Making a Boot Diskette

It is crucial that you make a boot diskette with the MS-DOS version that is currently on your hard drive. Also, copy your CONFIG.SYS and AUTO-EXEC.BAT files and any files that might contain device driver information for your hard drive or other devices. This is especially important if your hard drive uses a third-party partitioning program such as DiskManager. To see exactly which files you should copy, use a text editor to view the contents of CONFIG.SYS and AUTOEXEC.BAT. In the CONFIG.SYS file, any file with an .SYS extension, such as DMDRVR.SYS, is a file you need to copy to your boot diskette. In the AUTOEXEC.BAT file, look for drivers used by special graphic cards. These files might not be as easy to find, but they are usually found in the directory created especially for these drivers.

To make your boot diskette, insert a blank (formatted or unformatted) diskette in drive A:. At the command prompt, type

format a:/s

Press ↵, and the format begins. The switch /S transfers the information MS-DOS needs for its operating system. After the diskette is formatted, copy your CONFIG .SYS and AUTOEXEC.BAT files from the root directory in C:. Next, copy any of the drivers that we have already mentioned. If either startup file calls a file from within a directory, you must change it to reflect its location on the diskette in your A: drive.

For example, the following line from an AUTOEXEC.BAT file shows a video driver being loaded from its own directory:

```
c:/ mirage / smonitor -A1 -B3 -D1
```

This file is needed to access the graphics adapter, so copy the file SMONITOR.EXE to your boot diskette, and make the following change in the AUTOEXEC.BAT file:

```
smonitor -A1 -B3 -D1
```

Now when AUTOEXEC.BAT calls the program, it can find it. Make any needed changes in the CONFIG.SYS file to reflect the files' new location.

Using Setup

When upgrading to MS-DOS 6.22 on a hard drive, the Microsoft MS-DOS Upgrade SETUP.EXE program should be run in the MS-DOS version installed on your computer. Booting the machine with another version of MS-DOS can cause improper access of the hard drive that can lead to file corruption. After your computer has started with its current version of MS-DOS, insert the setup diskette in the A: drive, and type **setup** at the A> prompt. After pressing the ↵ key, Setup checks your system for any incompatibilities.

MS-DOS releases older than 4.0 limited hard drive partition size to 32MB. You may want to make your partitions larger. If you change your drive partitions, back up your data files before proceeding. Also, if you are upgrading from a release before 4.0, you will not be able to return to the previous release because of incompatibility in the partition structure.

OUT WITH THE OLD DOS

During installation, Setup creates the directory OLD_DOS.X and moves all current MS-DOS files into it. If you decide you do not want to keep these files, you can remove the files and directory by typing **del old_dos.x** at the C> prompt.

If you are not using a third-party memory manager, you will want to run MemMaker to optimize your upper memory access.

Upgrading from DOS to Windows 3.1

Windows 95 is the latest operating system, but don't let that dissuade you from installing Windows 3.1 on your PC. Windows 3.1 is a viable interface because it's a popular, well-supported product with a few years of maturity under its belt.

System Requirements

Though not as demanding as Windows 95, Windows 3.1 has some minimum system requirements for operating at maximum performance. You must use DOS 3.3 or newer; we recommend using release 5.0 or newer. (See the earlier section on "Upgrading Your MS-DOS"). Microsoft recommends at least 3MB of RAM, but as with all applications, the more RAM your computer has, the better the system operates. Ideally, you should have at least 8MB of RAM.

You need at least a 386-class processor to run in a 386 Enhanced mode, which lets you run DOS in a Windows environment and can simulate expanded memory for DOS-based applications. Windows 3.1 will run with a 16MHz 386SX processor, but the faster the processor, the better.

 NOTE   You must have a memory manager file such as HIMEM.SYS installed for Windows to use Enhanced mode. The file EMM386.EXE is needed if you use the DOS memory management commands on a 386-based computer.

A fully installed Windows package consumes about 20MB of hard drive space, so be sure you have at least that much available. Windows also needs additional drive space to set up either a permanent or temporary swap file.

Making Setup Changes

During Setup, Windows alters your AUTOEXEC.BAT and CONFIG.SYS files by adding commands it needs for startup. Typically, the values used in these command lines are maximized for Windows and do not take into account available memory or how you plan to use your system.

This is a good time to prune both of these files of any unnecessary command lines. Use a standard ASCII text editor when working with these files. To prevent your computer from reading and executing a command line, you can either erase it or use a REM (remark) command to remove it. For example, to disable the following CONFIG.SYS file command line

```
device=c:\dos\ansi.sys
```

type **rem** in front of it.

Skill 22

After saving the file, you must reboot your computer for the change to take effect. Now when your system reboots, the ANSI.SYS driver will not be loaded. In fact, this is a driver you may want to consider removing; Windows does not use it.

Windows adds a `stacks=` command line to the CONFIG.SYS file. The line will read: `stacks=9,256`.

This translates to 9 stacks with 256 bytes each. DOS stacks store and switch stacks for hardware interrupts. You can save about 3KB of memory by changing the setting to: `stacks=0,0` (NOTE: zero, zero).

If you see a *Stack Overflow* or *Exception error 12* message, or your computer crashes unpredictably, increase the size of the stacks.

You also may want to edit the `buffers=` line. An optimum setting for Windows is 28, but if you are using the cache program SMART-DRV.EXE, use the command line: `buffers=10`.

SMARTDRV.EXE is a special program that monitors hard drive activity and diverts a portion of the data into memory. This program is called a *cache* and substantially improves the performance of your system. There is no need to use the LOADHIGH (LH) command for SMARTDRV.EXE, because it automatically loads into memory.

 NOTE   There are some duplicate files between DOS and Windows. Look in the DOS and Windows directories, and always check the file dates and use the most recent version of the HIMEM.SYS, RAMDRIVE.SYS, and SMARTDRV.EXE files. If two files exist on your system, use the file with the most recent date.

Working with TSRs

Load only the terminate-and-stay-resident (TSR) programs that are necessary to run Windows. (TSR programs are loaded in MS-DOS memory even when they are not running so they can be called on for a task while other applications are running.) Typically, the only programs in this category are CD-ROM and network drivers loaded from your AUTOEXEC.BAT file. If you are mainly working in Windows, you don't need to load a mouse driver because Windows uses its own. If you frequently work with DOS-based programs while in Windows, and those DOS-based programs have mouse support, you may want to load the driver, since the Windows mouse does not work in DOS.

Windows 3.1 is still a popular platform to work with. It is easy and fairly intuitive, but can be a bit cantankerous when working with programs that misbehave.

Perhaps, instead of using Windows 95 with its catch phrase "Start me up," you would rather have a system that's "started and running." Less taxing equipment requirements than Windows 95 and a huge selection of programs make Windows 3.1 a winner.

Upgrading from DOS to Windows 95

There are two reasons to upgrade to Windows 95 from DOS: either you've never had Windows on your computer, or you have deleted everything and decided to install the new operating system from scratch. In either case, your equipment must fulfill these minimum system requirements: 33MHz or higher, a 386DX processor (a 486 is preferred), 8MB of RAM, 50MB to 55MB of free hard drive space, and a Video Graphics Array (VGA) or higher resolution monitor and video adapter.

Because you are upgrading from DOS and your computer is not loaded with a previous Windows version, you'll want to buy the Windows 95 package that's labeled "For PCs without Windows!" and not the one marked "Upgrade." The package is available on CD-ROM or 3.5-inch diskettes.

Preparing Your System

Windows 95 installs its own system, including MS-DOS, so it doesn't matter which DOS version you currently have. If Windows has never been installed on your system, you probably are considering upgrading your current applications to their Windows counterparts.

 NOTE   Before starting installation, make a complete backup of your data files. With a DOS-based computer, there is no benefit to backing up all of your application files unless you want to reuse them in Windows.

Because Windows 95 requires up to 55MB of free hard drive space, be sure your disk partition is large enough to support Windows and all its directories, especially if you are working with an MS-DOS version older than 4.0. Before 4.0, the partition size of DOS was limited to 32MB. In this situation, you must make your disk larger by repartitioning so you can install Windows 95.

The following section describes how to repartition your hard drive.

Skill 22

Using the Boot Diskette

The diskette version of Windows 95 includes a boot diskette containing an operating system and the files necessary to partition (FDISK.EXE) and format (FORMAT.EXE) your hard drive.

 **WARNING** Changing hard drive partitions will cause data to be lost. Back up all important data before proceeding with these instructions.

If you are using a computer without an operating system, or the hard drive partitions are too small to install Windows 95, follow these steps.

1. With the boot diskette in drive A:, reboot your computer.

2. When the command prompt appears, type **fdisk,** and press ⏎.

3. From the FDISK screen, select Option 4, Display partition information. This screen displays the distribution of space on your hard drive. If your drive has more than one partition, each is displayed as EXT (extended) DOS under the Type heading. The heading Mbytes displays the size of the drive, and Usage indicates the percentage used by each Type.

4. After returning to the FDISK screen, select Option 3, Delete partition or Logical DOS Drive.

If your hard drive is divided into logical drives, you must delete the logical drives in the extended DOS partition before deleting the primary DOS partition. After you delete all partitions, you may want to look at the partition information again (Option 4).

Partition size depends upon your hard drive capacity. To limit cluster size, make your partitions 128MB or less. Creating a large partition has its pros and cons. We like to divide the drive into smaller "chunks" for efficiency and performance. Setting aside a single drive partition to maintain your swap file contains fragmentation to a single location, which makes defragmentation easier and faster.

After partitioning your drive, from the FDISK screen set the active DOS partition (always drive C:). Next, using the FORMAT.EXE program, format each drive letter that partitioning created. Remember to add the /S switch to the format command when formatting drive C:. This transfers the operating system so that your computer will boot.

INSTALLING WINDOWS 95 ON A 386

Installing Windows 95 from 3.5-inch diskettes on a 386 computer with 4MB of RAM is extremely slow. To speed the process, you can copy the files on the diskettes to a temporary directory on your hard drive. Because these files (.CAB) are compressed, you will need to use the EXTRACT command located on Disk 1 to copy the WIN95_XX.CAB files to your hard drive, in order to copy files from Disks 2 through 12. The .CAB files are Microsoft Distribution Media Format (DMF), and MS-DOS commands such as COPY and XCOPY won't work on these diskettes.

To copy a .CAB file from a diskette to your hard drive, use the following command:

extract /c a:win95_xx.cab c:\\<*tempdir*>

with <*tempdir*> being the location of a temporary directory on your hard drive.

If possible, don't install Windows 95 or the Windows swap file on a compressed disk. Often, the free drive space reported by the utility is more than what is actually available. Also, using a compressed disk for the swap file may seriously degrade system performance.

DOS users who upgrade to Windows 95 have an advantage in that they don't have to relearn Windows, while users with Windows 3.*x* must prepare for a new interface. Either way, you now have the latest technology Microsoft offers.

Downgrading from the Upgrade Version of Windows 95

Microsoft correctly assumed that not everyone would be enamored with Windows 95. Fortunately, the upgrade version of Windows 95 maintains a copy of the old Windows and DOS files precisely for this situation. To downgrade, follow these steps:

1. Close all open applications on the Windows 95 Desktop.

2. Click the Start button on the Desktop to open the Start menu.

3. Use the mouse to highlight Settings on the Start menu, and then click it.

4. Highlight the Control Panel option, and then click it. This will open the Control Panel window.

5. Double-click the Add/Remove Programs icon. This will open the Add/Remove Programs Properties window.

6. At the Install/Uninstall page of the Add/Remove Programs Properties window, highlight the Windows 95 option, then click the Add/Remove button.

 NOTE If you click the Old Windows 3.x and MS-DOS System Files option, you'll delete the earlier versions of Windows and DOS that remained on the hard drive.

7. A warning screen will appear, telling you that you're about to remove Windows 95 from your computer and restore previous versions of Windows and DOS. It warns that you may have to reinstall some applications and reconfigure your swap file. It also tells you not to uninstall Windows 95 if you have compressed your hard drive since installing it on your system. After reading the warning, click Yes if you're sure you want to proceed.

 NOTE Any time the Cancel button is displayed, you may click it to stop the downgrade process immediately.

8. A second warning screen informs you that Windows 95 will check your disk for errors and that any long file names created by Windows 95 will be removed. Again, click Yes to continue.

9. The ScanDisk window will open and begin checking your hard disk for errors. You don't have to do anything at this point; the computer will automatically run ScanDisk. Don't try to change the ScanDisk settings; the computer will take care of it for you. When ScanDisk is finished, a warning screen will tell you Uninstall is ready to proceed. Click OK to continue.

10. The computer screen may go blank for a short time as the Uninstall program prepares to delete all Windows 95 information from your computer. A Windows 95 Uninstall screen will soon appear and on-screen messages will explain the uninstall process. During the process, the computer will check all files and directories for changes made by Windows 95 so it can return them to their original Windows (non-Windows 95) and DOS configuration.

 NOTE
The entire uninstall process will usually take less than 15 minutes to complete, but the actual time required will depend upon the size of the hard drive and the number of files stored on it.

11. When the uninstall process has finished, the computer will tell you that Windows 95 Uninstall is ready to restart the computer. Remove all diskettes from diskette drives, and press ↵ to restart the computer in its pre-Windows 95 condition.

12. The computer will restart, but it will take you to a C> prompt rather than the Windows 95 Desktop. If you have any problems when restarting the computer, turn it off, let it sit for a few seconds, and then turn it on again.

13. Type **win** at the C> prompt, and press ↵ to make sure your previous version of Windows is still loaded on your computer and that it works, noting any error messages when you restart. If you can get into Windows and it seems to run well, you should be able to ignore these messages.

Try running the applications installed on the computer and reload any that were affected, corrupted, or lost during the uninstall process. Contact the system manufacturer or software developer to resolve serious configuration problems.

Skill 22

DOWNGRADING FROM A FULL VERSION OF WINDOWS 95

You cannot downgrade to DOS from a full version (as opposed to an upgrade version) of Windows 95 without completely removing Windows 95 from your computer, formatting the hard disk, and installing a full version of DOS.

Upgrading from DOS to OS/2 Warp

OS/2 is a full-featured, 32-bit operating system unlike anything else on the market. Though not as popular as Windows, OS/2 has a loyal following of users who firmly believe it is the operating system to own. OS/2 Warp offers easier installation, fewer system requirements, and better device driver support than previous versions.

Besides supporting file names up to 256 characters, OS/2 also has Extended Attributes (EAs). An EA is information attached to a file but it is not part of the file's contents. EAs can contain information such as file type, comments, keywords, icons, and special file information.

EAs are a good place to store information about user preference and default settings. In a High Performance Files System (HPFS), the EAs are stored with the file on which they contain data. In a file allocation table (FAT) system, EAs are stored in a file named EADATA.SF that resides on each FAT drive. The HPFS is a file system that uses a high-speed cache to speed up disk access. A FAT tracks the status of disk space used to store files.

System Requirements and Preparing Your System

OS/2 requires a 386SX or higher processor with at least 4MB of RAM, but it's better to have 8MB. Hard drive space requirements vary according to your installation, but usually you need about 40MB of hard drive space. If installing with an existing version of DOS, it must be 3.1 or newer.

If you plan to install OS/2 as the only operating system, which means using Boot Manager to create HPFS partitions, back up all important data. OS/2 is compatible with the DOS version of BACKUP on version 3.3 and newer releases. The alternative is to use a third-party backup program, but be sure you can restore it from OS/2 before saving your data with it.

Installing OS/2

If you have DOS and want to install OS/2 on your system, you can either use OS/2 as the only operating system on your computer, or use OS/2 and DOS on the same partition using a dual-boot system.

With OS/2 as the only operating system on your computer, the system boots directly into the OS/2 environment without being sidetracked by the Boot Manager or dual boot. Your hard drive space is used more efficiently because there are no redundant or rarely used files taking up disk space. You also eliminate the danger of damaging OS/2 files by using DOS-based utilities. With this setup, you can use either the enhanced 32-bit FAT or HPFS on your hard drive.

This single operating system approach is recommended for more experienced users, especially those with OS/2 experience. Using OS/2 as your only operating system all but eliminates the possibility of reverting to your old DOS operating system.

 NOTE   If you have a peripheral such as a CD-ROM drive or scanner that is not supported by OS/2, you may want to consider using OS/2 and DOS as shared systems.

If you decide later you want to install Windows or DOS, you will have to reformat your C: drive.

With a dual-boot system, your current version of DOS stays in its location, and OS/2 is installed in its own directory. With this installation, it is easy to switch between DOS and OS/2, and you can run a DOS window while in OS/2, which gives you access to both operating systems. OS/2 "remembers" the last operating system used before shutdown, so the next time you start your computer, it boots up in that mode.

FAT and HPFS

As mentioned earlier, you can partition your hard drive under OS/2 with either FAT or HPFS. The FAT system is similar to the one used in DOS systems and is accessible by DOS and, in some cases, is actually faster than a DOS FAT. The FAT partition is more prone to fragmentation, and runs more slowly than HPFS when dealing with larger disk partitions.

Though HPFS is not recognized by DOS, DOS does recognize HPFS drives when running in an OS/2 session. HPFS is faster and far less likely to fragment than the FAT. DOS cannot take advantage of long file names on HPFS. But because of the speed of HPFS, some DOS applications may actually run faster under OS/2 than under their native environments.

OS/2 is an excellent operating system that lacks third-party support and native applications. OS/2 also does not support as many devices as other operating systems, and it is wise to check OS/2 forums on CompuServe and America Online frequently for updates.

The current release of OS/2 does not support Windows 95, and there does not seem to be a move in that direction. How that will affect the future of this product is anybody's guess.

Upgrading from Windows 3.1 to Windows 95

Installing Windows 95 if you have Windows 3.1 is more than a mere upgrade. Windows 95 is a new operating system with new needs and features. Windows 95's ability to run existing applications is the only similarity between it and previous Windows versions. Once you look past the important backward-compatibility issue, you'll see that the two programs chart new courses.

Microsoft recommends a minimum of a 20MHz 386DX processor and 4MB of RAM to run Windows 95. But to fully reach its operating potential, Windows 95 should be run on a 33MHz or faster 486DX microprocessor with a minimum of 8MB of RAM (and 16MB is better). A typical installation requires 35MB to 40MB of hard drive space, and if you plan to access the Microsoft Network and Microsoft Exchange, you'll need another 20MB of hard drive space.

Finding Room on Your Hard Drive

There are a couple of ways to regain some hard drive space to make room for Windows 95.

If your Windows 3.1 swap file is permanent, disabling it frees the space it now occupies on the hard drive. To change the virtual memory setting, go to the Control Panel, double-click the 386-Enhanced icon, then click Virtual Memory to open the Virtual Memory dialog box. Windows 3.1 uses one of two methods to deal with its swap file—Permanent or Temporary. The other setting is None. The Size area displays the amount of drive space occupied by the swap file. If the Type is set to Permanent, that is the amount of drive space you will regain on the swap file's resident drive. If the Type is Permanent, select None from the Type list from under the New Settings area.

After changing the setting, you must restart Windows for the change to take effect on your computer.

N **NOTE**   Another way to clear hard drive space is to delete unnecessary files.

Protecting Your Data

It is important to back up all your important data files when upgrading to Windows 95. We recommend that you also back up these files:

- All initialization (.INI) files in the Windows directory
- All Registry data (.DAT) files in the Windows directory
- All password (.PWL) files in the Windows directory
- CONFIG.SYS and AUTOEXEC.BAT files
- All critical Real mode drivers specified in the CONFIG.SYS and AUTOEXEC.BAT files
- Proprietary network configuration files and logon scripts
- All Program Manager group (.GRP) files in the Windows directory
- Any file crucial to the operation of any part of your system

Managing Startup Files

Because of the nature of Windows 95, the AUTOEXEC.BAT and CONFIG.SYS files are no longer required in the startup process, except for drivers specifically used for certain hard drive controllers. If your CD-ROM drive and sound card are supported by Windows 95, you should delete any references to your 16-bit drivers in the CONFIG.SYS and AUTOEXEC.BAT files. Do not load any memory resident (TSR) programs unless it's absolutely necessary. Windows 95 uses VCACHE for disk caching, so make sure you are not loading SMARTDRV. You can remove the following commands from CONFIG.SYS:

```
stacks=
buffers=
files=
```

You can remove MSCDEX from your AUTOEXEC.BAT file although Windows 95 should have already placed a REM command before it. You also can remove the Set Temp= line since Windows 95 will automatically set the Set Temp= line variable to the Temp directory it created in the Windows directory.

If you run memory resident programs, you will probably want to load them into upper memory. In this case, you must load a memory manager such as HIMEM.SYS from CONFIG.SYS.

If you are loading a video card refresh rate utility from the AUTOEXEC.BAT or CONFIG.SYS files, do not remove this command line. Windows 95 does not support ANSI.SYS, so if a program requires this driver, you will need to keep it active for loading from CONFIG.SYS.

Choosing a Setup Scenario

Windows 95 provides four installation options: Typical, Portable, Compact, and Custom. Each scenario installs a set of preselected files onto your system. Compact Setup installs the fewest files while Custom Setup, according to your selections, can install the most. Custom Setup requires the most user input, so if you are uncomfortable with providing your configuration information, then don't select this scenario.

Our experience shows that the Typical Setup suits a large number of users and is the one to start with. It is easy to add or remove applications after installation.

As we mentioned, installing Windows 95 is more than an operating system upgrade. That's why Microsoft uses the term "migration" to describe the move to Windows 95. It may take some getting used to, but you'll find Windows 95's new features worth the effort.

Upgrading from Windows 3.1 to OS/2 Warp

If you decide Windows isn't for you, OS/2 is your answer. Here is a true 32-bit multitasking operating system that is stable and less demanding on your computer's physical capabilities.

System Requirements

To successfully use OS/2, your computer must have as a minimum: an 80386 (SX or DX) processor, 4MB of RAM, 60MB of free hard drive space, a 3.5-inch 1.44MB diskette drive, a Video Graphics Array (VGA) or better video card, and a mouse.

 NOTE   Keep in mind that the recommended processor speed and amount of RAM are minimums. When dealing with any operating system, the faster the CPU and the more RAM the computer has, the better everything runs.

OS/2 uses system resources much more efficiently than Windows. A third-party memory manager is not needed because OS/2 accesses the complete range of RAM addresses and does not feel the squeeze of the usual DOS 640KB barrier. This unfettered memory management, coupled with OS/2's inherent stability, generally adds up to an overall system performance improvement when working with applications that aggressively use system resources.

When you move into OS/2 from Windows, you can either set up a dual-boot system that enables you to move between the two operating systems, or eliminate Windows altogether and use OS/2 as your only system. Your decision depends upon which applications you plan to use or already own. If you have lots of Windows-based programs with lots of data files, you may want to start with a dual-boot system. But if you are just beginning to put an application suite together, you probably will want to start with OS/2-compatible programs.

If you want to continue to run Windows, have the Windows installation diskettes handy. If your system came installed with Windows, you should be able to create a set of these diskettes. In either case make sure you have the diskettes before starting the OS/2 installation.

FAT and HPFS

A standard DOS partition uses a file allocation table (FAT). A DOS FAT system stores and tracks the file data on your hard drive. OS/2 has a FAT system that is similar to DOS, but it is more efficient in handling and tracking data and is less prone to fragmentation. Both FAT systems allow dual-boot systems to run.

The high performance file system (HPFS) in OS/2 maintains better file integrity, allows long file names (up to 256 characters), has faster access, and is less prone to fragmentation than its FAT counterpart. It requires more memory, however, and cannot be read by DOS. File system errors might be difficult to manage, and it requires that your hard drive be reformatted.

Windows Files

If you decide to keep Windows operational on your system, be aware that Win-OS/2 makes changes to several existing Windows files. The following is a partial list of the files and changes.

- WIN.INI—In the [Windows] section, if a Windows printer is not defined, OS/2 inserts GENERIC/TEXT ONLY in the `Device=` statement.

- In the [Desktop] section, it adds `Icon Spacing=100`.

- In the [Ports] section, it adds .OS2 ports

Installing OS/2

To start the installation process, insert the OS/2 installation diskette, and start or reboot your computer. After the initial boot, insert OS/2 Disk 1 as prompted. At setup, OS/2 gives you the option of an Easy or Advanced installation. If you want to eliminate Windows from your system, you must select Advanced. If you decide to keep Windows active on your equipment, select the Easy option. The Easy installation automatically installs OS/2 on the C: drive if DOS and Windows reside there. Easy installation does not format the partition and automatically sets up the dual-boot feature, allowing you to start your computer in either DOS or OS/2.

In the Advanced setup, you can format the existing partitions as a FAT or HPFS. Using either formatting scheme destroys all data on the target partition. If your drive has multiple partitions, you may want to install OS/2 on a drive other than C: and format OS/2's resident boot drive with HPFS. To make a dual-boot system work, only the boot partition must be formatted with a FAT system.

 **WARNING**

There are dangers in the dual-boot option. DOS does not recognize OS/2's Extended Attributes (EAs), which store information about a file's attributes and other important file information. Because DOS doesn't recognize this information, if a file is deleted or moved by a DOS utility or command, the attribute is not removed, and remains in the FAT. A new file could become attached to the attribute and not detect that it contains information about a now nonexistent file. Also, another file may place its EA at the same address as recorded in the now misplaced pointer. This means two files would show ownership of information in the same spot on the hard drive.

When upgrading to OS/2, preserve your data, and plan for future software installations.

Upgrading to Two Operating Systems

Your PC is a flexible tool. By adding devices and enhancements to your computer, it can be adapted to perform a wide range of functions. Working with such varied operating platforms gives you the ability to configure your computer to fit your needs.

Because of the PC's architecture, two or more operating systems can reside on the same computer. Until recently, though, users were limited to two operating systems: DOS and Xenix. But with the introduction of Windows 3.1, Windows 95, and OS/2, the operating system playing field has broadened.

If you are uneasy about using a new operating system, a great way to learn about it is to use both your old and new systems on the same computer. This lets you learn and work in the new system while maintaining a familiar interface with the old system.

Unfortunately, two operating systems consume an enormous amount of hard drive space. If you already have hard drive space problems, installing another operating system might not be possible. If you have space available separate from your computer's C: drive, you might be able to install the system there. There is a drawback to this: if you decide to make the new operating system your only system, it is a major headache to move all of the files or to reinstall the program.

Before You Begin

Make sure your equipment fulfills the new operating system's minimum requirements. We recommend a 486DX processor with 8MB of RAM, a hard drive with at least 200MB uncompressed capacity, and an Super Video Graphics Array (SVGA) (800 × 600) monitor and video card. A CD-ROM drive, though not required, is a worthwhile addition to your system. Ideally, you should use a version of MS-DOS or PC DOS that is 5.0 or newer.

Take precautions with your important data, no matter which operating system you plan to use. If you have tape backup capabilities, this is a good time to perform a total system backup. We recommend that at a minimum, you back up all important data files as well as the following:

- All initialization (.INI) files in the Windows directory

- All Registry data (.DAT) files in the Windows directory

- All password (.PWL) files in the Windows directory

- All Program Manager group (.GRP) files in the Windows directory

- All crucial Real-mode drivers specified in the CONFIG.SYS and AUTOEXEC.BAT files

- The CONFIG.SYS and AUTOEXEC.BAT files in the root directory

- Proprietary network configuration files and login scripts

Before installing any large program, check the integrity of your drives by using DOS ScanDisk or a third-party disk utility, and defragment all your drives. If you are using a compression routine such as Stacker, be sure to run the defragmenting routine on all compressed drives.

Be sure to disable all unnecessary terminate-and-stay-resident (TSR) programs loaded from the AUTOEXEC.BAT file. Disable any feature that suspends your computer's operation after a specified time interval. (A TSR is a program under MS-DOS that is loaded in memory even when it is not running so it can be called upon for a specific task.)

Make sure your partitions are large enough to handle the additional files required to load a second system. If they are not, your choices are limited. You must either delete files to free hard drive space or use DOS FDISK to repartition and reformat your drive. This should be used only as a last resort, because reformatting destroys all data.

Using Windows 95 and Windows 3.*x* Together

Although Windows 95 is very popular, many people are not quite ready to dump their current Windows setup for the newest kid on the block. Although Microsoft doesn't endorse it, this is the ideal opportunity to run a dual-based operating system. You can spread your wings and try Windows 95 while still having Windows 3.*x* to fall back on during a work crunch.

Your computer must operate with at least MS-DOS 5.0 or PC DOS 6.*x* in order to use a dual-boot setup. During installation, be sure to send the files to a directory other than the current Windows directory. Windows 95 Setup checks your AUTOEXEC.BAT and CONFIG.SYS files and makes the necessary changes.

Setup creates the hidden, read-only file named MSDOS.SYS in the root directory of the computer's boot drive. This file contains the paths, application file compatibility data, and other information required at startup. Through the [Options] section, this file also lets Windows 95 know if it resides with another operating system for dual-booting.

 NOTE Because the hidden attribute is on, the MSDOS.SYS file will not be displayed when using the normal DOS DIR command. Also, with the read-only attribute on, you cannot edit the file. You will need to use the ATTRIB command to turn off the hidden and read-only attributes.

While in the root directory of C:, at the command prompt, type

attrib -h -r msdos.sys

This makes the file visible and removes the read-only attribute for editing.

To enable the dual-boot feature, you must add this command line: `BootMulti=1`. The following example is the MSDOS.SYS file on one of our computers and should be a typical representation of this file's contents.

```
[Paths]
WinDir=C:\WINDOWS
WinBootDir=C:\WINDOWS
HostWinBootDrv=C
[Options]
BootGUI=1
DoubleBuffer=1
Network=0
```

Using an ASCII text editor, open the MSDOS.SYS file, and add the following command line beneath the [Options] heading:

```
bootmulti=1
```

 NOTE　　The numerical values 0 and 1 represent "on" or "off" using Boolean values.

When the machine reboots, you can select an operating system. After you finish editing and saving the file, return it to its original hidden, read-only status to protect it. To reset the attributes, at the command prompt, type

attrib +r +h msdos.sys

If you are using a disk compression program, be sure to make the changes on both the host and mounted drive.

During system startup, pressing the F4 key launches your current DOS, and pressing the F8 key opens the Windows 95 startup menu.

Booting from Windows 95 and DOS

If you have never installed Windows on your computer, you might want to start up Windows 95 with your old version of DOS.

Because Windows 95 is not being installed over an existing Windows 3.*x* directory, your old DOS directory and its contents remain intact. This enables you to start your computer using the older version of DOS. To get his dual-boot capability, follow the instructions in the preceding section to add the `BootMulti=1` command line to the MSDOS.SYS file. Pressing the F4 key when the Starting Windows message appears starts the earlier version of DOS. If you consistently start up in DOS and have DOS 5.*x* or newer on your computer, adding the line `BootWin=0` in the [Options] section of the MSDOS.SYS file changes the default operating system to DOS.

Using Win-OS/2 and Windows 3.*x*

It may seem strange to have two Windows-based programs as shared operating systems, but in this case, they complement each other. When running a Windows application during an OS/2 session, the application doesn't allow Win-OS/2 to take control of your computer. This means that when a program develops a problem, only that single session crashes while the rest of the OS/2 sessions remain stable. Windows, on the other hand, takes control of the computer for each active session. When a crash occurs in the active window, it may cause the computer to lock up, displaying the dreaded General Protection Fault (GPF) message.

NOTE   OS/2 modifies some Windows 3.1 and Windows for Workgroups files to make them compatible with Win-OS/2. Be aware that you will lose your networking capability when running WFW under Win-OS/2.

As you prepare to install a second operating system, we are assuming that your computer is already running Windows 3.1, and you want to add OS/2 to it. Before starting, find either the CD-ROM or diskettes you used to install Windows. If you do not have a set of Windows diskettes because the operating system came pre-installed from the computer manufacturer, be sure to create a set of Window diskettes before starting the OS/2 installation. Your computer's documentation should tell you how to do this.

If you are using a DOS compression program such as Stacker on the drive where DOS and Windows are located, you must decompress this drive. Also, if the compression program does not state that it is OS/2-compatible, assume that it is not. You will not be able to use the compression program after OS/2 is installed.

Win-OS/2 works with more than 90 percent of Windows applications. You may find that some features available under Windows do not work in OS/2. As mentioned earlier, running Windows under Win-OS/2 actually makes your operating system more stable.

Working with two operating systems is an excellent way to make the transition from one system to another. In some instances, such as with OS/2, the second system may actually improve the performance of some applications. When working with a dual system, however, be careful when using system-specific utilities. Using some DOS-based utilities on OS/2 or Windows 95 can have disastrous effects on your files.

If you use two operating systems, you probably will opt for a single system eventually. A dual-operating system gives you the chance to make a sound decision based upon your experiences.

Are You Experienced?

Now you can. . .

- ☑ **upgrade your old version of MS-DOS to a newer version**
- ☑ **prepare your system and upgrade from DOS to Windows 3.1, Windows 95, or OS/2 Warp**
- ☑ **take advantage of improved features by upgrading from Windows 3.1 to Windows 95**
- ☑ **try something different by upgrading from Windows to OS/2 Warp**
- ☑ **upgrade to running two operating systems**

Skill 22

Adding on to Your Web Browser

- ❑ Understanding Web browser add-ons
- ❑ Installing add-ons
- ❑ Getting the most from multimedia
- ❑ Using utility add-ons

Using a browser on the World Wide Web used to be a fairly straightforward proposition. You could open Web pages, follow links, and even download files, but that was about it.

Then came the first plug-ins. These programs could be attached to your browser, giving it additional capabilities. Sometimes simple, sometimes extremely clever, these add-ons opened a new set of windows from which to view the Web. Now it seems that every time you turn around, there's another way of looking at stock reports from your browser or using your browser to meander about a three-dimensional world.

Most of these add-on programs are free (or at least feature a free trial period) and easy to install, but there are so many of them that it's hard to know what they do and whether you'll even find them useful. We've waded through this sea of add-ons and broken them down into the major areas of user interest.

 NOTE The terms "add-on," "add-in," and "plug-in" are interchangeable; they all refer to programs that you can add to your browser in order to enhance its performance in some way.

Understanding the Add-on Story

There are two major areas of increased functionality provided by add-ons: multimedia and utility. Multimedia expansions can give your browser the ability to run animations, view video, or listen to audio files. The capabilities of utilities can range from being able to tell the time in Hong Kong to running Windows applications that are embedded into a Web page.

Add-ons are usually written by third-party developers who want browsers to be able to use technologies that they've developed or to be able to access information on certain types of Web sites.

Add-ons first came out for Netscape's Navigator 2.0, but now they're available for later versions of Navigator and Microsoft's Internet Explorer 3. There are a few that will function on *Mosaic* (the first graphical Web browser) and other older or more obscure browsers, but the majority of add-ons are made with the newest versions of the two most popular browsers in mind.

Some add-ons are available only for Navigator; others will work only with Explorer, but most developers have created versions for both browsers. Microsoft's add-on page (the ActiveX Component Gallery) is located at `http://www.microsoft.com/activex/controls/` and at the time of this writing it boasted 103 add-ons.

Navigator's page for add-ons (Inline Plug-Ins) is located at `http://home.netscape` `.com/comprod/products/navigator/version_2.0/plugins/index.html` and features 108 add-ons. Other Web pages that have add-ons can be found by searching at your favorite shareware site.

Installing Add-ons

While some add-ons are also available as standalone applications, most need to be installed into whichever browser you're using. With Navigator, this usually entails downloading an executable file, quitting the browser, running the file, and then restarting the browser. If the add-on is not packaged in a self-executing program, users may have to place it in Navigator's Plug-In folder themselves. Because these add-ons range in size from a few hundred kilobytes to several megabytes, this can be a time-consuming process.

Microsoft has an easier, yet possibly more dangerous, option for Explorer users. At most of the pages featuring ActiveX controls, the browser will automatically install the add-on in a few minutes. The user doesn't even have to restart the browser. However, there are some who think this automation is less secure. An ActiveX add-on can have access to a user's operating system, providing the potential for disastrous results if the control was written by a malicious programmer.

One well-known ActiveX control called Exploder was written to demonstrate how dangerous add-ons could be. Exploder simply shut down PCs, but it showed how easy it would be to inflict more serious damage. Microsoft has repaired the security breach Exploder demonstrated, though other breaches are under investigation.

Navigator also may be susceptible to these types of spiteful add-ons. Microsoft claims that its security for accepting or rejecting these add-ons and other security breaches is much better than Netscape's. In fact, when we were trying a demonstration of one of the add-ons described later (Stockwatcher), Explorer wouldn't let us open the page with the stock quotes. It gave us a warning that it could be unsafe.

We have some advice for users wanting to add on to their browsers. Installing add-ons is just like any other aspect of the Internet or real life; there are some malevolent people out there, so take a little care and make sure you know what you're doing before adding any extras to your browser. The add-ons on Netscape's and Microsoft's pages have been checked out by the companies, so they are the safest bets. Before you install add-ons that you find through other sources, you may want to run them by other users or your browser manufacturer.

Getting the Most from Multimedia

Every Web browser since Mosaic has been able to view graphics; that's what helped make the Web such an attraction in the first place. But thanks to certain add-ons, being able to do no more than view standard images has begun to go the mundane way of text-based Web browsers.

Animation

Java has been an Internet buzzword recently, and it promises to revolutionize the computing industry in the future. But for now, Java programs (called *applets*) are usually little more than entertaining animations in Java-enabled browsers. There are many add-ons that emulate this ability, the most famous being Shockwave from Macromedia (`http://www.macromedia.com/shockwave/`).

Browsers with the Shockwave add-on can view complex animations ranging from dancing bears complete with sound effects to online games, like the one designed for Conquest of the New World from Interplay Productions (`http://conquest.interplay.com`). Interplay centered its site on the add-on, featuring humorous animations, a Shockwave movie, and an engrossing online battle game.

 NOTE   If you go to a Shockwave-enabled Web site without the Shockwave add-on, your browser will ask if you'd like to link to a site where you can download Shockwave.

Unfortunately, Shockwave animations are quite time-consuming, even with a 28.8Kbps modem, because the animation won't play until it is completely downloaded. We tried another type of animation add-on, called Sizzler, that tries to compensate for this problem.

Totally Hip Software's Sizzler (`http://www.totallyhip.com`) is available for Windows (3.1, 95, and NT) and functions equally well with either browser. The installation for Explorer was painlessly completed for us through the ActiveX site, but the Navigator installation was also pretty easy. We downloaded the small (185KB) executable file, ran it, rebooted Navigator, and were ready to go. Sizzler animations get moving on-screen much more quickly than Shockwave or Java because they start their dance, bongo-beating, etc., before they are completely downloaded. You get a fuzzy image until it's loaded, but it's moving.

All these exciting new forms of animation show promise for what multimedia may soon deliver, but for now, they amount to little more than icing on a Web page cake.

Audio/Video

Sound and moving pictures have been two of the biggest detriments to rapid travel on the Internet. Audio and video files are too large to allow a transfer fast enough to support high-quality video-conferencing, movie watching, or music listening without a *dedicated connection* to the Internet. (Dedicated connections are high-speed Net connections that are constantly connected to the Net such as the T1 lines that transfer about one megabit per second and the Integrated Services Digital Network (ISDN) lines that transfer about 100Kbps.) But new technologies, especially the process of *streaming*, are moving the Internet one step closer to replacing television and radio. Streaming is the ability of an add-on to begin playing a video or audio clip as soon as it starts to download to your system. This results in nearly real-time viewing or listening with only a slight deterioration in quality.

One of the first add-ons to really take advantage of streaming was RealAudio (`http://www.realaudio.com`). RealAudio is available as an add-on or a standalone application for almost any platform, for use with any browser at any connection speed of 14.4Kbps or greater. A RealAudio-enabled browser lets users listen to news broadcasts, radio stations, and live concerts from around the world at near-stereo quality with a 28.8Kbps modem—and close to CD quality with an ISDN line.

We tested streaming video, which utilizes the same concept, except that it streams motion pictures as well as the audio. We installed the VivoActive player add-on (available at `http://www.vivo.com`) in both Explorer and Navigator. Again, Explorer automatically installed the add-on in a few seconds. For Navigator, we had to download the executable file, run it, and then restart the browser.

VivoActive, available for Windows (3.1, 95 and NT) and PowerMacs, worked equally well for both browsers. Appropriately, we watched a short video debate between Jim Barksdale of Netscape and Bill Gates of Microsoft about their future plans for the Internet. There was some delay every 20 to 30 seconds, as the player allowed the streaming to catch up, but the picture was clear and the audio was great. It was the best video we'd seen over the Internet on a 28.8Kbps connection.

NOTE   Until the Internet as a whole widens its *bandwidth* (the ability to transfer information), streaming audio and video lets those of us with slower connections enjoy some of its kilobit-hogging perks.

Skill 23

3D/VRML

Virtual reality (VR) has always been high on the wish list of those yearning for technological advancement. Its goals of creating environments that engulf users in worlds of 3-D sound, images, and tactile feedback have been achieved, but only in a limited manner. Available mainly for giant corporations and the ultra-rich, VR remains largely out of reach for the common dreamer. The Internet could make it a reality for average folks, but again, only with a successful quest for greater bandwidth. VR on the Web, which is still in its infancy, presents itself in the form of 3-D images and backgrounds through the use of Virtual Reality Modeling Language (VRML) and other means.

VRML is similar to Hypertext Markup Language (HTML), the language that most Web pages are written in, but it is used to create a more realistic environment. Most browsers are just beginning to be able to recognize these 3-D pages, so add-ons are often needed.

We tested the HotSauce add-on created by Apple Computing (`http://hotsauce.apple.com`) and available for Macintosh and Windows (95 and NT), but weren't impressed. HotSauce lets Web page creators display their links as buttons in a 3-D array, supposedly making them easier to circumnavigate. We found that it just put the links in a jumbled pile. We could move link buttons out of the way to get to others, but we had a problem when we tried following the links—they often failed. HotSauce was easy to install in both browsers but was also equally mundane in both.

We decided to give another 3-D add-on a go. We tried out WIRL from VREAM Inc. (`http://www.vream.com`), which is available for Windows (95 and NT), and were more pleased with its results (see Figure 23.1). Although the files for both browsers were huge (more than 5MB), we were able to have a smaller 500KB add-on installed through the Microsoft ActiveX page. It took about five minutes, and it was able to run all the WIRL demos.

The basic demo had three images that were activated with a mouse-click. A helicopter that took off, a cannon that fired, and a whirling WIRL logo showed the capabilities, but in a rather limited fashion. We traveled to the VREAM site for a more complete sampling. The best example we found was the "Isle of Morphos," where users could navigate either a bird or a kayak about the isle. While enjoying the view, users could control their vantage points in all three dimensions. WIRL's quality was good, the interaction was sensitive, and the extras were clever.

These add-ons indicate that virtual reality is on its way—and not just for a select few.

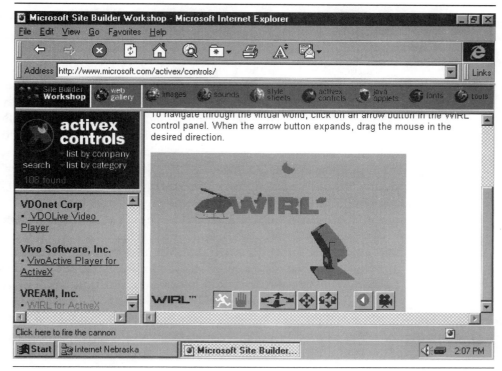

FIGURE 23.1: Microsoft's ActiveX Component Gallery installed this WIRL add-on so we could test its three-dimensional capabilities.

Using Add-ons

Browser add-ons are more than just glimmer and glitz. The majority are designed with a specific use in mind—something users might need or want that their browsers are currently incapable of doing. The possibilities are nearly limitless, and new, useful add-ons are being introduced every day.

Web Utilities

Of course, a major interest of browser users is how to increase the functionality of their browsers. Many utilities are just simple add-ons that slightly modify the browser, and make it more useful. For example, Cyberspell from Inso Corporation (`http://www.inso.com/consumer/cyberspell/cybrspll.htm`), which is available for Windows (3.1, 95, and NT) running Netscape Navigator, checks the spelling of any words, e-mail addresses, and e-mail messages that the user types.

Another useful example is EarthTime from Starfish Software (`http://www.starfishsoftware.com`), which is available for Windows (95 and NT). This add-on lets users check the local time in up to eight cities around the world.

Still others are much more complicated, such as DataViz's Web Buddy (`http://www.dataviz.com`), which is available for Mac and Windows 95. Web Buddy functions like other "offline" browsers; it will grab entire Web pages and let you peruse them at your leisure while disconnected from the Internet. But Buddy is more powerful than most. You can schedules pages for it to download, convert HTML pages into word-processing documents or images for use in graphics programs, and organize all the pages with its own bookmarking feature.

We tried Buddy for both Explorer and Navigator. It was a large download for either (more than 2MB), and we had to quit the browser and install the add-on after the download was completed, even for Explorer. But we found good uses for Buddy. If you don't have unlimited connection time and have certain pages that you regularly visit on the Web, Buddy can save you time and money.

Many of these browser-enhancing add-ons will no doubt be added to future versions of Explorer and Navigator, but until then, plugging them in may make your Web surfing easier.

Add-ons and Windows

Microsoft is dedicated to merging browser and desktop. The new upgrades to Windows 95 will implement some of this integration, and Microsoft's ActiveX and the latest version of Internet Explorer could make it happen soon. Until this bond is formed completely, however, there are many add-ons that attempt to bridge this gap.

The Word Viewer Plug-in, another add-on from Inso Corp. (`http://www.inso.com`), which is available for Windows (3.1, 95, and NT) and Navigator, lets users view any Microsoft Word 6.0 or 7.0 document from within Navigator.

In a similar vein, Acrobat 3.0 from Adobe Systems Inc. (`http://www.adobe.com`), which is available for Mac, Windows (3.1, 95, and NT), Unix, and OS/2 lets users read and navigate Adobe's Acrobat files in their browser. (Acrobat is a method of storing files that lets them be viewed on any PC with an Acrobat reader.)

ADD-ONS YOU DON'T ADD ON

Both Microsoft Internet Explorer 3.0 and Netscape Navigator 3.0 come with some pre-installed add-ons. Some of these are integrated so smoothly that you won't even notice them. Others open up their own windows and make themselves blatantly obvious.

Navigator has added e-mail and news capabilities since 2.0, and Explorer finally caught up with version 3.0. If you have a connection to both mail and news servers, this can save you from having to start up other programs to check and send e-mail or read the newsgroups. Having all three programs in one also lets them work together—jumping from Web page to newsgroup or newsgroup to e-mail.

Telephony, the combination of PCs and telephones, has recently created a lot of interest, most of it aimed at the use of the Internet as a way to make free or very cheap long-distance calls. If two users have the same software, they can communicate using PC microphones and speakers and only have to pay their dial-up connection charge. In short, that means you can call anyone in the world and talk as long as you want for the flat rate your Internet service provider charges, usually something like $19.95 per month. So it's no surprise that both browsers come with their own telephony software built in.

Navigator's CoolTalk provides an audio connection to anyone who also has the browser and the software. It includes a whiteboard (that lets users share graphical information as well) and a chat feature.

Explorer's NetMeeting works similarly, letting users share their voices, applications, and graphics. It also includes support for international conferencing standards and its own built-in chat capabilities.

As more add-ons demonstrate their usefulness for the average user, they will be incorporated directly into the browser platforms. Until then, we must pick and choose our add-ons to match our needs.

Skill 23

Citrix's WinFrame is much more ambitious. It lets browsers run Windows applications that are embedded on a Web page (see Figure 23.2). Regardless of the user's operating system, if they have Explorer or Navigator, they can run a Windows application. We ventured to `http://www.citrix.com/hotspot.htm` with both browsers. Explorer automatically installed the add-on, and we only had to download a small (130KB) file for Navigator.

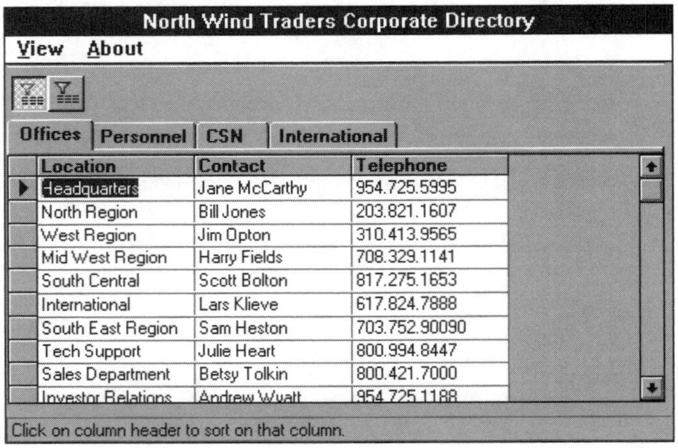

FIGURE 23.2: The WinFrame add-on from Citrix lets you run Windows applications such as this sample Rolodex embedded in a Web page.

The site featured demos of the Microsoft Access database, the group project package Lotus Notes, and others. It took a bit of time for each program to load, and they were a bit cumbersome to navigate (there was a tracer effect that led to overlapping when we moved up or down in the browser window), but this add-on demonstrated the inevitable merger between the desktop and the Internet that will soon change the way we compute.

Doing Business with Add-ons

Of all the different types of utility add-ons, those that cover the business side of things are the most focused. These add-ons address a specific need and address it completely.

About People from Now Software (`http://www.nowsoft.com/plugins/about_people.html`), which is available for Mac and Windows 95 using Navigator provides a browser address book. Any addresses posted to the Web with the Now Up-to-Date Web Publisher can be viewed in Navigator in a list or business card form.

Even more specific is Chemscape Chime from MDL Information Systems Inc. (`http://www.mdli.com/chemscape/chime/chime.html`), which is available for Mac, Windows (3.1, 95, and NT). Chime lets scientists view chemical information in many different structures using Navigator.

We tried out an add-on with a little more general interest. Wayfarer's Stock-watcher (`http://www.wayfarer.com`), which is available for Windows (95 and NT), gives you updates of the stocks that you have selected as they fluctuate throughout the day. It was quite a large download (more than 3MB), but it included the add-ons for both Explorer and Navigator. Unfortunately, Explorer's security kicked in, and it wouldn't let us run Stockwatcher without adjusting the safety settings.

We ran it in Navigator instead. But when we tried to run Stockwatcher from the Wayfarer site, it said we were missing some extensions and loaded them in, which took about 10 minutes. After we finally got Stockwatcher going, we were suitably impressed. There were a limited number of stocks to choose from, but you could e-mail Wayfarer and ask them to add stocks that you're interested in. By double-clicking a particular stock, we could view a 3-D chart that showed the peaks and valleys in that stock's price. As is standard in most online ticker tapes, the stock prices were delayed about 20 minutes, but we found this add-on useful—much more than a novelty.

People on the Web are as varied as people in life—different interests, goals, and dreams. There is no one set of options and abilities that could be included in a browser to match these needs. Add-ons are, and will be for some time, an excellent way to adapt your browser so that it caters to your unique desires during your travels on the Web.

Are You Experienced?

Now you can. . .

- ☑ **understand the hows and whys behind browser add-ons**
- ☑ **install add-ons without compromising your computer's security**
- ☑ **use add-ons to visit multimedia sites, including those using animation, audio, video, and virtual 3-D.**
- ☑ **use add-ons to increase the functionality of your browser**

Skill 23

SKILL

24

twenty-four

Troubleshooting Tips and Tricks

Many times, computer problems are far less severe than they first appear. Usually, they are caused by accidentally deleting a file or program required to access or launch a device. Fortunately, many of these problems are easily solved if you follow a specific plan and use tools and utilities available from the DOS operating system and third-party software manufacturers.

There are some tasks, however, best left to professionals. And even though you might be able to pinpoint a problem, if you are uncomfortable just removing the cover from your system—don't.

Information on troubleshooting computer and peripheral problems is found throughout the book. In this skill we've gathered some helpful tips for what to check first and how to solve common problems. For details on troubleshooting a particular component or peripheral, refer to the skill that covers installing or upgrading it.

The Essentials of Troubleshooting

Solutions to hard drive problems vary in complexity. To help diagnose a problem, you can run the DOS ScanDisk utility (type **scandisk** at the DOS prompt) to find and, in some cases, fix the problem. You can run this program and any optimization programs without harming your hard drive. If you are getting boot errors (when the computer won't start properly), programs such as ScanDisk won't help, and it is best to let an expert work on the problem.

 NOTE   Adding or installing hardware requires you to open the case. If you're uncomfortable doing this, don't. You could cause some damage if precautionary measures aren't taken. You can, however, install keyboards, mice, modems, monitors, and joysticks without any specialized knowledge.

If the problem is beyond your understanding, you have several sources of help. If you purchased your computer from a computer store or large chain, it is probably best to take it back. You also can usually find a third-party repair service in your town. If your hardware is still under warranty, some manufacturers will ask you to ship it back to them for repair. If the warranty has expired, try your computer manufacturer's telephone help line.

You also can find forums on online services, such as CompuServe and America Online, where users can get help and commiserate.

Before You Call Technical Support

If you've tried everything you can think of and you still can't get your computer to work, it may be time to call a technical support line. Manufacturers of software and hardware, as well as Internet service providers, maintain these lines so their customers can get the help they need. While it can take some persistence and the investment of quite a bit of time to get through to a tech support person, making a call to a support line may be the solution you're looking for.

Here are the things you need to know about your computer's setup before calling technical support:

Computer System

System purchase date (for warranty purposes)

System type

Error message(s) displayed

Any peripherals hooked into the system

System serial number

What applications were running when the problem occurred

Any system backup CDs or diskettes that are available

Online Service

Your name and address

Your user name and password

Error message(s) displayed

Your modem make and model

Hardware/Software

Your system configuration

Your product identification number and/or model number

Error message(s) displayed

Skill 24

Taking Precautions

Before you do anything with your computer, there are some basic rules to follow:

- Always make a bootable diskette with a copy of all the files that your system requires to get started.

- If you use a compression program, copy all files required to mount the compressed drive. (Compression programs create additional space on your hard drive by compressing data in files.)

- Back up all your files before delving into your system.

- Never install or remove interface cards with your computer on.

- Eliminate static by touching a metal surface before working on your computer.

- Never change jumper settings without knowing the possible effects. Always write down the current jumper settings of all interface cards.

- After you have turned the power off, always allow your hard drive to stop rotating before turning the power back on.

- Don't connect a printer that is turned on.

- Avoid using an A/B switch box with a laser printer when you have two printers attached to a single computer.

Following these simple steps will help you avoid trouble and the possibility of damaging functioning components.

Getting Started

When troubleshooting, it is easy to assume a cause-and-effect relationship that doesn't exist. For example, a faulty cable may cause symptoms that falsely indicate that either the device or its interface card is causing the problem. There is also the law of averages: Certain computer components, such as memory, are seldom faulty.

Retracing Your Steps

Determine when the computer last operated properly. Has anything changed since then? A problem might be related to adding or removing software or hardware.

DEALING WITH DUST

Maintenance is one of the keys of keeping your computer up and running. Dust is a common culprit in hardware problems. It is sucked through tiny venting grids into the computer by the cooling fan mounted on the motherboard. As the layer of dust thickens, it creates an insulation barrier around circuits and components that prevents heat from dissipating. Sustained high heat levels inside the computer quickly damage the processor chip and boards.

Preventing this heat buildup is easy. Every few months, remove the case and gently clean out the dust. Be sure you remove the electrical plug from the wall first, and be careful never to touch anything inside the computer before you discharge static electricity by touching a metal object. A great way to remove dust is by spraying compressed air onto the exposed motherboard. Another cleaning method is to use a small, battery-operated vacuum tool available at computer supply outlets.

When retracing your steps, you'll often find a small change can significantly change your system. For example, a device that worked the last time you ran your computer doesn't work now. Try retracing your steps back to the point where the problem began. In this example, the first thing to ask is, "Does the device require a special driver?" (Because device drivers are programs that let a PC and hardware components work together, they are sometimes the missing link.) If it does, did something happen to that driver? Is it corrupt? Has the file that normally loads it been changed? These are the questions to consider.

Many software installations alter your system's startup files such as CONFIG .SYS, AUTOEXEC.BAT, or Windows files (such as Windows 3.1's .INI files and Windows 95's Registry files). Usually, software programs ask if it's OK to edit the files and notify you of the changes, but some packages will edit startup files without telling you. If your problems started right after that new package was loaded, check your startup files for changes. Checking the time and date attached to the files is an easy way to determine if the new program edited them. If the date and time of any of the startup files match when you installed the program, odds are that the new program changed the file.

Skill 24

Using the Process of Elimination

Approach troubleshooting by identifying each potential problem and then investigating it thoroughly before moving on to the next potential problem. For example, if you add a device such as a modem, and your mouse stops working, you probably have an address conflict. The mouse worked before you installed the modem, but not after. Because both of these devices use serial port addresses, it's a good bet that they are both trying to access the same address.

Checking the Configuration

CMOS, which stands for *complementary metal-oxide semiconductor,* is where your system keeps information about the hardware connected to it. Hard drives have specifications that CMOS must match for the disk to boot. This drive matching is called *drive type* and is a numerical value. Each number lists a specific characteristic, and if the information in CMOS does not match the drive type, your system will not boot. Most of today's computers let you access the CMOS settings at startup. The typical message will be something like *Press the Del key to enter setup.*

If your machine won't boot and you are getting a message indicating it has lost its Setup or CMOS settings, chances are the battery that powers the CMOS is dead. Depending upon the type of battery installed on your system, these batteries last from two to five years. Most new systems have their batteries attached as an integral part of the motherboard and usually never need replacing.

Opening Your Computer

If you remove your computer's cover, remember our warning about static. Handle cables inside your computer's case carefully; they are tough, but not indestructible. Hard drives use different cables than diskette drives. Cables with twisted wires at one end are for diskette drives; hard drive cables are straight.

Also, when you're connecting cables to your interface card pin-to-plug orientation is crucial to your computer's proper operation. Hard drive and diskette drive controller cards are clearly marked to indicate which set of pins belongs to which type of drive. Also, pin number 1 is always marked to make sure you attach cables properly. Ribbon cables always have a single wire that is colored differently than the others to designate pin 1.

Troubleshooting Diskette Drives

If a diskette drive gives you read errors (assuming that the diskette is not the problem), remove the diskette, reinsert it, and try reading it again. If it still gives a read error, repeat the process two or three times. If you can finally make the drive read the diskette, two or three things may be occurring:

- The diskette drive may be dirty.
- The drive is not being read properly by the application.
- The drive head is out of alignment.

If you suspect your drive is dirty, run a cleaning diskette, which you can buy at a computer store. If the computer is near people who are smoking, the drive head may be coated with tar, which prevents the head from correctly reading the diskette. If the read errors are sporadic and do not seem to occur in only one application, this is probably the problem.

If you find that the error always seems to occur in a particular application, however, some part of the program may be corrupt. Reinstall the offending program, and see if that cures it.

If a drive on another computer has problems reading a diskette that was formatted on the drive in question, giving you read errors, this is a good indication that the drive's head is slightly out of alignment. Diagnostic programs can determine if this is a problem. If it is, it's best to replace the drive.

Basic troubleshooting, as you can see from these tips, is a process of elimination. Most problems leave footprints that lead you back to their origin—and give hints about their solutions.

Are You Experienced?

Now you can. . .

- ☑ **understand the basics of troubleshooting and how to avoid common computer problems**
- ☑ **get started with troubleshooting by evaluating your system**
- ☑ **check for potential configuration problems**
- ☑ **open your computer and examine the cables and connectors**
- ☑ **troubleshoot diskette drives**

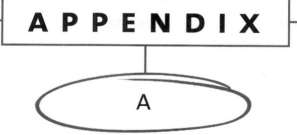

APPENDIX A

Manufacturer Index

In the course of this book we've talked about how to upgrade just about every part of a computer. Before you dive into an upgrade you'll want to check the prices and features of the components and peripherals you're considering buying. For example, you may want to contact some of the manufacturers on this list to find out about purchasing a new motherboard or the cost of upgrading your RAM.

 NOTE   Keep in mind that the computer marketplace changes constantly—some of the information on this list may have changed since we contacted these vendors.

CD-ROM Drives

Matsushita Electric Corporation

1 Panasonic Way
Secaucus, NJ 07094
(800) 726-2797
(201) 348-7000
Fax: (201) 392-6007
http://www.panasonic.com

NEC Computer Systems Division

1414 Massachusetts Ave.
Boxborough, MA 01719
(800) 632-4636
(508) 264-8000
Fax: (508) 635-4666
http://www.nec.com

Pioneer New Media Technologies Inc.

2265 E. 220th St.
Long Beach, CA 90810
(800) 444-6784
(310) 952-2111
Faxback service: (310) 952-2309
http://www.pioneerusa.com

Plextor Inc.

4255 Burton Drive

Santa Clara, CA 95054

(800) 886-3935

(408) 980-1838

Fax: (408) 986-1010

http://www.plextor.com

Sony Electronics Inc.

3300 Zanker Road

San Jose, CA 95134

(800) 352-7669

(408) 432-1600

Faxback service: (800) 766-9022

http://www.sel.sony.com/sel

CPUs

Cyrix Corporation

P.O. Box 850118

Richardson, TX 75085

(800) 340-7501

(972) 968-8387

Faxback service: (972) 968-8609

http://www.cyrix.com

Evergreen Technologies

806 N.W. Buchanan

Corvallis, OR 97330

(800) 733-0934

(541) 757-0934

Faxback service: (541) 757-7350

http://www.evertech.com

IBM

Route 100
Somers, NY 10589
(800) 426-2968
(914) 766-1900
Faxback service: (800) 426-4329
http://www.ibm.com

Intel Corporation

2111 N.E. 25th St.
Hillsboro, OR 97124
(800) 321-4044; (503) 696-8080
Faxback service: (800) 525-3019
http://www.intel.com

Kingston Technology Corporation

17600 Newhope St.
Fountain Valley, CA 92708
(800) 835-6575
(714) 435-2600
Fax: (800) 435-0056
http://www.kingston.com

Hard Drives

Conner Peripherals

See *Seagate.*

Insight Enterprises Inc.

6820 South Harl Avenue
Tempe, AZ 75283
(800) 927-2931
(602) 902-1000; (602) 333-3000
Fax: (602) 902-1153
http://www.insight.com

Iomega Corporation

1821 W. Iomega Way
Roy, UT 84067
(800) 697-8833
(801) 770-2028
Faxback service: (801) 778-5763
http://www.iomega.com

Maxtor Corporation

510 Cottonwood Drive
Milpitas, CA 95035
(800) 262-9867
(408) 435-7884
Faxback service: (800) 262-9867
http://www.maxtor.com

O.R. Technologies Inc.

42 W. Campbell Ave.
Campbell, CA 95008
(408) 886-3000
Faxback service: (888) 286-6422
http://www.ortechnology.com

Quantum

500 McCarthy Blvd.
Milpitas, CA 95035
(800) 624-5545
(408) 894-4000
Faxback service: (800) 434-7532
http://www.quantum.com

Seagate

3081 Zanker Road
San Jose, CA 95134
(800) 732-4283 (automated)
(408) 456-4500
Faxback service: (408) 456-4501
http://www.seagate.com

Western Digital

8105 Irvine Center Drive

Irvine, CA 92618

(800) 832-4778

(714) 932-5000

Faxback service: (714) 932-4300

http://www.wdc.com

Memory

Hewlett-Packard

3000 Hanover St.

Palo Alto, CA 94304

(800) 752-0900

(415) 857-1501

Faxback service: (800) 333-1917

http://www.hp.com

Intel Corporation

2200 Mission College Blvd.

P.O. Box 58119

Santa Clara, CA 95052-8119

(800) 628-8686

(408) 765-8080

Faxback service: (800) 525-3019

http://www.intel.com

Toshiba America Information Systems Inc.

9740 Irvine Blvd.

P.O. Box 19724

Irvine, CA 92618

(800) 334-3445

(714) 583-3000

Faxback service: (800) 457-7777

http://www.toshiba.com

Motherboards

American Megatrends Inc.

6145-F Northbelt Parkway

Norcross, GA 30071-2976

(800) 828-9264

(770) 246-8600

Faxback service: (770) 246-8787

http://www.megatrends.com

Micronics Computers & Orchid Technologies

4565 Northport Loop West

Fremont, CA 94538

(800) 577-0977

(510) 651-2300

Faxback service: (510) 661-3199

http://www.micronics.com

RAM

First Source International

7 Journey

Aliso Viejo, CA 92656

(800) 761-9866

(714) 448-7750

Fax: (714) 448-7760

http://www.firstsource.com

Ingram Micro Inc.

1759 Wehrle Drive

Williamsville, NY 14221

(800) 456-8000

(716) 633-3600

Faxback service: (714) 566-1900

http://www.ingrammicro.com

Kingston Technology

17600 Newhope St.

Fountain Valley, CA 92708

(800) 337-8410

(714) 435-2600

Faxback service: (800) 435-0056

http://www.kingston.com

PNY Electronics

299 Webro Rd.

Parsippany, NJ 07054

(800) 234-4597

(201) 438-6300

Faxback service: (800) 234-4597

http://www.pny.com

Multimedia Kits

ATI Technologies Inc.

33 Commerce Valley Drive E.

Thornhill, Ontario, Canada

L3T 7N6

(905) 882-2626

Faxback service: (905)882-2600

http://www.atitech.com

Aztech Labs

45645 Northport Loop West

Fremont, CA 94538

(800) 886-8859

(510) 623-8988

Faxback service: (510) 623-8989

http://www.aztechca.com

Creative Labs Inc.

1901 McCarthy Blvd.

Milpitas, CA 95035

(800) 998-1000

(408) 428-6600

Fax: (405) 742-6611

http://www.creaf.com

Diamond Multimedia Systems Inc.

2880 Junction Ave.

San Jose, CA 95134

(800) 468-5846

(408) 325-7000

Faxback service: (800) 380-0030

http://www.diamondmm.com

Graphics Cards

ATI Technologies

33 Commerce Valley Drive E.

Thornhill, Ontario, Canada

L3T 7N6

(905) 882-2626

Faxback service: (905)882-2600

http://www.atitech.com

Boca Research

1377 Clint Moore Road

Boca Raton, FL 33487

(561) 997-6227

Faxback service: (591) 994-5848

http://www.bocaresearch.com/

Diamond Multimedia Systems, Inc.

2880 Junction Ave.

San Jose, CA 95134

(800) 468-5846

(408) 325-7000

Faxback service: (800) 380-0030

http://www.diamondmm.com

Orchid Technology

See *Micronics Computers Inc.*

VideoLogic Inc.

1001 Bay Hill Drive, Suite 310

San Bruno, CA 94066

(800) 578-5644

(415) 875-4167

Faxback service: (800) 203-8587

http://www.videologic.com

Sound Cards

Aztech Labs Inc.

45645 Northport Loop East

Fremont, CA 94538

(800) 886-8859

(510) 623-8989

Faxback service: (510) 353-4325

http://www.aztechca.com

Creative Labs Inc.

1901 McCarthy Blvd.

Milpitas, CA 95035

(800) 998-1000

(408) 428-6600

Fax: (405) 742-6611

http://www.creaf.com

Logitech Inc.

6505 Kaiser Drive

Fremont, CA 94555

(800) 231-7717

(510) 795-8500

Faxback service: (800) 245-0000

`http://www.logitech.com`

Turtle Beach Systems

5 Odell Plaza

Yonkers, NY 10701-1406

(914) 966-0600

Faxback service: (914) 966-0600

`http://www.tbeach.com`

Operating Systems

IBM

Route 100

Somers, NY 10589

(800) 426-2968

(914) 766-1900

Faxback service: (800) 426-4329

`http://www.ibm.com`

Microsoft Corporation

One Microsoft Way

Redmond, WA 98052

(800) 426-9400

(206) 882-8080

Faxback service: (800) 936-4100

`http://www.microsoft.com`

Index

Note to the Reader: First level entries are in **bold**. Page numbers in **bold** indicate the principal discussion of a topic or the definition of a term. Page numbers in *italic* indicate illustrations.

e

n

O

P

q

r